Montgomery in Europe
1943-1945

Montgomery in Europe 1943-1945

SUCCESS OR FAILURE?

Richard Lamb

BUCHAN & ENRIGHT, PUBLISHERS
LONDON

First published in 1983, reprinted 1984, by
Buchan & Enright, Publishers, Limited
53 Fleet Street, London EC4Y 1BE

British Library Cataloguing in Publication Data available

ISBN 0 907675 77 8

Photoset in North Wales by
Derek Doyle & Associates, Mold, Clwyd
Printed in Great Britain by
The Guernsey Press Co. Ltd., Guernsey, Channel Islands

Contents

Illustrations

All illustrations are from the Imperial War Museum, except those
marked*, which are kindly loaned by John Henderson Esq, MBE.

Maps

'Good-morning; good-morning!' the General said
When we met him last week on our way to the line.
Now the soldiers he smiled at are most of 'em dead,
And we're cursing his staff for incompetent swine.
'He's a cheery old card,' grunted Harry to Jack
As they slogged up to Arras with rifle and pack.
                    *
But he did for them both by his plan of attack.

                                Siegfried Sassoon, 'The General'

Foreword

Field-Marshal the Viscount (Bernard) Montgomery of Alamein was the best known and the most controversial general of the Second World War. Under the thirty-year rule his archives in the Public Record Office were made available to historians six years ago, and only a short period remains while those close to him during the war will be available to comment on the secrets disclosed – sadly, many are already dead. Surprisingly, no work of military history based upon these documents has so far been published. This is therefore an appropriate moment to write a study of his generalship in Europe from 1943 to 1945, when he fought his most important campaigns, using these key fresh documents and other archives, as well as the views of those close to him during the period.

In some ways I found it easier to write about Napoleon than Montgomery. Both commanders wrote a great number of letters and orders each day during their campaigns. Napoleon's are all collected and in print; Montgomery's are scattered. Meanwhile, members of my own generation who took part in his campaigns are becoming fewer, and I had much looked forward to meeting and discussing Montgomery's conduct of these battles with Maj-Gen Sir Kenneth Strong, KBE, CB, and Maj-Gen R.F.K. (David) Belchem, CB, CBE, DSO. Alas, they have both died since I embarked on this work, although both left behind valuable books.

Although Montgomery for most of his life had little interest in money, he caught the publishing itch with the success of his post-war books, and in 1962 sold his diaries and personal papers to the *Sunday Times* for a capital sum and an annuity. In this archive there may be some documents relating to his campaigns, as well as to his personal life, of importance to military historians. No date has been fixed for their release, and meanwhile those of us who knew about and took part in the Second World War are growing older.

I have thus not read Montgomery's so-called diary for the period covered by this book. I have not missed much. Lt-Col Christopher (Kit) Dawnay,* who was Montgomery's Military Assistant from shortly after the Normandy landings until the end of the war, told me that his general was too busy to write a daily diary. Instead he instructed Dawnay to keep a series of Twenty-First Army Group files giving a description of the main events and Montgomery's reasons for his decisions; the result was known as 'the Log'. Dawnay had frequent conferences with his commander on what to insert and how to phrase it, but the whole record was in fact written by Dawnay in the third person. In addition, these files contain duplicates of important letters written by Montgomery and Eisenhower, and of key directives.

There were at least six copies of the Log, and the Prime Minister, the Chief of the Imperial General Staff, and the Secretary of State for War were each sent one. There are copies in the Dawnay archives, in Churchill College, Cambridge, and in the Public Record Office. At other periods of his life Montgomery wrote a daily diary, but for the North-West Europe campaign his 'diary' probably consists of inserts added after the war to the Log kept by Dawnay. Extracts referred to as 'diary entries' in his post-war books do not correspond exactly with the Log.

Brigadier Sir Edgar (Bill) Williams, Montgomery's head of Intelligence, helped his chief with his memoirs, and rewrote substantial chunks from drafts in the Field-Marshal's own handwriting. Normally, Bill Williams told me, Montgomery would accept his alterations, but when there were queries he would never produce his sources. According to Williams, Montgomery's diaries would tend to show history as he would like it to be written, not as it actually was. Williams continued: 'My chief interest in the Montgomery diaries when they are eventually released would be to see what boasts Montgomery made about events in which he and I were intimately involved together.' Kit Dawnay told me that Montgomery always wanted the Log written to show events as he liked to view them in retrospect.

* He was Montgomery's G (Ops) officer at Twenty-First Army Group Tac HQ, and was in charge of the liaison officers and the whole of Tac HQ.

The Eighth Army files for the period I have covered are reasonably complete, but the Twenty-First Army Group files have been ravaged; I suspect that the Field-Marshal was partially responsible. After all, Winston Churchill, when Prime Minister after the war, gave Montgomery virtual approval when he defended him for keeping the original Lüneburg surrender document. In the House of Commons Churchill refused to take complaints about this 'liberation' seriously, saying: 'If such trophies became the personal property of the Commander-in-Chief in the field it would be an incentive to all young officers in the British Army.' He went on to tell the late Dick Stokes, Labour MP for Ipswich, that if he (Stokes) had secured the surrender of half a million enemies 'he could keep the receipt for the transaction, but I can assure the House there is no chance of anything like that happening' (*Hansard*, 17.6.1954, Col. 2277).

Fortunately, however, I have found the key records missing from the Twenty-First Army Group archives by searching in the files of other British formations and of SHAEF at the PRO, or in American archives and other archives at home.

I have unearthed a great number of Montgomery's letters and notes, mostly in his own handwriting. I have quoted copiously from these both because they reveal him as a man, and because they give the background to his often crucial decisions far better than his own post-war writing and speeches. His letters, notes and orders written in the heat of battle show dramatically his frame of mind at the time, and the considerations behind his actions and decisions.

His sometimes inflammatory correspondence with Eisenhower, much of which I have reproduced, demonstrates the at times bitter hostility between them. These internecine quarrels threatened the Anglo-American alliance, and the enmity between Twenty-First Army Group and the War Office, on the one hand, and SHAEF on the other, has never been fully underlined before. I have not taken sides, but have produced the facts for the reader to make his own judgement on the controversy. Nevertheless, I feel that the contrast between Montgomery's clear views on how the war should be conducted and Eisenhower's compromise and lack of decision emerges very clearly from their letters.

I give my sincere thanks to David Montgomery, the present

Viscount, for his kindness and his valuable help, and for permission to quote from his father's writings. He has been good enough to say that he welcomes this book.

Bill Williams is a very old friend of mine. We were both at Merton College, Oxford, as undergraduates fifty years ago, and it was a very small college then. It has been for me a great pleasure to resume our friendship, and the help he has given has been beyond value. He was close to Montgomery throughout the period I have covered and, with his acute academic mind and his experience in editing the *Dictionary of National Biography*, his comments have been most illuminating. I have included many quotations from Williams as they reveal much about Montgomery and the other British and American commanders; he has also been kind enough to read much of the manuscript.

I am deeply grateful to General Sir Frank Simpson, GBE, KCB, DSO ('Simbo'), Director of Military Operations at the War Office during the campaign in Europe. His memory and clarity of mind are exceptional, and he kindly gave me access to his important archives, which include 150 letters from Montgomery. He was a close personal friend of both Montgomery and Alanbrooke, and got on well with Eisenhower and Bedell Smith and the other American generals. From his position at the War Office he had a unique ringside view of the campaigns, and of the allies fighting them.

I am also very grateful to Kit Dawnay. As head of Twenty-First Army Group Tac HQ he knew Montgomery intimately, and was to a certain extent his confidant. He kindly gave me the run of his archives, which contain important and hitherto unpublished material, including the transcript of Montgomery's speech at the vital St Paul's School conference in April 1944, where security was so tight that no notes were allowed to be taken; other historians have had to rely on the memories of those who were present.

John Henderson, who was Montgomery's ADC from El Alamein in 1942 to the end of the war, has been most helpful, and my thanks are due to him for telling me about the Field-Marshal, for his reminiscences of recorded and unrecorded events, and for his courtesy and kindness.

My thanks are also due to Major Charles Messenger for his help. His recent experience at the Staff College and of the Staff

College battlefield tours has been most useful to me, and he kindly read in manuscript my accounts of the battles of 'Goodwood' and Arnhem and suggested improvements.

I would like most sincerely to thank all those who have given me the benefit of recollections and comments. Such is the interest in the Field-Marshal that as soon as it was known that I was writing this book I was proferred considerably more material than I could use; nevertheless, all of it proved of great value.

I am most grateful to the following, whose observations, besides the other help they have given me, have been of great value and add much to this book. I have, in accordance with usual practice, edited their comments for clarity, while scrupulously preserving the sense of their remarks: Maj-Gen Hew Butler, CB; Field-Marshal the Lord Carver, GCB, CBE, DSO, MC; Lt-Col C.P. Dawnay, CBE, MVO; Richard Du Vivier, Esq, CBE; General Sir David Fraser, GCB, OBE; the late General Sir Richard Gale, GCB, KBE, DSO, MC; Brigadier Michael Gordon-Watson, OBE, MC, MA; Brigadier Sir Geoffrey Hardy-Roberts, KCVO, CB, CBE; John Henderson, Esq, MBE; Brigadier A.G. Heywood, CBE, MVO, MC; Brigadier J. Hunter, DSO, OBE, MC; Wing-Commander Asher Lee; General Sir James Marshall-Cornwall, KCB, CBE, DSO, MC; The Viscount Montgomery of Alamein, CBE; General Sir Nigel Poett, KCB, DSO; Robert Priestley, Esq, MBE; General Sir Charles Richardson, GCB, CBE, DSO; Maj-Gen G.P.B. Roberts, CB, DSO, MC; Lt-Col G.A. Shepperd, MBE; General Sir Frank Simpson, GBE, KCB, DSO; Brian Urquhart, Esq; Brigadier Sir Edgar Williams, CB, CBE, DSO.

Bill Williams and General Sir Frank Simpson kindly lent me their recent correspondence with the late Maj-Gen Belchem, who was contemplating another book on the Second World War to follow his *Victory in Normandy* when he died; I am most grateful to Mrs Belchem for permission to quote from these letters in part.

Michael Olizar and the staff of the Sikorski Museum and Polish Institute, Kensington, have been most helpful over the Polish Army, and I am very grateful to them. I am also indebted to the staffs of the London Library and the Public Record Office, Kew; to Patricia Methuen, the Archivist, and the Trustees of the Liddell Hart Centre for Military Archives, King's College,

London; and to the staffs of Churchill College, Cambridge, the Imperial War Museum, London, and the Ministry of Defence Library, Whitehall.

I wish to thank most warmly those in America who gave me their help: Dr Forrest C. Pogue and John Wickman of the Dwight D. Eisenhower Library, Abilene, Kansas; Dr William Snyder, University of Texas; Professor Louis Galambos, Johns Hopkins University; Richard J. Somers, Archivist-Historian, US Army Military History Institute, Pennsylvania; Wilbert B. Mahoney, National Archives, Washington.

My thanks are due to the publishers of the Canadian Official History for permission to quote from the work of Colonel C.P. Stacey, and also to Messrs Batsford for permission to quote from Belfield and Essame's *The Battle for Normandy*. These and other useful works are listed in the bibliography. Of recent books I have found Russell Weighey's *Eisenhower's Lieutenants* an excellent, complete and well documented analysis of the North-West Europe campaign written from American sources. David Irving's *The War Between the Generals* provides many sidelights on the in-fighting between SHAEF, on one side, and the War Office and Twenty-First Army Group on the other. He does not give detailed references, but quotes outspoken extracts from the unexpurgated and unpublished originals of the Patton Diaries, the Butcher Diaries, the Courtney Hodges Diary, the Kay Summersby Diaries, and the diary kept for Air Chief Marshal Sir Arthur (later MRAF Lord) Tedder by Wing-Commander Scarman.

General Sir Miles Dempsey, who commanded XIII Corps in Sicily and Italy in 1943, and British Second Army in North-West Europe, played a key role in these campaigns, yet Montgomery mentions him little in his writing. Dempsey, a modest and unselfish man, never courted publicity or renown. His diary or daily log of the campaign in North-West Europe, deposited in the PRO, is a useful factual account; but he did not, however, put into it his views on controversies. For example, he does not mention the sacking of Bucknall, nor his argument with Montgomery about 'Goodwood', nor the controversy with the Americans over their taking Second Army's road on the way to the Seine. He makes it clear that he wanted the airborne drop at Wesel, not at Arnhem, but does not write a word of criticism of the way in which Montgomery frequently by-passed him and dealt directly with Horrocks, the XXX Corps commander. I am grateful to my cousin Geoffrey Hardy-Roberts and to Robert Priestley for their help over Miles Dempsey's role. Until his death Dempsey corresponded with certain historians, but under the thirty-year rule his letters will not be available until the year 2000.

Finally, I give warm thanks to Mrs Joan Moore and to John Mark for their secretarial help, and to Toby Buchan for his meticulous editing, and for his encouragement throughout.

Transcripts of Crown Copyright material in the Public Record Office appear by kind permission of the Controller, Her Majesty's Stationery Office.

Preface to the Paperback Edition

I am deeply grateful to the following for corrections and amendments to the first and second editions – Field-Marshal Lord Carver, Brigadier Michael Gordon Watson, Commander C.G. Crill, RN, Brian MacDermot, Esq., General Sir Charles Richardson, and Major-General G.P.B. 'Pip' Roberts.

The correspondence between General Alexander and Field-Marshal Alanbrooke about the US Army in North Africa was not released by the Alanbrooke Trustees in time for the English editions, although an extract is included in the American edition. It reveals Alexander's poor opinion of the fighting qualities of the US troops in North Africa.

An extract is now included on page 446, and should be read in conjunction with the account of the preparations for the invasion of Sicily on page 21. In light of this correspondence, it is not surprising that Alexander agreed to Montgomery's request that Patton's army should land side by side with the British in the south-east corner of Sicily – contrary to Patton's wishes. In the letter he showed to Montgomery, Alexander had stated that American troops would be 'quite useless in Europe'; Montgomery was therefore confident that Alexander would agree to his demand to take over Patton's road west of Etna. This incident was the first in the saga of hostility between Montgomery and Patton.

Of course, Alexander's prediction proved false. In Sicily Patton's army out-performed Montgomery's in the eyes of the world.

Since publication of the hardback editions Montgomery's private papers have been fully catalogued by Dr Stephen Brooks and made available to researchers at the Imperial War Museum. They add little to my research and do not cause me to alter my conclusions.

As I suspected (see page 11) Montgomery kept no diary for the campaign of 1944/45. References to his 'diary' in his published memoirs are to the 'log' written for him by Colonel Dawnay, on which I drew extensively. I am most grateful to Colonel Dawnay for his kindness in giving me access to the copy of the 'log' in his personal archives, because this is the key to Montgomery's thinking during the campaign and contains as appendices important letters and memoranda which had not been used previously as source material by any historian.

Other important clues to Montgomery's thinking can be found in his numerous letters from Twenty-First Army Group to the late General Sir Frank Simpson. Again these had not been used by any previous historian. I am most grateful to the late General Sir Frank Simpson and Lady Simpson for their kindness in having given me privileged access to their important archives which are now available to researchers in the Imperial War Museum.

June 1987

1

Sicily and After

Under the thirty-year rule, the Public Record Office has disgorged most of its secrets of the Second World War, and only for a few years more will it be possible to obtain the views of the survivors of those in high places during that tragic period. This is therefore the appropriate moment to attempt a definitive historical verdict on Bernard Montgomery's performance as commander in Sicily, Italy and North-West Europe between July 1943 and May 1945.

The key to understanding Montgomery's guidance of the campaigns is his complicated character and temperament. His devoted official biographer, Nigel Hamilton, writes: 'Bernard quarrelled savagely ... and scandalised the family by his treatment of his mother ... insulted and injured colleagues, seniors, subordinates, friends ... and turned against his son David.' For generations stories have circulated at Sandhurst that both Montgomery and the late Sir Oswald Mosley were sadistic while cadets, and the story of Bernard burning another boy and nearly being sacked from the Army when aged nineteen is authenticated by his official biographer.

Bernard admired his father, an Anglican bishop, but hated his mother, of whom he wrote in 1944 'She is a menace with children.' At Mons in September 1914 he had been badly wounded, lay in no-man's-land for four hours, and after his recovery stayed in staff jobs; he would otherwise probably not have survived the First World War.

His marriage was a great success and he was devoted to his son and stepsons. Influenced by ten happy married years in India, England and Egypt he became more affable, but his wife's tragic early death, in his arms, in October 1937 accentuated his abrasiveness, a characteristic which made him unpopular with many in the British Army.

Field-Marshal Lord Gort, CIGS in 1938 until he became C-in-C of the BEF in 1939, disliked Montgomery and refused to give him command of a division because of his reputation. However, thanks to his friend Lt-Gen Sir Alan Brooke, Bernard became a divisional commander as war broke out, and returned from the shambles of Dunkirk with a well-earned reputation as the most efficient of the British generals — his great personal courage had (and has) never been in doubt.

But although he was disliked by many of his contemporaries, Montgomery had admirers and friends in high places — notably Brooke, CIGS from 1941, Maj-Gen Frank Simpson, Director of Military Operations in 1944, and Sir James Grigg, Secretary of State for War from 1942. There was unparalleled efficiency in the armies he commanded, and his staff always worked devotedly for him.

Montgomery was brilliant at organisation; all his working life was devoted to studying how to make army staff work more efficient. He understood every branch of the army and its weapons; he was expert at moving great numbers of men and huge quantities of stores and vehicles at great speed across large distances; above all, his personality was always good for the morale of his troops. He understood how to co-operate with the RAF and the Navy, and appreciated the immense value of interpreting and using Ultra signals* and other intelligence about the enemy. And, provided he was in sole charge, he was good at commanding the troops of other nations.

Any errors he made were in strategy; his armies were always highly efficient technically. No departmental head under Montgomery could pull the wool over his eyes; they had to do the job properly or he would find them out. He devoured and understood statistics of vehicles, stores and ammunition, and always knew the current reinforcement position. As a result his

---

* At Bletchley Park, near London, certain enemy signals were tapped and decoded by experts using Enigma machines. The decrypts were sent to the armies in the field and were known as 'Ultra'. It was imperative that the enemy did not know that their most vital and sensitive signals were being interpreted, and the existence and use of Ultra remained the most closely guarded secret of the war, one which was not revealed until thirty years afterwards.

decisions were soundly based on a proper appreciation of what it was possible for his army to do, provided that the intelligence about the enemy was correct. His successes were due to this professional brilliance. His mistakes were due to his temperament, notably in dealing with others, to sudden swings from optimism to gloom, and to extreme jealousy and dislike of any criticism of his plans. Apart from Arnhem, he tended to be over-cautious.

Montgomery's greatest moment was his victory at El Alamein in October 1942, and the triumphant advance of his Eighth Army into Tunisia early in 1943. Once in Tunisia he had to co-operate both with the British First Army and the US Army. For the first time his over-caution began to show, and his arrogance alienated the American generals.

At the Casablanca Conference in January 1943 Roosevelt and Churchill had decided upon an Allied invasion of Sicily later that year, once the Germans had been cleared out of North Africa. Montgomery expected to be in sole charge of the Allied armies in Sicily, and General Sir Harold Alexander, C-in-C in the Middle East, proposed him for the post. General Dwight D. Eisenhower, C-in-C Allied Forces in North Africa, was against him and was backed by Churchill. As a result Montgomery was left in command of the British Eighth Army, and General George Patton had a separate command, the US Seventh Army. Both were to be under Alexander's Fifteenth Army Group with Eisenhower in overall command at Allied Forces HQ in Algiers. Eisenhower set up his planning team for the Sicily campaign, codenamed 'Husky', in the Ecole Militaire in Algiers in February 1943. From the start he and Alexander made it plain that Patton and Montgomery were to be on an equal footing. This cooled the Eighth Army commander's ardour. In his own words it was no longer to be 'a private war conducted by the Eighth Army. Instead we had to adjust our way of doing things to a larger canvas and this would mean compromise'.[1]

Curiously, in addition to the Algiers effort other planning staffs were at work in London, Cairo and Rabat. Montgomery, not liking what he heard from these sources, demanded an urgent conference with Eisenhower in Algiers, which took place on 19 April 1943. There he asked for Eighth Army HQ to be withdrawn from the fighting in Tunisia as soon as possible in order to undertake the planning in Cairo while X Corps controlled the Eighth Army front. In a memorandum he wrote: 'Some sort of compromise will be necessary to get ourselves out of the mess we are now in.'[2]

Montgomery was correct in describing the planning for 'Husky' as a 'mess'. There had by now been seven different plans, and Eisenhower's staff were working on Plan 8. Montgomery had not been consulted at all, although Eighth Army was to play a major part. In Cairo his Chief of Staff, Freddie de Guingand, recently promoted Major-General for the Sicily planning, showed him Plan 8.

The Eighth Army was to land in the south-east corner of Sicily around Syracuse and Gela; Patton's US Seventh Army was to land at the north-west corner around Palermo and Trapani. Out of hand, Montgomery turned down Plan 8 and insisted that the Eighth Army assault must be concentrated around Syracuse and the Pachino peninsula, immediately to its south.

A conference was held in Algiers on 2 May. According to Montgomery he buttonholed the American Lt-Gen Walter Bedell Smith, Eisenhower's Chief of Staff, in the lavatory and persuaded him before he went back to the conference room that the two armies should land side by side; in other words that instead of sending the Americans to the north-west they should land on Montgomery's left flank at Gela. During the conference, according to the shorthand notes, Montgomery insisted there would be severe opposition from the Germans, agreed emphatically with Air Chief Marshal Sir Arthur Tedder, commanding the RAF in that theatre, that the airfields around Gela must be captured during the initial assault, and laid down that the armies must above all be concentrated. He concluded: 'The answer to the problem is to shift the US effort from the Palermo area to land on either side of Gela. The invasion of Sicily will then be a complete success.'[3] The next day Alexander signalled Montgomery that Eisenhower had agreed to his plan.

General Sir Charles Richardson (at that time Brigadier, General Staff, Eighth Army HQ), told me that he went with Montgomery to the Algiers Conference, and that the tale of the lavatory incident is substantially correct. Before the conference Montgomery rehearsed his arguments to Richardson, insisting that the British and American landing beaches must be close so

*See Preface to Paperback Edition page 17 and Appendix page 446.

that the two armies could give each other mutual support. He had kept on saying: 'Is that clear, Charles?' and Richardson assured him it was. According to Richardson, Montgomery put his arguments to the conference so crisply and cogently that he won the day easily. Patton, however, had set his heart upon acting independently in Sicily, and was bitterly disappointed at this turn of events, which meant that his US Seventh Army had to assault on beaches adjoining the British. He was full of resentment against Montgomery, though he loyally accepted the decision.

As soon as the Tunisian fighting finished, with the surrender of all the Germans and Italians on 13 May, General Sir Bernard Montgomery went home on leave. He was hailed as a conquering hero. He stayed at Claridges, where crowds flocked to see him going in and out; letters and presents poured in – so many that he had to employ extra ADCs to deal with them – and the national papers covered acres of newsprint with his praises. Britain had lost so many battles in the early stages of the war that they were starved of a military hero, and Montgomery filled the bill admirably. The War Office encouraged him to show off, since they considered it good for the Army, which desperately needed a successful general to boost its morale.

Fame, alas, is a heady business, and without doubt Montgomery got a whiff of *folie de grandeur*. De Guingand, who knew Montgomery intimately, wrote: 'He lost a little of his simplicity and realised that he was a power in the land and that there were few who would not heed his advice. In fact he realised he could afford to be really tough to get his own way.'[4]

Alan Moorehead, then a war correspondent in North Africa, had ample opportunity to observe Montgomery, judging that 'He always had a certain intensely serious determination to impose his will on other people.' From that time on this domineering trait was markedly accentuated, and there is little doubt that this brief trip to London, with its rampant publicity and admission to exalted circles, produced a subtle character change. He became more difficult to deal with and keener than ever to dominate the scene.[5] This was to have sad consequences – especially in his relations with the American generals.

Montgomery returned to Algiers on 2 June to meet the Prime Minister and the CIGS (with them came the King, who knighted Montgomery in an aerodrome tent on 19 June). The Sicily invasion was scheduled for early June.

Brooke, the CIGS, had advised Churchill that Montgomery's lack of tact and tendency to arrogance made the American generals dislike him, and that they refused to back him as sole commander of 'Husky'. While in Algiers Brooke recorded his opinion of Montgomery in his diary:

He requires a lot of education to make him see the whole situation outside the Eighth Army orbit. A difficult mixture to handle; brilliant commander and trainer of men, but liable to commit untold errors due to lack of tact, lack of appreciation of other people's outlook. It is most depressing that the Americans do not like him and it will always be a difficult matter to have him fighting in close proximity to them. He wants guiding and watching continually, and I do not think Alex is sufficiently strong and rough with him.

Brooke was a close friend and admirer of Montgomery, and remained devoted to him until the end of the war, which makes his criticism revealing. He was always disparaging about Alexander who, according to one historian, acted in Sicily and Italy only as 'Monty's glorified road manager'.[6]

Montgomery's task with Eighth Army was to land XIII Corps (Lt-Gen Miles Dempsey) just south of Syracuse, and XXX Corps (Lt-Gen Oliver Leese) astride the Pachino peninsula to capture the airfield there. Both the American and the British landings were to be preceded by airborne assaults, with British 1st Airborne Division landing in gliders and US 82nd Airborne parachuting in.

Morale in the Italian Sixth Army, defending Sicily, was low and their fighting troops were in poor condition, while the Italian battle fleet was at La Spezia, 400 miles away, and reluctant to leave port. But the German 15th Panzer Division had nearly 100 tanks, and the Herman Goering infantry division was on its way – German morale was high. There were 315,000 Italian and 50,000 German troops on the island.

More troops and ships took part in the Sicilian invasion than in the initial Normandy assault. 2,500 naval vessels carried 115,000 British Empire and 66,000 American assault troops in the largest amphibious operation in history.

At 0245 on 10 July Montgomery's Eighth Army assault went

in, and made good progress against light opposition. The enemy, however, reacted more strongly against Patton's US Seventh Army and made counter-attacks with tanks against the Americans at Gela. These were beaten off with the help of naval guns. By the evening of the 10th Eighth Army held forty miles of coastline, and the port of Syracuse – so important to the Allies – was captured without opposition. Montgomery himself landed at 1700 on 12 July (D + 2); Brigadier Sir Edgar (Bill) Williams, head of Eighth Army Intelligence, told me they both bathed in the sea at Syracuse that evening.

Montgomery signalled Alexander at Fifteenth Army Group on 12 July: 'Battle situation very good. Everything going very well. No need for you to come unless you wish', but to his own Main HQ he reported: 'Most of Airborne Brigade landed in sea and thus could not contribute to the operation.'[7]

Although the seaborne operations were successful, Montgomery's airborne landings had been disastrous. On the night of 9 July 1,200 men of British 1 Airlanding Brigade were flown into Sicily in 144 gliders. The American pilots of the towing aircraft were inexperienced and most of them loosed their gliders far too early. Sixty-nine gliders fell into the sea, fifty-six were scattered along the southern coast, and only twelve gliders with around 100 men landed on the target, the Ponte Grande bridge near Syracuse. Eight officers and sixty-five men held the bridge until they were relieved, but the proportion of casualties amongst these scarce, highly trained elite troops was tragic.

1 Parachute Brigade, which Montgomery sent in to attack the Primosole Bridge between Augusta and Catania on the night of 13 July, fared worse. Although Montgomery had captured Syracuse and Augusta the German armour held up his advance through the plain to Catania, and he badly needed the Primosole Bridge. 1,900 parachutists in 126 Dakotas piloted by Americans, together with nineteen gliders carrying anti-tank guns, dropped at the same time as the Germans dropped their redoubtable 4th Parachute Regiment from the air almost into the same dropping zone. Of the British, only 250 of all ranks could be assembled after landing. They captured the bridge, but after removing the mines and detonators they ran out of ammunition and were forced to leave the bridge to the Germans. It was not recaptured until 16 July – Montgomery had wasted his airborne troops.

After this failure Montgomery contemplated using airborne troops for another drop but Alexander, firm for once, vetoed this, signalling: 'Not prepared to sanction further use of airborne troops until training of pilots improved. Do not contemplate further use.'[8]

The best commentary comes from Maj-Gen John Frost, who dropped on Primosole:

> The Germans fully realised the importance of denying the easy run across the plain to the narrow route between Mount Etna and the sea, which was the key to the defence of Sicily. In fact Catania was never taken, but was outflanked as a result of very hard fighting elsewhere. The Catanian plain was an ideal DZ, and with the whole of it in our hands Catania and the key would have quickly been at our mercy. I consider that if the whole of the 1st Airborne Division had been put down on the Catania plain, from the Primosole Bridge to Catania, the whole campaign in Sicily would have been won within ten days.[9]

This is a valid criticism of Montgomery.

At first Montgomery gravely underestimated the strength of the German reaction. On 13 July he informed Alexander: 'General battle situation excellent. Am making a great effort to reach Catania tomorrow night 14 July, and with some luck hope to do so.' On 16 July his signal to Alexander read: 'Hope to get to Catania tonight.'[10] But he had misread the situation, for Catania did not fall until 6 August.

Now the Eighth Army commander created grave trouble between himself and the Americans. On 14 July, with the failure of the parachute drop, Montgomery found himself held up in the Catanian Plain by 29th Panzer Division, reinforced by the two regiments of paratroopers flown in from Avignon in France, one of which, the 4th, had coincided on the Primosole DZ with the British. Without warning Patton or asking Alexander for authority, Montgomery decided to usurp Route 124, running west of Etna towards Messina, although this had been assigned to Patton for his advance up Sicily. Late on 14 July Alexander signalled that he agreed Eighth Army was to have Route 124 and that US Seventh Army was to relinquish it. Patton and the Americans were furious, feeling that Montgomery, backed by

Alexander, had arbitrarily relegated their role to guarding his left flank.

Montgomery tried to encircle Etna by sending XXX Corps round the west on Route 124, while XIII Corps on its own attacked along the east coast. With insufficient weight to their attacks and with Eighth Army's artillery and tanks divided, both corps soon became bogged down. If their commander had sent both his corps along the east coast and allowed Patton to attack in full strength to the west of Etna, the Allied thrust would have been too powerful for the Germans.

A livid Patton flew to Tunisia to see Alexander, who soon realised how deep was the American resentment; as a consolation prize he agreed that Patton could manoeuvre to the west and capture Palermo. Alexander, by allowing Montgomery to divide Eighth and Seventh Armies, condemned them both to a slogging match; the German defences around Etna have been compared with Torres Vedras. Patton fared better than the British. In four days with a brilliantly executed operation he captured Palermo in the north-west tip of the island, and on the next day, 23 July, he attacked east along the north coast. Despite bitter resistance his troops entered Messina on 16 August, the day before the British, after thirty-eight days of fighting. He had stolen Montgomery's colours, and was thrilled to have his revenge for the dirty trick he felt the latter had played on him by pinching *his* Route 124.

As the Eighth Army began to make some progress Montgomery sent signal after signal to Algiers to enquire about 'My Fortress' – a four-engined bomber which Eisenhower had offered him for his personal use. It arrived in Malta, but then got lost because it was sent to North Africa for a new engine. On 23 July Montgomery sent a telegram of congratulations to Patton for capturing Palermo, and accepted an invitation to visit him there on the 27th. By now the Fortress had arrived, and after cabling Patton to warn all his anti-aircraft defences on the coast route, the British general flew in it to Palermo. On the way back there was nearly a nasty accident, and to Montgomery's relief, Bedell Smith replaced it with a C47 Dakota which was more suitable for the short runways available.

When on 13 July Montgomery had decided to use Eighth Army in a two-pronged attack around Etna, instead of letting Patton come up on his left flank on Route 124, the Sicilian

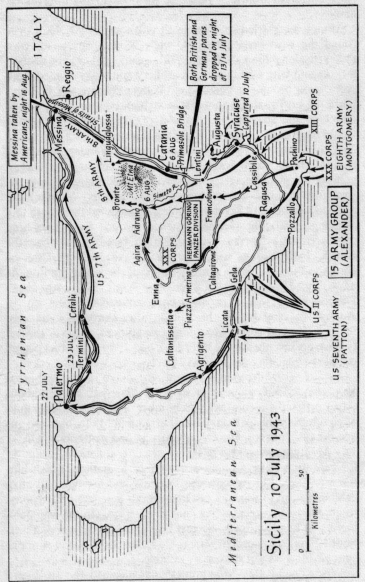

Sicily 10 July 1943

ITALY

Messina taken by Americans, night 16 Aug

Both British and German paras dropped on night of 13/14 July

8TH ARMY

Reggio

Straits of Messina

Messina

Linguaglossa

Catania
6 AUG
Primasole Bridge

Syracuse
Captured 10 July

Augusta

US 7th ARMY

Mt Etna

Bronte
6 AUG

Lentini

XIII CORPS

Simeto R.

Adrano

Francofonte

Cassible

Agira

HERMANN GORING PANZER DIVISION

Ragusa

EIGHTH ARMY
(MONTGOMERY)

Enna

XXX CORPS

Caltagirone

Pozzallo

XXX CORPS

Pachino

15 ARMY GROUP
(ALEXANDER)

Piazza Armerina

Gela

Caltanissetta

Licata

US II CORPS

23 JULY
Termini

Cefalù

Agrigento

Palermo

22 JULY

Tyrrhenian Sea

US SEVENTH ARMY
(PATTON)

Mediterranean Sea

0   50
Kilometres

campaign shed its early hopes of brilliant success. Alexander erred greatly in endorsing Montgomery's decision to use Route 124, and the Germans at Messina had time to evacuate their troops and equipment across the Straits to Italy. Correctly Maj-Gen Hubert Essame wrote: 'Monty was too strong a personality for Alexander, and only one man, Alanbrooke, could ever control him.'[11] Alas, in Sicily Alanbrooke was not at hand.

Eisenhower and Alexander had made no master plan for the two armies, preferring to leave it flexible. They failed to understand what a hideous omission this was, for Montgomery was temperamentally incapable of consulting with Patton to construct such a plan. As a result of the hard fighting on each side of Etna Eighth Army suffered nearly 12,000 casualties, against the Americans' 7,500. Maj-Gen David Belchem, Montgomery's BGS in Sicily and Italy, wrote: '... if Monty and Patton had made a co-ordinated drive around Etna to Messina they would have got there more quickly with less loss of life.'[12]

Here Belchem is deliberately contradicting his former commander, for in defence of his decision to put XXX Corps on Route 124 Montgomery himself had written: '... to persist in the advance to Catania would have meant very heavy casualties ... the object could be achieved with less loss of life by operating on the Adrano axis [to the west] with the added advantage that on that flank we would be in close touch with our American Allies.'[13] This excuse does not hold water, since Patton was only too ready to fill XXX Corp's role on the west slopes of Etna. If Montgomery had kept all his armour and strength on the east coast while Patton made the left hook, the result would have been much happier for the Allies, and in all probability the Germans would not have succeeded in evacuating their troops so successfully from Messina.

Not only did Montgomery upset Patton and the Americans, he also provoked Lt-Gen A.G.L. McNaughton, GOC Canadian Army Overseas, who wanted to visit the Canadian Division in Sicily commanded by Maj-Gen Guy Simonds. Montgomery rudely forbade him to come and said he would be arrested if he landed. McNaughton was furious, as was the Canadian Government. Alexander backed Montgomery up completely, saying that because of the shortage of transport the decision was justified. McNaughton complained bitterly to Eisenhower who, concerned, took the matter up with Alexander during a bathe in the Mediterranean at Amilcar, Tunisia. But with Alexander backing his general, all the diplomatic American could do was to tell McNaughton that 'he could not interfere in a family matter between Britain and the Commonwealth.'[14]

Lord Tweedsmuir, who commanded a Canadian regiment in Sicily and Italy, told me that Simonds asked Montgomery to keep McNaughton away. Bill Williams states that Montgomery said to him at the time 'he would not have parades with a C-in-C while they were fighting battles under his orders'. This Williams felt was 'absurd and just an excuse for being high-handed'.

Montgomery showed at least some consistency in keeping McNaughton out, for he refused to have the observers from Cairo sent by GHQ, Middle East Forces. During the planning stages in Cairo de Guingand, without consulting Montgomery, had arranged with his opposite number at MEF for them to send into Sicily three observers — a gunner, an infantryman, and a tank soldier. The gunner observer, Colonel Godfrey Jeans, stayed in Sicily for three weeks at Eighth Army Main HQ with Montgomery's Major-General, Royal Artillery, Alan Hornby. At first Montgomery thought Jeans was one of Hornby's staff, but when he learned that he belonged to MEF he immediately sent a message that he must leave at once or he would be arrested and deported. Godfrey Jeans told me: 'At the time we felt Monty just could not stand any interference from outside.' Tragically, the tank observer, Lt-Col Archie Little, was killed just as he got *his* marching orders, and the infantry observer never got further than Malta because Montgomery, as soon as he learnt of his presence, told him to go back to Cairo. Montgomery was in fact cutting off his nose to spite his face, since the job of the observers was to transmit back to the training schools in the Middle East valuable information about the Sicily beach landings and other aspects of the fighting, and these training schools were supplying the Eighth Army's reinforcements.[15]

The Allied Military Government Officers, responsible for civil affairs in captured Italian territory, did not come under Montgomery's direct command. He was equally high-handed with them. He refused to allow them in his early loading schedules, and when in his opinion they failed to take over captured towns quickly enough he complained strongly to their head, Maj-Gen Lord Rennell of Rodd, in charge of Civil Affairs

Administration for Italy and the Middle East. When Lord
Rennell replied that they were short of transport Montgomery
said to him: 'Why can't they get cracking on a bicycle?'

Lord Rennell found Montgomery so unco-operative that he
complained to Grigg, the Secretary of State for War. Grigg and
Rennell were friends, and both enjoyed making outspoken
criticisms in private. Grigg passed on Rennell's complaint to
Montgomery, and got back this amusing letter:

> Rennell, dressed as a Major-General, arrived at my Tac HQ.
> He was given tea and greeted. He asked me how AMGOT
> was going. He was very pompous and rather superior; he
> gave the impression that it was good of him to have come. I
> told him AMGOT was going very badly and hampering our
> operations. He disagreed and said it was going very well, and
> became rather argumentative.
>
> He resented any criticism of his show. In my opinion they
> have a very poor lot of chaps in AMGOT; old school ties, the
> peerage, diseased guardsmen, etc.[16]

Montgomery had found the thirty-eight days of the Sicilian
campaign frustrating. He had so enjoyed being in sole charge in
North Africa that it was a step down to share the command and
what glory there was with the fire-eating George Patton. He was
disappointed, too, when his forward commando troops entering
Messina found Patton's infantry already there, having covered a
considerably greater distance while his army had bogged down.
Sicily was an anti-climax for him, and only a partial success.

Now, with his laurels stolen during 'Husky', Montgomery was
desperately anxious to be the 'overlord' of the Allied invasion of
Italy. He wanted a new triumph, and felt discredited because the
Germans had successfully evacuated to the mainland the bulk of
their forces, and were now preparing for the defence of Italy
under the overall command of Field-Marshal Albert Kesselring.
Although the Allies had complete air supremacy and the Royal
Navy dominated the sea, the Germans with 60,000 men and
10,000 vehicles had crossed the Straits of Messina before the
city fell on 17 August.*

---

* On 17 August General Alfred Jodl, Hitler's Chief of Staff, telephoned
Field-Marshal Erwin Rommel, commanding the German armies in north

The next step, the invasion of the toe of Italy, like Sicily, was planned as a joint British and American operation. This, in Montgomery's view, required an 'overlord' to co-ordinate the operations, though the chain of command remained the same: Eisenhower, Supreme Commander in Algiers with Alexander his deputy at Fifteenth Army Group, Admiral Sir Andrew Cunningham, Naval C-in-C, and Tedder, Air C-in-C. But Eisenhower and Alexander refused an 'overlord' despite the crying need for one, and the clear evidence from Sicily that Montgomery would not voluntarily co-operate satisfactorily with an American commander.

Originally the invasion of Italy was to be carried out only by the Eighth Army on a two-corps front, with a direct assault across the Straits of Messina (Operation 'Baytown') and another landing in the area of Gioia Tiro on the north coast of the toe (Operation 'Buttress'). This plan appealed to Montgomery, who would then have been in sole charge of a dramatic invasion of Europe. But with the fall of Mussolini and the probability of an Italian surrender the Allies in late July planned another seaborne landing at Salerno ('Avalanche') and an airborne landing by US 82nd Airborne on the Rome airfields. This last operation ('Giant 2') was called off because of a last-minute panic by the Italian General Carboni, in command of the Italian armoured divisions who should have defended the Rome airfields against German attacks during the airborne landings. The operation would have been a success, according, to the American generals involved, and also in the view of General Siegfried Westphal, Kesselring's Chief of Staff.[17]

To Montgomery's annoyance 'Buttress' was cancelled on 17 August and X Corps, which would have undertaken it, was taken away from him and put under the command of the US Fifth Army (General Mark Clark) for 'Avalanche' (US Seventh Army had been replaced by US Fifth Army). The new plan, for two armies to invade Italy simultaneously in place of his Eighth Army on its own, annoyed Montgomery, especially as 'Baytown' was downgraded to a minor four-battalion operation with a slow build-up. He demanded at least two divisions for 'Baytown' and protested so vigorously to Alexander that

---

Italy: '90 to 95 per cent of the troops' had been safely evacuated to Messina and nearly all the trucks and guns.[18]

eventually the Eighth Army assault across the Straits of Messina was upgraded to two divisions under XIII Corps – 5th Infantry and 1st Canadian, together with 231 Independent Brigade. The US Fifth Army force for Salerno was far larger and consisted of British X Corps and US VI Corps, both under Clark's Fifth Army HQ.

General Patton, commanding the replaced US Seventh Army, had gone back to America under a cloud following two unfortunate incidents with patients in field hospitals who he suspected of malingering, and Seventh Army's next assignment was to be the invasion of southern France in August 1944, codenamed 'Anvil', under General Alexander Patch. US Seventh Army had been formed in Algiers on 5 January 1944 under Mark Clark, and had been trained for amphibious operations – for landing near Gibraltar if Spain entered the war, then for Sardinia and now for Italy.

No one realised more clearly than Montgomery the crying need for a master plan and a single commander to co-ordinate 'Avalanche' and 'Baytown', because of the strong German forces in Italy. General Heinrich von Vietinghoff-Scheel's German Tenth Army had redeployed to meet a possible Allied landing in central Italy, General Hans Hube's XIV Panzer Corps with two Panzer divisions and one Panzer Grenadier division having taken up positions near Gaeta and Salerno, while Herr's LXXVI Panzer Corps had been withdrawn to a line Scalea-Taranto-Brindisi, leaving only a single battalion south of Catanzaro to oppose the Eighth Army landing. Montgomery disliked playing second fiddle – instead of planning to go all out to help 'Avalanche' he preferred to build up his forces in the toe of Italy with a view to mounting a successful campaign once Eighth Army was firmly established in strength on the mainland of Europe. He was genuinely worried by the German strength in Italy, estimated at twenty divisions, and feared a disaster in the early stages.

On 19 August he signalled Alexander that he would be so short of landing-craft that 'any invasion of Europe in face of opposition would be impossible.'[19] He complained also that he had been given no 'object' for the operation, and had no information about the resistance likely to be encountered. This last observation was incorrect, since Eighth Army Intelligence knew that only Herr's Panzer corps was near the toe of Italy, and a 3 Commando patrol had crossed the Messina Straits to reconnoitre.[20] Intensive air reconnaissance over Reggio and the surrounding countryside had confirmed that there were few German soldiers, while the Italian troops were unlikely to fight.*

Alexander replied on 20 August:

Your task is to secure a bridgehead on the toe of Italy ... in the event of the enemy withdrawing from the toe you will follow him up with such force as you can make available bearing in mind the extent to which you can engage the enemy in the southern toe of Italy, the more assistance you will be giving to Avalanche.[21]

Montgomery, however, ignored this instruction about helping 'Avalanche' at his Eighth Army staff conference held on 26 August, where he said: 'The limit of operations will be the capture of the toe as far as the neck at Catanzaro.'[22] The Catanzaro neck is the isthmus between the Gulfs of San Euphemia and Squillace, eighty miles north of Reggio, and this was an incorrect interpretation of Alexander's instructions. However, all Montgomery's administration and build-up was based on this limited objective, with plainly a minimum intention of rendering immediate help to 'Avalanche'. It is quite clear that Montgomery planned his own campaign in Italy as something separate from 'Avalanche', but blame for allowing this falls also upon Alexander and Eisenhower who, with a sad lack of foresight, invaded Italy without proper co-ordination of the operations of their two armies. It was left to Alexander at Fifteenth Army Group HQ in Africa to do his best in the situation, and he was too weak with his Eighth Army commander.

On 23 August Eisenhower called a conference with Montgomery and Mark Clark, the two army commanders, in Algiers. Montgomery asserted that the earliest he could carry out 'Baytown' was the night of 4/5 September, not 30/31 August as ordered by Eisenhower. Eventually, however, he agreed to cross the Straits on the night of 2/3 September after Admiral

---

* Major (now Brigadier) Peter Young, the well known author, took a patrol of Durnford-Slater's 3 Commando over the straits to Bova Marina on 26 August. They radioed messages to XIII Corps, and sent an officer back with Italian prisoners to Sicily. Their reports made it clear the coast of the toe was not garrisoned by Germans, and there were few Italian soldiers.

Cunningham had promised to fly to Italy to hurry on the naval preparations. Eisenhower told the army commanders that the Allies were on the brink of an armistice with the Italians, after which it was hoped that the Italians would immediately join the fighting on the Allied side. On his return to Sicily Montgomery moved forward from his luxurious villa at Taormina to a tent and caravan encampment hastily set up for his Tactical HQ on the Messina coast.

A few commandos who crossed the Straits and landed at Bova Marina on the night of 27/28 August reported no enemy anywhere near, and the German artillery fire was almost non-existent – only a few shells arrived at Messina, probably from mobile 88-mm guns, on the evening of 2 September.[23] All the signs were that the landing would be unopposed.

Montgomery's orders to 5th Division were: 'Establish a bridgehead ... be prepared to move north-east to enable beachheads to be developed for maintenance, capture San Giovanni and Cannitello to open the Straits for the Royal Navy.'[24] There was no mention of advancing along the road to Salerno.

Montgomery's intelligence officers considered that there was not more than one German brigade group in southern Calabria and that the Germans were unlikely to resist invading forces until the latter reached the Gioia Plain, thirty miles north of Reggio. All this notwithstanding, Montgomery insisted on a creeping artillery barrage on the undefended north shore of the Straits of an intensity recalling the Battle of the Somme. An elaborate fire plan was drawn up by the CCRA, XXX Corps, although no enemy positions had been identified. A considerable portion of the fire was directed on forts shown on the maps, but when British troops landed they found there had been no guns in most of these forts since 1915; most were either abandoned or used as magazines.[25] Senior officers went to the artillery HQ in a villa overlooking the Straits and selected targets. Then the CCRA would call down fire on them to demonstrate his preparedness.

600 Eighth Army guns fired from the mainland at 0345 on 3 September, as did the big guns of *Nelson, Warspite, Rodney* and *Valiant*, with destroyers and gun-boats joining in at short range – American field guns joined in as well. Over 400 tons of shells were fired by Eighth Army alone, though Montgomery never explained why he indulged in this useless and prodigal barrage.

The war correspondent Christopher Buckley wrote:

> British commandos had reported from the further shore and
> in view of their reports and other indications of no serious
> opposition on the beaches the bombardment seemed rather
> unnecessary and wasteful. There was little evidence of any
> guns near the enemy beaches. Personally I believe this heavy
> bombardment could have been perfectly well dispensed with,
> but it had been elaborately planned and I suppose it was not
> easy to call it off.[26]

Buckley expresses the consensus view, held by those present at
the time, of this extravagant barrage on which Montgomery had
insisted.

3 September was a perfect Mediterranean morning. As the
barrage lifted 5th Division and 1st Canadian crossed the Straits
in a flotilla of boats and quickly occupied a little chain of fishing
villages and the small town of San Giovanni. The large town of
Reggio further south was occupied without opposition, and none
of the beaches were wired. Italian soldiers emerged from their
few pill-boxes and trenches with their hands up, and helped the
invaders to unload their stores. Reggio had been occupied by
0930, and within four hours RAF fighters were using the
aerodrome. Most of the inhabitants had fled into the hills, and
the town was heavily damaged by shelling and bombing.

In his intelligence report up to 1900 on 3 September Bill
Williams wrote: 'No effective resistance was encountered.
Civilian Reports say Germans retreated two days ago to Bagadi
and Gambaria. From Air Recce it appears this is only
temporary line ... During the day there was no contact with
German troops.'[27]

The invasion was like a naval regatta. Hundreds of boats
crossed and recrossed the three miles of dead calm sea of the
Straits of Messina — motor- and steam-boats and warships. On
the Sicilian side Italians gave or sold flowers and fruits to the
Allied soldiers as they embarked. It was a beautiful scene except
for the horror of the thick palls of smoke rising from Reggio
after its unnecessary bombing and shelling. During the morning
Montgomery crossed in his own launch and then transferred to
a DUKW, loaded in advance with cigarettes to give away to the
troops. He received an enthusiastic welcome both from his own

men and the Italians as he returned to Europe, more than three years after his ignominious departure from Dunkirk.

Bill Williams, crossing with his General, found him

> relaxed and happy as a schoolboy. When he got into Reggio Montgomery went into the local Fascist HQ and there found a fantastic amount of good writing paper, which he immediately appropriated because it was so much better than the Eighth Army issue paper. He was normally strongly anti-looting, but that morning was a 'relaxed magpie'.

Montgomery used this Fascist stationery for his letters,* and many Eighth Army files are encased in thick cardboard marked in Italian 'various subjects' and 'curriculum vitae'.

Telephone calls made by obliging Italian local government officers revealed that 29th Panzer Division had been withdrawn to the north; Montgomery had the toe of Italy to himself. That night a signal announced that the Italian surrender had been signed secretly, yet he issued no orders to his troops to advance quickly or urgently to reconnoitre the road to Salerno. Had Montgomery himself been responsible for 'Avalanche' as well as 'Baytown' he would have had his troops scampering up the approach roads from the toe to the Salerno beach-head to secure the south flank of 'Avalanche'. Now he deliberately ignored Alexander's instructions of 20 August about assisting 'Avalanche', and instead concentrated on building up his supplies in preparation for a German counter-attack which, since they had pulled back, could never come. The Canadian division marched north-east through the hills via Aspromonte, enjoying the cool upland air, and reached Locri on the east coast. They met no opposition, and for the next few days advanced leisurely along the pleasant coast road, arriving at Catanzaro Lido on the evening of the 10th with no battle casualties.

The western coastal route was the direct link with Salerno, and 5th Division following it met no Germans on the first day.

---

*Montgomery loved appropriating captured stationery. At the end of April 1945, after Twenty-First Army Group captured Munster, he used the writing paper of the GOC, German Sixth Army Corps, for his letters to the War Office.

By dark on the 3rd the line San Stefano-Scilla had been reached, and commandos landing at Bagnara that night found they were cutting off the withdrawal of light German rearguards. The leading infantry of 5th Division soon linked up with the commandos, and the remaining Germans retired. By noon on 6 September Gioia Tauro was reached after 'slight German resistance'; at 1425 there was contact with the enemy at Rosarno, but by 2330 leading troops of 13 Brigade were beyond Rosarno. Demolitions caused some delays, and it took 5th Division HQ nine hours to travel eighteen miles.[28]

In an effort to pinch off the German retreat the XIII Corps commander, Lt-Gen Miles Dempsey, ordered 231 Independent Brigade Group, consisting of 2nd Devons, 1st Hampshires and 1st Dorsets, with 3 and 40 Commandos, to land at Santa Venere just south of Pizzo early on 8 September. Their arrival on the beach coincided with the withdrawal of the German 29th Panzer Grenadiers along the coast road. The Germans took up positions in and around Pizzo, which stands on a bold sandstone promontory, and their mortar and artillery fire caused casualties on the beach soon after dawn; one LCT was knocked out, though it managed to unload its lorries. There was fighting around Pizzo for most of the day, during which a German counter-attack was repelled with the help of naval guns. A war correspondent who landed with 231 Brigade at Santa Venere wrote:

> The Brigade's landing showed remarkable conservativeness ... and was not used as boldly as they might have been ... early in the morning, had its orders permitted, the Brigade might have established itself at Pizzo securing more far reaching results. As it was assigned a semi-passive role, the enemy later in the afternoon got additional troops to Pizzo by way of the secondary road. Our failure to attempt to capture Pizzo which was at no stage strongly held and get us to the important road junction beyond it is less apparent.[29]

There was similar criticism from other observers.

The 231 Brigade convoy had left Messina on the evening of 7 September but lost its bearings and landed at San Venere in considerable confusion, with the Dorsets on the right and the Hampshires on the left. The Dorsets, once off the beach, ran into German half-tracks carrying four-barrelled 20-mm guns, and one Mark IV tank. Their 6-pdr anti-tank guns knocked out the tank, and in a well known incident (the subject of a painting), Sgt Evans threw a grenade into a half-track, for which he was later awarded the Military Medal. On the evening of the 8th 5th Division infantry arrived from the south through Vibo Valentia, and the Germans abandoned Pizzo. On the 9th 231 Brigade, with the Devons in the lead, advanced quickly for twenty miles to the Amato River. They met little opposition, although the brigade commander, rashly motoring ahead in his jeep, was wounded in an encounter with a mobile detachment of Germans. On the 10th the Devons crossed the Amato followed by the 5th Division infantry; the Dorsets were ordered to drop out and remained for three days near Nicastro for rest and reorganisation.

Montgomery sent no orders to push on urgently, so 5th Division and 231 Brigade enjoyed the beautiful Italian countryside in fine weather. The local people were friendly and showered gifts of grapes and other fruit on the British soldiers, while chickens and even sheep could be bought to supplement the army rations. It was like a holiday picnic after Sicily and Africa. The mainland of Italy, even in the toe, is softer and more attractive than Sicily, and the troops bivouacked beneath olive or pine trees or in the thick scrub, and the nights were cool although the days were warm. At last Eighth Army's soldiers were enjoying the fruits of their African and Sicilian victories, and the cheers of the civilian population in the villages and towns was warming. The Italian Army in the area had unofficially surrendered and thousands of its soldiers worked as labourers to repair the roads and bridges damaged by the Germans, although the indiscreet use of radio links by Italian generals caused Montgomery to take away all radio sets from Italian headquarters.

After the battle at Pizzo on 8 September, 5th Division reported the 9th as 'a quiet day with very slight opposition', and on the 10th patrols of 5th Reconnaissance Regiment were near Nicastro and Tiriolo, where they contacted the left wing of the Canadians in the narrowest part of the 'neck'.[30]

Then the incredible happened. On 11 September, just as the Salerno landings ran into desperate trouble, Montgomery ordered 5th Division to rest for two days in the area of Nicastro, although 5th Recce were to send patrols forward to investigate the bridges and try to reach Cosenza to report on the airfields.[31] On the same day the Dorsets reported Nicastro clear of Germans, and on the 12th patrols from 5th Recce reached Amantea without meeting any enemy. On 13 September patrols from the same unit were in Cosenza – so peaceful were the conditions that one patrol had gone by train. The records now available show that Montgomery simply failed to tell his subordinate commanders to push on quickly. As the Eighth Army War Diaries reveal: 9 September, 'Army Commander intends pause a few days at neck to pull up tail of army. Fifth Division will hold Catanzaro-Tierno.' On 12 September the XIII Corps Commander, General Dempsey, had 'not yet decided future intentions, but possibly Fifth Division would advance up the coast.' Yet on 8 September Monty had signalled Alexander: 'after three days' fighting my line is Delianouva-Bovalina Marina which represents nearly one thousand square miles of Italy. Inform Winston this is my present to him.'[32] This was ridiculous bombast unworthy of Montgomery, because apart from the engagement at Pizzo there had been almost no opposition.

A signal to Alexander dated 9 September typified Montgomery's attitude: 'My Divisions are now strung out, have fought and marched 100 miles in seven days, are tired and must be rested ... two days rest with intensive recce Cotrone Rossano Belvedere Strezzano.'[33] Alexander was not pleased. He knew some of Montgomery's infantry had advanced on foot, but even by 6 September 5,000 vehicles had crossed by ferry from Messina to the mainland and many were available to transport troops by road.

General Sir Frank Simpson told me:

Whenever I discussed Messina to Salerno with Monty I got the impression that he thought the whole Italian operation was badly planned and irresponsible, and that the Salerno landings could never have been a success, in which he was right because the casualties were unacceptable. He also had confirmed Intelligence Reports that the Germans had sufficient mobile armour and infantry divisions of good quality in the Italian peninsula to see off his tiny Eighth Army if they were suddenly deployed against him. He did not want

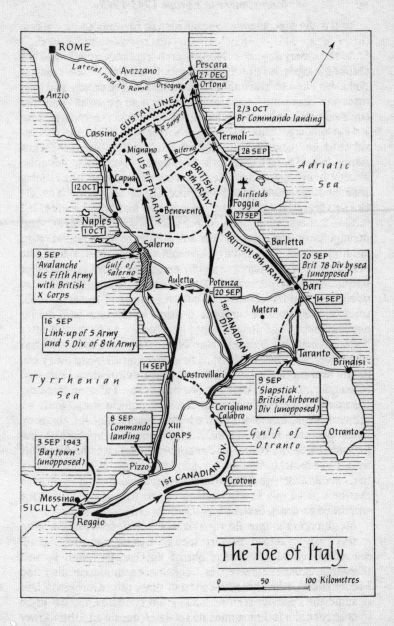

The Toe of Italy

ROME

Anzio

Lateral road to Rome   Avezzano

Pescara
27 DEC
Orsogna   Ortona

GUSTAV LINE

2/3 OCT
Br Commando landing

Cassino   R. Sangro

Mignano   R. Biferno   Termoli
28 SEP

Capua   BRITISH 8th ARMY

US FIFTH ARMY

12 OCT

Adriatic Sea

Airfields
Foggia
27 SEP

Naples
1 OCT   Benevento

Barletta

9 SEP
'Avalanche'
US Fifth Army
with British
X Corps

Salerno

Gulf of Salerno

Auletta   Potenza
20 SEP

BRITISH 8th ARMY

20 SEP
Brit 78 Div by sea
(unopposed)

Bari
14 SEP

16 SEP
Link-up of 5 Army
and 5 Div of 8th Army

1st CANADIAN DIV.

Matera

14 SEP   Castrovillari

Taranto   Brindisi

Tyrrhenian Sea

9 SEP
'Slapstick'
British Airborne
Div (unopposed)

8 SEP
Commando
landing

Corigliano
Calabro

XIII
CORPS

Gulf of Otranto

Otranto

3 SEP 1943
'Baytown'
(unopposed)

Pizzo

1st CANADIAN DIV.

Crotone

Messina
SICILY

Reggio

0   50   100 Kilometres

to risk disaster, therefore he decided to be cautious.

Montgomery, with his tidy and cautious mind, acutely disliked having his forces 'strung out', and the enemy out of sight. He liked to know the exact position of the enemy and their strength. He wanted, too, to be able each day to visit any of his units and still be back in time for an evening conference with his liaison officers at his Tac HQ; when he was unable to visit his forward units he had no wish to give authority to divisional commanders to seize opportunities for a spectacular advance. Worried by the potential German strength on the Italian mainland, he found 3-16 September a type of battle which did not suit his temperament and for which he had little appetite.

On 5 September Alexander had flown to Reggio, and Montgomery met him on the airfield there. The senior man confirmed that the Italian Government, who had signed the armistice on 3 September, would announce it on 8 September and immediately commence fighting on the Allied side. He also confirmed that 'Avalanche' would take place at Salerno at 0430 on 9 September; one airborne division would land at Taranto simultaneously and it was hoped the Italian Army would seize Taranto, Brindisi, Bari and Naples. According to Montgomery, Alexander was over-optimistic; he asked him to move away out of the hearing of the other officers. Once out of earshot he told Alexander: 'Italian morale is so low that they will never fight the Germans. The Germans are in great strength in Italy, while we are very weak. Therefore we must not dissipate our resources by opening up too many fronts.'[34] Montgomery also claimed that he forecast, in the course of the conversation, that the Germans would concentrate against 'Avalanche'; yet if he was so sure that 'Avalanche' would run into strong opposition it is strange that he was so dilatory in pushing up the west coast to join the embattled forces at Salerno.

Montgomery continued to Alexander: 'Before we embark on a major operation on the mainland of Europe we must have a master plan and not being told of any master plan, I must therefore assume there is none.' Again according to Montgomery, Alexander listened but obviously disagreed. This demand for a master plan was really a request for himself to be in sole charge – a forerunner of similar requests to Eisenhower in 1944 and 1945.

In his memoirs, Montgomery excused his slow progress towards Salerno, writing 'We marched and fought 300 miles in seventeen days in good delaying country against an enemy whose use of demolition caused us bridging problems of the first magnitude.' Now that the official War Diaries in the Public Record Office are available his statement does not hold water; the inevitable conclusion is that Montgomery made little effort to reach the southern flank of the Salerno beach-head in as short a time as possible. He wanted to take no risks in face of the potential strength of German divisions in Italy and concentrated instead on a slow, massive build-up.

It is true that there were narrow hairpin bends on many of the roads, slowing transport, but most were passable. There had been also a good number of demolitions, chiefly on road bridges, but in that part of Italy in the summer the river beds are level and dry and the sappers reported it was easy to bypass damaged sections. For example, on 11 September the CRE (Commander, Royal Engineers), 5th Division reported 'No bridge blown on the road Gioia-Cittanuava', and on 12 September 'A few bridges blown on coast road towards Belvedere'. But a typical report from CRE 5th Division reads: 'Two bridges blown at Corali are passable and bulldozer will take one hour to repair another.'[35]

Two parties of Eighth Army war correspondents were able to motor the 120 miles from Nicastro to the Salerno bridgehead in forty-eight hours; they met no opposition. Christopher Buckley with four other journalists set out at 0630 on Tuesday, 14 September, and soon passed the forward elements of 5th Division at Scalea and Maratea, to find another party of war correspondents had preceded them. They sped on beyond Maratea, everywhere receiving an enthusiastic welcome from the Italians with flowers, fruit and eggs, so that their car began to resemble 'a church at harvest festival'.

When they reached Policastro, where the main road crosses a river and turns inland, they found the bridge had been thoroughly destroyed, but some small boys quickly guided them to a ford where, as usual, the bed of the river was composed of firm gravel and they were able to cross in their staff car. Hearing that the main road had been mined, they turned off to the left through side roads towards Agropoli. At Bugheria they found the other party of war correspondents, led by Evelyn Montague of the *Manchester Guardian*, supported by Eighth

Army's Public Relations Officer. That night they were all at Vallo on the American flank, and at 1050 on the morning of 15 September they met American patrols at Castagneto. The Americans were on the point of demolishing another bridge, but when they heard the road was open to the Eighth Army they left it alone. The war correspondents motored on to the lovely Greek temples of Paestum, within a few hundred yards of US Fifth Army HQ. General Alexander was there and insisted on seeing them, demanding a detailed account of the condition of the roads which they had traversed. Plainly he wanted to find out if there was any excuse for Montgomery's dawdling.

Not until twenty-four hours later, on the 16th, did Eighth Army patrols link up with the US Fifth Army. As there were no demolitions to stop the advance and there was no enemy in the area, obviously 5th Reconnaissance Regiment from 5th Division could have linked up with the Americans at least forty-eight hours before they actually did, and probably by 12 September. Buckley wrote:

> Wednesday, 15 September, was the turning point on the Salerno front and the last day on which the situation was critical ... If the 8th Army had pushed forward along their route sooner General Clark would have received the news that there were no German forces between the two armies, the unnecessary demolition of several bridges would have been avoided and Commanders at the beach-head might have felt in a position to go over to the offensive rather earlier than they did. At the very least the considerable tension prevailing at the beach-head would have been relieved.[36]

Although there were no US troops in Vallo, the village formed the southern edge of the 'Avalanche' perimeter. Buckley and his party, by motoring 120 miles through no-man's-land in one day, had linked up one army with another, a feat which makes nonsense of Montgomery's excuses for not advancing. Buckley rightly wrote:

> This episode strengthened my previous conviction that a quite unnecessary slackness had developed in the British forces in following up and maintaining contact with the retreating enemy; demolitions were accepted as an act of God, and

although the sappers worked as hard and fast as they could the command took it for granted that there were no means of circumventing them.

The slow progress was due entirely to Montgomery failing to give orders to push on as far and as fast as possible to relieve the hard pressed beach-head at Salerno. (Indeed, in each town Buckley's party had got the mayors to telephone to the north to make sure the road was passable and that there were no Germans.)

It was shaming for Montgomery that unarmed war correspondents should have reached US Fifth Army so far in front of his troops, for as the Salerno landings ran into trouble Alexander urged him to hurry; in addition, intelligence reports reaching Eighth Army HQ made it clear from the first that Salerno was a risky business. Montgomery virtually ignored Alexander's orders to do his best to relieve the pressure on US Fifth Army.

As a result of this lack of pressure from Eighth Army, 26th Panzer Division was able to take up battle positions on the Salerno perimeter between Eboli and Battipaglia on 14 September, and their arrival increased the Americans' problems. Earlier, at midnight on 8/9 September, 26th Panzer had been ordered to pull back to Castrovillari, seventy miles north of Catanzaro. 29th Panzer Grenadiers were already there, and sent a detachment north to Lagonegro to counter a rumoured British landing at Sapri. The remainder of the division should have been en route for the Salerno front, but the whole force was halted because of the false news of a landing at Sapri. Nevertheless, 29th Panzer reached the line Sala Consolina-Eboli on 11 September; had it not been for the scare about a British landing 29th Panzer would have been available to Hube on the Salerno perimeter just at the moment when US Fifth Army was in deepest trouble.

On 7 September Alexander had asked Montgomery to take command of 1st Airborne Division when it landed at Taranto, and also of 8th Indian Division, which was to follow. Montgomery's signal in reply was typical:

Appreciate no firm decision regarding use of 8th Army Taranto for few days. Consider possibilities which might arise. If enemy have 20 Divisions in Italy we must ensure that we do not have disaster ... only first class troops must be in Italy ... 8 Indian not in this category.[37]

It is surprising that Alexander did not give Montgomery a firm order to use the troops landed at Taranto to help 'Avalanche', and in view of 8th Indian's performance later the latter's critical comment is unjustified. Of course at that time the division was untried, having come direct from the Middle East to Italy; later, however, Montgomery was to wax enthusiastic over its performance.

This attitude was unacceptable to Alexander, and on 10 September he signalled Montgomery: 'Utmost importance that you maintain pressure upon Germans so they cannot remove force off your front and concentrate against Avalanche ... next few days crucial.' Montgomery ignored this signal, and in spite of Alexander's emphasising the need for pressure allowed 5th Division to complete its two days' rest. On 12 September he signalled Alexander: 'My admin very stretched but will take every justifiable risk.' Alas for Alexander and 'Avalanche', Montgomery had no intention of taking risks. While it was touch-and-go at Salerno Alexander became so unhappy with Eighth Army's slow movements that he sent his Fifteenth Army Group Chief of Staff, Brigadier David Richardson,* on 12 September to explain the crisis to Montgomery and to direct him to press on regardless of administrative difficulties; he also allocated twenty-seven extra landing-craft in order to speed reinforcement from Sicily across the Straits of Messina.

Montgomery signalled back on the 13th: 'Increased shipping now available puts me in much better position and I hope by 17 September to be able to begin to launch a definite threat against south flank of Germans facing US Army.' But on the same day Alexander sent this ominous signal: 'Position of US Army not favourable ... your intentions very cheering, I entirely agree.' Alexander must have been cheered by any small thing, since an offensive not beginning until 17 September would not be much use to 'Avalanche', where by now the Germans threatened to divide the Americans and British (X Corps, attached to US Fifth

---

* Charles Richardson was with Eighth Army, while David Richardson was with Fifteenth Army Group.

Army for the landings) and reach the beaches. Certainly Montgomery had thrown dust over Alexander's eyes about the lack of opposition and the state of the roads between the toe of Italy and Salerno.

On 14 September Alexander met Montgomery at Reggio and agreed with him a plan to attack with 5th Division on a two-brigade front north of Castrovillari on 16 or 17 September. The only possible comment on this conference is that if Montgomery did not know the plain truth, that there were no Germans in front of 5th Division, he should have done. The Eighth Army intelligence summaries make it clear how weak was the opposition, and the local subordinate commanders knew almost exactly the whereabouts of the Germans since the telephone system was intact and, as Buckley's party discovered, co-operating Italian local officials obligingly found out how many Germans there were in other towns to the north.

The Americans felt that Montgomery moved with 'reprehensible slowness', and it is impossible to dispute this. His dawdling as the Germans counter-attacked at Salerno sowed the seeds of a bitterness between him and the Americans which lasted until the end of the war. General Mark Clark's force which landed at Salerno consisted of US VI Corps (45th and 36th Infantry Divisions), and British X Corps (46th and 56th Divisions). The crisis point came on 13 September when the Germans opened up a gap between the British and American elements on the beach-head; emergency measures had to be taken and any help from Eighth Army would have been a godsend on that day, but Montgomery was resting his troops 100 miles away. Men from General Matthew Ridgway's US 82nd Airborne Division were dropped as reinforcements and any available men on the beaches, including those unloading supplies, were drafted into the line. The British 7th Armoured Division was landed in a hurry and, late on the night of the 14th, 509th US Parachute Division was dropped behind the German lines. These desperate, last-minute measures were expensive in casualties, but the Germans were finally stopped five miles from the beaches at a cost of 9,000 Allies casualties, some of whom could have been saved by a dash forward by Eighth Army.*

* Recently much publicity has been given to the Salerno mutiny. Reinforcements from Eighth Army belonging to 50th and 51st (Highland)

Although the war correspondents had proved that there was nothing to stop Montgomery rushing 5th Division into the 'Avalanche' area, the British advance remained pathetically slow. After Alexander's messages Montgomery had to make at least some token efforts. He decided to concentrate XIII Corps in the neighbourhood of Nicastro-Catanzaro, with light forces extended northwards. 5th Division reached Castrovillari and Belvedere on the 12th, and patrols from the Canadian division entered Cotrone on the east coast.

Reports from 5th Division also give evidence of the easy path a speedy advance would have had up the west coast. On 12 September the division's 5th Reconnaissance Regiment from Amantea reported no enemy there because they had withdrawn beyond Belvedere, and on the 14th the regiment reported the road Paola-Castiglione 'fit for all vehicles'. The next day 5th Recce were ordered to move to Lagonegro, but when it was learnt there were Germans there the regiment was withdrawn and 13 Brigade was made responsible for patrols along the roads to Sapri and Vallo, and for making contact with US Fifth Army. On this day, too, 231 Brigade arrived south of Scalea by sea from Niconastro, and on 16 September 13 Brigade contacted 36th Division, US Army, five miles north of Vallo. The attack planned by Montgomery for 17 September never took place because by then the Germans had called off the battle for Salerno.

Eventually 5th Division's operational orders for 14 September contained the intention 'Advance at all possible speed to relieve U.S. Army', while 231 Brigade was ordered to remain in the Scalea area and patrol vigorously north and west, but 'no move likely until 19 September.'[38]

Immediately after the signing of the Italian secret armistice on 3 September, Alexander had sent orders to 1st Airborne Division to embark at Bizerta on 8 September to land at Taranto on the 9th, after the armistice had been announced. The plan was to follow them up with HQ V Corps and two more divisions, 8th Indian and 78th Infantry, together with four

---

Divisions were rushed to US Fifth Army; 200 men refused to fight with strange units, however, and had to be marched back to the beaches under arrest. Montgomery said firmly that if he had been consulted he would have refused to allow Eighth Army reinforcements to go to US Fifth Army (Ahrenfeld, *Psychiatry in the British Army in World War II*, p. 219).

squadrons of fighter aircraft. As the 12th Cruiser Squadron brought 1st Airborne into Taranto harbour the Italian battleships *Doria* and *Duilio* sailed out to surrender at Malta, in accordance with the armistice.

1st Airborne landed on the 9th without opposition, welcomed by the Italians who, thrilled at the news of the armistice, believed in vain that the war was over for them. The Italian Army co-operated in every way possible. Unfortunately, on the next morning HMS *Abdiel* struck a mine while at anchor and sank with the loss of forty-eight sailors and 120 soldiers of 6th Parachute Regiment drowned, and another 120 soldiers wounded.

Italian local government officials telephoned around the province and were able to give Maj-Gen Hopkinson, commanding 1st Airborne, the news that the German 1st Parachute Division was based at Altamura, west of Bari, with rearguards at Castellanata, Gioia del Colle and Ginosa, but that the whole formation, on hearing of the Italian surrender, was moving back towards Foggia. By the 10th Monopoli on the Adriatic coast was clear, but in the only serious fighting, at Castellanata on the 11th, Maj-Gen Hopkinson was fatally wounded. On 13 September Bari and Brindisi were taken without opposition.

There was no possibility of a counter-attack from the Germans. Frost noted: '1st Parachute Brigade were given very little to do, for the 8th Army was moving slowly in those days and while the 5th US Army fought desperately for its beach-heads at Salerno the 8th was maintaining its balance. We spent four days digging at Taranto in case the Germans produced a sudden riposte.'[39] This underlines Montgomery's wait-and-see attitude; he was not prepared to use 1st Airborne to create a diversion to ease 'Avalanche', although Taranto was only 140 miles from Salerno by a good road on which there were few demolitions.

1st Airborne could not manoeuvre in conjunction with the rest of Eighth Army because Reggio and Taranto are nearly 200 miles apart by road, but a threat to Potenza, the key road junction between Taranto and Salerno, must have drawn off German troops from 'Avalanche'. There was nothing to prevent an attack by 1 Parachute Brigade being made on Potenza, but not even a feint advance was attempted. Potenza, as the British knew, was only lightly held by troops of 1st German Parachute Regiment and 26th Panzer Division. Any serious movement towards Potenza must have forced Vietinghoff to divert troops from the Salerno perimeter.

On 16 September the Canadian Division, advancing slowly up the east coast road, linked up with 1st Airborne near Metaponto on the Gulf of Taranto. After a quite unnecessary bombing Potenza fell to the Canadians on the 19th with little resistance, but by then the urgent need to relieve Salerno had passed.

In his memoirs Montgomery claimed that 'he pushed on in reply to Alexander's cry for help', but this is not borne out by an analysis of the troops' movements. On 14 September, the last crisis day at Salerno, his troops were still seventy-five miles away and static, although by then the war correspondents had reached the southern edge of the Salerno perimeter. He went on to blame lack of supplies for his slow progress, though in fact virtually no ammunition was consumed because there was so little fighting, apart from the action at Pizzo. Although the British sustained 200 casualties in one day at Pizzo, total casualties for the campaign up to 16 September, including sickness and accidents, were only 635. True, transporting petrol forward was a problem, and there was a shortage of jerry cans, many of which were being stolen by the Italian civilians. Montgomery, moreover, could call on whatever supplies he wanted from his own *ad hoc* 8th Army supply base ('Fortbase') in Catania. Although Montgomery complained of petrol shortage, his 'Q' staff had not set a good example, because they demanded 1,000 gallons of high octane petrol for the Army Commander's private motor launch which, his ADC John Henderson told me, Montgomery only used once.[40] In any case, 5th Division carried fuel for 225 miles, and Reggio San Venere and Cotrone were in use as ports. 63,663 men, 24,512 tons of stores and 15,273 vehicles had been landed in Italy up to 16 September. Apart from the Taranto troops, XIII Corps had a total strength of 58,000 with only a few rearguards left in Sicily, but even with this massive force Montgomery failed to influence in any way the Salerno battle. He would have encountered no serious supply difficulties in pushing two brigades up to the southern flank of US Fifth Army between 11 and 14 September; at the same time 1st Airborne could have drawn all the supplies they wanted from Taranto if they had advanced towards Potenza.

In his memoirs, General Mark Clark is kind to Montgomery. He writes that he received several letters by courier from Eighth Army's commander detailing his progress up the coast towards the beach-head, and that Montgomery suggested on 15 September, 'Perhaps you could put out a reconnaissance along the road from Agropoli to meet my people who have already started from Sapri ... it looks as if you may not be having too good a time and I do hope all goes well with you. We are on the way to lend a hand and it will be a great day when we actually join hands.' Clark replied: 'It will be a pleasure to see you again at an early date, situation here well in hand.' Certainly the situation was in hand by 15 September, but Clark adds ironically: 'In view of the fact that we had narrowly escaped being pushed into the sea I didn't mention his optimistic idea of our sending out a reconnaissance party.'[41] His strongest anti-Montgomery observation was: 'Eighth Army was making a slow advance towards Salerno despite Alexander's almost daily efforts to prod it into greater speed.'

When, on 19 September, the Canadians took Potenza for Montgomery, the road from Bari to Salerno was opened, giving the Allies a firm line from which to launch an offensive up Italy. On 21 September, as soon as the Fifth and Eighth Armies had firmly joined hands on the Salerno-Bari line, Alexander issued a directive ordering Clark to capture Naples, and Montgomery the Foggia airfields on the Adriatic. Naples fell on 1 October, after the Germans had carried out heavy demolitions, and the Americans were then given Rome as a further objective, while Eighth Army, after Foggia, was to push up the east coast to Pescara, from where ran the most southerly non-mountainous lateral road to Rome.

The Allies now had eleven divisions facing Kesselring's nine, though the Germans had fourteen more in northern Italy ready for contingencies in Yugoslavia, France or the Balkans. The Allied divisions were much stronger numerically and had far more tanks, guns and ammunition. In addition the Allies had complete command of the air.

Kesselring's plan was to pull back his nine divisions first to the Bernhard Line (so called because it was meant to stop Montgomery) on the Volturno and Biferno rivers, and then to the Gustav Line along the Garigliano to Cassino, and on to the Sangro on the Adriatic.

At first Montgomery had in front of him only the badly depleted German 1st Parachute Division. Without much fighting he took the important Foggia airfields by 27 September, and had cleared the whole of the Gargano peninsula by 1 October.

He had little enthusiasm, however, for his difficult advance up the Adriatic coast, and became querulous about the non-arrival of supplies, for which he now had to rely on AFHQ in Algiers. He was looking for an excuse for slow progress. On 5 October he sent a personal signal to Alexander: 'My petrol situation is now most serious owing to non-delivery of my demands and unless you can get me some soon my army will not be able to operate efficiently.' He was told 8,000 tons were being unloaded in the ports in the heel of Italy, and Alexander asked Clark to give temporary help from US Fifth Army supplies. On the next day Clark sent this personal wire to Montgomery: 'Send trucks to Paestum for 100,000 gallons and I shall be able to give you more.'[42] In fact Montgomery issued no orders for rigid petrol economy, and his 'acute petrol shortage' must be taken with a pinch of salt.

Earlier, Montgomery had lent his BGS, Charles Richardson, to Clark's HQ as Deputy Chief of Staff, US Fifth Army, where his chief role was liaison. Alexander had asked him for the best officer available, for relations between Clark and Montgomery were delicate, and became strained as the two armies tried to advance side by side through the difficult Italian country. Charles Richardson told me:

Monty certainly did not like competition, and Mark Clark himself had a certain vanity. Monty used to emphasise that Clark had no battle experience, which was true, and in the First World War he only reached the rank of captain. Fortunately Clark's lack of knowledge of tactics was more than compensated by [Lt-Gen A.M.] Al Gruenther being his Chief of Staff [after the war he rose to command NATO]. I got on splendidly with Al Gruenther, who to my mind was a marvellous chap and a fine soldier. Fortunately, too, he was always pro Monty. With the Apennines dividing the two armies there was little we could do in the way of co-operation. One army had little influence on the other.

Thanks to Richardson and Gruenther, relations between Montgomery and Clark remained harmonious outwardly, although there was no love lost on either side. Montgomery's signals to Clark are cavalier. On 12 October he wired: 'Will come tomorrow for short talk and then see Naples and not bother you any more'; since American generals liked long conferences this was hardly calculated to please. Then, on 24 October, he invited Clark to Eighth Army and sent Noel Chavasse, his ADC, to Clark's HQ to make arrangements. Two days later he signalled Clark: 'Chavasse has told me your plans therefore no need for you to come.'[43] (According to Lord Chalfont, when Clark had visited Eighth Army Tactical HQ, shortly after the Salerno link-up, Montgomery pretended to be out, although Clark knew he was not. Bill Williams told me he could not remember this incident, but 'if it is true I find it too hideously in character'.[44] John Henderson too could not recall it, but said Montgomery intensely disliked unexpected visitors, and that the story could be true.)

At this time Winston Churchill coined the phrase: 'Whoever holds Rome holds the title deeds to Italy,' although these words had no meaning in a military context and little in a political sense. Montgomery was by now conscious that a decision must be made soon as to who should command the cross-Channel invasion, and he was desperately anxious to leave Italy for this much more important command. In an effort to allay any suspicions of Churchill's that Eighth Army's Italian performance was not as good as it should have been, Montgomery had signalled the Prime Minister direct on 4 October:

> We have advanced a long way and very quickly. It had to be done in order to help 5 Army but it has been a great strain on my administration which had to be switched from the toe to the heel during operations and which is now stretched to the limit ... When I have got control of Termoli Campobasso I will halt for a short period. After the halt I will advance with my whole strength on Pescara and Ancona. I shall look forward to meeting you in Rome.[45]

Since Montgomery had signalled Alexander on 29 September that he hoped to reach the Rome Line by 30 October, he obviously still had some hopes of good results. However, the signal to the Prime Minister was intended more as a subtle reminder of his claims to command in North-West Europe than an optimistic forecast of victories, and in the remaining weeks he was to spend in Italy his enthusiasm waned fast.

Eighth Army Intelligence discovered that the Germans were preparing defence positions at Termoli, behind the Biferno river. Accordingly, Montgomery sent 78th Division ahead at top speed and planned a daring commando raid from the sea with over 1,000 men for 20 October. The raiders landed north of Termoli behind the German positions almost without opposition and swiftly captured the town; indeed, they achieved such surprise that German lorries were still arriving in Termoli with supplies after its capture and were ambushed one after another. Kesselring counter-attacked the Termoli bridgehead with 16th Panzer Division, equipped with Tiger tanks. The Germans had practically broken through into Termoli when, after some desperate fighting, and helped by reinforcements landed by sea, the Eighth Army held them at the eleventh hour. The Germans withdrew northwards to the River Trigno. Montgomery's unusually bold tactics had paid off handsomely, though it had been touch and go at Termoli. Hitler took a great interest in 16th Panzer's counter-attack and was so cross at its failure that he sacked the divisional commander, General Stettinius.

With Termoli in Eighth Army hands, the Foggia airfields, captured by Eighth Army by 27 September, were now safe from counter-attack and operational. Eighth Army regrouped, and the RAF and USAAF sent floods of aeroplanes and supplies into the Foggia airfields complex not only for tactical support of the armies, but also for long-range bomber raids as far afield as the Ploesti oilfields in Rumania.

The air forces made huge demands on shipping space for their large-scale operations, and the supply services, now under the mammoth Anglo-American HQ in Algiers, came under severe stress. AFHQ was inexperienced and inefficient, and Montgomery found his supply situation much more difficult than in Africa and Sicily, when it had been under his own control. He complained continuously, and became increasingly unenthusiastic for the unglamorous role which lay ahead of him up the Adriatic coast.

At the end of October, Montgomery decided that an extra division would speed his advance. He wired Alexander on 29

October that he needed this reinforcement (1st Infantry Division) 'to smash through Sangro line and get to Pescara. Definite limit to the distance I can go if resistance continues as at present.' He realised almost immediately that he had insufficient supplies for these troops, and insufficient room to deploy them on his single axis; two days later he told de Guingand to inform Alexander's HQ that he no longer required an extra division.[46] This sudden change of mind is uncharacteristic of Montgomery. Normally he was so incisive and positive, but now the strain of fighting a long winter campaign against a determined enemy in the mountains was telling upon him.

As the weather broke, Eighth Army had to contend with horrific mud, which covered the roads and made them so slippery that they became death traps for incautious drivers. After hard fighting on the Trigno at the beginning of November, Eighth Army reached the south banks of the Sangro by the middle of the month. Now they faced the German winter Gustav Line, and the daunting task of crossing the Sangro river, 400 feet wide in flood with a flat plain, 2,000 yards long, to the north ending in a steep escarpment 150 feet high. Montgomery was to have no more victories in the Mediterranean, and his heart was no longer in the Italian campaign. Although Alexander, his immediate superior, complied with his every request, he disliked having equal status with Mark Clark, and had resented Rome, Churchill's 'title deeds to Italy', being allocated to the Americans.

On 18 November he wrote to the CIGS:

I am preparing a heavy blow on the Adriatic side. All I want is good weather. I have gone all out for surprise and have concentrated such strength on my right that given fine weather and dry ground under foot, I will hit the Boche a crack that will be heard all over Italy ... I fear the Fifth Army is absolutely whacked. So long as you fight an army in combat teams and the big idea is that everyone should 'combat' someone all the time you do not get very far. My own observation leads me to the conclusion that Clark would be only too delighted to be given quiet advice as to how to fight his Army. I think he is a very decent chap and most co-operative; if he received good and clear guidance he would do very well.

The above letter to Brooke gives an insight into Montgomery's mind at that time. He felt strongly he should be the 'overlord' of the Italian campaign, and was frustrated because his efforts on the Adriatic, which were very costly in casualties, were not properly co-ordinated with those of the Americans. Alas, his 'heavy blow ... and crack' to be heard all over Italy on the Sangro misfired. He rightly criticised the higher command for sending him slogging up Italy with no master plan; 'we risk an administrative breakdown,' he continued to Brooke. That was untrue except for the strain imposed on transport by the colossal amount of field artillery ammunition he deemed necessary for his assault over the Sangro. It was only after he had left Italy that the Eighth Army was starved of supplies during the build-up for the cross-Channel invasion.*

Montgomery launched his attack over the Sangro on 28 November, announcing to his troops 'We will hit the Germans a colossal crack'. Both the 27th, during which the German positions were bombarded, and the 28th were fine for a change, and Montgomery quickly secured a bridgehead over the Sangro. But although he had broken into the German winter line, he could not breach it. With his usual bombast he announced that 'my troops have won the battle as they always do. The road to Rome is open.'[47] This was untrue, for there had never been any chance of a break-through to the Rome lateral road at Pescara in winter. Indeed, it was not reached until June 1944, after Rome fell to the Americans, and the Eighth Army never forgave Montgomery for this false optimism. Casualties were heavy in December as the British made attack after attack over the Sangro, with only limited success. Bitter weather and snow caused grave hardship, and there were many cases of frostbite.

The CIGS visited Montgomery in Italy on 14 December. In London, the Prime Minister had been critical of Eighth Army's slow progress, and scathing about the failure to use the landing-craft available for amphibious landings behind the German lines. Brooke noted in his diary:

Frankly I am rather depressed about what I have seen and

---

* The author remembers 25-pounder field guns being rationed to three rounds per day in early 1945.

heard today. Monty is tired out, and Alex fails to grasp the
show ... Monty strikes me as looking tired and definitely in
need of a rest ... I can see he feels Clark is not running the
5th Army right; nor that Alex is grasping the show
sufficiently. Monty saw little hope of capturing Rome before
March ... no longer any talk of turning left by his forces to
capture Rome.

The next day he wrote: 'The offensive is starting badly ...
something must be done about it as soon as I get back,' and on
the day after, following a visit to US Fifth Army, he wrote
'Clark is planning nothing but penny packets'.

Montgomery undoubtedly felt that his luck was running out,
and both Churchill and Brooke were aware that the Italian
campaign was not to his liking. He was giving a poor impression
which might well have jeopardised his chance of command of
the Second Front. Fortunately for him, the decision was by
now almost made.

Bill Williams gave me this recollection of that period:

Monty definitely 'played the monkey' with the facts after the
Sangro crossing when he said the road to Rome was open
and, soon after establishing bridgeheads, he had to halt the
offensive with heavy losses. This was all part of his business
of 'enthusing the troops', which is why he went out on a limb
at times. You must remember that in the very bad winter in
Italy morale was low; we were crawling about in yellow mud
which even covered all the roads. It was very cold and
Monty's reaction on the Sangro was to call it a victory to
encourage the troops, even when he had failed.

In Italy both Mark Clark and Monty were showmen. They
didn't see much of each other but Monty realised that the
Eighth Army front on the Adriatic would never yield
dramatic results. He was terribly egocentric and discussions
went on about shifting the weight of the Allied offensive in
Italy from the Adriatic to the Fifth Army's front in the west.
Monty was bitterly opposed to taking any British troops
away from the Eighth Army and giving them to the US Fifth
Army [X Corps and other British troops had been sent to US
Fifth Army].

Still, even in this depressing winter in Italy, his spirits were always up. With the front static he was always showing himself to the troops and boosting their morale, which in turn elated him and kept him happy.

I am afraid he did run down the First Army, comparing their performance unfavourably with the Eighth Army in North Africa, and Monty was responsible for some of the antipathy which existed between the former Eighth and First Army divisions during those early months in Italy.*

John Henderson told me: 'As the Eighth Army got bogged down in Italy it became clear to Monty that this campaign was a stalemate, and his mind wandered to the Second Front, as we called the cross-Channel invasion, where he had a good idea he might get command. All our minds were fixed on it, and Italy became a second consideration.'

In the end, Montgomery was chosen by Roosevelt and Churchill to command the cross-Channel invasion, though it was a near-run thing. He received instructions to return to England on 24 December, in the nick of time to save his reputation as the Sangro operations ground to an unhealthy halt – a stalemate which had to last until the spring. He was lucky. If he had stayed in Italy his reputation as a victorious commander must have faded, and Italian campaigners never held him in such esteem as the rest of the Army. They felt he had left them in the lurch.

Sir Charles Richardson told me:

Our little gang at Eighth Army HQ took a poor view of the Sicily and Italy invasions. After doing so well in Africa we could not see why we should be wasted on an uphill struggle through the mountains of Italy. We thought, 'poor old Eighth Army, labouring up the east coast of Italy along one main road'. That is what Monty felt too. We felt we should be the élite of the British Army for the much more important invasion of France, although we had no idea it was so far off.

---

* The feuding between former soldiers of the British Eighth and First Armies in the Italian campaign was extraordinary and shaming, and was fanned not only by Montgomery, but also by Alexander. On one occasion I heard Alexander telling officers it was important to put '1' or '8' on their Africa Stars to show which army they had been in.

And so, on Christmas Eve 1943, Montgomery received a coded signal 'for his eyes only' that he was to command the invasion of Europe. He had already decided that if the call came he would take with him his Chief of Staff, de Guingand, Maj-Gen Miles Graham, his Chief Administrative Officer, and Williams, his head of Intelligence. They all lived at Eighth Army Main HQ, while Montgomery, with his hand-picked liaison officers were at Tac HQ. The news came through to the Main HQ on the late BBC bulletin during dinner on the 24th, and on Christmas Day the staff officers were all agog to hear which of them would go back with their general. Montgomery's high spirits and school-masterish sense of fun immediately returned. Bill Williams takes up the story:

That night we heard on the BBC radio that Monty was to command what was then known as the Second Front. Every morning before breakfast I had to go from Main Eighth Army HQ to Monty's Tac HQ to brief him about the enemy. I was most excited about the Second Front because I was sure Monty would want me to go with him. I told my driver that I was probably going back to England and that he would come with me; he was thrilled. That day I remember well there was no news whatsoever about the enemy, and all that Monty would discuss with me was how to prevent Bernard Freyberg [Maj-Gen Sir Bernard Freyberg, VC, GOC New Zealand Forces] swimming the River Sangro to see exactly what was going on on the other side. Freyberg was keen on swimming exploits and we both agreed he shouldn't be allowed to do this. Both I and my driver were disappointed men when we drove back to Main Eighth Army HQ, but as soon as I got out of the jeep I got a message that 'Master' wanted to speak to me on the 'phone. Then in his piping voice he told me that he was going back to London and that I was going with him. Our talk about Freyberg before breakfast had been a school-boyish leg pull.

2

Montgomery and the Invasion

On 31 December 1943 Montgomery flew from the improvised airstrip near the Sangro river on the Adriatic coast of Italy to Marrakesh in Morocco, where Churchill was convalescing after an attack of pneumonia. Eisenhower, just chosen as Supreme Commander for the invasion, was a fellow guest, and immediately told Montgomery that basic changes were needed in the existing plan for invading Normandy across the Channel, now code-named 'Overlord'.

Arriving on New Year's Day 1944, Montgomery saw Churchill, who was lying in bed surrounded by official papers. The Prime Minister greeted him warmly, then handed him a bulky document entitled 'Operation "Overlord"' and told him to read it. By the next morning, after staying up half the night, Montgomery had briefed himself on the contents and was, like Eisenhower, unhappy about it. Churchill asked him what he thought of the plan, and received from his general a typed report which condemned the plan because the front for the landings was too narrow. Montgomery considered that the Channel Islands should be retaken to provoke an air battle, and made to Churchill the important point that for the Sicilian landings he had only needed special craft for the initial assault, and that once the beaches were taken he had been able to land large numbers of troops from liners five miles out to sea.[1]

Montgomery's memorandum had the effect of weakening Churchill's faith in Lt-Gen Frederick Morgan, Chief of Staff to the Supreme Allied Commander, who had been responsible for drafting the original 'Overlord' paper. Indeed, so pleased was Churchill with the memorandum that he wrote to the Chiefs of

Staff heartily endorsing it. He went on to tell Montgomery that, in his view, it was an advantage to invade a long Continental coastline from an island because 'our forces are concentrated at the start while the enemy are forced to spread themselves out over a wide range'.

Churchill insisted that the Allies must not use the word 'invasion' until they had crossed the German frontier. He also objected to Roosevelt's use of the phrase 'fortress of Europe' in a recent speech, telling the Chiefs of Staff that they must eliminate all expressions such as 'Invasion of Europe' or 'Assault upon Fortress of Europe' – instead he insisted upon: ' "Liberation of Europe from Germans" ... We must not make a present to Hitler of the idea that he is the defender of Europe which we are trying to invade.' Churchill also wrote to the Air Ministry on 2 January that he was pleased to hear from Montgomery that 'many landing points ought to be chosen instead of concentrating as at present proposed through one narrow funnel.'

The Prime Minister loved talking about strategic details, and Montgomery indulged him as they both went on a picnic with Churchill's wife, Clemmie. Altogether, Churchill was highly pleased with Montgomery and his memo, while his general was at his most cordial and delighted him by explaining the technicalities of an amphibious assault. This was right up the PM's street, since he loved being an amateur soldier.

General Morgan, with a secret staff known as 'COSSAC' (Chief of Staff to Supreme Allied Commander) had been working on the plan for invading across the Channel since March 1943, having established a combined American/British headquarters, also known as COSSAC, at Norfolk House in St James's Square in London. Originally, when an early invasion appeared more likely, a British C-in-C for the invasion was considered essential, and Churchill had originally promised the job to the CIGS, Brooke. As the months went by, however, it became clear that the invasion could not be launched until 1944 and that the United States would have to provide most of the troops and resources once the campaign of the Continent was under way. Churchill was considered by the Americans to be lukewarm about a cross-Channel attack because of his keenness on attacking the 'soft underbelly' of the Axis in the Mediterranean; it was therefore agreed that there should be an

American Supreme Commander.

Morgan's planning had been handicapped throughout by lack of a Supreme Commander. At the Quebec Conference in August 1943 his draft proposals had been accepted, but five precious months were allowed to slip away before the overall commander was appointed, and thus final plans could not be drafted until that appointment.

Roosevelt and Churchill had agreed unofficially at Quebec that General George Marshall, the American Army Chief of Staff, should be Supreme Commander, but no decision was recorded. At the first Cairo Conference in November 1943 Churchill had pressed for Marshall, but Roosevelt could not make up his mind since he was anxious to keep Marshall with him in Washington. Finally, at the Teheran Conference on 1 December 1943, Roosevelt offered Marshall the post, but to the President's relief he was reluctant to accept. Thus the appointment went to Eisenhower, while Marshall stayed at the President's side in Washington.

Eisenhower wanted Alexander as Field Commander, for he knew he would find him more amenable than Montgomery, though he overrated Alexander's ability and powers of decision. Brooke and Grigg, the Secretary of State for War, wanted Montgomery because they knew he had a quicker brain and was better at decision-making; he had additionally the gift of boosting the morale of troops by the exercise of his strong personality. Brooke recorded in his diary several times his low opinion of Alexander's ability, while Churchill, who also overestimated Alexander, remained neutral about the choice of Field Commander. Montgomery, with such backing, got the job, to the disappointment of the American generals.

Stimulated by the Prime Minister's admiration in Marrakesh, Montgomery flew to England (in a four-engined bomber provided by Eisenhower, who thought two engines risky) on 2 January 1944. The supreme challenge of his lifetime faced him. He was fifty-six, extremely fit, expert in all modern war technology and utterly confident of his own ability to lead a combined US/British Army to victory. Above all, he had a clear and incisive mind. As a result his orders were always understood, while his personality ensured that they were carried out. Undoubtedly he was the right choice, and although he was to make mistakes and to incur much criticism during the next eighteen months, no other serving British general was so well equipped for the job. The rundown of the British Army in the 1920s and 1930s had had deplorable effects on the calibre of Regular officers, and in 1943 there were few men of outstanding ability, ambition and foresight in its upper echelons.

Eisenhower changed COSSAC into Supreme Headquarters, Allied Expeditionary Force (SHAEF) and told Morgan that he wanted his former Chief of Staff, Bedell Smith, to be in charge. Morgan gracefully accepted the position of Deputy Chief of Staff.

Eisenhower was by now in America, having relinquished command of AFHQ, Algiers, on becoming Supreme Commander. Montgomery took charge of reshaping the 'Overlord' plans, and immediately set up his headquarters in his old school, St Paul's in Hammersmith. The chain of command was now: Eisenhower, Supreme Commander; Air Chief Marshal Sir Arthur Tedder, Deputy Supreme Commander; Bedell Smith, Chief of Staff; Admiral Sir Bertram Ramsay, C-in-C, Allied Naval Forces; Air Chief Marshal Sir Trafford Leigh-Mallory, C-in-C, Allied Air Forces. There was no C-in-C, Allied Land Forces, but Montgomery was Commander, Twenty-First Army Group, with operational control of all land forces during the assault phase. Eisenhower would assume direct command when an American Army Group was formed under Lt-Gen Omar Bradley once the assault phase was over, and the American troops considerably outnumbered the British. Meanwhile, Bradley would serve under Montgomery as Commander, Twelfth Army Group, though it was always intended that he would have equal status with the British general once the assault phase was completed.

Morgan's COSSAC plan had postulated three divisions landing on the Normandy beaches close to Cherbourg. In his hurried memorandum to Churchill written at Marrakesh Montgomery had stated:

This is just not an operation of war. By D plus 12 twelve divisions would have been landed on the same beaches as were used for the initial landings. This would lead to appalling confusion on the beaches ... further divisions would come pouring in all over the same beaches; confusion instead of getting better would rapidly get worse ... initial landings must be made on the widest possible front.[2]

Montgomery, with his orderly mind, had grasped immediately that an assault on the scale of 'Overlord' needed several beaches for the massive build-up of supplies and the onward movement inland of huge numbers of troops, and at Marrakesh Churchill had agreed with him in principle. Now, instead of COSSAC's three-division assault, Montgomery insisted on a fifty-mile front from the River Orne to Cherbourg. There were to be five landing beaches, each under a corps commander, and on D-Day one division, backed by ancillary troops, would land on each beach, to be followed by a second division on each beach on D-plus-1. From the start Montgomery wanted British Second Army to attract and contain German armour to the east while the Americans first took Cherbourg and then overran the Cherbourg peninsula on the west to reach the Brittany ports. There were no quarrels with the US generals over this vital principle at the time, though it was to become the subject of controversy later.

Montgomery claimed in the early discussions that the wider front would permit more divisions to penetrate inland, and minimise traffic and administration difficulties. He always emphasised the paramount importance of capturing Cherbourg early, showing his characteristic concern for the supply build-up; he emphasised also the need for capturing Brest and other Brittany ports.

The COSSAC planners from the start had misgivings about their proposed three-division assault, yet some of them disputed Montgomery's arguments for a wider front on the grounds that the initial beach assault might fail because naval and air support fire would be dissipated instead of concentrated on three beaches. Montgomery, flushed with his African victories, with Sicily and Italy behind him, and with his reputation at its highest point, was backed by Eisenhower and insisted on wider amphibious landings. Here he was clearly correct.

With Eisenhower still absent, Montgomery held his first London conference at St Paul's on 7 January,[3] where he announced that 'the British have reached the limits of their manpower' and would be unable to form an extra army group. Two armies must be committed in the assault as the areas for the landings were now extended to stretch from Varreville to

Cabourg. The Americans were to be on the right, and the British on the left; the former were to take the Cherbourg peninsula and the town and port of Cherbourg. The British would operate to the south to prevent any enemy interference with the American army from the east. He added that he hoped eventually to get a firm lodgement from Caen to Nantes, with the British army being supplied and reinforced through the Cherbourg peninsula and the Americans through Brittany.

Owing to limitations imposed by problems of mine-sweeping, naval support and craft, only eight brigade groups could be employed initially, he said. The allotment of these groups between the British and the Americans had not yet been decided, although it would probably be three American and five British. Montgomery stressed that he wanted to land everywhere at once rather than spread the assault over two days, and that the heavy shore batteries at Le Havre set a limit to the area of landing on the east. In discussion, he stated that his reasons for wanting five British brigade landing groups and only three American was the urgency of securing airfields, which were in the British sector. Bradley commented that it would be difficult to explain away the smaller initial American effort, and a decision was postponed until the next meeting, set for 10 January.

At this second conference – Eisenhower was still in America – Montgomery said that his ideal would be five divisions landed on the first tide, followed by the essentials of two divisions on the second, including the British 7th Armoured Division. He also needed one airborne division on D-Day ahead of the American landing on the Cherbourg peninsula, to be followed by a second airborne landing at a place to be selected. Ramsay, the naval commander, said the expansion of the front on Montgomery's lines would expose the navies to more fire from coastal defence guns, and that the soldiers would have to stay aboard the ships longer because they would be embarked at ports further from the landing beaches; 'more naval escorts would be required,' he added. His remarks, as recorded in the minutes of the meeting, do not sound enthusiastic; he was not prepared to commit himself at this stage but said that if extra resources could be provided 'the new concept might be possible'. The air commander, Leigh-Mallory, said the extension of the front might mean more damage inflicted on the invasion force by the Luftwaffe.

Montgomery went on to say that he favoured 1 May for D-Day. Ramsay contradicted him, saying that 1 May was not possible, and that the earliest suitable moonlight period (thought to be necessary for a night approach) would be a month later. Hitherto Ramsay had considered the dark period, which followed the fortnight after each moonlight period, to be unsuitable owing to the difficulties of marshalling shipping in the dark, but now admitted that with further training it might be possible to accept a dark period. This meant the first possible dark period would be in the middle of May; more realistically, the beginning of June.

Montgomery stated that it was essential to put the French railways out of commission for a radius of 150 miles from D-Day to D-plus-14, and he wanted no bombing of the area itself before D-minus-1, but then 'everything possible on area with daylight bombing at communications and later railways'. By now his final plan was taking shape, but he became alarmed that there might be a shortage of landing-craft for a five-division assault. He wired Eisenhower on 10 January, the day of the conference, that the 'Anvil' landings proposed for the South of France at the same time should be reduced to a 'threat', and asked the Supreme Commander to 'hurl himself into the context to get us what we want'.[4]

In his opening remarks, Montgomery emphasised rather too strongly that he would be commanding the US troops during the invasion. Some of the Americans became somewhat resentful at this and in the interval Bradley went up to Montgomery and asked him to tone down his remarks. In a statesmanlike way Montgomery then said that he would command the British and Canadian troops, but that he would suggest to General Bradley the scheme of manoeuvre for American troops.

On 21 January, at Eisenhower's first meeting with the invasion commanders, Montgomery opened the proceedings by declaring that the COSSAC plan to invade Europe with three divisions was 'just not on'. Once more he insisted five divisions plus one airborne were necessary, and emphasised that Cherbourg must be captured quickly. He continued: 'It would be the task of the US to capture Cherbourg; then drive for the Loire ports and Brest, while the British and Canadians deal with the main enemy body approaching from the east and south-east.' This clear-sighted vision of the invasion was the core of his master plan which eventually defeated Hitler.

Eisenhower agreed, and suggested he send a telegram to Marshall saying that in his view 'Anvil', which would draw men and resources away from the assault on North-West Europe, was impossible, though Bedell Smith feared this would give the impression that they had changed their minds too quickly. Montgomery insisted, however, that a ten-division 'Anvil', as originally proposed, was out of the question, saying: 'We must plan for a real and proper Overlord. Leave in the Mediterranean enough lift for one division.'

Upgrading the mass of the invasion forces meant that the original date, 1 May, was also 'not on' because there would be insufficient landing-craft available by then. Ramsay told this conference that he believed early June was the right date, but that the number of landing-craft required was still daunting – one million soldiers, he emphasised, had to be delivered to the beaches with their equipment. The conference reluctantly agreed to postpone D-Day until June, although this meant a shorter campaigning season. And now the folly of the heads of state in not appointing the invasion commander in August 1943 became apparent: there was little time in which to alter the plan to suit the invasion commander's wishes.

Montgomery was a great success with those present at the 21 January meeting, while the American generals appreciated the clarity and force of his arguments. Above all, Eisenhower made it clear at the conference that he was relying on Montgomery, and blessed all his proposals. At the lunch following the meeting all was harmony between the British and the Americans.

Twenty-First Army Group had been closely controlled by the War Office. This did not suit its new commander, who was not prepared to refer his decisions to higher authority, and anyway was convinced that such a course would be both time-consuming and inefficient. He immediately began to make changes, without, in his own words, 'waiting for War Office approval'. The Secretary of State for War, Grigg, soon received complaints from several Heads of Departments, and he himself expressed strong disapproval. Montgomery lunched with Grigg, explained that there was much to be done in a short time, and apologised if he had 'gone too fast'. Grigg fell for Montgomery's almost mesmeric charm, and all was well. The two men became firm friends, and Grigg endorsed the general's short-circuiting of the War Office from them on.

This great personal charm had already served Montgomery well. Soon after his arrival in London in January he had had an audience with the King at Buckingham Palace. Montgomery had heard on the grapevine that some of the 'old school' – especially the Brigade of Guards – had put the King up to objecting to his black beret, which by now had become famous. He had immediately told the King that the black beret was an important factor in building up morale and that, as all soldiers knew it was worth 'at least an Army Corps', it was vital that he should go on wearing it. The King, like Grigg later, succumbed to Montgomery's charm, and raised no objection to this unorthodox use of uniform. He greatly liked Montgomery and thoroughly enjoyed his later visits to Twenty-First Army Group Tac HQ in France.

Montgomery had quickly reassembled his old team from the Mediterranean – de Guingand, Williams, Belchem, Richardson and Graham, and Eisenhower and Bedell Smith gave this staff and their commander a fairly free hand over planning. SHAEF and Twenty-First Army Group were very friendly in these early stages, although Morgan at SHAEF resented the criticism of his original invasion plan.

Unfortunately, de Guingand's health was deteriorating, but otherwise he was an excellent choice as Chief of Staff. A Regular soldier, ten years younger than his chief, he loved staff work, was content as a subordinate, and was utterly and invariably loyal to Montgomery during the war. He had been at the War Office in 1939/40 as Military Assistant to the then Secretary of State for War, Leslie Hore-Belisha, and this civil service experience was invaluable during the planning of 'Overlord' with the necessarily involved War Office so close to Twenty-First Army Group HQ. De Guingand was gregarious and tactful; Eisenhower and Bedell Smith liked him greatly, and at this stage he was able to sort out any misunderstandings between Montgomery and the Supreme Commander and his staff.

Bill Williams, Montgomery's BGS (I), an able Oxford don, had a flair for Intelligence work and, being twenty years younger than Montgomery, enjoyed a happy working relationship with him. David Belchem had commanded 1st Royal Tank Regiment in the Desert in 1943, and had joined Montgomery's staff for the planning of the invasions of Sicily and Italy. He now became head of the Anglo-American Planning Staff (BGS, Ops), in which key role he was responsible for co-ordinating the Allied naval and air forces. He was an excellent linguist and entirely loyal to his general.

Charles Richardson, in charge of Montgomery's planning (BGS, Plans), was extremely capable, a Sapper who had obtained a First Class Honours degree at Cambridge. Miles Graham, the Chief Administrative Officer, lacked flair, according to Bill Williams, but was ably backed by Colonel Fielden and Oliver Poole (after the war, the latter achieved distinction as head of the Longman Financial Times Group). Twenty-First Army Group's commander always tended to be abrasive, but his talented team were tactful and charming, and credit must go to Montgomery for choosing them and inspiring their devoted loyalty.

As has been said, a limiting factor on more assault divisions and a wider front was the shortage of landing-craft, and as early as 5 January Bedell Smith had cabled Washington to inform Eisenhower that Montgomery insisted categorically on the wider front, and that this presupposed more landing-craft which could only be made available by postponing 'Anvil', then planned to synchronise with 'Overlord'[5] (at Teheran Stalin had said he favoured a simultaneous 'Anvil', and it was vital that the Western Allies should sustain Russia in its desperate battle against vast Nazi forces.) Eisenhower agreed reluctantly to postpone 'Anvil' in view of the statistics of landing-craft available for 'Overlord', and there was heated argument between Eisenhower and Montgomery about the numbers of ships to be earmarked for the postponed 'Anvil'. The British Chiefs of Staff backed Montgomery and wanted to downgrade it to one division, as he had suggested on 21 January. At a SHAEF meeting on 16 February Montgomery presented an ultimatum, saying the 'Overlord' shipping proposals were 'unacceptable' and that he must have 'the craft and shipping essential for a successful Overlord'. Eisenhowever would not agree to give up 'Anvil', and sent a memorandum to Montgomery three days later:

I am convinced that Anvil will be of great assistance to Overlord by diverting German Divisions away from the lodgement area and by opening a way for the French and US Divisions now in the Mediterranean to join the decisive effort against Germany. Hence we must make a maximum effort to mount Anvil.[6]

Montgomery, Churchill and Brooke continued to oppose 'Anvil'.* They were right, as it proved, for in the event the South of France landings, some two months after 'Overlord', did not draw a single German division away from Normandy. But in the haggling over 'Anvil' Eisenhower realised, not for the first time, how difficult a colleague Montgomery could be. There followed a debate at head-of-state level as to whether 'Anvil' should be mounted or not, but Montgomery was no longer directly involved in this controversy.

Quantifying Montgomery's plans for a five-division assault for 'Overlord' produced a demand for an extra 72 LCIs, 47 LSTs and 144 LCTs.† By postponing D-Day from 1 May to 1 June it was just possible to accumulate the necessary amounts of landing-craft in time. De Guingand claimed that the American planners overestimated the carrying capacity of landing-craft under assault conditions, and complained that the major reason for the shortage was the American hoarding of them in the Far East – their preferred theatre. The Americans countered this complaint with one of their own: hundreds of US-built landing-craft lay unrepaired in the UK because the British Government would not pay overtime for their repair.

De Guingand called a landing-craft conference at Norfolk House (HQ SHAEF) on 15 February, and a satisfactory compromise between the British and American points of view was reached. The British agreed to try heavier loading for the assault and to improve the repair position, although de Guingand warned that extra loading would mean double bunking for soldiers, with many staying on board for as long as sixty hours before disembarking on the invasion beaches. The Americans promised to divert craft from 'Anvil', and to send from the USA

---

* At Marrakesh on 1 January Montgomery had told Churchill it would be ninety days before 'Anvil' had any effect on 'Overlord'. The PM accepted this argument, and stuck to it.

† Respectively, Landing-Craft, Infantry; Landing Ship, Tanks; and Landing-Craft, Tanks.

seven more 4,000-ton LSTs, each capable of carrying 2,000 tons of cargo, including twenty medium tanks on the main deck.

Montgomery's planning for the assault proceeded at the bare minimum lift of five divisions, and despite all his pleadings, tactfully and skilfully conducted by de Guingand, there was to be no spare capacity on D-Day, although in the event the Americans delivered more extra craft than they had promised. Eventually there were 168 LSTs (61 British), 245 LCIs (equally divided), and more than 1,000 LCTs (664 British). Montgomery had had to fight a tough battle for his extra landing-craft, but thanks to his determination he won the day.

A revised detailed invasion plan was completed, under Montgomery's chairmanship, by syndicates representing Twenty-First Army Group, British Second Army, General Bradley's US First Army, the joint Naval/Air Force HQ, SHAEF, and all interested commands. It was published on 1 February, under the code-name 'Neptune'; this referred to the assault only, and was initialled by Montgomery, Ramsay and Leigh-Mallory. US First Army produced its detailed plan on 25 February, and British Second Army its plan on 20 March.

The dread of the coming battle in Europe lay like a black cloud over Britain. The country had been at war for more than four years, and memories of the blood-bath on the Somme in 1916 and the years of trench warfare worried the older generation. But, once the invasion plans had been decided in principle at the 21 January conference, Montgomery embarked on a much-needed morale-raising tour of the Forces and the armament factories. (So happy was he with his staff and the atmosphere of mutual confidence that he held only weekly conferences and spent most of his time out of London, living in a special train. This, known as 'Rapier', was based on Addison Road, and had sleepers and a restaurant, a saloon for conferences, and was able to carry staff cars.) Montgomery understood how public relations could raise morale, and he enjoyed the limelight. He had a flair for dramatic personal appearances, and his speeches to the troops, using a loudspeaker from a jeep, were successful beyond expectation. He had, after all, spent a lifetime with soldiers, and he loved and understood them, especially young men; he could mesmerise them by his speeches, and he revelled in his popularity. Now he found that the average young soldier expected to die in the coming assault, and he sought to dispel their gloom by instilling a revivalist fervour. In this he was right, for morale in Britain was low.

The home army – which was chiefly British Second Army – was frustrated. It had spent four years in training, yet was untried in battle. A small proportion were survivors from the Dunkirk fiasco, and memories of that 1940 disaster still loomed large throughout the army, fuelled by these veterans. The best divisions had toiled away too long at exercises which produced only artificially the atmosphere of war. There were, too, many veterans of the First World War, unable to understand why they had won in 1918 and then been defeated in 1940; younger men were puzzled why their own generation had lost all the land battles until Alamein in 1942. Those senior officers who were survivors of the First War bored and horrified their juniors with reminiscences of trench warfare, which seemed entirely out of date to young men now expert in mobile warfare, tank movements and RAF support.

Now, in Montgomery, they saw a survivor of the First World War who *had* mastered the art of modern warfare, and who had won his battles against the Germans. They felt he knew how to use in action the modern technology in which they had been training for so long, and that he had the authority and knowledge to lead them to victory over Hitler's armies, armies that had been invincible until they had crumbled before this same commander in Africa. And, instead of going to France, as in 1940, with bayonets to face men with sub-machine-guns and feeble Boys anti-tank rifles to fire uselessly against armour, here was a properly equipped, well-trained army which would sweep all before it. This was the message Montgomery put over, and he did a magnificent job in raising morale just when it was essential to do so.

So popular did Montgomery become as a result of his tours that Churchill and other politicians worried that he might become almost a military dictator, for he addressed factory workers as well as soldiers. The BBC cut down his invitations to speak, and unofficial messages were sent to ask him to stop his tours. He refused. He knew he was doing good, and that the assault would test the morale of the troops. He had confidence in his staff, and felt that the best use of his time was to make personal appearances so as to get to know the commanders and to inspire his soldiers.

Early in March he visited the Polish Army in Scotland, but here his address did not go down so well. Several of those present on that day have told me they regretted that he said nothing about liberating Poland and that they did not like his remark 'together we shall kill a lot of Germans'. Many of the Polish soldiers had been German or Austrian citizens themselves before the war and although they were vehemently anti-Nazi, they had many German relations and friends.

In a letter dated 14 March to General Casimir Sosnkowski, C-in-C of the Polish Army, Montgomery wrote about the visit: 'I met quite a number of men who had fought *against* me in the Africa Corps under Rommel; I now know why the Africa Corps was so good.' This was tactless. Only 400 were recruits from North African POW camps, and these mostly came from Silesia – a part of Poland which Hitler had incorporated in the German Reich, and where young men of conscript age were forced to join the German Army under threat of reprisals against their families. They had been, for the Nazis, anyway, unwilling warriors who contributed little or nothing to Rommel's effectiveness.[7]

A few weeks, later Montgomery again revealed himself to the Poles in a poor light. General Sosnkowski had told the War Office that he would only put the Polish Parachute Brigade at 'the disposal of the Supreme Allied Commander for operations in Western Europe' provided it would be withdrawn if it sustained 25 per cent casualties, which would endanger its use in Poland, and that it must not be used with Twenty-First Army Group if 'an opportunity arose for its employment in Poland'. Sosnkowski wrote that he feared high casualties might reduce its effectiveness to that of one battalion, just 'at the very moment when the Brigade will be badly needed in Poland'. Brooke, as CIGS, was prepared to agree, but as soon as Montgomery heard of these reservations he wrote this unattractive letter to Simpson, the Director of Military Operations at the War Office:

20th March 1944

Freddie [de Guingand] has shown me your letter of the 19th March, and enclosures, referring to the Polish Para Brigade. I have decided to answer you myself as I feel very strongly in this matter.

The conditions put up by General SOSNKOWSKI are unacceptable. I feel the time has come for us to adopt a more realistic attitude towards our Allied nations. To be dictated to by nations who have been under the heel of Germany as to how their forces should be used is, to my way of thinking, quite wrong. We have got a difficult problem ahead, and to employ the forces of these Allies circumscribed by various restrictions is militarily unsound, and appears to me to be politically unwise. Some of these countries who did very little to help us against the enemy, e.g. France, now appear to be laying down conditions because they see the end in sight. I consider that nations who have been under the heel of Germany *must do as we tell them* until the war is over and Germany is defeated; they will probably have to do as we tell them even after that.

My view is, if I am to be saddled with Allied troops tied down by various restrictions, I would rather not have them at all; this applies to the Polish Para Brigade if they cannot be employed otherwise than in accordance with General SOS-NKOWSKI's conditions. I suggest you tell SOSNKOWSKI accordingly, and have no more nonsense about it.[8]

Montgomery's firm line was accepted completely by the War Office, and on 12 April Sosnkowski withdrew his reservations, expressing his 'complete confidence in General Montgomery'.[9] But the incident did not endear Montgomery to the Poles, whose patience with him was already short. (On his visit to Scotland he had addressed one senior Polish officer, through his interpreter, with the tactless question 'Do you speak German or Russian?' – forgetting that the Poles had their own language. And towards the end of the war, when a Polish general told him, at an official lunch, that he could not return to Poland, Montgomery replied: 'Why not? They will probably make you one of their generals.')

On 7 April 1944 a Presentation of Plans was held in the lecture hall at St Paul's School. Only 111 passes were issued, amidst great secrecy since any leaks would have been disastrous. Churchill and the British Chiefs of Staff were present, and all generals of the four armies – British, American, Canadian and Polish – together with their naval and air force counterparts. Montgomery, allowed only thirty minutes in which to put over his views, again made an excellent impression, radiating an infectious confidence. Much of the criticism later levelled at him over the Normandy campaign arose from this briefing, so it is appropriate to examine in detail how he defined his plans.

No minutes were kept, but Lt-Col Dawnay holds in his archives a copy of the transcript of Montgomery's statement, which was given out to those present with rigid injunctions about secrecy.*

He told the conference that there were fifty-five identified enemy divisions in the west, of which eight were armoured.

Since Rommel toured the 'Atlantic Wall' the enemy has stiffened up his coastal crust but the movement of his mobile reserves is south i.e. away from the assault area; this shows that our target area is not yet known to the enemy. Rommel will hold his mobile divisions back from the coast until he is certain where our main effort is being made.

By D plus 5 the enemy will have brought in six Panzer type divisions. By then we will have fifteen divisions ashore. After about D plus 8 I think the enemy will have to consider a roping off policy i.e. trying to stop our expansion from the lodgement area ... I suggest we should plan in general on the enemy having a round total of sixty divisions of which ten will be Panzer ... the armoured divisions are being kept directly under Rundstedt, and delay may be caused before they are released to Rommel. This in fact may help us and quarrels may arise between the two of them.

This vision of enemy movements was prophetically accurate, and demonstrates how well briefed Twenty-First Army Group was kept by Ultra about German intentions.

Montgomery's address continued:

There are four armies taking part in the operations:

First U.S. Army	Assault Armies
Second British Army	
First Canadian Army	Follow Up Armies
Third U.S. Army	

---

* The only records kept were the guest list, and a note that Twenty-First Army Group provided lunch and tea.

The order of battle can be seen on the diagrams. The tasks given to the armies are as follows:

First U.S. Army
  (a) To assault astride the CARENTAN estuary.
  (b) To capture CHERBOURG as quickly as possible.
  (c) East of CARENTAN, to develop operations southwards towards ST LO in conformity with the advance of Second British Army.

After the area CHERBOURG–CAUMONT–VIRE–AVRANCHES has been captured, the Army will be directed southwards with the object of capturing RENNES and then establishing our flank on the R. LOIRE and capture QUIBERON BAY.

Second British Army
  To assault to the west of the R. ORNE and to develop operations to the south and south-east, in order to secure airfield sites and to protect the eastern flank of First U.S. Army while the latter is capturing CHERBOURG.

  In its subsequent operations the Army will pivot on its left and offer a strong front against enemy movement towards the lodgement area from the east.

First Canadian Army
  This Army will land after the Second British Army and will take over from it the left or northern sector of the lodgement area. The troops of Second British Army in the area so taken over, probably one Corps, will come under command First Canadian Army.

Third U.S. Army
  This Army will land after First U.S. Army and will have the tasks:
  (a) of clearing the BRITTANY peninsula and capturing the BRITTANY ports.
  (b) as soon as the BRITTANY and LOIRE ports have been captured, of covering the south flank of the lodgement area while the First U.S. Army is directed N.E. with a view to operations towards PARIS ...

The Sea-borne Assault

17. The existing resources in landing ships and craft are contained in five Naval Assault Forces, and two Naval Follow-up Forces. These forces have been allotted in support of Armies as follows:

First U.S. Army
Two Assault Forces   Lift of approximately
One Follow-up Force   8,700 vehicles.

Second British Army
Three Assault Forces   Lift of approximately
One Follow-up Force   10,900 vehicles.

    The total lift is some 20,000 vehicles, all of which will be landed on the first, second, or third tides.

18. The forces to be carried in the initial lift are as follows:

First U.S. Army
    Three Infantry Divisions (Assault)
    Five Tank Battalions (Assault)
    Two Ranger Battalions
    Army and Corps Tps and Naval and Air overheads.

Second British Army
    Three Infantry Divisions (Assault)
    Three Tank Brigades (Assault)
    One Armoured Brigade
    One Infantry Division (less two Inf Bde Groups)
    Two S.S. Bdes
    Army and Corps Tps. and Naval and Air overheads.

19. The assault will take place on D day on an eight Brigades, Regimental Combat Team, front.
H hour will be nautical twilight + 90 minutes, but this time may change.

First U.S. Army
    Assaults on a front of three Regimental Combat Teams.

Second British Army
    Assaults on a front of five Infantry Brigades.
Details are shown on the diagram, and Army Comds will explain the plans later.

Montgomery detailed the planned drops for the American and British airborne troops which were eventually successfully executed, and which are described later, and added:

> The problem with airborne troops is to land enough troops to do the job, and to land them in the right place. I have laid down that the smallest number to be landed in any one place, at one time, is a Bde; and far better to land a whole Division. Once airborne troops have done their job, they must be collected into reserve for use again as soon as they are refitted.

During the actual campaign, however, he was unable to follow this dictum because he was short of infantry. The British 6th Airborne Division fought from D-Day until they reached the Seine late in August, and the US airborne divisions dropped for the Nijmegen and Arnhem operation continued to fight with Twenty-First Army Group for months afterwards, to the consternation of some American generals.

He also forecast that 'once the initial operations are over airborne troops will be used to keep the battle moving by means of "air hooks" of not less than a Brigade', and he specified other likely operations, such as an attack on the Brittany ports by up to two airborne divisions, and an operation in conjunction with the crossing of the Loire.

To help Montgomery to outline his plan, a phase map was hung on the wall showing the estimated position at, among others, D-plus-20, D-plus-35, D-plus-60 and D-plus-90. According to Maj-Gen Belchem, Montgomery never wanted to be committed to the phase map but was rail-roaded into it by the US planners; after the campaign it was used by his critics as an argument that his master plan had gone astray. On the map, he forecast that if all went well by D-plus-90 the Canadian First and British Second Armies would hold the Seine between Paris and Rouen, while US First Army would drive over the Seine for Paris, with US Third Army on the most southerly flank.

According to the phase map exhibited on 7 April, by D-plus-20 the Allied front line would form an arc from the River Orne to Avranches; by D-plus-35 the line would be from the River Dives east of Caen through Argentan and Le Mans to Nantes on the Loire estuary. Commenting on the phase line for D-plus-35, Montgomery said: 'The British Second Army will push its left out towards the general lines of the River Touques. At the same time the army will pivot on Falaise and will swing with its right towards Argentan-Alençon.' When later, these targets were not achieved, Montgomery said that they had had no real importance for his master plan, which led to grave misunderstandings with Eisenhower and SHAEF.

His closing comment was:

> Given close co-operation between the airforces and the land armies, I do not see how the enemy can stop us from developing the operations as we plan – if only we can get a good lodgement in the first four days and capture Cherbourg quickly.

In the afternoon, Bradley told the conference that he had to tackle the *bocage*, the countryside of wide hedges and banks and tiny fields around the Cherbourg peninsula which was appalling terrain for tanks. That morning Montgomery had rather recklessly suggested that Bradley should explore the possibility of a 'tank knock about' after Omaha Beach* was taken; clearly he had underestimated the difficulties for tanks in the bocage.

The conference confirmed the original placing of the Americans on the right and the British on the left, but anyway this could not now be altered since the US supply depots, training schools and reinforcements were all based in the west of England. The deception plan – 'Fortitude' – was also discussed on 7 April. It was to prove to be one of the greatest triumphs of the invasion, for not only was Hitler successfully deluded into guessing that the main invasion would come in the Pas de Calais, but he also kept considerable forces in Norway and Denmark against a possible invasion there. The implementation of the complex deception plan alone was responsible for keeping twenty German divisions in the Pas de Calais until too late to throw back the invasion in Normany, more than 150 miles away. Indeed, Field-Marshal Gerd von Rundstedt, the German C-in-C West, later admitted that until D-plus-14 he had

---

* US First Army was allotted two landing beaches in the western sector, codenamed 'Utah' and 'Omaha'. East of 'Omaha', the three British and Canadian beaches were, from the west, 'Gold', 'Juno', and 'Sword' (see map, p. 95).

expected another invasion in the Pas de Calais.[10]

Selected journalists were briefed about the coming invasion, and then forbidden to write anything more for their papers before D-Day, while diplomatic bags to neutral countries were suspended. Montgomery pointed out that security arrangements had to be stringent, emphasising that if any of the participants at the conference betrayed their secrecy vow the invasion would be in jeopardy.

Slightly discordant notes were struck by Ramsay and Leigh-Mallory. Ramsay again stressed the difficulties for the Navy, but redeemed himself by agreeing with Montgomery that the combined navies could land the troops in the right places and afterwards maintain the required supplies.

Leigh-Mallory, for the air forces, emphasised that on D-Day the German Air Force could be well controlled with relative ease, but he spotlighted the need for the early seizure of the 'good' airfield area beyond Caen. This was a sore point with Montgomery, for he knew his difficulty would lie in getting beyond Caen; privately, he thought that the air forces could operate efficiently from home bases.

Montgomery made it clear to the conference that he was worried about the underwater obstacles which the Germans were planting under the cliffs on the chosen invasion beaches. He explained that he now planned to land at half-tide, three hours before high water, to give the engineers time to make paths through the obstacles. The Americans observed that this would be expensive in casualties, and Montgomery said that he would employ armour along with infantry in the first wave, using new tank 'gadgets'. He then entered into details about these gadgets, or 'Hobart's funnies' as they were sometimes known. His brother-in-law, Maj-Gen Percy Hobart (known as 'Hobo') was, like Montgomery, one of the few officers in the thirties who understood the enormous potential of modern tanks. Although he had officially retired in 1940, Hobart had, with Churchill's backing, designed tanks equipped with new devices which were to be of enormous value in the invasion. Given, at the Prime Minister's insistence, access to considerable research and manufacturing capacity, Hobart developed, among others, the DD amphibious tanks, tanks equipped with flails to pass through minefields, and the invaluable armoured bulldozer. The DD tanks were made amphibious by equipping them with floating detachable canvas 'bloomers' – pleated screens for buoyancy. These tanks, adapted from standard, had a duplex drive (hence 'DD') which consisted of twin propellers for swimming as well as the normal track-laying drive for land. The British had ordered 650 DD Valentines and 900 DD Shermans, and they were to prove invaluable. Eisenhower fell for the DDs, and found Montgomery's enthusiasm for their use infectious. Unfortunately, other American generals were more sceptical, and on D-Day, to their cost, had only three tank battalions equipped with DDs against the seven British battalions so equipped. Marshall had sent General Charles H. Corlet to England as a consultant for the invasion plans because he was expert in amphibious landings after considerable experience in the Pacific. Corlet had reported that he found senior British officers appreciative of his knowledge and advice, but the Americans not so receptive. After the 21 January conference, however, Eisenhower insisted on ordering a further 300 DDs, to be delivered from the USA within two months.

Churchill, on 7 April, looked tired and old. He was worried, for that week he had suffered his worst Cabinet squabble ever, over the proposed bombing of the French roads and railways. However, he wound up the proceedings with a pep talk and as the conference dispersed there was a friendly atmosphere amongst British, Canadians and Americans, and a confidence that all would go well.

In his diary, Brooke commented on this conference: 'Monty started with a good speech. Churchill was in a weakly condition looking old and lacking vitality.' In an entry four days earlier he had written: 'PM aged tired and failing to grasp matters. It is a depressing sight to see him gradually deteriorating. I wonder how long he can last – not long enough to see the war over I fear.' The CIGS's diary entries provide a telling commentary on some aspects of these invasion conferences. Maj-Gen Gerard Bucknall, GOC, XXX Corps, had also spoken at the conference. Brooke was unimpressed with him and wrote prophetically: 'Bucknall very weak and unfit to command a Corps.'

After the 7 April conference, Montgomery issued important instructions to British Second Army and US First Army about the use of armoured groups on D-Day to penetrate inland from the beaches quickly. He set great store by them, writing:

The best way to interfere with the enemy concentrations and countermeasures [on D-Day] will be to push forward fairly powerful armoured force thrusts on the afternoon of D-Day.
If two such forces consisting of an Armoured Brigade Group were pushed forward on each army front to carefully chosen areas it would be very difficult for the enemy to interfere with our build-up ... to be successful such tactics must be adopted on D-Day: to wait until D plus 1 would be to lose the opportunity and also to lose the initiative ... I am prepared to accept any risk in order to carry out such tactics.

Unfortunately, on D-Day itself the traffic congestion on the beaches was far greater than anticipated, and his armoured thrusts could not be made in strength. A small detachment of Canadian tanks did, however, reach the outskirts of Caen by the evening, but they had to withdraw as they had no support.

The final top-level conference was held on 15 May at St Paul's with the same senior officers and their staffs present; King George VI also attended. Montgomery was again supremely confident, his comments and speeches lucid. The only copy of his address is in the Dawnay archives, written in pencil with almost no corrections. In it he emphasised that Rommel* would try to defeat the invasion on the beaches, and that he had sixty divisions in France including ten Panzers, of which four were in or close to the invasion area – 21st Panzer, 12th and 17th SS Panzers, and Panzer Lehr; he added that five German divisions would oppose the assault initially. He forecast that by dusk on D-Day the Allies would be fighting hard against six divisions, with another Panzer division approaching from Rennes to be effective on D-plus-1. By D-plus-2 Montgomery expected the Germans to have nine divisions opposing the invaders, of which five would be Panzers, and that thirteen more divisions might be approaching.

He expected a 'full-blooded counter-attack' at any time after D-plus-5, with a total of twenty-four enemy divisions engaged against eighteen Allied.

* Von Rundstedt, as C-in-C, West, had under his command Field-Marshal Erwin Rommel's Army Group 'B', which comprised nearly two-thirds of the operational German troops in France, and General Blaskowitz's Army Group 'G', stationed on the Biscay coast and on the Riviera.

Rommel, Montgomery said, had made a world of difference to German defences and morale since he took over, and was best 'at spoiling attacks as he is too impulsive for a set-piece battle, and he will do his best to Dunkirk us ... by preventing our tanks landing'. He went on to say that armoured columns must penetrate deep inland and quickly on D-Day; 'this will upset the enemy plans and tend to hold him off while we build up strength.'

Montgomery predicted that Rommel would try and hold Caen, Bayeux and Carentan, and he emphasised the menace of the minefields and hidden obstacles, which meant that the invaders must touch down on the beaches thirty minutes before the incoming tide reached the obstacles, while the latter were still exposed and thus ineffective.

He concluded: 'We shall have to send the soldiers in to this party "seeing red". We must get them completely on their toes, having absolute faith in the plan, and imbued with infectious optimism and offensive eagerness.'

Air Chief Marshal Sir Arthur Harris, C-in-C, Bomber Command, even at this late hour told the conference that the strategic bombing of Germany was an adequate substitute for invasion, and the King embarrassingly stammered out a few words. This time Churchill did not speak. He arrived in time for lunch, and afterwards became cheerful and genial. In the afternoon Montgomery lifted his smoking ban in deference to the Prime Minister. This relieved the tension and the conference broke up with the smell of victory in the air.

Brooke commented in his diary about the 15 May St Paul's conference:

The main impression I formed was that Eisenhower was a swinger and no real director of thought plans energy or distinction – just a good mixer and international co-operator. Monty made excellent speech. Ramsay overwhelmed by his own difficulties. Leigh-Mallory very clear description. Spaatz read out whole of poor statement. Monty was in very good form.

At this stage Brooke had already made up his mind that Montgomery was head and shoulders above everyone else, and he never altered his poor opinion of Eisenhower.

In his own mind, Montgomery had decided that, after landing and consolidating the beach-head, British Second Army would do its best to capture Caen and the airfields beyond it. If, as he anticipated, however, Rommel flung too many of his Panzers and infantry divisions into the defence of Caen, the British would attempt just to hold and contain the enemy, and to attract as much of the German armour as possible to the Caen sector so that the Americans thrusting down the Cherbourg peninsula would meet weaker resistance. He did not intend at this stage to risk the sacrifice of his British divisions in a desperate effort at a break-out in the Caen sector. He knew only too well that the British and Canadian reserves of manpower were too low for such a slaughter, and that no fresh British divisions could ever be raised because of the country's already daunting commitments, although more US divisions were available.

Conscious of the disaster of the Dieppe raid in 1942, both Montgomery and the American commanders insisted on overwhelming fire support. Montgomery therefore plumped for forty-five minutes of daylight before touch-down on the beaches, so that the fire support could be observed and adjusted. It was to prove a wise decision. The landings, he noted, must be made at full moon and low tide, and this meant only 5, 6, or 7 June, allowing a margin of two days' postponement for bad weather.

Montgomery and de Guingand were still having difficulty in keeping Tedder, Leigh-Mallory and Air Vice-Marshal Arthur Coningham (commanding the Tactical Air Forces) happy, so they again glibly promised the air force commanders the airfields beyond Caen which, in their heart of hearts, they knew were unlikely to be to be taken for some time after the landings. This promise, and the use of the unrealistic phase map, gave ammunition to Montgomery's critics later, when the Normandy battle hung fire. The verdict of history, however, on Montgomery's planning for the landings, and his conduct of the subsequent operations in Normandy, should allow no such criticisms. His achievement was magnificent, and the way in which he delegated the details to his planning staff and went on his successful morale-boosting tours stamps him with greatness. So confident was he that he did not attend Eisenhower's conferences on 3 May, 22 May or 29 May, preferring to stump the country while his staff handled details.

One of Churchill's quirks was that he liked to have a pet

aversion on which he could let off his tensions, a fact which became clearer as the invasion drew near. With the strain of waiting for D-Day, the Prime Minister worried more and more about the large numbers of administrative vehicles and personnel which showed up on the charts of loading priorities. He now began to query the loading programme. The War Office could give him no satisfactory answer; all they were able to say was that Montgomery's planning staff had certified that these scales were essential.

A week before D-Day Churchill went down to Twenty-First Army Group HQ, which had now moved to Portsmouth, and there suggested to Montgomery that he (Churchill) should address the latter's staff on the subject of unnecessary vehicles and unnecessary clerical personnel. Characteristically Montgomery would have none of it, and said to Churchill:

> It would be unwise for you to speak to my staff. Even if I have made mistakes it is now too late to put them right. The loaded trains are on the way to the ports and many of the boats are already loaded. To alter things now would dislocate 'Overlord'. I myself am sure that every single man and vehicle is necessary. If you do not believe me and insist on last-minute alterations you must have lost confidence in me.[11]

It was a tense moment. Suddenly Churchill saw that he had left things too late, and that 'Overlord' was beyond his control. He could not afford a quarrel with Montgomery at this eleventh hour. He was in fact almost certainly right about the loading priorities and the unnecessary personnel, and undoubtedly he still thought so, but now he bowed to the inevitable. Montgomery led him out of his office and introduced him to his waiting staff, all of whom knew what the two men had been discussing. Churchill rose to the occasion and acknowledged defeat, saying with an impish grin: 'Gentlemen, today I must not talk to you.' A clash between these two dedicated leaders had been averted, but it had shown that Montgomery knew how enormously powerful was his own position vis-à-vis the Prime Minister. It was an incident that did nothing to make him more modest.

The main Twenty-First Army Group HQ had moved to Southwick House, Portsmouth at the end of April, leaving only the rear echelon in London. Montgomery had his office and mess in a charming small house, where he and de Guingand had bedrooms while the rest of his generals lived in tents and caravans, though they messed with their commander.

D-Day was now set for 5 June, but on the 2nd the weather experts became pessimistic about prospects for the invasion. The decision whether or not to postpone because of bad weather was not, however, Montgomery's responsibility, but Eisenhower's, as Supreme Commander. At 0430 on 4 June Eisenhower held a conference at Southwick Park, and asked the assembled commanders for their views now that they had heard gloomy reports from the meterologists. Tedder, Leigh-Mallory and Ramsay all advised a postponement. Only Montgomery wanted to go, despite Leigh-Mallory's especially pessimistic view that his crews would have to bomb on instruments without seeing their targets. Eisenhower decided to postpone for twenty-four hours.

Tedder was furious, and asserted later that Montgomery had been ready to risk his armies knowing full well that, because of the weather, the air forces could give only very reduced support. From this point Tedder became one of Montgomery's severest critics, egged on by the disappointed Morgan, Eisenhower's Deputy Chief of Staff. (Morgan became such a thorn in Montgomery's flesh that the latter accused him of automatically supporting Eisenhower's ideas at the expense of his own.) Tedder had lost 2,000 aircraft and 12,000 men killed in the two months before D-Day, and Montgomery's implied assumption that the air forces were of little value to the invasion force was like a red rag to a bull to him in the tense hours before the invasion.

By now, 4 June, some submarines were already in position on the invasion routes to act as markers. As each craft surfaced, it had immediately to dive again in response to urgent signals about the postponement. The submarines spent another uncomfortable twenty-four hours, eleven fathoms under the surface.

Bradley and the other US generals had already embarked on ships with their troops, and in the afternoon they sent a message to Eisenhower recommending that at all costs the invasion should go ahead on 6 June. Eisenhower reconvened the conference at 0430 on the 5th. Tedder and Leigh-Mallory were still against going, and Ramsay added that a decision was needed within half an hour if 'Overlord' was to take place on Tuesday, 6 June. The meteorologist said: 'There is a glimmer of hope. A clear spell is possible for 24 hours from late on 5 June.' Montgomery was as keen as ever, and with many misgivings Eisenhower told the conference that the invasion would go ahead as planned on 6 June. According to his ADC, Eisenhower was so worried that he immediately drafted the bulletin which he would have to issue if the invasion was a failure.

The troops landed on the invasion beaches at 0430 on 6 June. Montgomery spent the whole day quietly at his HQ in Portsmouth reading the signals as they came in; he was especially delighted when Leigh-Mallory reported that aircraft casualties had been low in the airborne landings. Then, at 2230, after recording a message for the BBC, General Sir Bernard Montgomery embarked on the destroyer HMS *Faulkner* for Normandy.

3

Normandy Assault

Montgomery spent D-plus-1 at sea. The British and American assault on the beaches had been successful, despite the rough sea and, in places, strong resistance. The airborne divisions had accomplished their main task; the massive air superiority and the bombardment by naval guns had softened up the opposition and the armies had taken full advantage of this. German reaction was slow, because Hitler was still duped by the deception plan and believed the main assault would come later in the Pas de Calais. As a result no reinforcements were rushed from the German Fifteenth Army Group, based on the Calais coast to Eighth Army Group fighting desperately in Normandy. Nor would Hitler allow von Rundstedt to throw his powerful Panzer reserves into these early battles.

Although Montgomery would not admit it, the German infantry opposition on the beaches was weaker than anticipated except on Omaha Beach, where American troops were unlucky enough to encounter a crack division which had just arrived in Normandy from the South of France.* The German infantry mostly consisted of inferior troops, with little mechanised transport; there was, too, a large element consisting of Russians and Silesian Poles who had 'volunteered' for the German Army mainly to escape starvation. These soon became POWs. Hitler had thought it too dangerous to send them back to the Russian front, and there were as a result good numbers of them in Normandy under senior German officers, although the junior

---

* Williams had felt this division might be present, but there were no confirmed reports of its location.

officers were mostly Russians.

During his interrogation after the war von Rundstedt said that the Atlantic Wall was 'largely a fake'. 'Twenty of our divisions had no mobility and were equipped with a hotch-potch of foreign artillery and filled with personnel from older age groups and low physical categories, plus thousands of Russians who were a menace and a nuisance.'[1]

Nominally the Germans had fifty to sixty divisions to oppose Montgomery, but that was only on paper. Some were skeleton divisions, 'with a Commander, a medical officer and 5 bakers'. Von Rundstedt added that a lot of the minefields were dummies, and that Hitler had indulged in intensive false propaganda about the strength of the 'Atlantic Wall', propaganda which was passed on to the Allies by agents in Paris and Switzerland. But von Rundstedt confirmed the strength of the underwater obstacles beneath the cliffs on the actual invasion beaches used, which vindicated Montgomery's continual underlining of the importance of careful preparation to deal with them.

Madame de Vigneral who, with her family, was living at Colombières-sur Seuilles, three kilometres from Sword Beach, wrote in her diary that by 1300 on D-Day the Germans defending her village were running away, and that the cooks had told her that they would kill their commanding officer when the invasion started. Apparently they did so, for by 1330 the car in which the commanding officer had driven away at dawn, and in which he had died, was brought back by a Canadian to her house when she was opening bottles of champagne. In the orchard, her father found sixty rifles belonging to Germans who had run away without fighting.[2] It took the Canadians until 1200 to cover the three kilometres from Sword beach.

John Henderson told me that at 0530 on the morning of D-plus-1 Montgomery woke him up in his cabin on the destroyer and said: 'You had better come on deck. The captain has just told me that he is outside the channel which has been kept clear of mines.' So Henderson and his chief stood looking over the side for mines until, at 0630, they reached Bradley's ship, the USS *Augusta*, off the French coast; Montgomery took it as a great joke. He now went on board the *Augusta* and asked Bradley to make every effort to link up the two American beaches. Utah and Omaha. Shortly after Montgomery had left Bradley's ship, Eisenhower arrived on *Augusta* and complained bitterly to Bradley that he had received almost no news on D-Day. All signals had to be decoded at Twenty-First Army Group HQ at Portsmouth, and the Royal Signals had grossly underestimated the amount of wireless traffic involved. At 0900 Dempsey came aboard HMS *Faulkner* and briefed Montgomery on Second Army's situation.

Montgomery had reason to be pleased with the early results of the invasion, apart from the failure to take Caen, and he was particularly gratified by the airborne successes. Throughout the planning he had insisted on using three airborne divisional drops, and this had aroused considerable opposition from the air marshals. Bradley and Montgomery had agreed, however, that if the Utah Beach landing was to be successful and the Cherbourg peninsula cut in half, both the US 82nd and US 101st Divisions must land west of the beach near Ste Mère Eglise. This meant that 915 transport aircraft (most of them towing gliders) had to cross the Cherbourg peninsula on a moonlit night on a steady course, their flight path taking them directly over heavy enemy AA installations which would quickly be alerted.

During the initial airborne planning session at St Paul's, Leigh-Mallory had agreed to this plan, but later objected strongly and claimed that 80 per cent casualties in aircraft and troops would be likely. He stressed that, since the C47s to be used had not been fitted with self-sealing petrol tanks, many aircraft would fall in flames, taking the gliders with them, and 'that a substantial part of the force would not be available after the landing'. Montgomery and Bradley refused to yield, and Leigh-Mallory therefore went over their heads to Eisenhower to try and persuade him to cancel the plan. Eisenhower, however, backed his two generals. On the evening of D-Day Leigh-Mallory had enthusiastically let Eisenhower know that his objections had been groundless, and that not more than twenty aircraft had been lost; indeed, on D-Day itself, the American fight to take Utah Beach was made considerably easier because of the successful Ste Mère-Eglise air landings. Leigh-Mallory also reported that, in the vital period between 2200 on D-minus-1 and 0400 on D-Day, only fourteen out of ninety-two enemy radar stations were operating because of jamming and bombing; on the night of the 5th Luftwaffe night fighters had flown around Amiens fruitlessly searching for non-existent Allied aircraft.

Montgomery's enthusiasm for Hobart's tank 'gadgets' was

abundantly justified. According to Dempsey's papers, 129 DD tanks were launched by the British on D-Day, of which eighty-four landed and forty-five foundered. The War Office Report criticised the escape hatch, but in fact most of the crews of the foundered tanks escaped by dinghy: additionally, aimed fire at the floating tanks was less then expected. DD tanks floated in with the first wave of British soldiers and blasted the defences, providing fire and protection in vivid contrast to the failure at Dieppe. On the British beaches, fascine, carpet-layer and flail tanks made ways through the minefields almost without casualties and with great speed, where it would have taken hours for sappers on foot to clear them; additionally, the tanks were immune to small-arms fire, which at Dieppe had almost wiped out the engineers. On the British Gold and Juno Beaches it was too rough to float in all the DD tanks which had been carried in the landing-craft, but flail tanks were a great success. On the third British beach, Sword, where the water was calmer, twenty-one out of twenty-five DD tanks landed ahead of the infantry, together with the mine-clearing tanks, and this helped the troops enormously. Montgomery had also conceived the idea that some of the field guns should be able to bombard the coast from the decks of the landing-craft as they approached the shore, and this addition to the attackers' fire-power was of considerable help in silencing the defences. The Germans possessed a massive fire capability, and the minefields and underwater obstacles were formidable; the success of the British assaults was therefore a triumph for the detail Allied planning of which Montgomery had been chief architect.

On Omaha Beach US 29th and 1st Infantry Divisions faced near-defeat. Out of thirty-five amphibious tanks only five arrived safely, because of the high seas. Unfortunately, the American planners had been unimpressed by other Hobart specialist tanks, and in consequence had decided not to use flails nor the other devices, a decision that proved nearly disastrous. For hours the American troops on Omaha were pinned down by accurate observed German fire, and at one stage were on the point of being evacuated. Even by mid-afternoon, after considerable naval and air support, troops were crossing the shingle in single file because of the almost impossible task of clearing wide tracks through the minefields by hand under observed fire, though with the Hobart tanks the mines could have been cleared quickly and with few casualties. Montgomery had ordered Hobart originally to offer one-third of his gadgets 'to the Americans', but sadly Bradley and his staff were not interested, except in the DDs. The American military historian Russell Weigley claims this colossal error arose because the Americans, unlike the British, had not suffered the ghastly casualties in frontal assaults like those on the Somme or at Passchendaele, and tended therefore to look on tanks merely as instruments for break-through and mobility.[3] The contrast between the success of the British mine-clearing and the failure of the Americans at Omaha proves Montgomery's foresight in his all-out support for the Hobart tank devices.

By nightfall on D-Day British troops had advanced for up to six miles inland. They had not reached all their objectives, and Montgomery's optimistic view that Caen might fall on the first day had proved a wild dream. British 6th Airborne's daring landing had created a bridgehead east of the Caen canal and the River Orne, and after rushing the guards at Bénouville bridge they seized unguarded bridges on the only lateral road between Caen and Sword Beach. British 3rd Division had been given the task of capturing Caen, eight miles from Sword, while Canadian 3rd Division was expected to take Carpiquet airfield, eleven miles inland from Juno Beach and immediately west of Caen. The Canadians nearly took Carpiquet, but the planners had underestimated the traffic congestion on roads out of the beaches:[4] when, at 1000, a half-squadron of Canadians tanks reached the Caen-Bayeux road at Bratteville they found no opposition, and they were almost at Carpiquet airfield when they realised that they were alone, having completely outrun all the rest of the supporting Canadian divisions. Such had been the traffic delays on the beach exits that the follow-up troops were held up for hours. The isolated tanks had to withdraw, although had the Canadians arrived at Carpiquet in strength on the afternoon of D-Day they, with British 3rd Division, could have taken Caen.

3rd Division landed at Sword and swiftly overcame the beach opposition, but after that their progress was disappointing. Montgomery had insisted on battle-experienced troops for all the landings, and it is possible that their previous experience had made the troops over-cautious. Not until 1900 did the division link up with 6th Airborne at the key bridgehead of Bénouville, three miles from the outskirts of Caen. Forty tanks of 21st Panzer Division had counter-attacked 6th Airborne strongly at 1600, but fortunately by then 20th Anti-Tank Regiment had deployed its 17-pounders, and glider-borne reinforcements had arrived. The 17-pounders knocked out over twenty German tanks, while the glider reinforcements had doubled the fighting strength of 6th Airborne, but with 3rd Division behind schedule no determined effort could be made to chase 21st Panzer and take Caen. Nevertheless, Montgomery had a bridgehead over the river north-east of Caen for follow-up attacks into the best tank country, although it was not strongly held.

On D-Day, General Sir Nigel Poett (later a DMO) was the brigadier commanding 5 Parachute Brigade of 6th Airborne Division. The brigade crash-landed its gliders within a few yards of Bénouville Bridge, and General Poett told me:

Our operation on D-Day was a complete success and Monty's plan to capture the vital Bénouville bridge by a spectacular air operation was completely justified. The sergeant-pilots of the gliders did a magnificent job in guiding the gliders to within yards of the bridge so that my men achieved complete surprise. I was dropped one mile away and lost my signals officer and when I reached the bridge it was in our hands.

This was the first divisional strength air landing in the history of the British Army. In the preliminary plans it was to be only brigade strength, but Monty rightly upgraded it to a full airborne division.

It was well on the cards that Monty could have taken Caen on the first day, but 3rd Division were late in joining up with us from Sword Beach. At first light one of my companies could have taken Caen; in the afternoon it would have needed a whole battalion, and by night a division.

When I met General Gale (my divisional commander) at dawn I was able to tell him that my brigade had taken all their objectives. Our worst moment was at 0730 when we found 21st Panzer moving fast up to their start line to attack us down both banks of the Orne. Then they realised from the noise and smoke and lights from the beaches that the invasion had started so they only left one armoured regiment to attack us, and with well dug-in anti-tank guns we kept them off.

Instead 21st Panzer went down to the sea at Lyons-sur-Mer. Then they saw our glider reinforcements landing in the afternoon and, frightened of being cut off, they went back towards Caen. By 1900 3rd Infantry Division were able to give us great help in fighting off attacks by 21st Panzer Division tanks. We were heavily attacked during the first few days, and not until we took Breville, where the Germans were strongly lodged, were we at all safe. There were very heavy casualties in the night attack we made on Breville in conjunction with Lovat's commandos — it was put on too hastily for a complicated night attack.

Breville was the one hole in the perimeter of the bridgehead over the River Orne. Montgomery had always emphasised how vital this bridgehead was for future attacks, and when the town was occupied, by midnight on 11 June, his relief was great.

General Sir Richard Gale, the commander of 6th Airborne Division, informed me that

Monty would have liked to think he was responsible for planning our very successful Bénouville operation on D-Day. He was not. I planned it with my divisional staff, greatly helped by General David Belchem from Monty's staff. As we went in first during the night of D-minus-1 we came directly under Twenty-First Army Group, and Monty must be given credit for approving our overall plan, if not for the details. I did not come under command of General Crocker's I Corps until they landed [on D-Day itself].

In the struggle for the bridgehead over the Orne the battle for Breville, which we fought with the help of Lovat's* commandos, was the turning point. Neither from the north nor the south were we attacked seriously again.

And Sir Charles Richardson added:

Monty certainly took a keen interest in the main points of the

---

* Brigadier the Lord Lovat, DSO, MC, commanded 1 Special Service Brigade during the invasion. It was the task of this commando to push forward after landing and link up with 6th Airborne Division, which was successfully accomplished by the afternoon of D-Day.

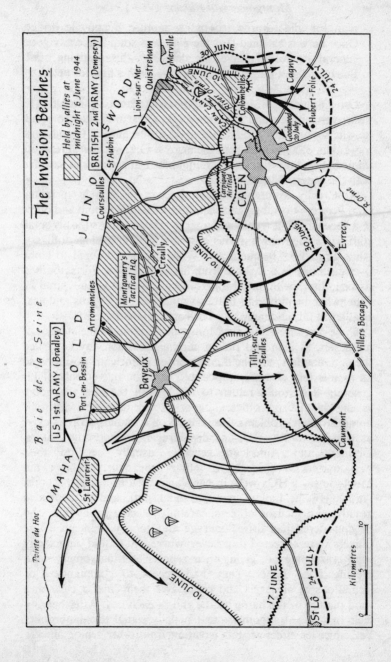

The Invasion Beaches

Held by allies at
midnight 6 June 1944

BRITISH 2nd ARMY (Dempsey)

US 1st ARMY (Bradley)

Baie de la Seine

Pointe du Hoc

OMAHA
St Laurent

GOLD
Port-en-Bessin
Arromanches

Bayeux

JUNO
Courseulles
St Aubin

SWORD
Lion-sur-Mer
Ouistreham
Merville

CAEN CANAL
River Orne

Crepon

CAEN
Carpiquet
Airfield

Montgomery's
Tactical HQ

Creully

Tilly-sur-
Seulles

Villers Bocage

Caumont

10 JUNE

17 JUNE

24 JULY

St Lô

30 JUNE

Evrecy

R. Orne

30 JUNE

10 JUNE

Colombelles
Cagny
Goodwood
20 July
Hubert-Folie

24 JULY

Kilometres
0   5   10

plan for glider-borne troops to capture Bénouville bridge. Once he was satisfied that the plan was sound, like any good general he would leave the details to his planning staff. Belchem was a magnificent executive, with a flair for detail.

On D-plus-2, 8 June, Montgomery landed himself. His destroyer ran aground in trying to get close in to the shore, but he was soon at his Tac HQ set up in an orchard at Creully, not more than 3,000 yards from the nearest German lines. He wrote immediately that day to de Guingand: 'I am very well satisfied with the general situation.'[5]

At Creully Montgomery found ready for him his personal (and very comfortable) caravan, his mobile map room and office in a specially built truck, and a large tent as a mess for his small staff. He settled down to this cosy life with his younger officers, while Brigadiers Belchem and Williams were ordered to come over each day in a Dakota from his Main HQ at Portsmouth in order to liaise with him. Montgomery stayed at Creully until 22 June, when he moved to Blay, six miles west of Bayeux and near Bradley at Grandchamp, not far from Omaha Beach.

Once on shore in France Montgomery resumed the lifestyle of his desert, Sicilian and Italian campaigns. Each day he visited the commanders, and held conferences in forward positions so as to interfere as little as possible with the movements of his generals. He would return to his HQ in the late afternoon, receive his liaison officers' reports, and then deal with his administration problems. He insisted on a landing strip as close as possible to Tac HQ, and discouraged unimportant visitors. German and American generals usually set up their headquarters in châteaux or other prominent buildings, but Montgomery's HQs were in caravans, sited in fields or woods. At his HQ he had a small personal staff, and he depended greatly on his liaison officers, carefully selected young men who he considered had drive, courage and good judgement. These officers were expected to go everywhere and to find out exactly what was going on, giving their reports to Montgomery each evening after dinner. They had access to commanders of formations at all levels and could give their chief a clear and vivid picture of the battle by the end of each day. After hearing their reports, Montgomery sent a daily signal to Alanbrooke. Yet, however effective, this isolation from other senior officers and from people of his own age contributed to Montgomery's failure to understand the criticism and jealousy which his conduct was arousing amongst the British and American chiefs at SHAEF, and at Bradley's US First Army.

Montgomery found time to write in his own hand to Simpson on 8 June, and to de Guingand on the 10th. These letters are clear, frank and revealing:

TAC HQ
June 8 1944

My dear Simbo,
You may like the following news of our battle.
1. There is no doubt that the Germans were suprised, and we got on shore before they had recovered. The speed, power and violence of the assault carried all before it.
2. Generally, the beach obstacles presented no difficulty; where they were troublesome it was because of rough weather – and on some beaches it was pretty rough.
3. DD Tanks
    (a) Used successfully on Utah beaches;
    (b) Failed to reach the shore on Omaha beaches and all sank – too rough;
    (c) Were not launched on 50 Div front as it was too rough; were landed 'dry' behind the leading flights; casualties to AVRE sappers high as a result, and to leading infantry;
    (d) Landed dry Canadian front.
    (e) Used successfully on 3 Div front.
Generally it can be said that the DD tanks proved their value, and casualties were high where they could not be used.
4. At a guess prisoners about 6,000 so far.
They consist of Germans, Russians, Poles, Japanese and two Turks.
5. British casualties about 1,000 per assault Division. American casualties not known. High proportion of officer casualties, due to sniping behind our front. Two infantry brigade commanders wounded: Cunningham, 9 Bde: Senior, 151 Bde. Good many infantry CO's killed including Herdon, OC 2 Warwicks. No general officers are casualties.
6. The Germans are fighting well; Russians, Poles, Japanese

and Turks run away, and if unable to do so, surrender.

7. Our initial attack was on a wide front, and there were gaps between landings. The impetus of the assault carried us some way inland and many defended locations were by-passed; these proved very troublesome later. In one case a complete German Bn, with artillery, was found inside 50 Div area; it gave some trouble, but was eventually collected in (about 500 men). There is still one holding out – the radar station west of Douvres; it is very strong and is held by stout-hearted Germans.

8. Sniping in back areas has been very troublesome, as a result of para 7. The roads have been far from safe and we have lost some good officers. I have been all right myself, though I have toured the area all day. There have been women snipers, presumably wives of German soldiers; the Canadians shot four women snipers.

9. The Germans are doing everything they can to hold on to Caen. I have decided not to have a lot of casualties by butting up against the place; so I have ordered Second Army to keep up a good pressure at Caen, and to make its main effort towards Villers Bocage and Evrecy, and thence S.E. towards Falaise.

10. First US Army had a very sticky part at Omaha, and its progress to Utah has not been rapid. I have therefore ordered it to join up its two lodgement areas and to secure Carentan and Isigny. It will then thrust towards La Haye du Puits and cut off the Cherbourg peninsula.

11. The two Armies have now joined hands east of Bayeux. No time for more.

PS. – The country here is very nice; green fields; very good crops; plenty of vegetables; cows and cattle; chickens, ducks etc. The few civilians there are appear well fed; the children look healthy; the people have good boots and clothing. The locals did not believe the British would ever invade France or come over the Channel; they say that the German officers and men thought this too, which may account for the tactical surprise they got.

Yours ever,

B.L. Montgomery.[6]

Headquarters
21 Army Group
10.6.44.

My dear Freddie,

I cannot possibly come out to Ramsay's ship tomorrow, nor is there any need for me to do so; for one, beyond the pleasure of seeing Ramsay, it would be a waste of time. You have my letter sent by Johnnie, and my intentions and plans will now be clear to you.

It is quite impossible to send any commandos back yet. I am directing the left of First Army on CAUMONT as a first priority, then ST LO next. Everything is going very well and I am well satisfied. The Canadians are a bit jumpy just at present, but they will settle down as they gain experience.

I have issued enclosed Personal Message. Give it to the press your end, and have it given out by the BBC. Send copies to Second Army Main for distribution to Second Army formations still in England, and send a copy to First Canadian Army.

Do not let any VIPs visit me, or anyone not actually concerned with the operations on land e.g. War Office PM 'B' etc. etc. I have two Army Commanders who have never commanded Armies in battle before, and a large number of inexperienced Divisions and Generals, and my time is very fully occupied; I have not time to spare for visitors. I would like to see Miles Graham, and also Slap White.

The roads have been far from safe, due to snipers left behind by the enemy. So far 8 women snipers have been killed.

Night bombing is going to be a nuisance; we had a very near miss at Tac HQ last night, and Sgt Ship had a narrow escape in the Mess tent.

Yrs ever
B.L. Montgomery.

If you want to discuss things come over and see me.[7]

A second short letter to Simpson – written on 14 June – is quietly confident:

All still quite OK and I am very happy about the situation. I had to think again when 2nd Panzer suddenly appeared last night. I think it had been intended for offensive action against 1st Corps. But it had to be used to plug the hole through which we had broken in the area Caumont-Villers Bocage. As long as Rommel uses his strategic reserves to plug holes that is good.

A third letter to Simpson, dated 18 June, stated that 'My own view is that we have got the Germans in a very awkward situation, and if we rub in our advantage heavily in the next two weeks we will be very well pleased. I am sending this letter over by P.J. Grigg.'[8] Montgomery knew that, by his writing to Simpson, Brooke would see the letter, and could thus brief Churchill on the situation if necessary.

These letters from the battlefront illuminate many aspects of Montgomery's character. On 12 June he wrote to de Guingand: 'I am enjoying life greatly and it is great fun fighting battles again after five months in England.'[9] At least this was frank, but admitting enjoyment in battles that were causing such enormous loss of life to the youth of England and of America was not an endearing trait – especially to those whose families suffered. It can be excused by looking on Montgomery as someone so dedicated and so anxious to win the war for Britain that he could only be happy when his talents were being used to the full; furthermore, he was never callous about the loss of his men. Later critics have, however, taken such comments as examples of hard-heartedness.

In the same letter Montgomery wrote:

My views about accommodation, messes, etc. I have decided that the only Major-Generals to be members of my mess will be yourself and Miles [Graham]; the others are all to be elsewhere. I will not have a crowd in my mess; my personal staff, Chief of Staff – and no more. You must set up another mess down the road. I cannot have B Mess at Tac overcrowded. In fact Tac HQ has got to remain small and self contained. We cannot supply vehicles to officers from Main. [Main HQ was still in England.]

The fact that Montgomery was able to write like this during

the anxious early stages of the invasion shows his determination to keep anyone of his own age group out of his mess, so that he could lead his personal life surrounded by the younger officers and unworried by criticisms and complaints from his contemporaries. De Guingand replied obligingly: 'I will bring plenty of jeeps and tents.'[10]

On 13 June Montgomery wrote, in his own handwriting, as he usually did, to P.J. Grigg, inviting him to the Allied positions but stating: 'It is not a good time for important people to go sight seeing; I have made this clear to the PM. My Corps and Divisional Commanders are fighting hard and I do not want their eyes taken off the battle. Have lunch with me and depart in the afternoon. It will be good for the troops to know you have been here.' By now the two men had become good friends. Grigg, outspoken and irritable, appreciated Montgomery in every way, and for the rest of the campaign they exchanged uninhibited letters in which both made contemptuous remarks about people in high places.

By now, Tac HQ had turned out to be too close to the Germans. John Henderson told me: 'The odd shell did land round about and one was pretty close to the tent. What is more, after we had been there five days they found a German soldier hiding in a trench, too frightened to come out, and he had been there within fifty yards of Winston, Smuts, and Ike, when they came out from England.' Thus we find Montgomery writing to Grigg on 25 June: 'I have been shelled out of the HQ you came to, and am now in a more peaceful area.' Later he told Grigg: 'I live in a very pleasant forest. You will find it most restful.'[11]

On D-Day alone, 75,000 British and Canadians and 57,000 Americans had landed, but within a week the landing of vehicles and stores was lagging far behind schedule, at around 75 per cent of the target. Montgomery therefore ordered the AA to be left behind, since in the virtual absence of the Luftwaffe it was not required. The main weakness felt by the troops, however, was in medium artillery, which also was given low priority. Churchill's remarks before the invasion about unnecessary military personnel and their corollary of surplus stores and vehicles may well have been correct, although it cannot be proved.

Even on D-Day, it was clear that the German tanks were superior to those of the Allies, and especially that American anti-tank guns were not up to the mark. The best German tank, the 50-ton Panther, could travel at 30 miles-an-hour on the road for 100 miles, and carried a special long-barrelled 75-mm high-velocity gun, together with two heavy machine-guns. Its main armour was 120mm thick and well sloped, which made the tank immune to most A/T guns and could only be pierced frontally by the British 17-pounder. Nearly as feared was the Tiger, with breast armour 180mm thick and a long-barrelled 88-mm gun as main armament in its heavy round turret.

Montgomery knew from his desert experience that he must rely on the 17-pounder anti-tank gun if he was to destroy the Panthers and Tigers, and he insisted that as many as possible of his British-operated lend-lease Shermans should be fitted with this weapon; when so equipped they were known as Fireflies. The Americans had brought to Europe Shermans equipped with only a 75-mm gun, short-barrelled and of low muzzle velocity, which was ineffective against the heavy frontal plate of the Tigers and Panthers. Only by flank shots could the US tanks knock out either a Panther or a Tiger, and American generals used to say that it cost them two tanks to destroy one German tank. Too late the Americans imported a 76-mm gun, but this also had too low a muzzle velocity to be really effective. On 5 August the American High Command asked the War Office to convert 700 of their Shermans to 17-pounder armament for Normandy. The work was to be carried out in Royal Ordnance factories at the rate of 100 tanks per month, but the request was refused on technical grounds.[12]

Montgomery, however, was in favour of giving limited help to the Americans over anti-tank guns, and on 6 July he had written to Lt-Gen Sir Archibald Nye, Vice-CIGS, saying:

> It is important to get USA armoured units equipped with the best tank gun as soon as possible. Some help from British sources may be required and if so I suggest it be given.
>
> Possibly when we have equipped our British units with two 17 pdrs per tank troop we might then concentrate USA units with one 17 pdr tank per platoon, and then proceed with third 17 pdr per tank troop for British units and so on. Such action would contribute towards more effective employment in battle of USA Armoured Divisions.[13]

At this stage Montgomery could still be generous towards his ally.

The Americans equipped eight battalions with long-barrelled 90-mm towed guns, but for most of the campaign in Europe they were at a grave disadvantage against German tanks. Montgomery knew that the British 25-pounder artillery piece had too low a muzzle velocity to be effective other than at close range, which had been proved in France in 1940 and again in the desert, and he was not going to rely on this weapon to destroy the Panthers and Tigers in Normandy. For although on D-Day the 17-pounder guns of 20th A/T Regiment had knocked out thirteen Panthers and Tigers, among other enemy armour, near Caen, rumours swept through Twenty-First Army Group that the Panthers, in particular, were invulnerable. All newspaper stories about the inferiority of British and American tanks were therefore censored on Montgomery's orders, as a counter to this decline in morale. In addition, he had one captured Panther and one captured Tiger tank towed to his Tac HQ, as proof that the monsters could be overcome. When Eisenhower visited Montgomery for the first time the latter claimed bombastically that he had destroyed 300 enemy tanks – probably an over-estimate, but one likely to encourage Allied troops facing German armour.

Eisenhower wanted an investigation into the failure of the American anti-tank guns, though of course nothing could be done immediately, and Bradley later admitted that his army only coped with German tanks because of its great superiority in numbers, and not because of its quality. But thanks to Montgomery's insistence on 17-pounders mounted on Shermans the British and Canadian troops could – and did – destroy heavy tanks. Montgomery was always incensed at tales of German superiority, for he considered it vital to the morale of his troops that they should consider themselves to have as good weapons as the enemy. (He was also concerned about tank numbers, and on 13 June sent a long memorandum in his own handwriting to Grigg listing the numbers of tanks in each British and US division – 1,540 British and 750 American in all.) On 14 June he wrote to de Guingand:

I am very disturbed at some of the reports which compare British armour unfavourably with German ... full information as to the relative performance of guns and tanks were made known to all troops over Overlord ... Only a proportion of enemy tanks are Tigers and Panthers. We estimate they have:

Tigers	80
Panthers	250
Mark IV	350
French tanks	100

There are, of course, others outside the Neptune* area.

We have around 250 17 pdr tanks in France plus large numbers of 17 pdrs (trailed), around 800. If we are not careful there will be a danger of the troops developing a Tiger and Panther complex ... Grigg rang last night and said there might be trouble in the Guards Armoured Division re the inadequacy of our tanks. He suspects the MP Anstruther-Gray† in the 6th Coldstreams.[14]

In the House of Commons, rumours about German tank superiority were upsetting Churchill.

Montgomery was also angry because General Bucknall, GOC, XXX corps, (on whom Brooke had commented so unfavourably after the 7 April St Paul's conference) had sent a report direct to the War Office about the defects of the 17-pounder – 'Bad show writing direct' was Montgomery's comment to Brooke, though he had been known to do the same thing himself when a divisional commander. On 24 June he wrote to Grigg: 'Reports are circulating about the value of British equipment, tanks etc. as compared with Germans ... anything which undermines confidence must be stamped on ruthlessly.'[15] Twelve days later, however, after further fighting, Montgomery took a more sombre view of British tank performance. He wrote to the War Office (6 July) with his considered views 'after consultation with his responsible commanders', and declared:

The Tiger has superior armour to any Allied tank ... Panther has superior frontal armour to British tanks – side and rear

---

* The invasion area, 'Neptune' being the code-word for the actual assault on D-Day.

† Major W.J. (later Sir William) Anstruther-Gray, MP for North Lanark.

armour is in no way superior. German Mark IV in no way superior to Sherman or Cromwell. Sherman tank is unquestionably more reliable mechanically than any other. Tiger and Panther have short life and spend a lot of time in workshops. Cromwell up to date has proved quite reliable.

With introduction of Sabot ammo we have caught up with, and possibly passed the enemy in ammo design. The 17 pounder tank is most popular. 75mm gun is becoming out of date. It cannot take a Panther frontally, and crews consider themselves out matched by the Tiger. Churchill crews have little experience of battle; they like their tanks but want 17 pounder instead of 75mm. Sherman and Cromwell tanks would like more armour on their tanks. Cromwell tanks must eventually go.[16]

This report erred on the side of optimism, though there can be no doubting its author's enormous technical competence. But every officer who served at this time in British armoured divisions that I have questioned replied that Allied tanks were inferior to those of the Germans. Montgomery knew he was up against a nasty morale problem, which explains his anger over Anstruther-Gray and Bucknall.

Further evidence of his sensitivity about rumours of poor British equipment is provided by his order to Second Army dated 25 July:

Where adverse comment is made on British equipment such reports are likely to cause a lowering of morale and lack of confidence among the troops ... when the equipment at our disposal is used properly and the tactics are good we have no difficulty in defeating the Germans. I have therefore decided that GSO 1 Liaison [Lt-Cols] will write no more reports for the present. You will issue orders at once that further reports are forbidden until I give permission ... Alarmist reports written by officers with no responsibility and little battle experience could do a great deal of harm. There will therefore be no reports except those made through the accepted channels of command.[17]

Montgomery had more problems with the morale of his infantry. On 20 July a Second Army intelligence summary contained a translation of a captured German document in which were several derogatory remarks about the British infantry: 'A successful break-in by the enemy is almost never exploited to pursuit. If our own [i.e. German] troops are ready near the front for a local counter-attack the ground is immediately regained.' The German conclusion was that they should occupy the main line of resistance very thinly, holding behind every sector a local reserve supported by tanks ready to advance as soon as the British artillery fire lifted. 'It is best to attack the English who are very sensitive to close combat and flank attack at their weakest moment – that is when they have to fight without their artillery.' The report described the fighting morale of the British infantry as being 'not very great', and continued: 'They rely largely on the artillery and air forces support. In the case of well directed artillery fire by us they often abandon their position in flight. The enemy is extraordinarily nervous of close combat. Whenever the enemy infantry is energetically engaged they mostly retreat or surrender.'

The report, from Panzer Lehr Division HQ, was more admiring of British armour, described as having 'a good offensive spirit' and liking 'to attack in pairs'. It also said that the Cromwells, with their high tracks, were more mobile in the bocage than German tanks, but 'battle recce [sic] advances very cautiously in spite of strong artillery support directed by Forward Observation Officers with the infantry'. It went on to say that the Germans could generally tell exactly where a British attack was coming because artillery fire was concentrated on the target usually for three hours beforehand.[18]

If Dempsey, as GOC, Second Army, authorised the circulation of this document he was courageous. The sentences derogatory to the British infantry have since been widely quoted, but they are in fact a short excerpt from a long German document, and it is possible that they slipped into the summary without the GOC's authorisation. But while there was an element of truth in the German appreciation, there was also an element of propaganda. The Germans too, had their own weaknesses, especially with their numerous Polish conscripts, who would desert wholesale from forward positions. One Polish deserter told his interrogator: 'I had a sympathetic German NCO. When I volunteered for duty in a forward post he said "You are asking me for a passport to Britain".'[19]

With his experience of the First World War and of the collapse in France in 1940, Montgomery was very conscious of the need to take every possible step to improve the British infantryman's morale, and to prevent flight or surrender. This was his main reason for visiting and addressing every unit before D-Day, and on his tours of the battlefront in Normandy he would always stop to talk to small groups and give out handfuls of cigarettes; everyone agreed that his optimism and personality were good for morale. Adolf Hitler had an advantage in that so many of his soldiers were devoted to his magnetic personality and were fanatic supporters of the Nazi party. The British soldier, however, had to rely on his sense of conscience and duty; and nearly five years of war, with air raids, separation, food rationing and other deprivations had produced a profound war weariness. Only the spirit of companionship and the dedicated leadership of officers maintained the courage of the British infantry in the dark days following the landings and before the Normandy break-out.

Hubert Essame found the difficulties that faced stretcher-bearers in finding and picking up wounded in the Normandy standing corn to be detrimental to the troops' morale.

A soldier who is hit when advancing through corn of this height ($2\frac{1}{2}$ feet) will fall to the ground and be invisible to the stretcher-bearers looking for him. His comrades know this and have to go on with the advance. They are also well aware that a wounded man may die if left unattended for any length of time ... The sights and sounds of the wounded can create tensions too great for soldiers unused to battle ... When a man was hit a comrade stopped briefly, took his rifle and bayonet and struck it in the ground beside him and placed his steel helmet on top of the rifle butt to guide the stretcher-bearers ... it was a poignant sight to gaze on these rifles surmounted by their tin helmets looking like strange fungi sprouting up haphazardly throughout the cornfields.[20]

Old hands from the Great War, like Montgomery and Essame, knew well the difficulty of keeping infantry attacking, especially after the young officers who trained the soldiers were killed or wounded. The break-out from Normandy could only be achieved by a hard slogging match with high infantry casualties;

in consequence, maintaining morale was never out of
Montgomery's mind. His perpetual, supreme confidence,
coupled with his theatrical behaviour, was a continual boost to
morale, one which was desperately required after the initial
exhilaration of the successful landing had passed.

With British infantry in unceasing contact with spirited Nazi
formations from 6 June onwards, many soldiers became
mentally, as well as physically, tired. Essame wrote: 'Their stock
of courage could soon be exhausted, leaving them bankrupt and
bereft of bravery. After the first few weeks in Normandy about
10 per cent of Second Army casualties in June and nearly 50 per
cent in the case of one of the veteran divisions were classified as
battle exhaustion.' Again according to Essame, a battalion
commander himself:

> One of the gravest psychological problems was the way in
> which one or two neurotics could infect a whole formation.
> Sometimes this occurred when incompletely trained
> reinforcements were used as front line troops, and panicked.
> Equally difficult to combat was the shock effect when really
> good officers were killed or gravely wounded. Such leaders
> had usually built up a sense of personal respect and trust
> which replacement officers could not quickly re-create. Often
> too officers were suddenly called upon to take over in a crisis
> and found that they were not able to cope with the demands
> made upon them. An example of this kind of thing happened
> when a good commanding officer was wounded at the height
> of the battle and the second-in-command moved up from the
> rear to take over. At Brigade HQ he was given 'an
> erroneously optimistic view picture of the situation' and when
> 'faced by a desperate military situation which would have
> taxed the skill of the most experienced commander he became
> distraught of course and had to be removed'.[21]

Desertions mounted, though offenders were severely punished
if caught. The death penalty for desertion had been outlawed in
April 1930, largely thanks to the efforts of the Labour MP
Ernest Thurtle, but in the Second World War both General Sir
Claude Auchinleck and Alexander had been in favour of its
reintroduction. Montgomery, however, stood out against it.
More cautious soldiers in Normandy just reported sick, and

were soon interviewed by a sympathetic psychiatrist. In July, Montgomery sanctioned the opening of exhaustion centres for 'battle happy' soldiers in Normandy, so that men no longer had to return to England for treatment; he also saw to it that a general psychiatric hospital was set up. (Self-inflicted wounds occurred less often than in the First World War, in so far as such statistics can be accurate.[22]) Essame, in common with many other Great War veterans, thought that there was a lack of moral fibre in the younger generation of soldiers. 44 per cent of Montgomery's men in Normandy served in non-fighting arms, where they rarely came into contact with the enemy; the infantry were exposed to the most danger. Even in 'Goodwood', largely a tank battle, the one-and-a-half infantry divisions involved suffered heavier casualties than the three armoured divisions.

There are instances to justify the German assertion, quoted above, that the British infantry were inclined to surrender or retreat. The most tragic which can be documented is the sad case of an infantry battalion in 49th Division. On 30 June the battalion was withdrawn from the line, and seven days later it was broken up. The original battalion commander had been sacked a few days before, as was the brigade commander six days later. Montgomery, having seen the new CO's report, wrote calmly to Grigg that he had been forced to withdraw the unit as being no longer fit for battle, and added in his own hand 'I consider the CO displays a defeatist mentality and is not a proper chap.' This was hardly fair. The CO who wrote the report, a copy of which went to Grigg, had only been with the unit for ninety-six hours.[23]

Grigg drafted this reply: 'I am surprised. What have Brigade and Divisional Commanders done about it? What happened to the original CO? ... It is a sad state for a Bn to get into and I hope you will get an experienced and mature CO to pull it together.' On reflection, however, Grigg decided not to send this draft to Montgomery. Instead he let the matter drop.

Ir is surprising that Montgomery sent the report to Grigg. Field-Marshal Lord Carver suggests (letter to the author) that it might perhaps have been a backhanded criticism of the state of training of units arriving from the UK; or perhaps his motive was to demonstrate, should the Army be slow in achieving a break-out, that it was not for want of trying on

Montgomery's part.

The report of the newly arrived CO, dated 30 June and written after four days with this unhappy unit, starkly reveals their tragic situation:

CONFIDENTIAL

Report on state of —— (49 DIV)
as on 30 Jun.

1.   I arrived at —— on the evening of 26 Jun. From am 27 Jun until am 30 Jun we have been in contact with enemy and under moderately heavy mortar and shell fire.

2.   The following facts make it clear that this report makes no reflection on the state of —— when they left UK:–
   (a) In 14 days there have been some 23 officer and 350 OR casualties.
   (b) Only 12 of the original officers remain and they are all junior. The CO and every rank above Cpl (except for 2 Lts) in Bn Hq have gone, all coy comdrs have gone. One coy has lost every officer, another has only one left.
   (c) Since I took over I have lost two 2 i/c's in successive days and a coy comdr the third day.
   (d) Majority of tpt, all documents, records and a large amount of equipment was lost.

3.   *State of Men.*
   (a) 75% of the men react adversely to enemy shelling and are 'jumpy'.
   (b) 5 cases in 3 days of self inflicted wounds – more possible cases.
   (c) Each time men are killed or wounded a number of men become casualties through shell shock or hysteria.
   (d) In addition to genuine hysteria a large number of men have left their posns after shelling on one pretext or another and gone to the rear until sent back by the MO or myself.
   (e) The new drafts have been affected, and 3 young

soldiers became casualties with hysteria after hearing our own guns.

(f) The situation has got worse each day as more key personnel have become casualties.

4. *Discipline and Leadership.*

(a) State of discipline is bad although the men are a pleasant cheerful type normally.

(b) NCO's do not wear stripes and some officers have no badges of rank. This makes the situation impossible when 50% of the bn do not know each other.

(c) NCO leadership is weak in most cases and the newly drafted officers are in consequence having to expose themselves unduly to try and get anything done. It is difficult for the new officers (60%) to lead the men under fire as they do not know them.

5. *Organisation and Adm of Bn.*

(a) Bn Hq and battle procedure generally is in a state of complete disorganisation for various reasons, but mainly because all key men have gone. It will take some time to put right.

(b) Major items of equipment are mostly made up, but tpt and all the essential minor items, which make for smooth running of the HQs, are missing.

(c) QM has an impossible task as if he manages to get a return it is out of date if the bn moves, as numerous articles are then left behind.

Conclusions.

(a) —— is not fit to take its place in the line.

(b) Even excluding the question of nerves and morale —— will not be fit to go back into the line until it is remobilised, reorganised and to an extent retrained. It is no longer a bn but a collection of individuals. There is naturally no esprit de corps for those who are frightened (as we all are to one degree or another) to fall back on. I have twice had to stand at the end of a track and draw my revolver on retreating men.

Recommendation.

If it is not possible to withdraw the bn to the base of UK to re-equip, reorganise and train, then it should be disbanded and split among other units.

If it is not possible to do either of the above and if it is essential that the bn should return to the line, I request that I may be relieved of my command and I suggest that a CO with 2 or 3 years experience should relieve me, and that he should bring his Adjutant and a signal officer with him.

Being a regular officer I realise the seriousness of this request and its effect on my career. On the other hand I have the lives of the new officer personnel (which is excellent) to consider. Three days running a Major has been killed or seriously wounded because I have ordered him to help me to 'in effect' stop them running during mortar concentrations. Unless withdrawn from the Div I do not think I can get the bn fit to fight normally and this waste of life would continue. My honest opinion is that if you continue to throw new officer and other rank replacements into —— as casualties occur, you are throwing good money after bad.

I know my opinion is shared by two other commanding officers who know the full circumstances.

In the Field.	(Sgd) ——, Lt-Col,
30 Jun 44.	Commanding, ——[24]

While this incident may have been the worst case of collapse of morale, I fear that it was not unknown for other COs, 2 I/Cs and company commanders to draw their revolvers to stop men running away. Montgomery's bombast was all designed to keep up his troops' courage and to prevent such instances, and he did a job in this respect which no other British general could have equalled.

Having failed to take Caen on D-Day, General Dempsey's British Second Army continued with fruitless direct assaults on the town. These met with so little success that, on 9 June, Montgomery decided to send XXX Corps in an encircling movement on his right through Bayeux and Tilly-sur-Seulles to Villers Bocage on the Caen-Avranches main road; this would be followed up by dropping 1st Airborne Division south of Caen to link up with the Villers Bocage force around Evrecy, thus enveloping Caen. Americans holding the high ground at Caumont would help the advance on the British right flank.

7th Armoured Division (the famous 'Desert Rats') led the

drive, and took Villers Bocage by 13 June. The division was mostly equipped with Cromwell tanks designed for speed, and had only a few Shermans with 17-pounders. These Cromwells were not entirely suitable for action in the bocage because they were under-gunned, having only 75-mm and not 17-pounder guns. When they met Panther and Tiger tanks of 2nd Panzer and Panzer Lehr on the morning of 13 June, one kilometre north-east of Villers Bocage, they suffered severe losses and had to withdraw, abandoning the recently occupied town. The XXX Corps Commander, Bucknall, had both of his escort tanks knocked out by Tigers when he visited 7th Armoured and, to the disappointment of the Americans, called off the attack on the next day after 50th Division failed to advance against Panzer Lehr. The American Lt-Gen Leonard Gerow, commanding US V Corps on XXX Corps' right, considered Bucknall to be overcautious; 50th Division's failure had exposed Gerow's left flank to counter-attacks.

The Americans had done their best to help XXX Corps on the west flank, but this battle, known as Caumont Gap, was Montgomery's first real failure in France. He was bitterly disappointed at the poor showing of the Cromwells against the Tigers and Panthers, and was displeased with Bucknall who, he thought, had almost panicked. It was six weeks before Villers Bocage was retaken. Montgomery's opportunity of encircling Caen from the north-west was lost, and the battle for that town went on to become his most expensive and controversial encounter with the Germans in Normandy. From this point on the Americans began to criticise Montgomery for lack of drive.

On 9 June Montgomery had written to de Guingand suggesting that one airborne division should drop south of Caen, and that the ground troops would move on Cagny and Evrecy, respectively to the south-east and south-west of the town. Leigh-Mallory vetoed this plan to land 1st Airborne Division, although its dropping ground would have been within range of 7th Armoured Division's artillery beyond Villers Bocage. Montgomery was furious, and on 12 June wrote to de Guingand:

... If we ... drop the Airborne DIV in Evrecy area we would be well placed and might get a big 'scoop' ... [Leigh-Mallory] cannot possibly know the local battle form here, and therefore he must not refuse my demands unless he first comes over to see me ... Obviously he is a gutless bugger who refuses to take a chance and plays for safety on all occasions. I have no use for him.[25]

Another unfortunate occurrence was Montgomery's issue of over-optimistic accounts of the Caumont battle; he had to eat humble pie after its failure. What also annoyed him was that his early optimism produced a spate of VIPs on visits to France.

As soon as it was clear that the Villers Bocage effort had failed, Eisenhower began to badger Montgomery to begin another attack on Caen. Montgomery replied that he wanted to tidy up his 'administrative tail' and to get all his supplies forward before he risked another attack. Eisenhower emphasised that the must keep the Germans 'off balance' and that the Allied drive should not falter.

On 14 June Montgomery asked Leigh-Mallory to visit him. At their meeting he convinced Leigh-Mallory that he needed the strategic bomber force to blast a path for the British Army into Caen. Leigh-Mallory agreed, but the Americans were immediately up in arms. General Carl Spaatz, commanding the US Strategic Bombing Force in Europe, lost his temper when Eisenhower asked for this use of the strategic bombers. He told Eisenhower: 'Leigh-Mallory and Monty have no imagination. They visualise the best use of our air potential as ploughing up several square miles for a few miles of advance. All that is necessary to move forward is sufficient guts on the part of the ground Commanders.'[26] (This echoed a similar row between Patton and Coningham in Tunisia.) Spaatz undoubtedly did not appreciate how much of Rommel's armour had been thrown into the battle of Caen to oppose Montgomery's advance, and Tedder and Cunningham also helped to kill the project. From this point there was open enmity between Montgomery and Tedder and Cunningham, but Leigh-Mallory and Montgomery became friends, despite their earlier differences.

Meanwhile, Eisenhower became impatient with Montgomery and his refusal to attack. On 18 June he wrote to him to hurry up, but Montgomery still hesitated over a big offensive against Caen.

Then, on the 19th, came three days of gales which closed the ports, and did untold damage to ships and stores. Montgomery postponed his attack once more, in spite of nagging by Eisenhower. The former had impetuously issued a directive to Dempsey and Bradley (M 502) on 18 June calling for the capture of Caen and Cherbourg by the 24th; in it he wrote: 'Caen is the key to Cherbourg. Its capture will release forces now locked up on our left flank.'[27] When Patton, staying for a few days with Bradley, read the directive he said derisively: 'Let's ask Monty to send us the key.' But on the 19th Ultra showed that German reinforcements were moving towards the Caen sector, and Montgomery felt that Dempsey would have a harder task than anticipated. He decided to delay again so as to increase his build-up, and wrote to Eisenhower in his own handwriting:

Bad weather and other things have caused delays in Divisions arriving here and marrying up with their vehicles, etc and becoming operative. Operations have begun in a small way on 2nd Army front; they become more intensive on 22 June, and on 23 June I shall put 8 Corps through in a blitz attack supported by great air power as at El Hamma.

(On 26 March 1943, at El Hamma in Tunisia, Montgomery had used air power to good purpose to turn the Mareth Line.)

Obviously Montgomery had hopes of success on the scale of El Alamein, and was pinning much on the Strategic Air Force being able to destroy or subdue the German front line so that the initial attack on Caen would be successful. On 20 June he signalled de Guingand that he would deliver a 'blitz attack' with VIII Corps on the 25th. The attack would be codenamed 'Epsom', since 25 June was Derby Day.[28]

On that day the British XXX Corps began 'Epsom' by attacking in the Caen sector with 11th Armoured and 15th Infantry Divisions, but without the air blitz Montgomery had wanted originally. 675 guns supported the push, but by now two new Panzer divisions had arrived in the Caen sector. Montgomery signalled Eisenhower: 'I will continue battling on the eastern flank until one of us cracks; it will not be us. If we can pull the enemy on to the 2nd Army it will make it easier for 1st Army when they attack southwards.' His signal on the next day read: 'Weather very bad with heavy rain and low cloud ... fighting will go on all day and all night and I am prepared to have a show-down with the enemy in my eastern flank as long as he likes.'[29] Yet Dempsey's attack was stopped along the line from Villers Bocage to Caen with heavy losses to the British, and a simultaneous 3rd Division attack north of Caen was also stopped by 27 June.

Into 'Epsom' Montgomery had sent 60,000 troops, many of them fresh from the UK. They achieved some initial success, and took the northern slopes of Hill 112, from where they would have been able to observe all German movement around Caen. But on 29 June German Panzers counter-attacked in strength with over 200 tanks, and the British had to evacuate the hill. By the 30th both sides were exhausted, but the British had won a tiny but important wedge into the German positions. Casualties on both sides were horrific; in more than one place the Odon stream had been dammed by corpses.

For Montgomery the result was disappointing. He needed a large-scale map to point out the territory he had gained, and he had claimed too much before the offensive started. In fact 'Epsom' *was* a success, for it had compelled Rommel to switch the bulk of his tanks from the American (western) sector to halt the British threat to Caen. But the newspapers in London and the USA were clamouring for Caen to fall; they could not know that by 29 June there were only 140 German tanks facing the Americans in the western sector, against 725 facing the British and with virtually none in reserve. Critics hailed 'Epsom' as another failure due to over-caution and to not risking enough troops.

Montgomery confidently went on telling everybody that the battle was going well and according to his plan, since he had drawn off so much armour from the US front. But he had promised airfields to the air marshals, and an advance well beyond Caen, which he could not deliver. Another valid criticism is that he overlooked how much easier it was for German tanks to fight in the open country in front of the British than in the bocage in which the Americans were operating.

On 4 July 3rd Canadian Division attacked Carpiquet. They were not entirely successful, and Dempsey recorded in his log: 'They secured and held the village of Carpiquet but on the right the operation was not well handled and the airfield remained in enemy hands.'

Meanwhile, Cherbourg had fallen to the Americans on 27

June, and although Bradley's army was technically under Montgomery's control this was strictly an American victory. Montgomery had hoped that the Americans would strike south simultaneously with their attack on Cherbourg – he was desperately anxious for them to form up on the start line for the decisive attack planned from the beginning to produce a break-out into Brittany. On 29 June he wrote to the CIGS: 'I tried very hard to get First US Army to develop its thrust southwards towards Coutances at the same time as it was completing the capture of Cherbourg ... but Bradley did not want to take the risk; there was no risk really; quick and skilful regrouping was all that was wanted.'

On 6 July Patton arrived in France, ready to take command of the US Third Army which he was to lead after the planned break-out into Brittany and Normandy. On the 7th Patton and Bradley lunched with Montgomery; Patton commented afterwards that 'Monty went to great length to explain why the British had done nothing,' and noted that Bradley was frightened of Montgomery.

At SHAEF, Eisenhower and Tedder became increasingly worried about the failure to take Caen, knowing that the planned break-out would have to be attempted by the US Army on the west front in the bocage, with its attendant problems for tanks. On 1 July Eisenhower told Tedder that he was worried by 'Monty's dilatory behaviour outside Caen,' and emphasised that Montgomery's 18 June Directive M 502 to Bradley and Dempsey had been over-optimistic. Part of the Directive read:

We have gained a good lodgement, kept the initiative, replaced our casualties in personnel, tanks etc. After the very great intensity of the first few days we had to slow down the tempo of operations to meet counter-attacks and build up our strength ... we are now ready to pass on to other things and reap the harvest ... enemy mobile reserves becoming exhausted ... he lacks good infantry to replace his Panzer Divisions for a full blooded counter-attack ... First Army's immediate task is to capture Cherbourg ... I hope to see Caen and Cherbourg captured by 27 June.

Neither was Eisenhower pleased by Directive M 505 of 30 June, which said:

My broad policy has been always to draw the main enemy forces on to our eastern flank and to fight them there so that our affairs should proceed the easier on west ... our policy has been so successful that Second Army is now opposed by a formidable array of 8 German Panzer Divisions identified between Caumont and Caen ... a full blooded counter-attack is imminent ... we welcome it ... it will be between Caen and Villers Bocage.

At this stage 7th Armoured had been put in reserve and Montgomery had asked the Americans to widen their front eastwards in order to support his operations.

On 3 July Montgomery wrote a long letter to Eisenhower boasting of how he had drawn Rommel's Panzers to the British sector, thus enabling the Americans to take Cherbourg and regroup without the menace of Panzer attacks from the Germans. When, however, the British general called for massive bombing by the Strategic Air Command before he could advance on Caen again, Eisenhower became angry. On 6 July he held a conference with Tedder and Cunningham, both of whom were sarcastic about Montgomery. On the day following this conference Eisenhower wrote and rebuked him for only attacking with two or three divisions so far; he added that what was needed was a full-dress attack with all forces committed, and offered an American armoured division for use on the British left flank. Montgomery refused the offer, and emphasised that there would be no 'stalemate'. This letter, and Montgomery's reply of the next day,[30] marked a breakdown in relations between the two generals, and the beginning of an antipathy that was to last for the rest of the campaign. The letters are reproduced in full in the Appendix.

After the war, Montgomery himself – and some historians – argued that Eisenhower never understood that his plan was to draw the German armour to the east and to keep it engaged there while the Americans attacked in the west. This argument is, however, untenable in view of Eisenhower's sentence in the fourth paragraph of his letter: 'I am familiar with your plan ...'

When Tedder read the words 'You can be sure there will be no stalemate' he commented that Dempsey's operations were 'company exercises'. General Morgan and Lt-Gen Sir Humfrey Gale (Deputy Chief of Staff and Chief Administration Officer at

SHAEF) were also scathing about Dempsey's slow rate of advance, and Gale pointed out that unless the Allies soon captured a second deep-water port in addition to Cherbourg 'the whole build-up could collapse'.[31] This was a false judgement, for in fact no other deep-water port was properly in use until late November, by which time the Allied armies were preparing for the battle for the Rhineland, more than 300 miles to the east.

On 8 July Dempsey had attacked again, helped by 6,000 tons of bombs dropped by Allied aircraft, and by nightfall on the 9th the enemy had been pushed back across the River Orne. But the Germans still held all Caen south of the river, and Montgomery could go no further. The battle for Caen had ended in stalemate.

On 10 July Montgomery signalled Eisenhower:

Operations on eastern flank proceeding entirely according to plan and will continue without a halt. 8 British Corps joins in tomorrow. Have ordered 2nd Army to operate southwards with left flank in Orne ... all this will help expedite affairs on western flank. Have had good conference with Bradley today and he will crack ahead hard tomorrow.

Eisenhower was unhappy at this, because he mistakenly believed that Rommel had transferred his Panzers from the British to the American sector so as to be ready for the American attempt southwards down the Cherbourg peninsula. Montgomery had been right, however; Ultra decrypts had revealed that between 1 and 4 July all the Panzer divisions except for a single battered one were in the British sector, and could not be transferred either to reserve or to the American sector since Rommel was so worried about the British attacks.

Montgomery's Directive M 510, also dated 10 July, to Bradley and Dempsey included the statement: 'Now that Caen has been captured ...' This was untrue. British Second Army's attack of 8 July had largely failed, and the Germans were still holding the part of the city south of the Orne. The Directive continued: 'The Faubourg de Vaucelles lying on the south side of the Orne opposite Caen will be secured and a bridgehead gained if this can be done without losses; I am not prepared to have heavy casualties to obtain this bridgehead over the Orne as we still have plenty elsewhere.'

The failure of this latest assault on Caen placed Montgomery in a dilemma. While Eisenhower always doubted the certainty of a breakthrough by the American First Army in the bocage, and kept on insisting on the need for an all-British attack in the east, the War Office continued to emphasise to Montgomery that he must not risk excessive casualties because there were no reserves of manpower for the British and Canadian armies.

Even on D-Day, the British Expeditionary Force had not been up to strength. On 12 June a Twenty-First Army Group appreciation stated that 'The army manpower situation is acute. Probable wastage exceeds probable reinforcements. The War Office have not been able to meet our full order of battle entitlements in unit establishments plus first reinforcements.' In May the War Office had forecast that, given the expected casualty rate during the invasion, the infantry position would be 'particularly unsatisfactory at the end of June and there would be a need for cannibalisation' on a large scale; one whole infantry division, the forecast continued, would have to be cannibalised by the second half of July, and another by the first half of September. In fact, by the end of July two tank brigades had been cannibalised, and by the end of August Twenty-First Army Group had, since D-Day, broken up twenty infantry battalions and five Royal Armoured Corps regiments, as well as making substantial cuts in anti-aircraft personnel, but it was still unable to keep infantry and airborne troops up to war establishment. On 10 August de Guingand ordered that all A1-classed men should be drafted from defence companies to infantry battalions, and that a reduction should be made in the strength of reconnaissance regiments by 100 men each; even after all these measures, he warned that there would still be deficiencies in infantry battalions.[32] Critics of Montgomery's caution following D-Day should take this serious manpower situation into account. The US Army at that stage had ample reserves available, and once British troops had run into heavier-than-expected opposition around Caen, Montgomery inclined more and more to the view that the Americans must incur the major part of the very heavy casualties inseparable from a successful break-out from the beach-head.

By now, Montgomery was aware that Eisenhower was becoming more and more critical, and he was warned by Brooke that the American Supreme Commander had complained in London to Churchill (on 5 July) that 'Monty was bogged down' and 'over-cautious'. Churchill, according to Brooke, had listened sympathetically to these complaints, which led to a furious, four-hour quarrel between the Prime Minister and the CIGS on the evening of 6 July. Churchill abused Montgomery because operations were not going faster, at which Brooke flared up and asked the Prime Minister 'why he could not trust his General for five minutes'. Brooke immediately told Montgomery of Churchill's attitude, and this was undoubtedly weighing heavily upon him on 10 July.

Eisenhower's letter of 7 July had not given firm and clear orders for an all-out attack although, according to his ADC, the Supreme Commander was smouldering with rage against Montgomery. Tedder, who thought the letter weak, and Bedell Smith urged Eisenhower to force an attack, saying that the letter 'was more of a "nudge forward" than "an ultimatum"'.[33] Portal had visited Montgomery on 9 July and, on his return to SHAEF, had told Tedder that: 'The problem is with Monty he can't either be removed or sacked.' But with Brooke and the War Office continually underlining that British reserves of manpower were in serious danger of exhaustion, Montgomery must be excused for hoping that the US Army, and not the British, would undertake the vital major break-out.

Thus Montgomery, always sensitive to criticism, was torn when on 10 July he held the conference with Bradley and Dempsey at his Tac HQ, to which he had referred in his signal to Eisenhower. Bradley agreed to plan a major offensive on his front, but expressed doubts about the outcome because of the difficulties of the bocage country and of flooded marshes. Dempsey, on the other hand, felt strongly that, instead of an American assault, Second Army should undertake an all-out armoured offensive in the favourable country around Caen, as Eisenhower was urging. At first Montgomery was indecisive, worried by the risk of too heavy casualties but attracted by the idea of using his armour in the good tank country. Late in the day he suddenly became bold and, after pondering for a few hours, gave orders to plan the offensive on the lines proposed by Dempsey. He gave the operation the code-name 'Goodwood'. A signal was sent to Eisenhower, who replied enthusiastically on 13 July and promised all possible air support. Everyone at SHAEF became happier after Montgomery's decision to put on 'Goodwood' which, they believed, would be an all-out attempt at a tank break-out to the south, beyond Caen.

But a letter from Montgomery to the CIGS, dated 14 July, is evidence that instead he had his main hopes for a breakthrough pinned on the Americans: 'Once 12 Army Group can get a footing on the road Periers-St Lo it will be able to deliver a real blitz attack ... I doubt if he [Rommel] can collect more troops to rope off again in the *west* and it is in the west that I want territory.'

Did Montgomery believe, as some American historians claim, that 'Goodwood' would be as big a personal triumph for him as El Alamein had been, and prove that the British were better troops than the Americans? I cannot agree with that claim.

Maj-Gen Philip ('Pip') Roberts, who commanded 13th Armoured Division in Lt-Gen Sir Richard O'Connor's VIII Corps during 'Goodwood', told me:

> I do not believe Monty was going for a real break-out. At the 10 July Conference Dempsey kept on emphasising to him that we had plenty of tanks, and said to Monty: 'Why not let us try for a break-out instead of the Americans?' When Monty refused, Dempsey tried again and said: 'Why not let both of us try?' Monty then decided to let Dempsey have a go and to synchronise the British attack with the main American attempt to break out in the west. Both Monty and Dempsey thought there was a good chance of a break-out; Monty rather less so than Dempsey, but Monty definitely was not going to commit many resources south of Bourguebus Ridge until, in his own words, he 'knew the form'. He would not chance his arm on that.

Field-Marshal Lord Carver told me:

> Monty was a realist who wanted a break-out in the east at Caen to encourage the Americans on the other flank. His attitude was that he was not sure he would win at 'Goodwood' but 'it will be marvellous if we do; if we do not win, then it is all part of my process of drawing German armour to the east and away from the forthcoming American attack at St Lo.'

Thus he had a double aim in mind. If he did not win he would not pursue a will-o'-the-wisp. Instead he would immediately seal that front off and try somewhere else.

Dempsey was more optimistic than Montgomery, and his operational instruction of 13 July gave VIII Corps' task as being to attack 'southwards and establish an armoured division in each of the following areas: Bretteville-sur-Laize, Vimont-Argentan, Falaise', which implied break-out; furthermore, he claimed that he 'would capture all the crossings of the Orne from Caen to Argentan'. Montgomery, with his usual caution, made Dempsey delete Falaise and Argentan from the written plan.

Montgomery's instructions for 'Goodwood' were dated 15 July; he insisted on giving them personally to Dempsey and O'Connor, and noted that he had done so on his top copy:

TOP SECRET
Notes on Second Army Operations
16 July – 18 July

1. To engage the German Armour in battle and 'write it down' to such an extent that it is of no further value to the Germans as a basis of the battle.
   To gain a good bridgehead over the ORNE through CAEN, and thus to improve our positions on the eastern flank.
   Generally to destroy German equipment and personnel, as a preliminary to a possible wide exploitation of success.

2. *Affect |sic| of this operation on the Allied policy*
   We require the whole of the Cherbourg and Brittany peninsulas.
   A victory on the eastern flank will help us to gain what we want on the western flank.
   But the eastern flank is a bastion on which the whole future of the campaign in NW Europe depends; it must remain a firm bastion; if it became unstable the operations on the western flank would cease.
   Therefore, while taking advantage of every opportunity to destroy the enemy, we must be very careful to maintain our own balance and ensure a firm base.

3. *The enemy*
   There are a lot of enemy divisions in the area SE of
   CAEN:

21 PZ	272
1 SS	16 GAF
12 SS	

   Another one is coming and will be here this week-end.

4. *Operations of 12 Corps and Cdn Corps – 16 & 17 July*
   Advantage must be taken of these to make the Germans
   think we are going to break out across the ORNE between
   CAEN and AMAYE.

5. *Initial Operations 8 Corps*
   The three armoured divisions will be required to dominate
   the area BOURGUEBUS-VIMONT-BRETTEVILLE,
   and to fight and destroy the enemy.
   But armoured cars should push far to the south towards
   FALAISE, and spread alarm and despondency, and
   discover 'the form'.

6. *Canadian Corps*
   While para 5 is going on, the Canadians must capture
   VAUCELLES, get through communication, and establish
   themselves in a very firm bridgehead on the general line
   FLEURY-CORMELLES-MONDEVILLE.

7. *Later Operations 8 Corps*
   When 6 is done, then 8 Corps can 'crack about' as the
   situation demands.
   But not before 6 is done.

8. *To sum up for 8 Corps*
   Para 5.
   Para 7.

9. *Finally*
   Para 6 is vital.

   Above given to General Dempsey on 15 July. He gave a
   copy to General O'Connor, 8 Corps [in handwriting on top
   copy only].

   B.L. Montgomery
General[34]

15.7.44

The tone of these instructions is cautious, although they mention armoured cars pushing far to the south towards Falaise creating 'alarm and despondency', and VIII Corps armour 'cracking about'. Montgomery stressed that it was vital that the Canadians should be successful in capturing Caen and pushing south down the Orne to Fleury, and that no armoured 'crack about' could take place otherwise; this heavy qualification is typical.

Another clue to Montgomery's real intentions during 'Goodwood' lies in a letter to Simpson dated 14 July and delivered personally by Lt-Col Christopher Dawnay of Montgomery's Tac HQ staff. Dawnay told Simpson that Montgomery's real objective for 'Goodwood' was 'to muck up and write off as many enemy troops as possible', and that if the drive to the Bourguebus Ridge was successful he would move west to surround and eliminate the enemy in the Villers Bocage-Evrecy area; 'Simultaneously he hoped the Americans would eliminate the Germans in the triangle Lessay—Coutances.' Simpson believes that Montgomery had no intention of rushing madly east or south, and his view is that 'Goodwood' was mainly intended to help simultaneous American attacks in the west.[35]

The late Maj-Gen Belchem co-operated with Montgomery in the writing of the latter's book *Normandy to the Baltic*. About 'Goodwood' Montgomery wrote: 'The armoured divisions were to dominate the area Hubert Folie-Verrieres, Vimont, and Garcelles Secqueville,' places which are all north of Bourguebus. When, however, Belchem suggested that they should print the actual order to Dempsey and O'Connor, with its instruction to 'dominate Bourguebus,' Montgomery refused.[36] Clearly after the war he wanted to play down his expectations from the 'Goodwood' attack.

One of his chief difficulties with 'Goodwood' was that in order to persuade the air marshals to give him another dose of carpet bombing, he had to infer that this was an all-out attack leading to a break-out. The air commanders had told him that they would not take their aircraft off the strategic targets in Germany for a limited attack; Montgomery, therefore, had to bluff that he would break the German front. As a result he was criticised.

On 14 July he wrote to Brooke: 'The time has come for a real showdown ... to loose a corps of Armoured Divisions into the open country about the Caen-Falaise road ... the possibilities are immense with 700 tanks loosed to the south-west of Caen and armoured cars operating far ahead ... anything may happen.' And he had written even more optimistically about 'Goodwood' to Eisenhower than he had to London: 'This operation will take place on Monday, 17 July. Grateful if you will issue orders that the whole weight of the air power is to be available on that day ... my whole eastern flank will burst into flames on Saturday. The operations on Monday may have far reaching results.'

Eisenhower agreed enthusiastically, telling Montgomery on 13 July that all senior airmen agreed with the plan and that it would be 'a brilliant stroke which will knock loose our present shackles.'[37] Tedder promised Montgomery: 'All the air forces will be full out to support your far reaching decisive plan to the utmost of their ability.'

Eisenhowever definitely expected 'Goodwood' to be a decisive break-out in the east, which would mean that the Americans would not have to put so much into their drive through the bocage in the west. Some historians argue that because of his 13 July message to Montgomery, clearly designed to encourage a break-out, Eisenhower believed that Montgomery's original plan only to hold the German armour on the east had been abandoned. But in any case, on 14 July Eisenhower wrote to Montgomery:

> I would not be at all surprised to see you gaining a victory that will make some of the 'Old Classics' look like a skirmish between patrols ... You can count on Bradley to keep his troops fighting like the very devil twenty-four hours a day and provide the opportunity your armoured corps will need to make the victory complete.[38]

This time Leigh-Mallory co-operated well with the land commander, and the days of Montgomery considering him 'a gutless bugger' (letter to de Guingand, 12 June) were over. Leigh-Mallory declared that the bombing offensive at Caen would be 'the heaviest and most concentrated air attack in support of ground troops ever attempted'. Montgomery wrote to Simpson: 'We must definitely keep Leigh-Mallory as Air Commander-in-Chief. He is the only airman who is out to help us win the land battle and has no jealous reactions.'[39] Everyone, including Montgomery, hoped and prayed that 'Goodwood' would prove to be the armoured break-out for British Second Army. VIII Corps was to spearhead the attack with three armoured divisions; XII Corps and Canadian II Corps were to attack on the flanks.

'Goodwood' was an armoured thrust towards the heart of Normandy, and was launched from the bridgehead east of Ranville, which was not more than two miles wide. To start the attack three double Bailey bridges over the Orne and the Caen canal had to be crossed; these were in full view of the Germans perched on the tall chimneys of the Colombelles factory at Caen. Five miles to the south of Caen rose the high ground of Bourguebus and the woods near Garcelles Secqueville, which gave the Germans perfect observation of the British advance, and excellent fields of fire for their atillery. Some twenty stone-built villages along the line of advance, surrounded by thick hedges and orchards, provided the Germans with natural strongholds in between the city and the high ground to the south.

Rommel and General Hans Eberbach (commanding Panzer Group West) had organised their defence in five successive zones, not three as the British thought, with most of their available armour well forward – today, NATO experts cite the placing of these five zones as a classic example of defence. 194 German field guns were sited on the Bourguebus Ridge and the adjoining woods, supported by 272 Nebelwerfers (multi-barrelled mortars, known to the British as 'Moaning Minnies' from the noise of the finned projectiles through the air). Montgomery was sending VIII Corps to attack Rommel where he was strongest: observation and fields of fire were in the German's favour, but Montgomery was counting on his overwhelming air support to redress the odds which, otherwise, were clearly against him. 4,500 Allied aircraft were to blast the German positions and, if properly directed and backed by guns, this bombardment, it was hoped, would reduce the German infantry and tanks to helplessness. To veterans of the First World War it sounded too much like the Somme again.

Another handicap was that Dempsey's artillery would have to remain west of the Orne until all the armour had crossed the three bridges, and even then moving the artillery forward would be bound to produce a fearful traffic problem. The plan was for the tanks to form up at the start-line and pour down the pre-laid bombing carpet right up to their planned objectives, while infantry divisions were to widen the flanks of the breakthrough. Unfortunately, because of traffic queues the lorried infantry could not keep up with the tanks, and 11th Armoured Divisions's infantry were soon left behind in mopping-up operations. In spite of the bombardment, many German anti-tank guns in the stone-built villages survived and held up the British armour (incidentally creating traffic jams) until Panzer reserves emerged to seal off the penetration.

The artillery and air bombardments, arranged for first light on 18 July, went according to plan, and at first the armour had an easy run, with the stunned enemy putting up little opposition. But by 0900 the tanks had passed beyond the range of their supporting artillery, and the Germans began to recover. The first trouble was from a small wood at Cagny, where 88-mm guns knocked out twelve Shermans, and in the village of Cagny itself six or eight Tiger tanks, although buried for a time, had survived the bombing. To the north and west, stiff resistance was also encountered by the Canadians in the remains of the Colombelles steelworks on the eastern outskirts of Caen. And, unfortunately, the bombing programme had not included the German artillery in the wooded country around Garcelles Secqueville, which lay out of range of the British medium artillery during the fighting; from there the Germans poured shells on the British infantry. German troops in the area round Couverville and Demouville had virtually escaped the bombing, and held back 11th Armoured's infantry throughout the first morning when they were badly needed further forward, while the partial failure of the bombing of Cagny, already mentioned, took a heavy toll of the British tanks. The infantry asked afterwards why only light fragmentation bombs had been used against these targets, as they did so little harm to the enemy when well dug in. They considered that Montgomery had let them down by agreeing to the use of such bombs.

Between 1000 and 1200 on the 18th the Germans delivered an armoured counter-attack. Tanks of 1st SS Panzer Division, quite intact having been far away from the British bombing, descended Bourguebus Hill. As Panthers and Tigers destroyed British tanks wholesale with their high-velocity guns, traffic congestion over the Orne bridges made it impossible for Dempsey to send forward reinforcements. From 1100 onwards there was a tank mêlée which defied description. The front line was dust, confusion, smoke and flames; the approach roads were one long traffic jam which prevented 7th Armoured Division tanks reaching the fighting zone until evening.

The German Panzer division infantry travelled in armoured carriers; most of the infantry with a British armoured division (apart from the armoured brigade and the reconnaissance companies, which used half-track armoured cars and bren carriers) had to travel on lorries. As a result, and quite apart from the congestion on the bridges, Dempsey could not get enough of his vulnerable lorried infantry far enough forward during the tank battles, although an infantry battalion of 29 Armoured Brigade (11th Armoured Division) took Hubert Folie, well forward.

The British had 750 tanks against the Germans' 230, but the Tigers and Panthers, with their thicker armour and better armament again proved superior to the British tanks, apart from the Sherman Fireflies with their 17-pounder guns. Only one in four Shermans had 17-pounders, however, the rest being armed with 75-mm guns. As a result of this inferiority the British lost 413 tanks during 'Goodwood' to German losses of 140, although many British tanks were of course reparable. And, as Montgomery had always feared, German morale was as high or higher than that of the British.

Montgomery employed his armour, as he had on the unsuccessful first day at Alamein, as a giant battering ram to overcome German positions. This was most unorthodox, since in the Second World War virtually everyone, including Montgomery, believed armour should be used to exploit successes created by infantry and artillery; indeed, General Essame claimed that 'Goodwood' tactically was 'the least inspired and the most eccentric of Monty's battles'.[40] Although Rommel had left the field, seriously wounded after his car had been attacked by Spitfires on the day before 'Goodwood' began, the German general undoubtedly had the best of his last encounter with Montgomery.

Maj-Gen (later General Sir) George Erskine, commanding 7th Armoured Division, one of Montgomery's old tank hands from the desert, thought 'Goodwood' a 'gross abuse of armour';[41] he did not bring his division into action until 1930. Maj-Gen 'Pip' Roberts told me that at 1130 Brigadier Hinde, commanding 7th Armoured Division's Armoured Brigade, came up to his tank and said 'There are far too many bloody tanks milling around here. I am not going to advance until you have taken Couverville and Demouville.' Hinde stayed put until later in the day, according to Roberts.

By nightfall, Montgomery had lost 1,500 men and 200 tanks. All he had gained was a small bridgehead east of the Orne to a depth of six miles, and a wider base at Caen. In spite of the greatest air support and the largest British tank attack of the war, no more ground was gained after 1100 on 18 July.

At 1620 Montgomery, completely misinformed about the true situation, signalled the CIGS: 'Operations a complete success, have ordered armoured cars to reconnoitre towards and secure crossings over dykes between Mesidon and Falaise. Situation very promising. Few enemy tanks met so far and no mines.' It was all untrue. *The Times* carried these headlines: '2ND ARMY BREAKS THROUGH. Armed forces reach open country. Montgomery well satisfied [19 July]. Wide corridor through German front [20 July].'

How Montgomery could have been so wide of the mark has never been explained. His liaison officers must have been misinformed, although Pip Roberts told me that none of them got near him. His misleading communiqué did his reputation considerable harm when the true situation was revealed, and provided his critics with useful ammunition, while a statement he made to the BBC was equally ill advised, ending as it did, 'General Montgomery is well satisfied with the progress made in the first day's fighting of the battle.' Yet on the far side of the Bourguebus Ridge the enemy defences had survived the bombing intact.

Montgomery had arranged with Bradley that the major American offensive to the west (codenamed 'Cobra') should also start on 20 July, but unfortunately, the attack was postponed and did not start until 25 July. Montgomery later admitted that he had been 'too exuberant' at his 'Goodwood' press conference.[42] He felt that 'Goodwood' and 'Cobra' were one big operation; he wanted to make the Germans feel they must keep their armour on the British front, and did not realise that he was giving a hostage to fortune by exaggerating the first day's gains.

If 'Cobra' had jumped off according to schedule his critics would have had much less ammunition.

Pip Roberts recalled the first day of 'Goodwood' to me:

My division, 11th Armoured, was designated as the lead division for VIII Corps. My orders were to establish my division on Bourguebus Ridge, but at the outset I had to use my infantry to capture Couverville and Demouville. I also had to capture Cagny, close to the start line.

When I saw the plan I lodged objections with Dick O'Connor, my Corps Commander, and even put them in writing. I told him I could not be expected to push fast with my tanks if I had to leave my infantry behind heavily engaged near the start line. O'Connor would not budge, so I said: 'Why not ask 51st Highland Division, who are holding the front in the Orne bridgehead, to get out of their trenches to take the nearest villages so that my own infantry can roll further forward with me?' O'Connor replied that Monty would not hear of 51st Highland Divsion getting out of their trenches because that might put our tiny but vital bridgehead over the Orne in jeopardy, and this faced the finest tank going in all Normandy. O'Connor told me if I did not want to lead, another division could go, so I accepted the plan.

In the event we made a good start behind a creeping barrage, but as soon as we got out of range of our own field guns the Germans came to after the bombardment, and I had to use my own infantry to take Coumerville St Honoré and Cagny.

If we could have kept our own infantry with us we might have got further, but we had no chance of a break-out to the south of Bourguebus Ridge because the German defences were ten miles in depth. The trouble was the Germans came to after the air bombardment too quickly, and I could not silence their anti-tank weapons further forward with my infantry bogged down miles away from my objectives. It was a grave drawback that infantry belonging to armoured divisions had to travel in soft lorries. My only alternative would have been to put them on top of tanks – not feasible at 'Goodwood' in face of the German guns.*

* During 'Goodwood', an armoured division would have had four infantry

Technically Erskine was right in saying that it was a misuse of tanks, but it did not matter as we had any number of tanks but we were terribly short of infantry. It was really a dash forward with tanks to the Bourguebus Ridge after mass bombardment. Dempsey told me he did not mind if we lost 700 tanks in our three armoured divisions in his corps. I lost 200, but did not have heavy casualties in men, and a proportion of my tanks were recoverable.

General Sir Nigel Poett, then commanding 5 Parachute Brigade, had a grandstand view of the start of 'Goodwood' from a hill to the south-east of the start line. He told me that he sat in an armchair on the first floor of the house which was his HQ and that

the engineers had dug trenches all around our HQ house so that we should be safe during the massive bombardment before 'Goodwood'. In fact not a single bomb fell near us. I saw our tanks advancing splendidly until they got out of range of our artillery. Then they were picked off one by one.

The mistake was not using them in conjunction with infantry. The desert philosophy was that a tank is like a ship at sea, and they had not learnt that this simply did not work in Normandy ... When I was Commandant of the Staff College after the war I always told the students that 'Goodwood' was a misuse of tanks.

Of course Monty was right, as Pip Roberts said, in saying our bridgehead over the Orne was vulnerable, but it was nothing like as vulnerable at the time of 'Goodwood' as it had been on D-Day.

Lord Carver, who commanded an independent armoured brigade which was in reserve during 'Goodwood', disagrees with General Poett. He told me:

Monty did not misuse tanks at 'Goodwood'. He had plenty. On that ground infantry could do nothing except by night

---

battalions. Three of these would have been lorried infantry and the remaining battalion would have been motorised, which meant it travelled in armoured cars and bren carriers.

attacks, and we were very short of infantry. The ground was completely different from the bocage and only suitable for a tank to attack in daylight. Although the ground was right for tanks, the operation was a failure tactically … Anyone making judgements about 'Goodwood' must remember that infantry could only operate there by night. They would have been slaughtered in daylight attacks.

My criticism of Monty is that he had not learnt the lesson from El Alamein that you cannot in open country move infantry up to support armour in lorries. Soft vehicles are no good to carry them forward. They needed armoured protection en route in these tank battles. Guy Simonds, the Canadian Divisional Commander, improvised brilliantly in the next attack in the 'Goodwood' area by putting his Canadian infantry into tanks from which the turret had been removed. Then they could be deployed forward in a tank attack.

Not everyone who took part in 'Goodwood' thinks it failed. Brigadier Tony Hunter, who commanded the motorised infantry battalion of the Rifle Brigade which took Hubert Folie, told me: 'We rode in on armoured half-tracks and brens, and made a successful attack on Hubert Folie. We were part of Pip Roberts's 11th Armoured Division infantry. In my view 'Goodwood' was a success, and Montgomery achieved what he set out to do, and what General Dempsey's Second Army orders said.'

The next day, 19 July, Dempsey tried to advance again with his tired and depleted troops. He still had superiority in numbers of tanks and men, but he made only limited progress although the Germans were near the end of their tether. 7th Armoured attacked Bourguebus, only to find that it 'bristled with Tigers and 88s' – they accomplished little.

On the 20th, the day of the bomb plot against Hitler, 7th Armoured attacked Bourguebus again, and found that the Germans had retreated. On their right flank the Canadians had taken their objectives in the town of Caen and had advanced along the east bank of the River Orne beyond Fleury, as set out in Montgomery's orders of 15 July. They had not, however, been able to give him 'the through communication' and the 'very firm bridgehead' he had asked for in his order to Dempsey because they were counter-attacked heavily during the afternoon by German armour, and VIII Corps tanks could not help them sufficiently; they had shot their bolt. The Canadians asked for air support, but a violent thunderstorm removed any hope of it. The torrential rain continued for forty-eight hours, filling slit trenches almost immediately with a foot of water, and hampering any movement. It was a scene of considerable desolation. An officer wrote in his diary:

> I have never seen such bomb craters. Trees were uprooted, roads impassable. There were bodies in half; crumbled men; a tank lay upside-down, another was still burning with a row of feet sticking from underneath. On one crater a man's head appeared sticking out from the side. The place stank.[43]

With the coming of the storm Dempsey called off his attacks, and 'Goodwood' was over. Montgomery refused to admit failure, and at a press conference announced that 156,000 Germans had been killed or made prisoner since D-Day, a pretence that all had gone well. Strategically, and like 'Epsom', 'Goodwood' can be classed as a success because it drew to the east so much of Rommel's armour, and secured both Caen and a stronger bridgehead over the Orne. Tactically, however, it was a definite failure. Montgomery always insisted that because of 'Goodwood' the Germans retained six Panzer divisions on the British front, and that they were never able to withdraw even a single one of these divisions for a strategic reserve, as Rommel had always intended. Here he is right. Certainly if even a single Panzer division had been put in reserve, the American break-out at St Lô (25 July-4 August) would have been far more difficult.

Although the British Government had been informed about the plot to kill Hitler, its members were taken by complete surprise when, on the last day of 'Goodwood', the news came that Hitler had narrowly survived assassination. Overtures had been made by the anti-Nazis, led by Colonel Klaus von Stauffenberg, through Sweden, and as early as May 1942 Bishop Bell of Chichester had been sent there to meet Pastor Dietrich Bonhoeffer, a leading conspirator. So frightened was Churchill of alienating the Russians, however, that he refused to extend any helping hand towards the conspirators at all, and Anthony Eden, the Foreign Secretary, firmly told Bishop Bell that he would do nothing. This was a grave disappointment to von Stauffenberg and his collaborators, but they went ahead courageously with the plot, hoping that once Hitler was dead the Allies would quickly come to terms with them.

Eisenhower had been given no briefing whatsoever about the plot, and had no method of communicating with the German C-in-C, von Kluge, who had replaced the injured Rommel on 20 July. The blame for this falls squarely upon Roosevelt and Churchill; indeed so little was known, or had been told of the anti-Nazis that Brooke recorded in his diary on 21 July: 'Astonished to hear of attempt on Hitler's life.'

Both Rommel and his successor, von Kluge, were implicated in the plot to assassinate Hitler, and in having secretly promised to act against the Nazi regime. On 15 July Rommel had sent a signal to Hitler pointing out that the position of Germany was grave and that there were no reinforcements of any importance that could be brought to the Normandy front, whereas each day the Allies were bringing in new forces and masses of war material.

> It must be expected the Allies will succeed within fourteen days to three weeks in breaking our thin front and will push far on into the interior of France; the consequences will be immeasurable ... I must beg you to draw the political conclusions without delay. I feel it is my duty as the Commander-in-Chief of the Army Group to state this clearly.[44]

During the next few days, all that were left to him as an active commander, Rommel told his friends amongst the German commanders in his armies of his démarche to Hitler; beyond doubt, if Hitler were successfully assassinated Rommel would have been a ringleader and a key man in the struggle to destroy the Nazi regime. Unfortunately, on 17 July, when the Allies greatly needed to keep Rommel at the helm in Normandy, he was seriously wounded in the RAF attack on his car as he was returning from the front line to his HQ at La Roche Guyon. At first he was thought to be dead, and although he recovered he was out of action on the crucial day, 20 July, when von Stauffenberg so nearly killed Hitler and, for a few vital hours, had the chance to topple the Nazis. Had the attempt succeeded, it is likely that Rommel would have called for an immediate battlefield armistice, or even surrender, on hearing the news.

Early in July, with von Kluge's agreement, Rommel had made a trial of the possibility of a local suspension of hostilities in order to parley with his enemy. General von Luttitz made wireless contact with the Allies in the US 2nd Division sector. The Allies agreed to exchange German female personnel (medical and signals), kept in Cherbourg, for severely wounded Allied soldiers, and named a rendezvous. Two hours of local armistice were enough for this act of humanity, but Hitler was furious with Rommel when he heard about it. This story must, however, be treated with some caution, since it appears only in Lt-Gen Hans Speidel's autobiography, written after the war when he was seeking rehabilitation. There is no trace of it in the archives.[45]

It is a poor reflection on the Allied leaders that the assassination attempt took them by surprise, for if on 20 July the German Army had believed Hitler to be dead, there must have been a slackening of resistance. No instructions were given to the psychological warfare branches of the US or British armies to exploit the situation, nor was any attempt made to produce leaflets and broadcasts telling the German soldiers fighting at 'Goodwood' that Hitler was dead, the Nazi regime at an end, and peace in sight.

Like Rommel, von Kluge was implicated in the plot, but he was nervous and would not declare himself unless or until Hitler was dead. Von Rundstedt knew of the plot but would have nothing to do with it; General von Stülpnagel, Military Governor of France, was one of the ringleaders, and on 20 July arrested the Gestapo leaders in Paris.

Deliberately von Kluge stayed away from his HQ until he saw how the land lay. When he returned there, at 1800 on the 20th, he found a telephone message saying that Hitler was dead, and a note that German radio maintained that he was alive. General Ludwig Beck, ex-Chief of the General Staff and a leading conspirator, telephoned von Kluge from Berlin and asked him whether he would accept his (Beck's) authority as Acting Head of the Reich. Von Kluge did not refuse, but played for time in order to see whether Hitler was alive or not; meanwhile he asked von Stülpnagel to come from Paris. While the Military Governor was on his way, von Kluge telephoned the Wolf's Lair (Hitler's HQ in East Prussia) and in his War Diary it is recorded that he was informed by General Walter Warlimont, Jodl's deputy, that the plot had failed but that perjured officers had tried to form a new regime and to declare a state of emergency.

At dinner that night, von Stülpnagel tried in vain to persuade von Kluge to try and end the fighting in Normandy as, he claimed, Rommel would have done. But the army commander had no stomach for a hero's part, and told von Stülpnagel that he must release the Gestapo leaders in Paris, making it clear that these arrests were made without his (von Kluge's) authority. Von Stülpnagel left for Paris, and in the early hours of 21 July von Kluge, at the prompting of von Rundstedt's staff officers, agreed to suspend von Stülpnagel. He then sent a telegram of congratulations to Hitler.

In the end the plot had no effect whatsoever on the fighting in Normandy. The German Army in the field, hotly engaged on that day with British forces in the 'Goodwood' fighting, and with the Americans around St Lô, knew only of the broadcast announcement that an attempt to kill Hitler had failed. The background to the news was too obscure to affect their morale or lead them to think that the Nazi regime might tumble.

4

Near-Failure and
The Break-Out

Montgomery and Bradley had scheduled the main all-out attack by the Americans in the west as part of the 'Goodwood' offensive. In preparation, St Lô had been taken by Bradley's US First Army, after bloody fighting, by 18 July, and the major attack, 'Cobra', was due to start on 20 July. The American push to take St Lô had begun on 3 July, and other gains had been made all along the front.

Unfortunately for Montgomery, 'Cobra' had to be postponed because of the bad weather which had brought 'Goodwood' to a close, since a vital part of the plan was for the attack to be preceded by the same mass carpet bombing as for 'Goodwood' three days previously, and using the same aircraft. Leigh-Mallory, in charge of the Allied tactical bombing at SHAEF, crossed to Normandy alarmed by the bad weather forecast. 'Cobra' was immediately rescheduled for 1300 on 24 July, but visibility was again hopeless on that day. 'Cobra' was postponed until 0938 on 25 July.

This delay was nearly fatal for Montgomery. With the 'Goodwood' failure and now no American attack, the Normandy front was a temporary stalemate. Resentment against him boiled over. Maliciously, Tedder kept underlining to Eisenhower that Montgomery had not pressed the 'Goodwood' attack at the crucial moment, and had prevented his armour from pushing on; he wrote a letter to the Supreme Commander saying that Montgomery 'had no intention of making this operation the decisive one which you so clearly intended.'[1] Eisenhower was himself angry with his army commander, for he felt that Montgomery had led him up the garden path with his bombastic claims for 'Goodwood' and his misleading communiqués in the early stages of the battle. Certainly Montgomery had made a big mistake in creating, before the event, a scenario for one of the great victories of modern times.

Eisenhower had been fussed by the visit to London, on 18 July, of Henry Stimson, the US Secretary of War. Stimson had emphasised that the American press was making much of the disproportionate US losses compared with the British, and that in a presidential year it would be embarrassing if the impression was given that the British were letting the Americans do the bulk of the fighting. Stimson advised Eisenhower to set up his HQ in France as soon as possible, and to make it clear that he, Eisenhower, and not Montgomery, was in charge.

Morgan and some of the American generals pressed Eisenhower to ask for Montgomery to be sacked for over-caution, and for a few days all the talk among senior officers at SHAEF was concerned with who would succeed him. Gossip in the mess was that Montgomery would take over as Governor of Malta from the other 'failed' British general, Lord Gort. Eisenhower himself wanted Montgomery to go, but refused to take the initiative. His political intuition warned him of Montgomery's intense popularity both with the troops and the British public, and of the devotion to him of Brooke, who was so influential with the Prime Minister and the British Cabinet. Tedder remarked that 'The British Chiefs of Staff would support any recommendation Eisenhower might make for a change in the command of 21 Army Group,'[2] but this was manifestly untrue. Brooke would fight to the death to retain Montgomery, something which the cautious Eisenhower knew perfectly well.

Nevertheless Montgomery was in serious danger of being toppled from command not only because of pressure at SHAEF, but also because he had upset the temperamental Churchill who, at this stage of the war, was at his edgiest. V1 flying-bombs were causing intense damage in London, and the Prime Minister knew that this would get worse until the Allied armies overran the launching sites. Lord Cherwell had misled Churchill about the seriousness of the flying-bomb threat; by the end of June the V1s threatened to disrupt central government, and by 16 July had destroyed 13,000 houses. This was a far cry from the consoling advice originally given to the Prime Minister by Cherwell: 'about the new weapon – I believe its scale to be comparatively insignificant.'* How flustered Churchill was is demonstrated by one remarkable minute, which shows clearly that he was prepared to use poison gas in retaliation against the Germans, and to consider germ warfare in the form of Anthrax.[3]

Desperately anxious to see the Allied armies advance quickly from Normandy to the V1 launching sites on the northern coast of France, Churchill began to take seriously all criticism of Montgomery for being too slow. Brooke wrote that 'He was not always too fond of Monty', and recorded in his diary on 6 July:

> A frightful meeting with Winston after he had too much to drink. He was maudlin, bad tempered, drunken and highly vindictive against USA because he was annoyed by being told by Eisenhower that Monty was over-cautious. Winston started abusing Monty because operations were not going faster.

The CIGS flared up, and asked Churchill if he could not trust his generals for five minutes, adding that he, Brooke, was furious because Churchill had never uttered a single word of approval or gratitude for the excellent work which Montgomery *had* done. Exasperated with the Prime Minister, Brooke confided to his diary on 10 July: 'Winston is a complete amateur of strategy who swamps himself in detail which he should never look at.'

Brooke informed Montgomery of the lie of the land at 10 Downing Street but the latter, by now under the strain of fighting 'Goodwood', had severely blotted his copybook in Churchill's eyes. On 18 July, the Prime Minister sent a message to Montgomery that he wished to visit him; the latter immediately signalled Eisenhower that he did not want the Prime Minister to come. 'Goodwood' had begun to falter, and the last thing Montgomery wanted at that particular moment was Churchill breathing down his neck.

At once Eisenhower let it be known that Montgomery had asked him to keep the PM away, and fobbed Churchill off, suggesting that instead he went to Cherbourg and to Omaha

---

*Professor F.A. Lindemann, who became Lord Cherwell in 1941, was a noted physicist. He was a close friend of Churchill's, as well as being his scientific adviser during the war years.

Beach, and then sailed along the British beaches without, however, visiting Montgomery.[4] Churchill was livid, and for twenty-four hours Montgomery was in grave danger of losing his command.

On the same day, 18 July, Churchill informed Eisenhower that he would fly over on the 21st to drive around the Cherbourg peninsula and visit several of 'the alleged rocket strips'; he added ominously, 'I have no intention of visiting General Montgomery's HQ and he should not concern himself about me in any way.' And he told Brooke, with venom:

> With hundreds of war correspondents moving about freely this cannot be considered an unreasonable request from the Minister of Defence. If however General Montgomery disputes about it in any way the matter will be taken up officially, because I have both a right and a duty to acquaint myself with the facts on the spot.

Montgomery's fat was in the fire.

On the 19th, according to Brooke's diary, Churchill, still in bed at 0930, was raging against Montgomery for stopping his visit to him in France: 'Haig had always allowed him in the last war as Minister of Munitions. He would not stand it. He would make it a matter of confidence, etc. etc.' (At this stage Brooke was very annoyed with Churchill, noting in his diary on 20 July: 'Winston goes off skylarking instead of giving decisions months overdue'.)

Brooke, who had scheduled a visit to Montgomery for that day, realised that the moment of crisis had come for his friend. As soon as he landed at the airstrip at Tac HQ, Brooke informed Montgomery that Eisenhower 'Has been expressing displeasure and accusing Monty of being sticky and of not pushing sufficiently on the Caen front with the British while he made the Americans do the attacking on the right,' and that Churchill had taken these complaints very seriously. He firmly told Montgomery to go into his caravan and write to the Prime Minister, inviting him to Tac HQ. Montgomery wrote in his own handwriting:

Tac Hq
21 Army Group
19.7.44

My Dear Prime Minister

I have just heard from the C.I.G.S. that you are proposing to come over this way shortly; this is the first I have heard of your visit. I hope that you will come over here whenever you like; I have recently been trying to keep visitors away as we have much on hand.

But you are quite different, and in your capacity as Minister of Defence you naturally are above all these rules. So as far as I personally am concerned I hope you will visit Normandy whenever you like; and if I myself am too busy to be with you I will always send a staff officer. And if you ever feel you would like to stop the night and stay in one of my caravans – which will be held ready for you at any time.

Yrs sincerely
B.L. Montgomery

Montgomery did not show the letter to the CIGS – he dared not, since it contained the untruth that he had not 'heard' of the proposed visit. He repeated this to Simpson on the next day, obviously hoping that he would be believed in Whitehall.

According to Brooke, the letter worked 'like magic'; certainly it saved Montgomery. Churchill telephoned Brooke to say that he was delighted with the letter, and that he felt ashamed about all he had said in the morning. Late on the 19th he signalled Montgomery 'Thank you very much for your letter'. On the first draft of the signal he had dictated 'You may be sure that I shall never be a burden but only a prop if ever needed'. He put his fountain pen through this phrase, thinking perhaps that there might arise an occasion when he would have to be a 'burden', and also, perhaps, that he must not make his general any more conceited than he was.[5]

Churchill visited Montgomery on 20 July. All went well, for Montgomery, having seen the red light, exerted his mesmeric charm to convince the Prime Minister, successfully, that his campaign was going according to plan. Montgomery himself was genuinely optimistic, mainly because Ultra signals showed the Germans in the US sector to be in poor shape. Ultra also confirmed that 'Goodwood' had drawn almost all the German armour to the eastern front, so that the prospects for a swift American triumph with 'Cobra' were excellent. All this Churchill lapped up greedily; when he returned to London he said that 'all was going well in Normandy', telling the War Cabinet that he had never seen 'a happier army'. General Roberts told me that if Churchill had gone forward to visit his division at the end of 'Goodwood', he would have found morale high because, although they had lost a lot of tanks, casualties during the fighting had been low.

On 21 July Montgomery wrote to Simpson: 'The PM has just been here very friendly. I gave him a bottle of brandy as a peace offering.'[6] He could not have found a better present for the brandy-loving Churchill—at that stage of the war there was hardly a bottle of French brandy left in London.[7]

Dramatically, Churchill's visit to Montgomery at Twenty-First Army Group Tac HQ on 20 July had coincided with the explosion of von Stauffenberg's bomb in Hitler's command room at the Wolf's Lair. Williams told me, recalling Churchill's visit:

Upon that day I knew that something very strange was happening in Germany, and from the scraps of Ultra it was clear to me there was a sort of revolution: an attempt to topple Hitler, and that von Witzleben and Fromm were involved in the opposition. I knew that Fromm was in charge of the German signals network, which was encouraging. In Italy in the autumn I had interviewed a high-up Nazi deserter and asked him who was going to be the Nazis' Badoglio. He told me it would be Witzleben.

I told Monty that something dramatic was afoot and that at any moment he might get peace feelers from von Kluge that day, or even a battlefield surrender or armistice. Monty was most intrigued and like a schoolboy. When Winston Churchill arrived at Monty's HQ on July 20th, because of the exciting news from Germany Monty arranged a schoolboy plot with me. I was to tell Winston for five minutes exactly what the enemy was up to; then Monty for five minutes would tell the PM how he was going to defeat the Germans, and would then ask Winston 'What is going on with this news of a revolution in Germany?' Winston was completely nonplussed. He sat on the only stool in Monty's map caravan and looked at us in silence for a moment. Then I remember very clearly he produced a long chain with keys on it and unlocked two despatch boxes. They were full of papers all mixed up. He said: 'There is something about it in here – see what you can find.'

Monty and I scrabbled through these papers. They were Cabinet papers, Ultra signals, and other intelligence reports all muddled up. I quickly saw that von Witzleben was involved as well as Fromm.*

Winston Churchill then began to mumble to himself rhetorical sentences how he would deal with the overthrow of the Nazis and peace proposals, and began to coin phrases for a speech.

I suddenly realised that Winston had come from London with all this stuff in his despatch case unread, and that he was 'naked' in face of the possible sudden end of the war. I was amazed that he could have been as unbriefed about what was going on in Germany as he was on July 20th.

I am sure that von Kluge knew a great deal about the plot but didn't want to be contacted by the conspirators until he was sure Hitler was dead, and I feel sure that von Kluge was thinking of a battlefield surrender. Monty had never given any thought to it before July 20th but he was excited like a schoolboy at the possibility of a surrender that morning.

Perhaps Churchill recalled the dramatic surrender of the Austrian Army to the Italians on the Isonzo in October 1918, when a captain, accompanied by two private soldiers with large white flags, crawled up a railway embankment in the Austrian front line and walked gingerly through the forward Italian positions bearing an official surrender from the last Austrian Emperor, Karl. There might have been a repeat performance in Normandy on 20 July if Rommel, instead of von Kluge, had still been in command of the forces confronting the invasion.

The Ultra decrypts which had given Montgomery such

*Field-Marshal Erwin von Witzleben and Generaloberst Friedrich Fromm were both active conspirators against Hitler, Witzleben since as early as 1938. After the failure of the bomb plot Fromm sought exculpation by having a number of the chief plotters executed, but to no avail. Both men were executed for treason, Witzleben in August 1944, and Fromm in January 1945.

confidence after the 'Goodwood' failure were sent to Normandy from Bletchley as soon as the Enigma signals had been decoded, often within four hours of their German origination. Churchill saw the decrypts, and copies went to SHAEF, Twenty-First Army Group, Twelfth Army Group, British Second Army, Canadian First Army, and US First Army. They confirmed very positively that Montgomery's overall plan of drawing off the main strength of the German armour to the British front was paying off, despite the near disaster of 'Goodwood'. The Ultra intelligence gave undeniable evidence that the Germans on the American front would not be able to withstand the 'Cobra' attack, for the enemy infantry lines through which 'Cobra' had to drive a path were fragile. For instance, General Eugen Mendl, commanding II Parachute Corps, exchanged signals with General Kurt Student, commanding the Parachute Army in Germany, complaining that the fighting power of his parachutists was dwindling daily. His last two requests for reinforcements had been ignored and the critical situation forced him to commit the few replacements he received as soon as they joined, with the result that 90 per cent quickly became casualties because they were so young and had so little training. He declared to Student that most of them had never thrown a hand grenade, fired more than a few rounds of live ammunition, or learned much about machine-guns, entrenching tools or camouflage. No doubt this was partly the natural distortion of a general starved of trained reinforcements, but Montgomery believed it proved that the German divisions about to face the immense American assault were unlikely to be able to launch an effective counter-attack, and were anyway far below the normal standard of the parachutists who were usually the élite of the German infantry.[8]

Student promised 2,000 reinforcements, but Meindl asked that 1,000 should have further training in Germany – this proved 3rd Parachute Division would be well below strength when 'Cobra' started. Just before St Lô fell Ultra decoded a signal from Meindl forecasting that if the Americans attacked they must break through, since there was nothing to stop them. Ultra also showed that German LXXXIV Corps, further to the west, reported that artillery and air bombardment had so reduced its fighting power, and that casualties amongst officers had been so heavy, that the corps could no longer guarantee to hold the line;

some units were already giving ground. 2nd SS Panzer had kept the front from collapsing, but this division was dangerously short of petrol and the fighting for the St Lô start-line had cost it twenty-two tanks.

Ultra signals also showed that abortive Allied bombing before the false start for 'Cobra' on 24 July had led German LXXXIV Corps to believe, at least for a while, that their artillery had prevented a major ground attack. The guns had, however, used up far too much ammunition and were especially short of the 88-mm shells vital for destroying American tanks.

A signal from von Kluge to Hitler that he needed more tanks 'to stop the rot' was intercepted by Ultra, which also decoded a series of clear indications between 7 and 17 July that the Germans around St Lô, although still fighting hard, were not only nearing exhaustion but were becoming so thin on the ground that they would be in no shape to withstand the massed US First Army attack.

Montgomery and his immediate staff were convinced that Ultra intelligence guaranteed the successful result of 'Cobra' in advance, and that the attack would punch a hole through the German defences; since there were neither German reserves nor secondary lines of defence an Allied armoured break-out into almost undefended country must follow. Their optimism was enhanced by their faith in the new Rhinoceros tank attachment, which Montgomery felt would make American tanks far more effective in the bocage. US 2nd Division under Gerow had been so frustrated by the difficulties of operating tanks in the bocage that they had experimented with devices attached to the front of a Sherman. The most efficient was the Rhinoceros, which consisted of heavy steel tusk-like prongs welded to the front armour. When the tank butted into a hedgerow the prongs dug into the earth of the bank and pinned the tank down, preventing it from bellying up over the hedge and exposing its soft underside to German anti-tank guns; Shermans were able to drive through hedgerows by sheer force. In order to convert the tanks swiftly, iron from German underwater devices had been collected wholesale, and arc-welding equipment and crews were sent out from England. No Rhino tank was allowed to go into action before the start of 'Cobra', but by then three out of five American tanks had been converted. The chief result was that American tanks could operate off the roads, whereas the

German armour was confined to hard surfaces. Now the Allied deficiency in tank power could at last partly be made good, since the Rhinos could take the pockets of German armour in the flank, attacking the heavily armoured Panthers and Tigers from the side (normally a Rhino could cross a big hedge or bank in bocage country in three minutes). After their disheartening experiences in the bocage to date, when German tanks had proved greatly superior, it was a tonic for the Americans to know that their armour could undertake flanking movements across the fields.

Eisenhower and his advisers at SHAEF did not share Montgomery's optimism, which they considered to be quite unjustified after the failure of 'Goodwood' and all its high hopes. The Supreme Commander petulantly declared that it had taken Montgomery 7,000 tons of bombs to gain seven miles, and that he could not hope to go through France paying the price of 1,000 tons of bombs per mile.[9] Tedder continually talked of the 'British Army's failure', and Portal agreed that 'Monty was the cause'. Dempsey, during a visit to SHAEF, asked what all the fuss was about, claiming that there had never been any intention of achieving a break-out,[10] though this was hardly true either of his own plan, or of Montgomery's more cautious predictions.

Bradley, like Montgomery, sensibly preferred to look on 'Goodwood' as a preliminary to 'Cobra', and considered that the two operations should be judged as one. Because of the intense hostility to Montgomery at SHAEF, however, the 'Goodwood' failure was immediately seized on as a means of denigrating him. Yet if 'Cobra' had proceeded as originally scheduled, on 21 July, this agitation against Montgomery could never have occurred, since at that date there would have been no indication of a 'stalemate' in the British sector. Unfortunately, neither Eisenhower nor Tedder interpreted the Ultra signals as showing that 'Cobra' must produce a break-out without great loss, as Montgomery did correctly.

On 20 July Eisenhower visited both Twenty-First and Twelfth Army Groups. He found Bradley and Maj-Gen Lawton Collins, commanding US VII Corps, both very optimistic and enthusiastic for 'Cobra', and he happily discussed plans with them, feeling much at home. These two were the architects of the 'Cobra' break-out plan; Montgomery had no part in the details, although Twelfth Army Group was nominally under his control. Collins, a tough and aggressive commander, had the resilience and cheerful confidence which Bradley lacked, and together they made a good team.

Eisenhower went on to visit Montgomery, though the interview did not go well. The American found Montgomery complacent, his morale having been boosted by Churchill's visit, and did not like his attitude that the British had played their part in drawing Rommel's armour, and now it was up to the Americans. This was the line being taken by the American press, which Stimson had stressed to Eisenhower must be stifled. And, too, the openness and enthusiasm of Bradley and Collins was in marked contrast to Montgomery's cold defensiveness and arrogance. When Eisenhower got back to London he complained bitterly about Montgomery to his chauffeuse and confidante, Kay Summersby, who noted in her diary that he had said: 'Monty seems quite satisfied regarding his progress; says it is up to Bradley to go ahead ... Eisenhower is not pleased at progress made.'[11]

Not only was Eisenhower worried by what he termed Montgomery's 'excessive caution', but he was also pessimistic about the chances for American armour in the bocage, for he did not share Bradley's and Montgomery's faith in the Rhinoceros attachments. Ever since D-Day SHAEF had been very concerned at the deficiencies of the US Army's tanks compared with the Germans'. In a recent long report to Eisenhower Maj-Gen Maurice Rose, commanding US 3rd Armoured Division, had confirmed emphatically how inferior were American M4 and AM4 A3 tanks to Tigers and Panthers. Rose wrote: 'I have personally seen projectiles fired by our 75 and 76 mm guns bouncing off the front plate of Mark V tanks at 600 yards range.'[12] The whole report stressed that Panthers could only be destroyed by American tanks at very close range or from the flank, and that the bazooka (a hand-held recoilless rocket-launcher) had so little penetration that American soldiers were being trained to use captured German Panzerfaust anti-tank weapons, which could penetrate far thicker armour.

Fearful that Montgomery would add fuel to anti-British propaganda by not attacking hard enough, a problem exacerbated by the American tank weaknesses, Eisenhower wrote to him on 21 July: 'A few days ago I was extremely hopeful and optimistic that at last we were going to roll up the enemy. That did not come about.' The letter demanded that Dempsey should attack continuously in order to open up airfields and gain ground in the east, thus relieving one American flank. Significantly, Eisenhower commented that he knew that Montgomery was short of reinforcements, but he hinted very strongly that the British and Canadians were not pulling their weight: 'Eventually the USA ground strength will necessarily be much greater than the British. While we have equality in size we must go forward shoulder to shoulder with honours and sacrifices equally shared.'[13]

On 21 July, Montgomery's Twenty-First Army Group Directive (M512) emphasised his policy of 'holding our left.' But Eisenhower's letter, received later that day, alerted him to the need to heed the Supreme Commander's wishes, and he replied; 'There is not, and never has been, any intention to stop offensive operations on the eastern flank.' Dempsey was regrouping prior to another attack, he added – 'Does this above assure you that we see eye to eye?'[14]

At 0100 on 25 July Churchill telephoned Eisenhower, who was by then on the brink of asking for Montgomery's dismissal. During a half-hour conversation the American probed to find out Churchill's reaction to such a course, only to discover that the Prime Minister was now solidly on Montgomery's side. Next morning Eisenhower told his naval aide, Captain Harry Butcher, that Montgomery had sold the Prime Minister 'a bill of goods' at his Normandy HQ, and that 'the P.M. is supremely happy with the situation',[15] but he realised that no matter how maddening he found Montgomery, he must live with him for the time being. When, later that day, Tedder offered to come and discuss replacing Montgomery, Eisenhower told him that such a discussion would be fruitless in view of the Prime Minister's attitude.

Bradley's plan for 'Cobra', which he always stressed was his own and not Montgomery's, was to penetrate west of St Lô with VII Corps, pushing armoured and motorised troops deep into the German rear towards Coutances. 1,887 heavy and medium bombers and 559 fighter-bombers, carrying between them more than 4,000 tons of bombs, were to blast a hole in the thin German front line for American tanks to exploit. Unfortunately, when 'Cobra' was postponed for the second time, from 24 to 25 July, it was too late to stop all the bombers; many had bombed short, killing twenty-five and wounding 130 Americans. On the 25th, D-day for 'Cobra', the same thing happened when the red smoke marking the American front became obscured by dust and smoke. This time 111 US soldiers were killed and over 500 wounded; among the dead was Lt-Gen Lesley McNair, head of the US Army Ground Forces, who had gone forward to observe.

This second bomb attack by their own aircraft was so detrimental to morale that 'Cobra' got off to a slow start. In fact a good number of German infantry were shell-shocked by the bombardment and unable to fight, but Panzer Lehr and 5th Parachute Division were only slightly damaged, with the result that their by-now dreaded Panthers held up the Americans in the crucial early hours of the attack. By nightfall, however, US troops were making headway, although, as Lt-Gen Courtney Hodges, GOC US First Army, noted in his diary: 'It is not the breakthrough we had hoped for ... two successive days of bombing took the ginger out of our front line troops.'[16]

Eisenhower had crossed to Normandy to watch the start of the twice-postponed 'Cobra' attack. When he heard of the short bombing and of the casualties it had caused among his own troops, he told Bradley firmly that this was the last time he would allow the use of heavy bombers as a substitute for artillery in paving the way for a ground attack.

Back in London that evening, Eisenhower was depressed, and not even Bradley, who had accompanied him to the airstrip before his flight back to England, had been able to cheer him up. Although Bradley was very confident that he would make spectacular gains on the next day, Eisenhower had heard the same over-optimistic tale too often from Montgomery to allow his hopes to rise.

Happily for Bradley there were only two Panzer divisions facing him – Panzer Lehr, now reduced to forty-five tanks by battles with the British, and 2nd SS Panzer. Both had to hold the line, for there were no Panzer divisions in reserve for counter-attacks and, unlike the British during 'Goodwood', the Americans met no defensive positions in depth. On the second day of 'Cobra' German resistance weakened. Although their artillery had mostly survived the bombing, their armour, fortunately for the Americans, was chiefly deployed in pockets and could be outflanked by Rhinoceros tanks advancing through the meadows and hedges.

By the evening of the 26th Collins's VII Corps was on the brink of a breakthrough. With two armoured and four infantry divisions he was much stronger than the Germans facing him and, gambling with two of his mobile columns, he started to overrun enemy positions. Gerow's V Corps, on Collins's left, and Lt-Gen Troy Middleton's VIII Corps, on his right, made slower progress, however. But by 27 July the Americans were reaping a harvest denied to British Second Army, and were pushing their tanks and armoured cars into areas where there was no German armour. Many German soldiers simply ran away, and large numbers were made prisoner. On the third day Coutances fell, and Bradley told Eisenhower: 'Things on our front look good. Quesada [Maj-Gen E.R. (Pete) Quesada, commanding 9th Tactical Air Command, USAAF] has kept air formations over advancing columns continuously.'[17]

The Germans could not put in an armoured counter-attack to prevent disaster in the western sector because six of their Panzer divisions still faced the British; the American generals in the field were sincere in their gratitude to Montgomery for diverting so much German armour to the east. His plan to hold the enemy in the British sector now paid huge dividends. As the key road junction at Avranches fell on 1 August, Patton's Third Army HQ came into operation and his divisions, freed of the risk of heavy German counter-attacks, streamed into Brittany. US First Army turned east towards Vire and Mortain; Third Army secured Fougères and Rennes and then turned west towards the Brittany ports, away from von Kluge's army and into country almost empty of Germans.

Meanwhile, Eisenhower kept on nagging Montgomery to make certain that the British and the Canadians made their full contribution, insisting that the British general should follow his, Eisenhower's, policy of attacking all the time, all along the line.

Either in response to Eisenhower's prodding, or on his own initiative, Montgomery gave a great boost to 'Cobra' by ordering Lt-Gen Henry Crerar to launch an attack on 25 July with his Canadian First Army towards Falaise, where the strength of the German armour lay. This attack coincided with the start of 'Cobra', but it was doomed to failure and proved very costly – the Canadians suffered 1,500 casualties in one day's fighting. In spite of 1,700 Allied air sorties in support of the attack, Crerar's forces failed to make ground beyond the Bourguebus Ridge because there were strong Panzer forces in the woods behind La Hogue. No opening was secured by the British armour, and late on the first day Dempsey decided that the German defence was so strong that he must abandon the attacks. While it was yet another tactical defeat for Montgomery von Kluge was so worried by this threat that he came in person to the Canadian front on 27 July, even though that day was proving disastrous for his forces in the west, where the American attack was now achieving considerable success. Montgomery had been right to order this expensive Canadian attack, for it made certain that the German armour stayed in the east, and this ensured victory for 'Cobra'.

Back in London, Eisenhower had decided not to try and manoeuvre Montgomery out of the saddle – instead he would ask Churchill to use his influence to make his general move faster. At lunch at 10 Downing Street on 26 July he asked the Prime Minister 'to persuade Monty to get on his bicycle and start moving'. Churchill, his differences with Montgomery resolved, told Brooke that Eisenhower had complained both 'about your Monty's stickiness' and about the exaggerated reports in American newspapers that US troops 'were taking all the casualties'.

On the 27th, Eisenhower and Bedell Smith dined at 10 Downing Street, together with Brooke. Churchill had given the dinner in an attempt to bring Eisenhower closer to Brooke, and to help smooth the quarrels between Montgomery and the American. Brooke thought that the occasion did a lot of good, and himself offered to go to Normandy 'to assist in handling Monty', but in his diary for that day he made it clear how strongly he took Montgomery's side: 'Ike knows nothing about strategy. Bedell Smith, on the other hand, has brains but no military education in the true sense ... he falls short when it comes to strategic outlook. With that Supreme Command set up it is no wonder Monty's real ability is not realised.' And on the next day, 28th July, he wrote to Montgomery:

The trouble between you and the P.M. has been satisfactorily settled. Ike was worried at the outlook taken by the American press that the British were not taking their share of the casualties. Ike considers the British Army could and should be more offensive ... and that Dempsey should be doing more than he does. Ike has the very vaguest conception of war. He has some conception of attacking on the whole front which must be an American doctrine judging by Mark Clark with 5th Army in Italy. Unfortunately this policy of attacking along the whole front is one that appeals to the P.M. Ike may obtain some support in this direction. I feel personally quite certain that Dempsey must attack at the *earliest possible moment*, on a large scale. We must not allow German forces to move from his front to Bradley's or we shall give more cause for criticism than ever.

Montgomery replied immediately: 'Everything will be thrown in. Gave orders to Dempsey this morning that attack is to be pressed with utmost vigour, and all caution thrown to the winds and many casualties accepted and that he must step on the gas for Vire.' He was irritated that Eisenhower had complained to Churchill about him, but he fully realised the imperative importance of preventing the Germans from reinforcing the American front, as he also realised the need for more British attacks if he was to silence his critics, with their continual carping about his over-caution. Brooke's letter did little to curb Montgomery's cockiness, but it did bring to him a sense of reality, and the realisation that he was not completely his own master in Normandy.

On 25 July, a *New York Herald Tribune* headline had announced: ALLIES IN FRANCE BOGGED DOWN ON ENTIRE FRONT. Montgomery was again charged with 'over-caution', and *The Times* regretted his having used the word 'breakthrough' during 'Goodwood', indeed, the whole tone of press comment in the UK and the USA was critical of him. He attributed this, probably accurately, to Eisenhower, and felt strongly that he was being adversely commented on to journalists by staff at SHAEF in London. He sent two strong messages of complaint to Grigg, and received in reply this sympathetic if unorthodox letter from the Secretary of State for War:

PRIVATE AND PERSONAL

1st August, 1944

My dear Monty,

I have had your two messages about the Press and their alarmist stuff. The trouble for me is to know whether it comes from your side or from SHAEF. The particular item which infuriated you was from SHAEF and the Prime Minister has himself taken it up with Eisenhower and Bedell Smith (Brooke being present). I also spoke to Bracken [Brendan Bracken, Minister of Information] about it. The worst of it is, however, that both Bracken and Eisenhower seem to exist to give the journalists what they think they want and to support them against the soldiers at all costs. So nobody but the P.M. can do much there. However you can rely on C.I.G.S. and me beavering away at the old man, and I will certainly speak to the more reputable London editors and proprietors – but individually, I think, and not in a formal conference.

What happens on your side I don't know. They are a pretty scurvy lot anyhow but perhaps now that you have got Neville over there you may be able to induce them to be no more than a minor misfortune.

But none of this in my view goes to the root of the matter. The Americans at the best of times would do their damnedest to write down our effort and write up their own, to laud others and diminish you. But an election year isn't the best of times anyhow. And further I am convinced that Conyngham [*sic*] is continuing to badnam[e] you and the Army and that what he says in this kind is easily circulated in SHAEF via Tedder and again that Bedell – who seems to have become very conceited and very sour – listens too readily to the poison. If I am right then you will have no comfort until you have demanded and obtained the removal of Conyngham from any connection with OVERLORD whatever. He is a bad and treacherous man and will never be other than a plague to you.

If I may presume further I should force Eisenhower to come out into the open the next time you see him and refuse to put up with dark and fearful hints. Indeed I should make the accusation that the rumours are started in his own headquarters.

However giving advice is easy. You want me to *do* something. I will. I will try to get the SHAEF news arrangements right mechanically. At present the American No. 1 is sick and the British No. 2 is a bogus airman who is, I think, a relation of Archie Sinclair's. And I will also disseminate some wheat among the tares.

God bless and may your enemies be scattered – as well as your false friends.

By writing in this vein Grigg was deliberately fanning the quarrel between Montgomery and Eisenhower, as well as encouraging his friend to adopt an anti-American outlook. It was the worst possible kind of letter to send to the temperamental commander at this tense moment in the battle for the break-out, while the remarks about Bedell Smith and the demand for the sacking of Coningham, coupled with the advice to Montgomery to have a showdown with Eisenhower, are inexcusable. Furthermore, it was, or should have been, Grigg's task as Secretary of State for War to pour oil on the troubled waters; by now, however, he was a devoted supporter of Montgomery. Grigg himself was a strange character – though extremely able, he was bad-tempered and given to strong language, both in speech and on paper. (Evidence of Grigg's ill temper and rudeness can be found in the *Dictionary of National Biography*.)

Montgomery wrote back on the next day. By now he was much more buoyant and cheerful, for the American attack was going well and, after long weeks of anxiety, he could begin to see daylight at last. For the first time he addressed the Secretary of State as 'My Dear P.J.', and he was plainly delighted by Grigg's obvious enthusiasm for him.

PRIVATE, TOP SECRET & PERSONAL

TAC HEADQUARTERS:
21 ARMY GROUP
2.8.44

My dear P.J.

May I address you thus in my more personal letters. I will be very correct and official on other occasions!! I have your letter of 1 August. It is quite 1st Class and I had a real good hearty laugh when reading it; a good 'lash out' all round is an excellent thing. What we really need is an extensive use of

weed killer; we would then progress rapidly towards the end
of the war.

Here, the broad basic plan, on which we have been
working for so many weeks, is now unfolding in the exact
way in which it was intended. This is very gratifying. There
were some difficult moments; that must always happen in
battle, and it takes a little time to get the enemy where you
want him so that you can hit him a colossal crack *somewhere
else*.

It was the same at Alamein.

And it is at that time that the commanders in the field want
to be supported and encouraged, and the soldier's morale
kept high. In this case it was *at that time* that the Press began
a campaign which might have done great harm.

This is one great battle, directed by one commander, and
designed to produce a great dividend. But one cannot tell them
what you are trying to do, or how the battle is being forced to
swing; the need for secrecy is too great. However, we are off
now and I think the Bosche will find it very difficult to stop us
from bringing the full plan into effect i.e. the swing of the right
flank right up to Paris, and pushing the enemy armies up
against the Seine between Paris and the sea. And while this is
going on we open up Brittany.

Do come over and stay a night. That is the best time. I
have to be out by day a good deal. I would send my aeroplane
to Northolt for you any time, and return you to London in the
morning in time for work.

Yrs ever

Monty[18]

On 27 July Montgomery held a conference with his army
commanders, Dempsey and Crerar, and issued a new Directive
(M515) on the following day, which stated that 'the main blow
has now been delivered by the First US Army ... ' The attack
was making excellent progress, and everywhere else the object
was to help American progress. The British assaults on the Orne
in the Caen sector had compelled the enemy to bring such
strong forces to oppose them that any further large-scale attack
in that area was '*unlikely to succeed*'. Six out of the Germans'
total of eight armoured divisions were on the British front and
located east of Noyers – 'We must now deal a very heavy blow

west of Noyers where there is no German armour at all.' Second Army was to regroup and attack with not less than six divisions in the Caumont area.

On 29 July, spurred and excited by signals giving the extent of the American gains, Montgomery ordered Dempsey to start the attack on Vire, which he had mentioned to Brooke, on the 30th. Vire was the junction of seven roads, and the key point on the left flank of the American attack. On 28 July Eisenhower had sent a message to Montgomery approving of Directive M515, but urging more attacks by the British and Canadians and a speeding up of the main blow at Caumont: 'I feel very strongly that a three Division attack now on Second Army's flank will be worth more than a six Division attack in five days' time. Let us go all out on the lines of M515 and not waste an hour.'[19]

In this new operation, codenamed 'Bluecoat', Dempsey was ordered to attack south from Caumont with VIII and XXX Corps on 30 July. The plan was to capture the dominating hill of Mont Pinçon, six miles south of the Caumont-Villers Bocage line, and then try and insinuate British divisions behind the German forces facing Avranches. With so much of the German armour on the Canadian front south of Caen, Montgomery decided not to put on any more pressure in the east. He wanted to prevent Mont Pinçon and Vire from being used by von Kluge as a hinge for an orderly withdrawal of his defeated western divisions from the American sector.

As part of the 'Cobra' offensive, the Americans had been attacking strongly between Caumont and St Lô since the 26th, but in three days had only gained three miles. Here the bocage is at its thickest, and the Germans had laid large minefields and dug strong entrenchments on the slopes of Mont Pinçon.

On Dempsey's right, VIII Corps with 11th Armoured Division made an important gain of five miles on 30 July towards St Martin des Besaces, and took the feature Hill 309. The next day 11th Armoured advanced again and had the best of an encounter with a 21st Panzer battle group. Dempsey's forces had now driven a deep wedge between the German Seventh Army (General Hausser) and Fifth Panzer Army (formerly Panzer Group West, now under SS General Sepp Dietrich), and if they had occupied Vire in strength they would have threatened Hausser's right wing, which would have produced a gap of six miles between the two German armies.

On 1 August armoured cars of 11th Armoured Division, exploring undefended country to the south, had got to within two miles of Vire and could have captured the town. Dempsey, however, ordered VIII Corps not to press the attack in that direction because a modification of the inter-army boundaries had left Vire to the Americans. Unfortunately, the Germans quickly built up strong resistance round the town, and because of the rigid army boundaries the prize of Vire was not seized—a foretaste of what was to occur at Argentan fourteen days later.

Montgomery missed a tremendous opportunity in not taking Vire, for it lay on the line of German retreat from the American front to the key town of Mortain, thirteen miles further south. His set-back at Vire is evidence that, as a commander, he sometimes failed to take immediate advantage of unexpected opportunities thrown up in fighting, and this was especially so when the situation was complicated by the presence of defined battle zones for different, allied, armies. General Roberts holds this opinion, and told me:

My armoured cars got into Vire on 31 July, and we could have taken the town immediately and occupied it in strength because we had broken out to the south-west and were beyond the German lines. We would have been in the tip of an apex without anyone to back us up. Von Kluge definitely thought 'Bluecoat' was more menacing at first than the American break-out ... As a result [he] refused to shift any of his Panzers to the American front.

Once we had Vire we could have interfered very considerably with the German withdrawal from the St Lô front. Unfortunately the Americans complained heavily as soon as we got into their battle zone and used their roads.

The Americans in that sector were very slow. Monty could have changed the plan on the Vire front if he had wanted to. We sent back frequent and accurate sitreps so that those higher up knew exactly where we were and what was the opposition. Vire was a missed opportunity, and one of the reasons why I consider Monty was much better at set-piece battles than seizing opportunities. The good point about him was that he always stuck to his original intention, but when it became loose he never took advantage of the situation. Even at Alamein when it became loose he let it go haywire.

With 'Bluecoat' Montgomery felt that he was at last on the brink of a brilliant victory on the US flank which would put an end to the carping of his critics, and to the American newspaper stories that the British were not pulling their weight. Alas for his hopes, he was let down by XXX Corps, which made such slow progress between Villers Bocage and Mont Pinçon that VIII Corps' left flank became dangerously exposed. Even so, the extent of the VIII Corps advance had drawn to the Caumont front two German armoured divisions — 9th and 10th Panzer — which otherwise would certainly have gone to the American front; indeed Eberbach told von Kluge that the Caumont sector was the crucial one at that moment.

The commander of XXX Corps, Bucknall, had objected strongly to his Corps' part in 'Bluecoat', and had asked Dempsey if he could rewrite the plan; the latter, however, had refused. 43rd Division had only come under Bucknall's command thirty-six hours before the attack began, and he had complained that, since this division had never met 7th Armoured before, it was hard for the infantry and tank units to co-operate; he added that he considered that he had such a difficult axis of advance that it would not be easy to keep pace with VIII Corps.

On 31 July Bucknall sent back a complacent situation report, stating that he had captured the feature Bois du Homme and the high ground north-west of Aunay, his chief preliminary objectives. This, however, was not good enough for either Dempsey or Montgomery, who were determined that XXX Corps should take the road and rail junction at Aunay-sur-Odon, so that VIII Corps could continue a spectacular advance on the flank of the Americans.

Dempsey went forward to confer with Bucknall on the afternoon of 1 August, having heard that 43rd Division was held up by newly arrived troops of 10th Panzer, and that 7th Armoured had made no progress towards capturing Aunay, although Bucknall had told them 'to speed up action by taking any risks and by all means'. Montgomery had told Dempsey to be ruthless.

The 7th Armoured Division War Diary records that after the conference the BGS, XXX Corps sent this dramatic message to Maj-Gen Erskine, commanding 7th Armoured: 'You may lose

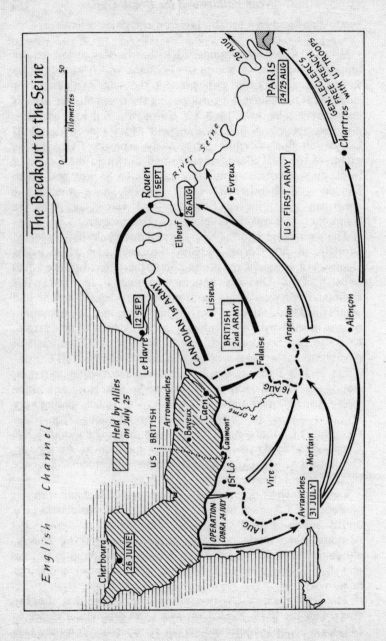

The Breakout to the Seine

every tank you have but you *must* capture Aunay by midnight.'

Next morning, Aunay was still not taken. Montgomery told Dempsey that Erskine must go, and Bucknall agreed with Dempsey that Erskine should be relieved of the command of 7th Armoured because that division had been 'most dilatory'. In the evening of the same day Dempsey told Bucknall that he too was sacked. The latter took his ill fortune like a gentleman, and later wrote: 'When I got to 21 Army Group HQ Monty delivered the coup de grâce gracefully and told me to carry on until my replacement arrived.'[20] But he considered that Dempsey was 'nervous and jumpy', and as he could not risk a fourth reverse he 'needed a scapegoat'. In fact, it was Montgomery who had insisted on the dismissals, and he made a clean sweep in 7th Armoured, replacing also the Armoured Brigade Commander, Brigadier Hinde, and the CRA. The division resented these sackings, which failed to bring about any 'rejuvenation', according to Chester Wilmot and others who were in a position to judge. Neither did Erskine's replacement live up to Montgomery's hopes.

Montgomery had always had great faith in 7th Armoured, his 'Desert Rats'. General Roberts, however, thinks that in this he was mistaken. He told me:

7th Armoured Division had been in battle too much and done too much fighting. At the time of 'Bluecoat' their tanks would reach a corner and then not go round it. Monty should have disbanded 7th Armoured and kept 9th Armoured [which was split up] who were fresh. I used to find when I was given an Armoured Brigade who had little battle experience it was like getting a fresh second horse.

On 2 August Montgomery had written to Simpson:

I fear I shall have to remove Erskine from 7th Armoured Division. He will not fight his Division and take risks. It was very easy in the desert to get a 'bloody nose', and a good many people did get one. The old desert divisions are apt to look over their shoulder and wonder if it is OK behind or if the flanks are secure and so on. The 7th Division is like that. They want a new General who will drive them headlong towards and through gaps torn in the enemy defence not worrying about flanks or anything. The big mass of German soldiery wants an opportunity to surrender. They must be given it. This does not apply to the SS troops. Great vistas are now opening up ahead and we want Generals who will put their heads down and go like hell.

I also have got to remove the Commander of 30 Corps. It is no good trying to make him change his character. He is too slow for this mobile business. Please show this letter to the CIGS.[21]

Montgomery replaced Bucknall as XXX Corps commander with his old friend Lt-Gen Brian Horrocks, who had, as it were, been waiting in the wings, recovering from a stomach wound received during an air raid on Bizerta before the Sicilian invasion. The appointment was something of a risk, for Horrocks was not yet fully recovered, but Montgomery knew that in him he had a dashing commander who would inspire the troops and 'put his head down and go like hell' when the opportunity arose. In a sense, Horrocks was Montgomery's answer to the charge of over-caution.

Montgomery had told Simpson that he wanted to bring Horrocks out to France as soon as he was well, and Simpson sent back briefiings about the lieutenant-general's recovery. After nearly dying in the Cambridge Hospital at Aldershot Barracks, Horrocks had been trying to get fit — even dressing up in marching order and going out for long tramps at night 'dressed up like a Christmas tree'. At the end of July Simpson told Montgomery that Horrocks was 'more or less fit for active service', and this precipitated Bucknall's dismissal.

Everyone serving in XXX Corps HQ at that time to whom I have spoken told me that there was a dramatic contrast between Bucknall and Horrocks. The former, a dapper figure of unquestionable courage, was precise and conscientious, if somewhat uninspiring, while Horrocks had enormous charisma. On his arrival he immediately gave his Corps HQ staff a pep talk, and then made a lightning tour of the formations. Morale improved enormously, although nearly everyone who saw him thought that he looked ill. (General Roberts told me that his troops always felt better after Horrocks had visited his division.) Whether thanks to Horrocks or not, 43rd Division had by 6 August captured the 1,200-foot-high Mont Pinçon, the most important tactical feature in Normandy, and from there XXX Corps observers could look down on the Germans, making effective use of artillery concentrations. Meanwhile, Patton's US Third Army was ranging almost unopposed through Brittany, while US First Army, turning east, had captured Mortain on 2 August.

'Bluecoat' kept three Panzer divisions and three battalions of heavy tanks away from the American sector, forces which would otherwise have been thrown against Bradley; now, with the advances of VIII and XXX Corps, Montgomery had made a large contribution to pinching out the Germans in what was becoming the Mortain salient. The American press, however, were more interested in Bradley's spectacular advances – the British and Canadians had scant credit for their efforts.

The following letters from Montgomery to Simpson reveal his planning and his supreme confidence. General Simpson told me that Montgomery wrote less inhibitedly to him than to the CIGS, and added: 'Monty knew that if I thought it would be useful I would show it to the CIGS, in which case Churchill probably saw it as well; but if it was at all delicate and confidential I would keep the information to myself and use it for Monty's advantage in any discussions with the PM or the CIGS and the Chiefs of Staff.' Certainly these letters are clear and frank:

August 1, 1944

My dear Simbo,

About the 6th Airborne*. I must throw everything into the present battle. The American Armies on the right and the British Armies in the centre are now in the process of carrying out the big wheel that will, I hope clear Brittany, push the Germans back to beyond the Orne and swing the right flank of the wheel. If the Second Army can progress steadily now we have the German roping off force cut in two. Once we get to Vire and Condé it will be awkward for the

---

* There were by now plans to withdraw 6th Airborne Division from the line and return it to the UK for refitting. The division had been fighting continuously since D-Day and had suffered heavy casualties as a result; Montgomery was criticised by the Airborne Corps in England for leaving 6th Airborne in the line for too long, thus wasting scarce and expensively trained parachutists. Interestingly, General Poett disagrees emphatically with this criticism.

Germans and I am working on that. On the left the Canadian Army must hold while the force pivots on that flank. I must take everything I can from the left and put it into the right swing. The Airborne Troops [ie 6th Airborne] must not be used offensively. Therefore they must be used on the left flank pro bono publico. I had taken the Division out to send home, but I have now put it back again into the line east of the Orne.

Everything is going very well. The whole plan which I have been working to all the time is now working out as planned. I hope to turn the right Corps of 12 Army Group westwards into Brittany tomorrow. 12th Army Group 9th US Army under Bradley assumed control at 1200 today.

On the next day he wrote again:

August 2

My dear Simbo,

The battle goes well and completely according to plan. Rennes is now ours and St. Malo. I doubt if there are many Germans left in the whole of Brittany except base wallahs, etc. George Patton should be in Brest in a day or two [here Montgomery was quite wrong, for Brest did not fall until 18 September].

The broad plan remains unchanged. I shall swing the right wing round towards Paris, and while this is going on I shall try and hold the enemy on to his ground in the Caen area. Then I hope to put down a large airborne [ie air transportable] force including 52 Division somewhere in the Chartres area and cut off the enemy escape through the gap between Paris and Orleans.

The big idea is to push the enemy up against the Seine and get a 'cop'. However, these things do not always work out as planned although the present operations are absolutely as planned.[22]

These letters are typical of Montgomery and give evidence of his clear forward thinking, while the racy language conveys his jaunty mood in those dramatic days when he knew that he was on the brink of a triumph.

In his important Directive M515 of 27 July, Montgomery had written: 'We must secure the Brittany ports before winter is upon us'. But now, in common with Eisenhower, he had his mind fixed on bigger targets than the continuation of his seaborne supplies. On 3 August Bradley decided, in Montgomery's words, 'to use Mortain as a hinge on which to swing his front to Le Mans and Alençon'. Three days later the Americans were at Le Mans, another seventy-five miles forward; unless the Germans withdrew immediately to the Seine they risked seeing their Army Group B destroyed in Normandy.

According to General Belchem, between 5 and 6 August Montgomery frequently told him that he was puzzled about von Kluge's next move, and expected the Germans to order a staged withdrawal first to the Orne and thence to the Seine.[23] Montgomery did not agree with Patton's surge through Brittany because it was diverting troops away from the main enemy; after the advance through Avranches he had wanted Patton to turn east across von Kluge's right flank in order to trap the German Seventh Army west of the Seine. The American drive through Brittany had been written into the original 'Overlord' plan because at the time the planners had been obsessed with the need to capture ports to maintain supplies to the invasion forces, but the swift Allied advance now made this need less urgent. The main prize in Brittany, Brest, did not fall until mid-September, and while St Malo was captured it could not be used because the Ile de Cezembre held out until 3 September.

Unless 'Anvil' was to be moved from the South of France to Brittany, as Churchill alone wanted, the best use of all available forces was to concentrate on destroying von Kluge's army. Montgomery was not concerned in the futile controversy which had suddenly arisen between Eisenhower and the Prime Minister about moving 'Anvil' to Brittany, a wild Churchillian suggestion, but he now rightly saw Brittany as an unnecessary diversion of resources. Eisenhower overruled him, however, preferring to stick to the outdated 'Overlord' plan, and coveting Brest and Lorient as ports in which to land the American reinforcement divisions now piling up on the other side of the Atlantic. The Americans had more divisions in France at this time than had been planned, but cargo unloading facilities were below estimates.

By now, Hitler had finally come to realise that there would be no second invasion in the Pas de Calais. Accordingly, in the first week of August he sent from there to Normandy one Panzer division, three infantry divisions and part of a parachute division. He unwisely insisted, however, that these divisions must be thrown piecemeal against the US Army, instead of being deployed sensibly from a firm base established in advance. Now, as Patton's Third Army moved far south of Avranches, Hitler conceived the plan of cutting it off by a counter-attack from Mortain to the sea. Far away from the battlefield he issued detailed orders, specifying – from maps, and without having seen the ground – concentration areas and roads to be used.

The Americans had met unexpectedly strong German resistance east of Mortain and around Domfront. Ultra revealed that Hitler had taken the decision to launch the Mortain counter-attack and that von Kluge had at first demurred, although he dared not argue too strongly because of his involvement in the abortive 20 July plot. Montgomery, however, was still sure that the next battle would be for the Seine crossings, because he thought that the enemy concentration at Domfront shown up by Ultra was not powerful enough for a successful counter-attack.

But if he was correct about the German strength, he was wrong about Hitler's intentions. Von Kluge launched his counter-attack from Mortain late on 6 August; his forces made initial advances and got within fifteen miles of Avranches. Six armoured divisions, some well under strength, led the way, encircling elements of US 30th Division, but one divisional commander, General Gerhard von Schwerin, was anti-Nazi and delayed the advance of his 116th Panzer.

Eisenhower, in Normandy at the time, held a hurried conference with Bradley on 7 August. Without consulting Montgomery they decided not to reinforce the divisions in front of Mortain, but to continue rushing as many troops as possible south through Avranches – if the worst happened and the Germans got through from Mortain to the sea at Avranches, Eisenhower guaranteed to provide 2,000 tons of supplies by air daily. This bold gamble paid off. Von Kluge gained a little ground, but at great cost, for the weather cleared and the Allied air force inflicted enormous damage on the attacking Germans. On the 8th von Kluge had to discontinue the counter-attack.

On the same day Eisenhower telephoned Montgomery from Bradley's HQ, with Bradley at his side. In a three-way telephone conversation the Allied commanders made plans to encircle 100,000 German troops, now in the Mortain 'pocket', which could be closed if the Americans advanced from the south through Argentan and the British from the north through Falaise. Montgomery agreed, and immediately began work on the directive needed to put the plan in operation.

A day earlier, on 7 August, the Canadians had begun a fresh attack towards Falaise, code-named 'Totalise'. Montgomery had noted from Ultra that some of the German tank divisions concentrating at Mortain had been drawn away from the Canadian front, which made the chance of a break-through beyond the Bourguebus Ridge more likely. 'Totalise' was entrusted to Canadian II Corps, and the plan was the brainchild of its commander, Simonds. He decided to attack by night without a preliminary bombardment, and to penetrate the forward German strong-points with two columns of tanks, accompanied by infantry riding in Priest tanks from which the 105-mm guns had been removed. This time the attack was a partial success, and by dawn the Canadian columns were three miles inside the German lines, where they were to be joined by the Polish Armoured Division in an attempt to break through. The Germans counter-attacked in strength, however, and by dark on 8 August the Canadian advance was halted. That night Eisenhower drove to Montgomery's HQ to urge him to continue the attack.

On the next day the Canadians attacked again, and lost forty-five tanks in attempts to penetrate the German defences, but during 9 August the Germans pulled back to a prepared defence line behind the River Laison. Montgomery had driven the enemy back nine miles, but his leading troops were still seventeen miles from Falaise. Once again he had been denied a spectacular break-through, though he had satisfied Eisenhower by keeping the German armour engaged. From a historical point of view, however, it is clear that if 'Totalise' had been a complete success, resulting in the capture of Falaise, then von Kluge would have ordered an immediate retreat to the Seine, with the result that many fewer Germans would have been trapped in the Falaise gap.

Montgomery's Directive M518, written on 11 August as the Canadian attack was grinding to a halt, outlined a plan for closing the 'sack' – through which German supplies were flowing – by a short envelopment. Twenty-First Army Group would thrust south and east to secure Argentan and Falaise, while the Americans would swing north from Le Mans to Alençon and then on to the general line from Carrouges to Sees, twelve miles south of Argentan. If the neck could not be closed by the Canadians and Americans meeting at Argentan they would revert to Montgomery's former plan, issued on 6 August, which was for the Canadians to capture Falaise and then swing east to the Seine through Lisieux.

Hitler now ordered von Kluge to launch another counter-attack, and German armour concentrated again in the Domfront area, well within the 'sack'.

On 11 August the Canadians were still eleven miles north of Falaise, but Patton's troops were advancing against light opposition at never-anticipated speeds. The US Army had a flair for rapid movement; its troops were first-class mechanics, and revelled in the swift advances. While the Canadians were bogged down north of Falaise XV Corps of Patton's US Third Army was racing up from the south towards Argentan, led by US 5th Armoured Division and General Jacques Leclerc's American-equipped Free French 2nd Armoured Division, which was fresh, having landed on the Normandy beaches on 30 July. '2ème Blindée' joined Patton at Le Mans on 9 August, and captured Alençon on the 12th.

In his Directive M517 of 6 August, Montgomery had left the inter-army boundary at Argentan; according to the Directive, when Patton reached Argentan he was to concentrate his troops and create a strong position from which he would be able to withstand all German attacks. On Saturday 12 August, Maj-Gen Wade Haislip, commanding US XV Corps, telephoned Patton and told him that US 5th Armoured was on the edge of Argentan and could take the town. The Canadians and Poles were still eighteen miles to the north and had not yet taken Falaise, which held out until the night of the 16th. Knowing this, Patton rang Bradley and remarked, 'We have elements in Argentan. Shall we continue and drive the British into the sea for another Dunkirk?'

There then ensued one of the biggest controversies of the war about Montgomery's tactics. According to the Americans, he should, in trying to close the pocket, either have reinforced his bogged-down Canadian corps, or asked Patton to advance north. The Poles and Canadians were inexperienced and were making poor progress, but Montgomery had more experienced British divisions available to reinforce them; moreover, these divisions did not suffer, as did the Poles, from the handicap of the language barrier.

Colonel Stacey, the official Canadian war historian, wrote:

> The Canadians would have done better if they had not been learning the business as they fought ... a proportion of officers were not fully competent for their appointments and their inadequacy sometimes had serious consequences. The capture of Falaise was long delayed. A German force far smaller than our own taking advantage of strong ground and prepared positions were able to slow our advance to a point where considerable German forces made their escape. Had our troops been more experienced, the Germans could hardly have been able to escape a worse disaster.
>
> 4th Canadian Armoured and 1st Polish Armoured Divisions had never fought before they were committed to Normandy at one of the highest and fiercest crises of the war ... Less raw formations would probably have obtained larger and earlier results. General Foulkes, Commander 2nd Canadian Infantry Division, wrote frankly: 'When we went into action at Falaise and Caen we found that when we bumped into battle experienced German troops we were no match for them ... it took two months to get the Division so shaken down that we were really a machine who could fight.'[24]

As Montgomery had noted in his letter (p.99) that the Canadians were 'jumpy' in the first few days of assault, it is surprising that he let the inexperienced Poles and Canadians alone take the full brunt of the vital drive towards Falaise and the south, instead of reinforcing them with more experienced divisions which were available. David Belchem felt this strongly, and wrote: 'Monty overestimated the speed of advance of the Polish Armoured Division and of the Canadians. He had forces available to reinforce them but did not do so.'[25]

Originally, Montgomery had had high hopes of the Polish Armoured Division. He had been enormously impressed (despite his occasional tactlessness) with their *esprit de corps*, and their fanatical will to defeat the Germans in revenge for Hitler's rape of their beloved Poland and the appalling treatment of their fellow countrymen after its conquest. But sadly, the Polish 1st Armoured Division's performance in battle against the strongest units of the Nazi army on the road to Falaise was disappointing.

This was no reflection on the valour of the Poles. Their commanders were elderly, of First World War vintage, and their experience during that war had been in the Russian, Prussian or Austrian armies. All of them had taken part in the triumphant campaign of 1920, when Marshal Josef Pilsudski's newly formed Polish Army had driven the Bolsheviks back from the gates of Warsaw to beyond the eighteenth-century Polish frontier to the east, inflicting a crippling defeat upon Budjenny's renowned horse army, and securing an enlarged Poland by the Treaty of Riga. But most of them had been brought up with horsed cavalry and, apart from exercises in the UK after their country's fall, they had no experience of the speedy deployment of armour under battle conditions, and did not appreciate the need for split-second decisions at crucial moments. Nor, militarily speaking, were they on quite the same wave-length as their Canadian comrades, with their New World techniques and attitudes, although they were on terms of great friendship.

The Polish Armoured Division was not up to full battle strength when it landed in Normandy. The divisional commander, Maj-Gen Stanislaw Maczek, had written to Montgomery about his great difficulties in getting 1st Polish Armoured up to strength:[26] 'In the national interest we have made great sacrifices to keep up our numbers', he wrote, but this had meant recruiting, as infantry privates, middle-aged Poles used to a sedentary life and without military experience. There were no reinforcements available in the UK, though the Polish Government-in-Exile in London had hopes for appreciable numbers of volunteers from Poles in the USA and Canada. They were not forthcoming. The second generation of North American Poles preferred to fight with American units, and calls for volunteers from London and America went unanswered.*

When the Polish High Command learned of the large proportion of Polish conscripts in the German divisions in

---

*In the First World War Polish volunteers for General Haller's Polish Corps from Canada and the USA found they were not entitled to hospital treatment and benefits, unlike their fellows in the Canadian and US armies.

Normandy, they had high hopes of mass desertions, which would enable them to make up their losses by recruiting POWs. Lorry-loads of British uniforms with Polish facings were brought up to the front lines, and POWs were asked if they could speak Polish. If they could do so to their captor's satisfaction, they were enrolled in the Polish Division; if not they were sent to a POW cage. 856 POWs were recruited in Normandy by the Poles, but their performance was 'disappointing', perhaps best summed up in a War Office report: 'They were not as good as anticipated, both from the morale and the training point of view. They had had enough of war already on the German side'.[26]

Because of high casualties, which could not be replaced, the Polish Armoured Division was so short of officers and men that it had to be given a six-week rest from 6 October. By then the division lacked ninety-two officers and 746 ORs and, since no reinforcements were available, for the rest of the campaign Montgomery had difficulty in keeping the Polish Division effective.

On 11 August Patton had told Haislip to push a division of his XV Corps north through Argentan. On the next day, however, Patton was firmly told by Bradley's Chief of Staff that he was not to cross the inter-Allied army boundary, fixed by Montgomery on 6 August as 'all inclusive Second Army at Tinchebray Argentan Laigle Dreux Mantes-Gassicourt. Tracings have been issued to Commanders showing the boundaries in greater detail.' In fact, Bradley never urged Montgomery to allow Patton to advance north of Argentan. Bradley's General Kleber telephoned de Guingand at 0950 on 13 August to seek Montgomery's permission for Patton to go north. De Guingand refused.* At 0657 US XV Corps had

---

This became widely known, and adversely affected Polish recruiting in the Second World War. After the war, however, the American Government gave full war pensions and benefits to all Polish volunteers.

*Bill Williams confirmed to me that in 1947 he had given Forrest Pogue, the American historian this recollection of the call from Bradley's HQ on 13 August: 'Monty said "Tell Bradley they ought to get back." Monty missed closing the sack. He was fundamentally more interested in full envelopment than inner envelopment. We fell between two stools. He missed the chance of closing the Seine by doing the envelopment of Falaise.' This interview has been quoted by a Canadian historian, but his anti-Montgomery argument based on it is not sound.[27]

informed Twenty-First Army Group that '5 USA Division were in outskirts of Argentan', but reported again at 1240 that Argentan was held by enemy tanks and anti-tank guns. On the next day, messages to Twenty-First Army Group showed US 5th Division to be north-east and south-east of Argentan, while the French 2nd Armoured Division was to the south-west of the town, about to move slowly north. Then came a report that elements of the French division who attacked Argentan 'late yesterday evening [13 August] were seen off by strong enemy forces of infantry and anti-tank guns.'[28]

These messages in the Twenty-First Army Group Log throw doubt on Patton's claim that he could not only have taken Argentan but that he could also have pushed on to Falaise. Patton recorded:

> I believe the order emanated from 21 Army Group Commander and was either due to jealousy of the Americans or to utter ignorance of the situation, or both. It is very regrettable that XV Corps was ordered to halt because it could have gone on to Falaise and made contact with the Canadians, north west of that point, and positively closed the gap.[29]

His first point is definitely incorrect – Bradley had made no strong representations to Montgomery to be allowed to advance beyond Argentan, and if he had pressed for permission for Patton to move north Montgomery would have had to agree.

Nor is Patton's second claim that he could have pushed north correct. Eberbach had swiftly concentrated 116th Panzer Division together with elements of 1st SS Panzer and 2nd Panzer in and to the north of Argentan; it was these formations that had repulsed both the Americans and the French at Argentan. Even so, according to German records these three divisions were reduced to only some seventy tanks, although these were Panthers and Tigers.

In his memoirs, Bradley wrote: 'In halting Patton at Argentan I did not consult with Montgomery. The decision to stop Patton was mine alone; it never went beyond my HQ.'[30] His memory is slightly at fault, however, having overlooked Kleber's call to de Guingand on 13 August. Bradley declared that he had never suggested to Eisenhower that he should intervene to force any inter-army boundary changes since he considered that, even if Patton had linked up with the Canadians, he could not have succeeded in keeping the gap closed because 'nineteen German Divisions were stampeding to get out of the trap.' Here he was wrong. On 13 August the Germans were *not* stampeding out of the pocket – on Hitler's orders they were concentrating inside it for another Mortain counter-attack. Bradley added, and here he may have been correct, 'I much preferred a solid shoulder at Argentan to the possibility of a broken neck at Falaise.'

Another imponderable is whether Leclerc's Free French division would have been prepared to accept major casualties to close the gap. De Gaulle had almost certainly ordered Leclerc to preserve his division for the assault on Paris, although once the latter had realised how close von Kluge's army was to destruction he might have ignored such an instruction.

But it is indisputable that if Bradley had ordered Patton to wait and build up reinforcements for XV Corps at Argentan, and Montgomery had sent fresh British divisions in to support the Canadian and Polish drive through Falaise, the sack would have been closed much sooner, and most of von Kluge's army would probably have been captured. In fact, more than half of it crossed the Seine, although all its heavy equipment was lost.

Some American and Canadian historians argue, like Patton, that Montgomery's obstinacy was responsible for the failure to close the gap earlier. This is not a valid criticism. It is true that he failed to initiate any fresh plan in order to seize the opportunity created by Patton's unexpected arrival at Argentan, but the major cause of the failure was Bradley's lack of initiative. These critics forget that if Bradley had reacted quickly to Patton's message, and had pressed Montgomery to move the inter-army boundary, then the latter would have been forced to agree. Montgomery was nominally in charge of Bradley, but in practice, at this stage of the Normandy campaign after the formation of US Twelfth Army Group, he no longer exercised the same control as he had after the landings. Colonel Stacey, the Canadian official historian wrote: 'There was an element of committee in the Allied system of command during this month of August.'[31] As a result, Bradley had been taking important decisions without reference to Montgomery; now, just when firm, precise timing and control were needed, they were lacking. For this Montgomery himself was partly to blame, for he liked to draw up his plans without consulting Eisenhower or Bradley, and refused to visit them, remaining aloof in his own Tac HQ.

There is little in the argument that it would have been hazardous to alter the inter-army boundary because of the danger of the Allies shelling and bombing each other. Gun lines for the artillery could have been fixed and altered at short notice, taking into account prominent and easily recognisable features. The nearness of the two armies would have made tactical bombing impractical, but there were plenty of targets for the air forces to the east and west of the bottleneck. Yet Bradley believed that 'To have driven into Monty's advance could have produced disastrous errors of recognition.'[32] The tale that time bombs had been dropped on the roads north of Argentan is also untrue.

On the morning of 14 August the impatient Patton, refusing to stand still at Argentan, requested that only two of Haislip's divisions should stay there, and that the other two should be allowed to make a dash towards the Seine. Bradley told him: 'If Monty wants help in closing the gap then let him ask us for it. Since there is little likelihood of him asking, push on east.'

On the 15th, therefore, US 5th Armoured and 79th Infantry Divisions moved rapidly eastwards towards Dreux. Resistance was light at first and there were fears that the bulk of the Germans had already escaped to the Seine. But on 16 August 116th Panzer counter-attacked at Bourg St Leonard, some nine kilometres east of Argentan and five kilometres south of Chambois. The village was lost and retaken in hard fighting, and evidence mounted that the Germans were on the point of escaping from the pocket.

On the same day the Canadians entered Falaise. Montgomery telephoned Bradley and urged that everyone should get moving to close 'the neck of the bottle'. He no longer wanted a link-up between Argentan and Falaise, but suggested instead that the armies should meet eleven kilometres north-east of Argentan, between Trun and Chambois on the Dives river, hoping to increase the bag by looping to the east.

On 17 August Field-Marshal Walther Model replaced von Kluge both as C-in-C, West and as commander of Army Group B. Von Kluge had done his best, but Hitler had consistently refused to send reinforcements or to order a retreat, and the imminent German collapse in Normandy was largely a result of this policy. Nevertheless, it angered the Führer, who suspected von Kluge of involvement in the 20 July plot, and was highly suspicious of his activities on 15 August, when he had been out of touch with his HQ all day. This mysterious lack of contact remains an unsolved riddle. It is just possible that von Kluge might have been trying to get in touch with the Allied Command in order to negotiate an armistice in the west, and certainly Hitler thought so. Von Kluge's radio truck had been silent since 0930 on the 15th, when he had set out for a conference with Eberbach, and at 1930 he was still missing. For a senior commander to vanish during a crucial battle is little short of catastrophic; this caused Hitler to comment that it was 'the worst day of his life'. Late that night von Kluge arrived at Eberbach's HQ, explaining that his radio truck had been put out of action in the morning by an air attack, and that the roads were terribly congested. The explanation dissipated the last of Hitler's trust in his C-in-C, West – he ordered von Kluge to command from outside the pocket, and relieved him of his command two days later. According to one historian, [33] an Allied radio signal seeking von Kluge's whereabouts was monitored, but this cannot be substantiated from Allied archives.*

Von Kluge's departure from the scene put paid finally to any chance of a German capitulation, for Model was a dedicated Nazi as well as a tough and ruthless commander who would fight to the end (in April 1945 he committed suicide rather than surrender, having first dissolved his army so that it would not be captured). But even if von Kluge had contacted the Allies with a view to an armistice, Montgomery had no instructions whatsoever from Churchill. In fact the idea of a German capitulation never entered Montgomery's mind after the abortive discussions with Churchill on 20 July.

The bulk of the German units crossed the Orne in relatively good order on 17 August, planning to move by night to the high ground east of the Falaise-Argentan road. One German commander said during interrogation after his capture: 'The British did not follow up very vigorously from the west.'[34]

---

* The most authoritative, and almost certainly true, account of von Kluge's conduct on 20 July can be found in Wilhelm von Schramm, *Conspiracy among the Generals*, English translation Allen and Unwin, 1956.

But on the 18th 4th Canadian Armoured Division took Trun, and recce elements advanced to the edge of St Lambert while, on their flank, the Poles secured Hordozeaux and Hills 258 and 137, and their reinforced recce troops got to within half a mile of Chambois. The pocket was almost closed.

A young Canadian pilot, Flight Officer (now Maj-Gen) Richard Rohmer, flew on a reconaissance mission over the narrowing gap at 1300 on 19 August. Crossing the main road to Falaise three miles north of Argentan, he was astonished to see

a column of every imaginable type of vehicle – a mixed bag of trucks, horse-drawn artillery, tanks, ambulances, anything that could move. They were two abreast on a road leading towards Pommainville. The head of the column was stopped at a fork in the road about 100 yards east of the paved Falaise-Argentan road. Around it the enemy had been gathering in the fields and under trees for 24 hours. At the head of the fork there were two staff cars. I could plainly see their occupants standing beside them apparently deciding which road to take. There was before me in the long double line stretching westward the largest, most valuable 'target of opportunity' I had or ever would see ... The order prohibiting air attacks in the Falaise Gap was in force ... two days later in a jeep I went down the four miles of road ... there was not a single destroyed or damaged vehicle.[35]

Montgomery had prohibited bombing in the area because of the heavy casualties suffered by Twenty-First Army Group from Allied bombers. 51st Highland Division complained of forty incidents on 18 August, with twenty-five vehicle casualties and fifty-one personnel. The Division's report stated: 'Continual bombing by own forces. Half the petrol being sent to 2nd Armoured destroyed. During a three day period 72 Polish soldiers were killed and 191 wounded: the Canadians lost 77 killed and 209 wounded from own bombing.'[36]

On the night of 19 August the Germans poured through the tiny Trun-Chambois gap. There was little cover for their columns, however, and artillery fire saturated the roads which, in daylight, were in full view of the Allied OPs. The casualties were prodigious. 1st Polish Armoured Division reached Mont Ormel during the night, but the Germans soon cut the roads to their rear, leaving them isolated. As soon as it became light the Poles saw every road on the plain to the west covered with German formations moving back. Polish artillery took a terrible toll but, on the 20th, German tanks attacked Mont Ormel all day, and succeeded in reopening the road to Champosoult. By now, the Poles had been without supplies for three days; enclosed in a pocket, they could neither receive supplies nor evacuate their 300 wounded and 800 prisoners-of-war. Finally, on 22 August, the Americans linked up with other Polish units at Chambois, and Canadian troops relieved the Poles on Mont Ormel, despite heavy German counter-attacks. The neck of the pocket was closed.

On 21 August the Allied artillery had wrought havoc among the Germans trying to escape through the encircling ring. The guns left in their wake a scene of utter carnage: the Germans lost at least 10,000 men killed, and the slaughter of horses was appalling. 50,000 prisoners were taken when the gap was finally closed, but a surprising number (estimates vary from 20,000 to 40,000) had escaped to fight again beyond the Seine, if they could get across. If the Argentan-Falaise gap had been closed when the opportunity presented itself on 13 August, very little of von Kluge's army would have survived, and if he himself had been made prisoner then a German surrender in the west might easily have become a reality.

For Montgomery, the campaign in Normandy had been at times intensely frustrating, although it had ended in triumph. In spite of overwhelming Allied air superiority, his three main Second Army offensives were conspicuous and publicised failures, while the fourth, 'Bluecoat', was only a partial success due to the poor early progress of XXX Corps. Both of the Canadian frontal attacks on the main German armour in front of Falaise were repulsed with heavy losses, and his biggest error of generalship was undoubtedly his failure to send fresh British divisions to reinforce the Canadian and Polish forces during the battle for Falaise.

In contrast, Bradley had enjoyed the glory both of the capture of Cherbourg, and of the spectacular break-out beyond St Lô and Avranches, so brilliantly exploited by Patton's Third Army. Yet Montgomery still had the satisfaction of knowing that his master plan to attract the German armour from the western sector and keep it in front of the British and Canadians had been a major contribution to victory, although it rankled with him that he never got the glamour of his longed-for armoured break-out by Second Army into the open country beyond Caen.

It is wrong to argue, as some have done, that Eisenhower never understood Montgomery's plan to draw Rommel's armour to the east to facilitate the break-out in the west. In fact, he understood it perfectly, but he overestimated the difficulties of the bocage for the American advance, and was worried by the US Government's insistence – in an election year – that casualties and sacrifices must be borne equally by the British and Americans. Besides this, he genuinely thought that Montgomery was over-cautious, and accepted, too readily, the continual complaints of senior British and American officers at SHAEF about slow progress.

Bradley, whose relations with Montgomery were good throughout the Normandy campaign, appreciated that the latter's master plan had worked well; no flatterer, he wrote after the war: 'Montgomery bossed the USA First Army with wisdom, tolerance and restraint ... I could not have wanted a more tolerant or judicious commander'.[37] Sadly, however, fierce disputes between the two generals were to flare up before Hitler was defeated.

Unfortunately, by the time the battle for Normandy was over Eisenhower had lost much of his confidence in Montgomery, mainly because his performance fell so short of his promises, and because he never produced proper explanations or excuses. If only Montgomery had consulted Eisenhower regularly about his plans a good working relationship might have been achieved. But Montgomery would never visit the Supreme Commander, nor would he let him know the reasoning behind his plans. He despised Eisenhower both as a strategist and as a commander in the field, and thus thought it not worth while wasting time on him – Bill Williams told me that throughout the campaign Montgomery kept saying: 'Ike is no battle general'. Unhappily, both Grigg and Brooke fostered this arrogance. Montgomery knew that these two powerful and influential figures, prodded by Simpson, would always back his decisions, as he also knew that, after their one serious disagreement, Churchill was on his side.

This conduct towards Eisenhower was inexcusable, and was naturally, and rightly, resented by the Supreme Commander. As a result, once Bradley took charge of his own Army Group there was no proper Allied chain of command. There was no considered examination of the wisdom of overrunning Brittany with strong forces while von Kluge's army remained undefeated further north. (Here Churchill further confused the issue by wanting, unreasonably, to switch 'Anvil' from the South of France to the still uncaptured Brittany ports, coining an absurd phrase: 'Why batter down the back door when we have the key to the front?') Perhaps most serious of all, the opportunity to close the Falaise gap and encircle more of the German army was also bungled by the Allies because of lack of co-ordination.

It is possible that if Eisenhower, as was strongly urged by Marshall, had himself taken command of the closing stages of the Normandy battles these mistakes would have been avoided, although making quick decisions was not his strong point. By then the Supreme Commander not only disliked Montgomery but was also frightened of him; he knew he could not rely upon his difficult subordinate to carry out the orders given to him. Yet Eisenhower baulked at a showdown with the hero of El Alamein, so immensely popular with the British people, although Tedder and Morgan, and his top American advisers, tried hard to get him to make a bid for Montgomery's dismissal.

Montgomery evidently envisaged the Supreme Commander as a figurehead in the background while he, in consultation with Bradley, made the plans and took the decisions. How deeply Eisenhower resented this bid to usurp his position is shown by a statement which he issued in the middle of August:

> No major effort takes place in this theatre by ground, sea or air, except with my approval, and no-one in the Allied Command presumes to question my supreme authority and responsibility for the whole campaign.[38]

Yet however unequivocal such statements, and however much his role was cut down to size, Montgomery felt strongly that *he* ought to be in sole command of the land battle, and that *he* was supremely qualified for the task. Brooke, Grigg and Churchill are greatly to blame for encouraging him in his attempts to assume a mantle of command which was not his.

The enmity and lack of communication between Montgomery and Eisenhower, coupled with the jealous hostility shown towards the British general by the forceful George Patton led, after Normandy, to strategic errors and misunderstandings which prolonged the war into 1945, with disastrous results for the future of Europe.

5

Eisenhower Takes Command

The American Government had always made it clear that Eisenhower, the Supreme Commander, must take over personal charge of the land operations in Europe once the assault and break-out phases were over; in this, Churchill had acquiesced. In the Mediterranean theatre in 1943, Alexander had been in sole charge of land operations as Deputy Supreme Commander under Eisenhower, but once Montgomery was chosen, in preference to Alexander, to command the Normandy assault, there was no chance of there being a British commander for the whole European campaign. Both Marshall and Eisenhower knew too well that Montgomery's personality would only be acceptable to the American generals for a short period—sooner or later there would be friction and, since Germany could not be conquered without the US Army, it was vital that the Supreme Commander should be acceptable to that army's generals. By way of consolation, Churchill promoted Montgomery Field-Marshal with effect from 1 September.

At the 12 January St Paul's Conference to co-ordinate 'Overlord' plans, Bradley had, as we have seen, queried Montgomery's 'commanding' both armies for the invasion; according to the American Maj-Gen Lewis Brereton, Montgomery had replied: 'I will command the British and Canadian troops but I will suggest to Bradley the scheme of manoeuvre for American troops.'[1] In practice however, he had gone much further and Bradley, appreciating both the clarity of his mind and his confidence in the plan to draw Rommel's armour to the east in order to allow an American break-out in the west, had accepted Montgomery's orders up to the time of the break-out.

The agreement was that once US Twelfth Army Group became operational under Bradley, Eisenhower would be in direct control of the land forces and Montgomery and Bradley would be equals. Eisenhower was reluctant to take over direct command too soon, mainly because of the difficulty of setting up his HQ in the constricted, battle-torn part of France available. He therefore decided to make US Twelfth Army Group operational before he moved to France and took over the reins; Montgomery remained in overall command of the land forces; however, and would do so until Eisenhower arrived.

Since the failure of 'Goodwood', there had been so much gossip about the likelihood òf Montgomery being sacked amongst senior officers at SHAEF and amongst the American field commanders that the war correspondents got wind of it. When, on 14 August, Eisenhower announced that Bradley was to command US Twelfth Army Group in accordance with the prearranged plan, inaccurate messages from journalists stating that Bradley would in future be taking orders direct from Eisenhower, and that Montgomery had been superseded, slipped past the censors. These reports originated on 15 August with a telegram from an American journalist in France, Wes Gallaher, saying that Montgomery and Bradley now had equal status. Gallaher later said that he obtained his information from staff officers at Patton's Third Army HQ, though here the wish may have been father to the thought, for Patton and his staff were the most hostile to Montgomery. Gallaher sent his message to the Associated Press news agency in London, and from there it was both relayed to America and put out on the nine o'clock BBC news. The BBC corrected it on the midnight news, but the early editions of the London nationals carried the story. On 16 August *Stars and Stripes*, the American servicemen's paper, carried the headline: 'Bradley Heads Army Group. Status Equal to Monty.'[2]

The confusion arising from these misapprehensions was disconcerting to Montgomery, just at the moment when the creation of Twelfth Army Group meant that he had less overall control of the battle.

The *Daily Mirror*'s leader on 18 August was vicious. Although it insisted that Montgomery was entitled to an apology, it made it clear that there was controversy about his leadership:

For some time past various statements which we need not particularise have been circulating about him, and these seemed to coalesce into something more than rumour when on Tuesday Reuter's special correspondent reported that Ike had taken over and Bradley was equal with Monty. This was denied by SHAEF at 2250. What is behind this confusing alternation of official assertion and contradiction we do not know ... something is clearly wrong which must have an adverse effect on the harmony of Anglo-American co-operation in the field.

The Chief Press Officer at SHAEF informed Washington that the *Daily Mirror* was 'not the most reputable of London newspapers'.

On the next day, SHAEF's Public Relations Department strongly denied that the activation of Twelfth Army Group gave Bradley and Montgomery equal status; it did not, however, make it clear that this equality would be achieved shortly. Meanwhile, London newspapers deplored Montgomery's 'demotion'.

The *Washington Times Herald*, however, wrote about 'British dominance of the Expeditionary Force', and the general tone of the American press was a complaint that the British held the principal command and that Eisenhower was little more than a figurehead. Marshall, angered by these comments, told Eisenhower on 17 August:

Stimson and I and apparently all Americans are strongly of the opinion that the time has come for you to assume direct command of the American contingent because reaction to British criticism has been so strong by USA journalists that it could become an important factor in the coming Congressional Elections. The astonishing success has produced emphatic expressions of confidence in you and Bradley, but this has cast a damper on the public enthusiasm.

Eisenhower, by now on the brink of assuming direct control of the land battle, as soon as he could set up his HQ in France, had no intention of taking command of just the 'American contingent', but he was irked by the credit given to Montgomery in the London newspapers which, since they held Montgomery to be responsible for all ground operations, acclaimed him as the tactical genius responsible for the victory.

The bickering about status and credit was, however, about to end, albeit temporarily. A suitable site for Eisenhower's HQ was found at Juleiville, close to the port of Granville and within sight of German-held Jersey. (German troops in Jersey staged a successful raid on Granville in the last few weeks of the war, but long after Eisenhower had left.) On 1 September SHAEF became operational at Granville, and Eisenhower, not Montgomery, was now in full charge of the land battle.

It was the day on which Montgomery assumed the rank of Field-Marshal, but this was cold comfort for him. He longed to retain command. Bill Williams told me that his chief hoped until the last moment that Eisenhower would leave him in overall command after 1 September; he would not believe Williams when he said: 'You can never command now. The numbers are such that it must be an American victory.'

Eisenhower and Montgomery had been more or less in agreement over the fundamental strategy for the assault and the break-out, but now they clashed head-on over plans for future operations once the Seine was crossed. Eisenhower wanted the two Army Groups, each under its own C-in-C, to advance towards Germany north and south of the Ardennes, under his sole overall command. Montgomery, strongly backed by the British Chiefs of Staff, wanted both Army Groups to advance north of the Ardennes under his sole command. There began a quarrel which lasted until the end of the war. This controversy – and the tactless way in which Montgomery handled it – led to a lasting enmity between himself and Eisenhower, and this in turn had an adverse effect on Anglo-American relations.

Montgomery and Brooke failed to realise that, for political reasons, it was no longer possible for Eisenhower to give a British general overall command of the American troops, since by now they so greatly outnumbered the British; nor did they understand that US generals might refuse to serve under a British colleague. So Montgomery continually bullied the Supreme Commander in an effort to force him to change his mind. His egotism, and his belief – assiduously fostered by the CIGS – that he was a better strategist than Eisenhower made him blind to prevailing circumstances, and the rest of the campaign was darkened by his disputes with the American.

On 17 August Montgomery had discussed future policy with Bradley. For some unexplained reason he had come away with the impression that Bradley agreed with his plan for a single thrust on the north front with a combined British and American force of forty divisions. In fact Bradley had already cooked up a quite different plan in consultation with Patton. This telegram of 18 August to Brooke reveals Montgomery's thinking, and his misapprehension about Bradley's opinion:

> Have been thinking ahead about future plans but have not (repeat not) discussed subject with Ike. My views are as follows. After crossing Seine 12 and 21 Army Groups should keep together as a solid mass of some 40 divisions which would be so strong that it need fear nothing. The force should move northwards. 21st Army Group should be on Western flank and should clear the channel coast and the Pas de Calais and West Flanders and secure Antwerp. The American armies should move with right flank on Ardennes directed on Brussels, Aachen and Cologne. The movement of American armies would cut the communications of enemy forces on channel coast and thus facilitate the task of British Army Group. The initial objects of movement would be to destroy German forces on coast and to establish a powerful air force in Belgium. A further object would be to get enemy out of V-1 or V-2 range of England. Bradley agrees entirely with above conception. Would be glad to know if you agree generally. When I have got your reply will discuss matter with Ike.

On the 19th Eisenhower informed his two Army Group commanders that he would soon take over command of the land battle; at the same time he made it clear that he wanted to cross the Seine 'on the run'. He directed Montgomery to strike northeast towards Antwerp and from there to the Ruhr, while Bradley was to advance from Paris towards Metz. Montgomery took a different view, and told Eisenhower that he wanted the Allies to concentrate by sending as large a force as possible towards Antwerp, under his command. They would then, he thought, be able both to clear the V-bomb sites and open up Antwerp as a supply port.

Shortly before Eisenhower's signal arrived, Bradley had informed Montgomery that 'Ike wants to split his force and send half of it eastwards', that is, away from the Pas de Calais and Antwerp. He did not, however, tell Montgomery that he favoured this plan. On 20 August Montgomery issued his Directive M520. He still had another eleven days as nominal overall commander, but now he had to be careful to agree his orders with Bradley and Eisenhower. He told the CIGS: 'I have so worded my directive that we shall retain the ability to act in any direction.' M520 ordered Bradley's right wing to 'assemble to the west and south west of Paris but not to take the city until the Supreme Commander decides it is a sound military proposition.' After Paris Bradley would advance to the general line Orleans-Troyes-Rheims-Amiens so that his forces could 'operate north east towards Brussels and Aachen with or without a portion directed due east to Saar.' But Bradley and Patton had no intention of going towards Brussels. They had plans to win the war on their own, by an advance straight into Germany far to the south.

On 22 August Montgomery sent de Guingand to Eisenhower with a memorandum which, with customary egotism, assured the Supreme Commander that the victory to date had been won by 'personal command'; it continued: 'The force must operate as one whole ... Single control ... is vital for success. This is a *whole time* job for one man.' Montgomery considered that the results of the Normandy campaign gave him an inalienable right to this privilege.

The memorandum was dictated on the 22nd, and was intended to serve as a brief for de Guingand in his talk with Eisenhower. There is no evidence that the tactful de Guingand ever showed it to the Supreme Commander, but Montgomery gave a copy to the Vice-CIGS, Lt-Gen Sir Archibald Nye, who visited him on the same day, Brooke being in Italy. It displays Montgomery's supreme confidence in himself, and his belief that this confidence should be shared by everyone else:

1. The quickest way to win this war is for the great mass of the Allied armies to advance northwards, clear the coast as far as Antwerp, establish a powerful air force in Belgium, and advance into the Ruhr.

2. The force must operate as one whole, with great cohesion, and so strong that it can do the job quickly.
3. Single control and direction of the land operation is vital for success. This is a *whole time* job for one man.
4. The great victory in N.W. France has been won by personal command. Only in this way will future victories be won. If staff control of operations is allowed to creep in, then quick success becomes endangered.
5. To change the system of command now, after having won a great victory, would be to prolong the war.[3]

Undoubtedly he had overlooked the fact that all the commanders considered the war to be nearly won, and that the Americans wanted as much glamour for themselves as possible.

For two hours de Guingand pressed Montgomery's case with Eisenhower, but found him adamant, although good-humoured. The SHAEF planners had decided, without consulting Montgomery, that they wanted 'a broad front both north and south of the Ardennes', and Eisenhower backed them to the full. He pointed out that it had always been agreed that he would take personal charge as soon as there were two army groups operating, and he added that now there were more Americans in the field than British and Canadians.

Montgomery was disappointed when de Guingand got back and told him of Eisenhower's reaction. In an attempt to sway the American himself, he invited Eisenhower for lunch on the next day, 23 August, at his Tac HQ, now in an apple orchard at Condé-sur-Noireau. At first light on the 23rd Montgomery flew to Laval to meet Bradley. He was seeking to persuade his fellow commander to lend US First Army for the northern drive,[4] and to halt Patton's Third Army so that Twenty-First Army Group could have the major share of road transport. He was still confident that Bradley would agree. Instead, Bradley, who had already consulted with Patton, surprised Montgomery by declaring that he favoured making the major Allied drive south of the Ardennes. He had already promised Patton two extra divisions 'for a push to the Siegfried Line', and he now told Montgomery that US First and Third Armies ought to advance through the middle of France to the River Saar and, once over it, to the Rhine near Frankfurt. Montgomery was aghast. If this plan was operated there would be such a shortage of transport for his own troops that he would play only a minor part in what, at that time, he expected to be the swift overrunning of Germany.

He was almost desperate when he got back to his own HQ to meet Eisenhower for lunch, and he was determined to swing the Supreme Commander round to his point of view either by threats or advocacy, for neither of which tasks was he well suited by temperament. Eisenhower dreaded the meeting. He disliked having to decide between conflicting views, since his preferred method of operation was to arrive at agreed, albeit compromise, decisions after committee-type consultations with his subordinates. He knew on 23 August that three choices were open to him: first, a broad-front approach with equipment and supplies rationed equally between Bradley's and Montgomery's Army Groups; second, concentration on a southern drive by the US armies; and third, Montgomery's plan for an all-out thrust in the north, with US First Army and the bulk of supplies allocated to the British commander. Eisenhower was well aware that this last alternative would infuriate the American generals, some of whom might even resign, and also that it was unacceptable to the American Government.

Even before the discussion began, however, Eisenhower had realised that there were merits in Montgomery's plan – SHAEF Administration kept on emphasising the need to capture other Channel ports nearer to Germany and, having been in London himself, he was acutely conscious of the dire threat to Britain from the V-bombs (several V1s had fallen close to him and had lost him a lot of sleep). Churchill had repeatedly impressed upon him the paramount need to overrun the launching sites since there was no possible defence against the V2s, and Allied intelligence had learned from Ultra and other sources that these were about to be launched against London. The V2s were rocket-powered ballistic missiles capable of rising to an altitude of sixty miles and falling at some five times the speed of sound – their 1-ton warheads caused considerable damage and casualties. The only way to stop them was to capture their launching sites. A fortnight after D-Day Churchill had said that he would not allow the V1s to interfere with the plans for the battle of Normandy, but now he emphasised to Eisenhower that the V2s were another matter.

Montgomery had little idea that these factors were already weighing upon Eisenhower's mind. He planned to railroad a reluctant Supreme Commander into accepting his point of view by a combination of military arguments and his own strong personality and reputation as a battle-winning general.

Bedell Smith arrived with Eisenhower but, to the latter's indignation, Montgomery insisted on excluding him from the conference, although he retained de Guingand. Montgomery began the meeting with a lecture in his usual Staff College style. Then, after describing his plan and the supply back-up it would need, he remarked that 'The immediate need is for a firm and sound plan,' and asserted that if Eisenhower's plan was followed it would lead to 'failure' — 'You must not descend into the land battle and become a ground C-in-C. The Supreme Commander must sit on a lofty perch to be able to take a detached view of the whole intricate problem which involves land, sea, air, civil control and political problems, and someone else must run the battle for him.' Eisenhower replied that both because of his instructions from Washington and of American public opinion, he had no alternative but to take command of the land battle. At this point Montgomery realised that his retention of overall command was a lost cause. Almost desperately, he told Eisenhower that he was willing to serve under Bradley because it was so vital that there should be unified control. The American interrupted him, however, saying that the argument was at an end and that he, Eisenhower would definitely assume personal control on 1 September.

Frustrated in his attempts to resolve the command controversy, Montgomery now tackled Eisenhower again over plans. He asked for Patton to be halted, and for all his US Third Army's supplies to be cut off and transferred to Twenty-First Army Group for its advance. He also asked for the use of First Airborne Army (the SHAEF strategic reserve) and for US First Army to be put under his command for the drive to Antwerp, explaining that he would have to shed the Canadians en route in order to capture the Channel ports, where the Germans had left strong garrisons. His arguments were, however, weakened to a certain extent because the British forces crossed the Seine four days behind Patton,[5] a cause for unfavourable comparison.

After an hour's argument Eisenhower conceded some points to Montgomery not so much because he was impressed with the cogency of the latter's arguments, but because he had come to the conference with his mind partly made up to give temporary priority to the northern drive because of the importance of capturing ports and overrunning the V2 launching sites.

Finally, the Supreme Commander told Montgomery that he would issue a SHAEF directive giving Twenty-First Army Group the task of pushing on to Antwerp, and thence eastwards to the Ruhr. Bradley would be ordered to advance on Montgomery's right, his 'principal offensive mission' being to support the British commander. Montgomery would be given First Airborne Army (consisting of one British and two US airborne divisions), and also the 'authority to effect the necessary operational co-ordination' between his right and US First Army.

An exasperated Montgomery expressed his frustrations, with his usual clarity, in a letter he dictated to Brooke as soon as Eisenhower had left his caravan:

Ike came to see me today. After a long and weary discussion he agreed on our left flank we must clear the channel coast and establish a powerful Air Force in Belgium and invade Ruhr. He also considers it necessary to invade Saar and would like to split the force. After further discussion he agreed that left flank movement must be strong enough to achieve quick success and it was then suggested there would not (repeat not) be enough left over for Saar operations at present. The problem of Command and control was then discussed. It seems public opinion in America demands Bradley shall hold his command directly under Ike and shall not be (repeat not be) subordinated to me. I said that left flank operations into Belgium and beyond would require careful coordination and control and that one Commander must do this. This was finally agreed. Bedell came with Ike but I insisted that Ike must settle big points with me alone and Bedell was excluded. They have now both gone off to draft a directive as a result of our conversation. I think discussion was valuable and cleared the air and there is a good hope that directive will be what is wanted. The draft is to be shown to me before it is issued. It has been a very exhausting day.

On the next day, 24 August, Eisenhower wrote to

Montgomery summing up their discussion; a copy was sent to Bradley.

Confirming our conversation of yesterday, the necessary directive will soon be issued to outline the general missions of the two Army Groups. It will be very brief, giving the Army Group of the North the task of operating north-east, in the area generally to the westward of Amiens-Lille, destroying the enemy forces on its front, seizing the Pas de Calais area and airfields in Belgium, and pushing forward to get a secure base at Antwerp. Its eventual mission will be to advance eastwards on the Ruhr. By the time Antwerp is reached the general strength and composition of the forces needed for the later task will have been determined.

Bradley's Army Group will be directed to thrust forward on its left, with its principal offensive mission, for the moment, to support the Army Group of the North in the attainment of the objectives noted above. He will likewise be directed to clean up the Brittany Peninsula as rapidly as possible, protect against any threat against our communications from the general area of Paris, and to begin building up, out of incoming forces, the necessary strength to advance eastward from Paris towards Metz.

You, as Commanding General of the Army Group of the North will be given the authority to effect the necessary operational co-ordination between your advancing forces and Bradley's left wing. Mechanical details for effecting this will be left to you and Bradley.

We must immediately prepare definite plans for the employment of the entire airborne force so as to speed up the accomplishment of the missions that you must attain rapidly in the north-east. Unless we use the Airborne Army, assuming it is practicable to do so, we will not be using all available assets and there would be no excuse for insisting upon the deployment of the major part of Bradley's strength on his extreme left.

Bradley is coming to see you this morning with instructions to bend every effort toward speeding up the deployment of his forces in that direction. The faster we do it the more certain will be our success and the earlier will come our opportunity to advance eastward from the Paris area.

All of us having agreed upon the general plan, the principal thing we must now strive for is speed in execution. All of the Supply people have assured us they can support the move, beginning this minute – let us assume that they know exactly what they are talking about and get about it vigorously and without delay.[6]

Unhappily, the letter was imprecise and woolly. For while it looked as if Montgomery would get the Airborne Army, as well as a measure of co-operation, Bradley and Patton wickedly interpreted it as meaning they could attack east towards Germany, although Eisenhower had stated Twelfth Army Group's 'principal offensive mission' as being to thrust forward on its left to support Montgomery's north-easterly drive to Antwerp. On 25 August Bradley ordered Patton 'to prepare to advance rapidly to seize crossings of the Rhine from Mannheim to Koblenz.' US Third Army's general was desperately keen to advance into Germany; to him, the word 'prepare' meant an immediate dash forward, thus effecting the two-front attack which Montgomery had persuaded Eisenhower, at least temporarily, to avoid.

Montgomery himself felt that Eisenhower's letter was a far cry from his own demands, but decided to make the best of it by interpreting its loose writing in his own favour. He wrote to Brooke as soon as he had received the letter:

Ike has now decided on his line of action. His directive to me is about all that I think I can get him to do at present. Ike has agreed that we must occupy the Pas de Calais and get possession of Belgian airfields and then prepare to move eastwards into Ruhr and he has given this mission to 21st Army Group. He has ordered 12 Army Group to thrust forward its left with what it can spare to assist 21st Army Group in carrying out its tasks and for this some six to eight U.S. divisions will possibly be available. The remainder 12th Army Group is to clear up Brittany and then assemble east of Paris. Eventually the whole 12th Army Group is to move eastwards from Paris towards Metz and the Saar. Ike is taking command himself of 12th and 21st Army Groups on 1st Sep. He has given me power to co-ordinate action of forces being used for northward drive to the Pas de Calais and Belgium including those divisions 12th Army Group which [word omitted?] taking part in this movement.

You will see that instead of moving combined might of two army groups northwards into Belgium and then eastwards into Germany via the Ruhr Ike proposes to split the force and to move American portion eastwards from Paris and into Germany via the Saar. I do not (repeat not) myself agree what he proposes to do and have said so quite plainly. I consider that directive which is being issued by Ike is the best that I can do myself in matter and I do not (repeat not) propose to continue argument with Ike. The great point is that I have been given power to co-ordinate and control movement of left wing northward towards Antwerp and Belgium.

Montgomery's hopes were to be disappointed, however, for the six to eight US divisions were to prove to be only a pipe dream. He would not, in any case, have interpreted Eisenhower's letter so favourably as he did if he could have seen what the Supreme Commander wrote on the same day to Marshall in Washington: 'I have TEMPORARILY changed my basic plan of attacking both to the north and east in order to help Montgomery seize tremendously important objectives in the north east.' He added that he considered the changes to be necessary, even though they interfered with his desire to push east through Metz, because Twenty-First Army Group had insufficient strength for its task: 'I do not doubt [he continued] 12 Army Group's ability to reach the Franco German border but see no point in doing so until we are in a position to do something about it.'*

There had been nothing about the plan being 'temporary' in Eisenhower's letter to Montgomery. But now SHAEF planners immediately began to study ways of transferring a corps from First Army to help Patton towards the Saar and the Rhine. The Supreme Commander was running both with the hounds and the hare; in supporting Bradley he was deceiving Montgomery, for his logistical situation did not permit of two major advances

---

* This message from Eisenhower to Marshall is quoted in Pogue, *The Supreme Command*, page 251, and Ellis, *Victory in the West*, but is omitted from the printed Eisenhower Papers.

into Germany simultaneously. Unable to satisfy both his Army Group commanders he refused to come down firmly on one side or the other. In the end, this lack of definition was to be a major cause of the prolongation of the war into 1945. Montgomery, however, by coupling his demands for a single thrust with a request that he himself should be put in full charge, had spoilt his own case.

On 28 August the British Chiefs of Staff met to discuss Eisenhower's proposed strategy, and decided that it was unsound. Brooke commented that 'This plan is likely to add three to six months on to the war', although he admitted that if Montgomery were to have operational control of US First Army, as seemed to have been agreed, then all might still be well.

Eisenhower did not issue his all important directive until 29 August. In the four days since his letter to Montgomery he had partially changed his mind after discussions with Bradley, who objected to giving control of US First Army to Montgomery, as did the SHAEF planners including the British Lt-Gen Sir Frederick Morgan, Maj-Gen Kenneth Strong, and Maj-Gen John Whiteley. The best that Montgomery would now have was 'authority to effect' any necessary co-ordination with First Army.

Meanwhile, Patton and Bradley had taken the law into their own hands, sabotaging the plan Eisenhower had agreed with Montgomery on 23 August. On the 26th, the day after his order from Bradley to advance to Rheims and prepare 'to seize crossings of the Rhine from Mannheim to Koblenz', Patton raced forward to the Meuse, which he crossed on 30 August. He was thus already 100 miles east of Paris and the same distance from the Rhine. But his sudden dash had used up all his petrol, for Eisenhower had given priority in American petrol deliveries to US First Army, which was to support Montgomery. Bradley and Patton were deliberately wrecking the Eisenhower plan, placing their divisions in positions where, to avoid disaster, Eisenhower would have to divert petrol earmarked for the priority northern thrust.

One of the chief problems at this time was that nearly all the senior commanders thought that the war was won; they all wanted to obtain the greatest possible glamour out of the final defeat of the Nazi armies. In the prevailing euphoria Montgomery was perhaps the most realistic, but neither British nor Americans believed that Hitler could stage a dramatic recovery which would extend the war until May 1945.

On 27 August, just as Patton's Third Army ran out of petrol and it looked as if he would have to halt his XII Corps, he captured 100,000 gallons of German petrol at Sens. He did not report the find, but instead sent his tanks advancing again, thus creating a yet more imperative need for supplies allocated to, and coveted by, Montgomery. US Third Army found two similar caches of German petrol on 29 August and 3 September, and, after reading its commander's over-optimistic signals about the prospects of his army's reaching the Rhine, Eisenhower changed his mind again and diverted 250,000 gallons of petrol to Patton on 5 September, and during the next three days another 1,400,000 gallons. Thus Patton was able to continue his onward progress towards Germany against light opposition. Both he and Bradley knew that transport and supplies would simply have to be diverted to them to keep them operational and, in their jealousy of Montgomery, this was exactly the state of affairs they were seeking.

On 2 September Eisenhower, Bradley and Patton held a conference at Chartres. The Supreme Commander reiterated that, because he needed to capture the Channel ports and the V2 sites, he must give priority in supplies to Montgomery. Patton protested strongly, and was supported by Bradley. As usual, Eisenhower compromised, and Patton recorded: 'We finally persuaded Ike to let V Corps of First Army and Third Army go on and attack the Siegfried Line as soon as the Calais area was stabilised. Eisenhower was impressed with the thought of a great battle in Germany. I finally got permission to cross the Moselle.'[7] Eisenhower's response to his two generals at Chartres was weak, and by permitting Patton to move so far towards Germany he seriously endangered his overall plan. With each mile that Patton's Third Army advanced towards the Siegfried Line the greater became the likelihood that it would be involved in heavy fighting, which would require resources of petrol and ammunition at the expense of the northern drive.

Patton and Bradley believed that they could cut through the Panzer divisions which Hitler was sending to their front before these had time to establish a defensive line. They hoped that their armies could then 'punch' into Germany, and thus bring the war to a swift and successful conclusion. It is certainly possible that they were right, but Eisenhower's decision to give them sufficient petrol for limited advances but not for a decisive battle proved to be the worst of both worlds. Patton called it 'the most momentous error of the war', because he was so certain of victory if he continued his push. It was indeed a 'momentous error', for it sealed the fate of both the southern and the northern assaults.

Bradley reinforced Patton with French 2nd Armoured and US 79th Infantry Divisions, taking them out of First Army. This so weakened First Army that it could not keep pace with Montgomery's advance on its left flank. By 10 September Patton had established two small bridgeheads over the Moselle south of Metz, but Third Army was then stopped dead by German reinforcements moved in by Hitler. Hodges's First Army had crossed the Meuse almost without opposition, and on 10 September he was approaching the Siegfried Line on a broad front between Aachen and Trier. But because of the removal of his two divisions, and because of supply difficulties, he was forced to turn right on to Patton's flank, instead of covering Montgomery on the left in his drive for the Ruhr. By dissipating his resources – against Montgomery's advice – and pandering to Patton and Bradley, Eisenhower had missed his chance of delivering a knock-out blow to Germany by thrusting enormously strong forces into the Ruhr from the north. Such an opportunity would not recur for months.

6

Over the Seine

Now let us see how Montgomery's troops fared after the battle of the Falaise Gap. On 26 August Montgomery issued his final directive (M520) as commander (or, perhaps better put at this stage, 'co-ordinator') of Twenty-First Army Group and Twelfth Army Group. His intention was for Twenty-First Army Group 'to destroy all enemy forces in the Pas de Calais and Flanders and to capture Antwerp ... to advance eastwards on to the Ruhr.' Allied First Airborne Army would be dropped in the Pas de Calais, while British Second Army was to cross the Seine with all speed and, irrespective of the progress of other armies on the flank, secure the area Amiens-St Pol-Arras, with a strong force of armour making a dash for Amiens.

In consultation with Bradley, Montgomery fixed the boundary between the two Army Groups as Mantes-Gassicourt – Beauvais – Albert – Douai – Antwerp, the American force having been ordered by Eisenhower 'to thrust forward on its left, with its principal offensive mission, for the moment, to support [Twenty-First Army Group] in the attainment of its objectives ... ' Montgomery expanded on this: '21 Army Group is employing First US Army for this task. It is to advance north-east on the general axis Paris-Brussels and establish itself in the area Brussels-Maastricht-Liege-Namur-Charleroi.' Wisely, he issued no directive for Patton's Third Army, which was in any case now over the Somme and quite beyond his control – indeed, Patton had been authorised by Bradley on the day before to prepare to drive for the Rhine.

As we have seen, Bradley was not interested in looping US First Army to the north to aid Twenty-First Army Group's drive to Germany; consequently he ignored Directive M520. His sights were firmly fixed on the Siegfried Line and a triumphant advance with Patton to the Rhine, well to the south and out of Montgomery's way. Ominously, Bradley asked Montgomery three days later (29 August) to include Brussels in the British boundary, and the latter had to agree; this meant that US First Army would stay further to the east.

On 25 August the Germans had surrendered Paris, not to the Americans, but to General Charles de Gaulle's provisional French Government. Patton's US Third Army and Hodges's US First Army had been approaching Paris as early as 19 August, but Eisenhower had not wanted to take the city because of the threat of its destruction, and because of the problems in feeding two million civilians. Instead, he wanted the American armies to encircle Paris and drive on for the German frontier.

With the Allied armies so close, Paris had risen in revolt against the Germans on 19 August, and on the next day the German Military Governor, Lt-Gen Dietrich von Choltitz, had asked the *résistants* for a truce until the 23rd. On 21 August de Gaulle had called on Eisenhower and asked him to send Leclerc's 2ème Division Blindée urgently into Paris. The Supreme Commander, after a day's agonised indecision, and without consulting Montgomery, ordered Leclerc, together with US 4th Division and a British contingent, to make for Paris. Leclerc, still 120 miles from the city on 22 August, urged his division forward throughout the next day, and entered Paris on the 24th. On 25 August von Choltitz surrendered formally to Leclerc. Hitler had ordered von Choltitz to reduce Paris to a 'field of ruins', like Warsaw, if the Resistance took to the streets. Fortunately von Choltitz, a cultured and civilised man, refused – though he would become a POW and be safe from Hitler's vengeance, his wife and family were still in Germany – and thanks to him Paris was spared.

Neither Montgomery nor Churchill had urged the Supreme Commander to send any British troops into Paris; Eisenhower afterwards agreed that he would have been much better advised to have left Paris to the Free French army alone, for de Gaulle flatly refused to hand over the city to the Americans, and in other ways caused difficulties. On 26 August de Gaulle ordered Leclerc to hold a victory parade in the Champs Elysées. Gerow, commanding US V Corps, told Leclerc to ignore this order and to send the French division in pursuit of the fleeing Germans. Leclerc refused to obey Gerow, however, and the parade was duly held. De Gaulle led the ceremony, rekindling the flame at the tomb of the Unknown Warrior, marching, after a four-year exile, in front of two million Frenchmen. It was both an historic and an emotional occasion, despite sporadic fire from German snipers which de Gaulle ignored completely.

Montgomery had been invited to attend the parade, but sensibly had refused.* Eisenhower, however, could not resist the temptation to have a look at the city, and asked Montgomery to meet him there on 26 August. Montgomery again refused – he had no interest in the liberation, in the architectural splendour, or in the fleshpots of Paris. The last soon became a paradise for rear echelon formations, and British and US supply service troops entered the black market in a big way. Montgomery's writ, however, no longer ran outside Twenty-First Army Group, which was unfortunate, since he would certainly have put a stop to the waste and corruption which sprang up among the Allied soldiers based in the city.

On 25 August, as Paris was liberated, Horrocks's XXX Corps began the British attack on the Seine at Vernon. Horrocks had been ill and out of action for nearly a week, and only resumed command a few hours after 43rd Division from his Corps crossed the Seine. Montgomery had been so concerned about Horrocks that he personally issued Maj-Gen Ivor Thomas, commanding 43rd Division, with his Seine attack orders, and had insisted that Horrocks should rest in a caravan placed next to his own at Tac HQ until the last possible moment before the attack. This is evidence of the faith Montgomery had in Horrocks, for he could have had the junior man invalided home. XXX Corps had been the laggards under Bucknall, but now Montgomery had chosen them to be the spearhead of a lightning advance, convinced that Horrocks's dash and charisma would produce the required results. In fact, it is arguable that Montgomery had made a mistake in bringing back

---

*Kit Dawnay told me that Eisenhower only invited Montgomery to Paris in a 'backhanded way which I [Dawnay] thought was rude and off-hand.' Montgomery, however, did not mind at all, for his thoughts were on other things. But he did instruct Dawnay to comment in the Log that 'the decision to enter Paris was undoubtedly premature and proved an embarrassment to the Allies for several days.'

Horrocks, because the latter's health broke down again in the crucial moments of the Arnhem battle.

For the crossing of the Seine, Montgomery had grounded VIII Corps at Vire and added all its transport to his general pool, so that Dempsey's Second Army now consisted of two corps, XII and XXX. Canadian First Army under Crerar, consisting of Canadian II Corps and British I Corps, was to cross the Seine west of Rouen and then attack along the coast, while Second Army made a dash for Brussels and Antwerp.

General Horrocks wrote in his memoirs:

On 29 August we burst out of the bridgehead on the Seine and set off on our chase northwards. This was the type of warfare I thoroughly enjoyed. I had upwards of 600 tanks ... and ... a frontage of fifty miles. Guards Armoured, 11th Armoured Divisions and 8th Armoured Brigade were scything passages through the enemy rear areas, like a combine-harvester going through a field of corn, with ... 50th Division clearing up the mess behind them.

In order to keep up with the battle, Horrocks took to a command tank, accompanied by three young officers; he did not see his Main Corps HQ for a week. On that first day XXX Corps advanced only twenty-nine miles, having started at dawn in torrential rain, but progress was faster on the 30th, and that evening Horrocks went to 11th Armoured Division HQ and ordered Pip Roberts to drive his division on through the night to capture the bridges over the Somme at Amiens, thirty miles further on, by first light on 1 September. 11th Armoured had already been on the move for thirty-six hours, but Horrocks's enthusiasm was infectious. By 0600 on 1 September Amiens was taken with some of its bridges unblown. During 11th Armoured's night advance the Nazi General Eberbach, now commanding Seventh Army, was captured with his Tac HQ, and SS General Sepp Dietrich, commanding Fifth Panzer Army, only narrowly escaped being taken. Horrocks described Eberbach as a 'scowling, unshaven and very ugly German officer dressed in black uniform', having been introduced to him at 11th Armoured HQ early in the morning – even a British general would not perhaps have been looking his best under the same circumstances. Eberbach gave valuable information to his interrogators, and agreed later to collaborate over negotiating a surrender.

On 3 September a 7th Armoured Division signals officer took a 'busman's holiday' in a Belgian telephone exchange. He managed to get a line through to Lille, and was told by the Belgian operator there that the Germans were pulling out. He then asked to be connected to Brussels and, on getting through, learned that the Germans had been moving out of the capital all day. The line was cut at 1930,[1] but by then the vital intelligence was being acted upon.

Horrocks lived up to Montgomery's expectations by quickening the pace, and during the night of 3 September British tanks rumbled into Brussels amid scenes of indescribable joy from the Belgians. The proud French had welcomed the British enthusiastically enough, but that had been tempered by the guilt many felt at their surrender to the Nazis in 1940. The Belgians, however, were uninhibited in their enthusiasm, and took their British liberators to their hearts. Queen Elisabeth the Queen Mother even offered her Palace of Laeken (where Napoleon had expected to sleep after the day of Waterloo) to Horrocks for his Corps HQ.

Next day, 4 September, Roberts sent his 11th Armoured Division triumphantly into Antwerp before the Germans could demolish the electrically operated sluice gates and cranes in the harbour. It seemed that the Allied armies, still operating on enormously extended supply lines from the Normandy beachhead, at last had their port.

But Montgomery now made a fundamental mistake. He ignored a signal from Ramsay, the SHAEF Naval Commander, which had been sent from Portsmouth to him and Eisenhower. Dated 3 September, the signal read:

> Both Antwerp and Rotterdam are highly vulnerable to mining and blocking. If enemy succeeds in these operations the time it will take to open ports cannot be estimated. It will be necessary for coastal batteries to be captured before approach channels to the river route can be established.[2]

The channel leading west from Antwerp to the sea is sixty-five miles long. German Fifteenth Army held both the south and north banks in strength, and their numerous and powerful guns dominated the water, so that no mine clearance could be undertaken. But Montgomery had fixed his sights on the Rhine and Germany, even though XXX Corps could have been turned left to seal off and defeat German Fifteenth Army to the west of Antwerp in early September, without heavy casualties. Montgomery gambled on his conviction that German resistance was crumbling so fast that the Allies could win the war without using Antwerp as a port of entry for supplies. As we shall see, no Allied ship entered Antwerp until 27 November; by then the full costliness of the mistake had been proved. The blame, however, is not all Montgomery's, for Eisenhower too had failed to appreciate the danger.

General Roberts told me:

Monty's failure at Antwerp is evidence again that he was not a good general at seizing opportunities. My thoughts, like Horrocks's and Monty's, on 4 September were east to the Rhine. We should have looked west towards Walcheren ... I made mistakes at Antwerp because I was not briefed that the Albert Canal was one of the most formidable obstacles in Europe. We only had small-scale maps, and I only saw it as a thin blue line on my map.

I heard the population of Antwerp were mobbing my troops, and tempting the officers into the best hotels. I decided not to go into the city because with my divisional flag on my tank I would have been drowned in champagne. During the celebrations in the town there was a considerable battle on the Albert Canal inside Antwerp, and we failed to capture the northern suburbs over the canal.

Unfortunately, I did not appreciate the significance of the fighting on the Albert Canal, and the Germans did not blow the crucial bridge for another twelve hours. If briefed before, I would have crossed the Albert Canal with tanks to the east of Antwerp and closed the Germans' route into Beveland and Walcheren.

At that time petrol was coming up regularly on lorries, and we saved space on lorries by not using much ammunition. I had enough petrol to continue my advance. Dempsey sent me a message: 'Push your recce north of the canal with armoured cars.' He did not realise we could not cross the Albert Canal so I had to tell him 'Message received but cannot comply.'

When I got near Antwerp none of Monty's liaison officers could possibly contact me. We were going too fast; Monty and Dempsey were many, many miles behind.

Horrocks himself wrote: 'If I had ordered Roberts, not to liberate Antwerp, but to by-pass the town on the east, cross the Albert Canal and advance only fifteen miles north-west towards Woensdrecht, we should have blocked the Beveland isthmus.' He was right, for as we shall see the Germans would not have been able to ferry Fifteenth Army troops over the Scheldt (which was to have disastrous results), and the port of Antwerp would have been usable far sooner. Worse still, on 4 September Montgomery ordered XXX Corps to halt for three days. It is true that some supplies were short (though according to Horrocks, on 3 September the corps still had 100 miles of petrol per vehicle) but he missed a marvellous opportunity to advance rapidly northwards on an enemy in near-rout; undoubtedly Patton in the same situation would have forged ahead.

The magnitude of the error was well summarised by Horrocks:

[The halt] was a tragedy because, as we now know, on the next day, 4th September, the only troops available to bar our passage northwards consisted of one German division, the 719th, composed mainly of elderly gentlemen who hitherto had been guarding the north coast of Holland and had never heard a shot fired in anger, plus one battalion of Dutch SS and a few Luftwaffe detachments. This meagre force was strung out on a fifty-mile front along the [Albert] canal.

To my mind 4th September was the key date in the battle for the Rhine. Had we been able to advance that day we could have smashed through this screen and advanced northwards with little or nothing to stop us. We might even have succeeded in bouncing a crossing over the Rhine. But we halted, and even by that same evening the situation was worsening.[3]

Hitler rushed troops, including Student's élite Parachute Army, to the Albert Canal, and by the time the attack was resumed on 7 September German resistance was strong, and

XXX Corps had great difficulty in securing bridgeheads over the canal.

Horrocks's book generously gives the impression that he was responsible for the stop at Antwerp, but this is incorrect. The decision was Montgomery's, and this is made clear by paragraph 6 of his Directive M523 of 3 September, which also demonstrates his extreme optimism about his proposed drive into Germany; plainly he anticipated low resistance on his route to the Rhine.

TOP SECRET
Copy No. 6
M523
3-9-44

21 Army Group
General Operational Situation and Directive

General Situation

1. Second Army is advancing to secure the area BRUSSELS-GHENT-ANTWERP. Its left Corps (12 Corps) is echelonned back to watch the left flank, until Canadian Army can get forward to the BRUGES area.
2. Canadian Army is moving forward, across the SOMME at ABBEVILLE, to its task of clearing the coastal belt.

Intention

3. (a) To advance eastwards and destroy all enemy forces encountered.
   (b) To occupy the RUHR, and get astride the communications leading from it into Germany and to the sea ports.

Forward Boundaries

4. All inclusive: 12 Army Group:
   WAVRE - TIRLEMONT - HASSELT - SITTARD - GARZWEILER - LEVERKUSEN (on the RHINE)
   All inclusive: 21 Army Group:

OPLADEN (on the RHINE) - WARBURG - BRUNSWICK

Canadian Army

5. Canadian Army will clear the coastal belt, and will then remain in the general area BRUGES-CALAIS until the maintenance situation allows of its employment further forward.

Second Army

6. On 6 September, the Army will advance eastwards with its main bodies from the general line BRUSSELS-ANTWERP. Before that date light forces will operate far afield, as desired.
7. The western face of the RUHR between DUSSELDORF and DUISBERG will be threatened frontally.
8. The main weight of the Army will be directed on the RHINE between WESEL and ARNHEM.
    The RUHR will be by-passed round its northern face, and cut off by a southward thrust through HAMM.
9. One division, or if necessary a Corps, will be turned northwards towards ROTTERDAM and AMSTERDAM.
10. Having crossed the RHINE, the Army will deal with the RUHR and will be directed on the general area OSNABRUCK-HAMM-MUNSTER-RHEINE.

Operations of 12 Army Group

11. First US Army is being directed to move its left forward in conjunction with the advance of 21 Army Group.
12. First US Army is directing its left two Corps (7 and 19) on:
    MAASTRICHT-LIEGE
    SITTARD-AACHEN
    COLOGNE-BONN
13. First US Army will assist in cutting off the RUHR by operations against its south-eastern face, if such action is desired by Second Army.

14. The Belgian and Dutch Contingents will be transferred at once from Canadian Army to Second Army.
15. The Armies of the Allies will soon be entering Germany; we shall then be in an enemy country, and must expect that the inhabitants will be hostile and possibly treacherous. Care will be necessary, and all officers and men will be warned to guard against spies, gestapo agents and treachery.

B.L. Montgomery

Field Marshal,
C-in-C,
21 Army Group.

Although it is not stated in this directive, Montgomery intended to use airborne troop drops in his advance to the Rhine. Even as news reached him on 4 September from XXX Corps that 3rd Royal Tank Regiment and 23rd Hussars, together with 8th Rifle Brigade, had entered Antwerp but had been unable to prevent harbour demolitions, a sure guide to the trouble that was to follow, Montgomery wrote to the CIGS: 'I intend to advance on Wesel and Arnhem (main Rhine bridges) and want to drop 1st British Airborne Divisions and Polish Airborne Brigade between Wesel and Arnhem.' So great was his optimism at this time that he wrote to Simpson that he expected to be in Berlin in two to three weeks.

There was by now considerable euphoria in the Allied camp. The then Brigadier Charles Richardson, BGS, Plans at Twenty-First Army Group HQ, sent the following signal from Main to Tac HQ on 11 September: 'If Germany should not surrender when Second Army reaches Osnabruck I suggest Arnhem is the most suitable location for our HQ after Brussels provided not destroyed in battle. If damaged I recommend we should move to either Munster or Bonn.'

General Richardson agrees that this was typical of the 'super-optimism' prevailing among senior officers in those few days after the giddy successes. After all, it was reasoned, the Kaiser had been overthrown in 1918, and the German armies had surrendered then when they had suffered nothing to equal the defeat in the west of 1944. Most people could not believe that the evil of Hitlerism had so entered the minds of the German people that they would fight until the bitter end, nor that the Führer would sacrifice his country in a vain effort to remain in power, with all his hopes pinned on his secret weapons being able to wipe out London and thus destroy the British ability to fight him. Hindsight is all too easy – these considerations must be borne in mind when passing any judgements on mistakes in strategy during this crucial short period.

On 3 September Maj-Gen Maxwell Taylor, GOC US 101st Airborne Division, rushed from the UK to Dempsey at Second Army HQ, to discuss with him the use of the airborne troops. He reported back to Lt-Gen Sir Frederick Browning (GOC I Airborne Corps and deputy commander of First Allied Airborne Army under US Lt-Gen Lewis H. Brereton) who held a conference at his Airborne Corps HQ at Moor Park, Hertfordshire, on the next day. There it was decided that 1st Airborne Division together with Polish 1 Parachute Brigade and 878th US Airborne Engineers were to crash land as close as possible to the bridges at Arnhem (Lower Rhine), Nijmegen (Waal) and Eindhoven (Wilhelmina Canal, north of the town), their landing areas having been marked first by the dropping of coloured smoke. The assault was to be similar to that which had resulted in the capture of Bénouville Bridge on D-Day, and the only criticism of the plan at this conference was that there might be heavy flak at Nijmegen.[4] This operation, known as 'Market-Garden Mark I', was planned for 8/9 September, that is, two days after the advance had started again from the Brussels-Antwerp line. The plan was abandoned by Montgomery almost as soon as it was made, however, because of the German resistance on the Albert Canal.

Montgomery stated in paragraph 8 of his 3 September directive that the weight of the army would concentrate on 'the Rhine between Wesel and Arnhem', but even at this stage his thoughts were already fixed on Arnhem bridge. This is interesting since, later, both Williams and Belchem considered that he should have made for Wesel.

On 4 September, having received Montgomery's directive, Horrocks stopped his Corps' triumphant march from the Seine with this jaunty signal: 'Top up tactically and administratively. Maximum economy petrol. Recce but not beyond 30 easting grid. Occupy Louvain. Recce but not across Dutch frontier. Major moves of main body for Guards Armoured and 11 Armoured unlikely before 7 September.'[5]

Montgomery was bent on by-passing German Fifteenth Army, and shooting straight on and over the Rhine. He might have been successful if he had continued on 4 September, but the three-day halt after that date gave the Germans their chance. For perhaps a day and a half Montgomery had an opportunity to push his armour into the almost undefended country up to the Rhine, but he delayed, and the cost of that delay was to be tragic.

By his heady advance from the Seine to Brussels and Antwerp in four days, Montgomery had proved that British armour could move as fast as American. The battlefields of the First World War had been crossed in hours, Belgium had been liberated, and the war seemed won. But with his troops short of supplies, Montgomery would take no chances, and he started a new polemic against Eisenhower, demanding priority in supplies for Twenty-First Army Group. On the afternoon of 4 September, after reading Eisenhower's directive dated that morning (which confirmed the decisions taken at his 2 September conference at Chartres with Patton and Bradley, and which agreed that Patton should continue his advance), Montgomery immediately drafted the following message to the Supreme Commander:

I would like to put before you certain aspects of future operations and give you my views.
1. I consider we have now reached a stage where one really powerful and full-blooded thrust towards Berlin is likely to get there and thus end the German war.
2. We have *not* enough maintenance resources for two full-blooded thrusts.
3. The selected thrust must have all the maintenance resources it needs without any qualification, and any other operation must do the best it can with what is left over.
4. There are only two possible thrusts: one via the Ruhr and the other via Metz and the Saar.
5. In my opinion the thrust likely to give the best and quickest results is the northern one via the Ruhr.
6. Time is vital and the decision regarding the selected thrust

must be made at once and para. 3 above will then apply.

7. If we attempt a compromise solution and split our maintenance resources so that neither thrust is full-blooded we will prolong the war.

8. I consider the problem viewed as above is very simple and clear cut.

9. The matter is of such vital importance that I feel sure you will agree that a decision on the above lines is required at once. If you are coming this way perhaps you would look in and discuss it. If so delighted to see you lunch tomorrow. Do *not* feel I can leave this battle just at present.[6]

This message was constructive, succinct and strong, if arrogant, but Eisenhower was determined to compromise, regardless of Montgomery's warning in paragraph 7 that this would prolong the war. Like many others, Eisenhower believed at the time that Hitler was beaten – he had no idea that new German armies were being created. In an office memorandum dated 5 September, written before Montgomery's signal arrived, Eisenhower wrote: 'The defeat of the German armies is now complete and the only thing needed to realise the conception is speed ... I deem it important to get Patton moving once again so that we may be fully prepared to carry out the original conception for the final stages of this campaign.' Such a course was the last thing that Montgomery wanted.

Significantly, the Supreme Commander added:

Two weeks ago when General Montgomery insisted upon a whole American Army moving to the north east on his right flank I told him he did not need that much strength to destroy the Germans still on his front. With his usual caution he felt it imperative that we make certain of no halt in operations towards Antwerp and Brussels ... I directed the First Army to advance closely along the boundary of the 21 Army Group. This forced Patton to stand still to the south east of Paris with his main bodies pushing only reconnaissances to the front.

This is clear evidence of Eisenhower's resentment at having to pander to Montgomery and thus hold up the American advance. Note that he forgot to write 'Field-Marshal'.

Because communications with SHAEF at Granville were so

bad, Montgomery did not receive a full reply to his signal of 4 September until the morning of the 7th, by which time he felt that he had built up sufficient supplies to start his troops moving on from Antwerp. On 5 September Eisenhower had signalled that it was essential to open the ports of Le Havre and Antwerp 'to sustain a powerful thrust into Germany', and that, while the offensive towards the Ruhr would always have priority, it was his intention 'initially to occupy the Saar and the Ruhr and by the time we have done this Havre and Antwerp should be available to maintain a deeper thrust into Germany.' This message incensed Montgomery, who considered that his lightning advance had so disorganised the Germans that he could push on to Berlin, if only Patton's transport and petrol were diverted to Twenty-First Army Group.

His reply was dated 7 September:

Have just received paras. 3 and 4 of your message of 5 September. First part of message has not arrived yet so do not know what it contains. My maintenance is stretched to the limit. First instalment of 18 locomotives only just released to me and balance still seems uncertain. I require an air lift of 1000 tons a day at Douai or Brussels and in last two days have had only 750 tons total. My transport is based on operating 150 miles from my ports and at present I am over 300 miles from Bayeux. In order to save transport I have cut down my intake into France to 6000 tons a day which is half what I consume and I cannot go on for long like this. It is clear therefore that based as I am at present on Bayeux I cannot capture the Ruhr. As soon as I have a Pas de Calais port working I would then require about 2500 additional 3-ton lorries plus an assured air lift averaging minimum 1000 tons a day to enable me to get to the Ruhr and finally Berlin. I submit with all respect to your para. 3 [about Le Havre and Antwerp as essential] that a reallocation of our present resources of every description would be adequate to get one thrust to Berlin. It is very difficult to explain things in a message like this. Would it be possible for you to come and see me?[7]

It was not only tactless but inconsiderate of Montgomery to ask Eisenhower to come and see him, for the latter had severely damaged his knee and was unable to walk. In fact, during the campaign Montgomery never offered to visit Eisenhower, and always expected the Supreme Commander to come to him.

Two days later, Montgomery received the missing part of Eisenhower's signal. It proved to be another compromise between the conflicting aims of Montgomery and Bradley because it said, surprisingly, 'I agree with your conception of a full blooded thrust to Berlin', but contradicted this by also stating, 'We must immediately exploit our success by promptly breaching the Siegfried Line crossing the Rhine on a wide front and seizing the Saar and Ruhr.' In response to Montgomery's answer of the 7th, Eisenhower agreed to a meeting at Brussels on 10 September. By now Montgomery was desperate, and thoroughly fed up with Eisenhower's indecision, generally expressed in messages from his HQ 400 miles from the battlefield. He considered the Supreme Commander to be 'completely out of touch'.

7

The Fatal Wrong Decision

Hitler, like Ramsay, appreciated the vital importance of holding both banks of the Scheldt, not only to deny Antwerp to the Allies, but also to provide an escape route for his 100,000-strong Fifteenth Army trapped on the coast west of Antwerp in the Dunkirk—Ostend—Bruges—Zeebrugge area. As long as German guns dominated the Scheldt these troops could be evacuated north to the port of Flushing on Walcheren Island. The only approach to Walcheren from the mainland is through the long and narrow South Beveland peninsula, which XXX Corps could have sealed off on 4 September. The Canadians were advancing along the coast, but had to take Le Havre, Dieppe and Boulogne en route, and they could not put much pressure on the still powerful Fifteenth Army.

On 4 September the German High Command admitted that the fall of Antwerp had closed 'the ring around the 15th Army, and that a threat to Breda at the neck of the Scheldt peninsula must be expected;' on the 6th the German Admiralty ordered energetic mining of the Scheldt channel. Hitler commanded Fifteenth Army to withdraw fighting on Boulogne, Calais, Dunkirk, Ostend and the Breskens pocket, designated them all as 'fortresses', and directed that strong forces were to cross the west Scheldt channel to Flushing on Walcheren Island. His personal directive stated that it was vital to hold the coastal fortresses, as well as Walcheren Island with Flushing harbour. Field-Marshal von Rundstedt was reinstated as C-in-C, West, while Model commanded Army Group B under him.

The Germans expected Montgomery to drive north from Antwerp immediately on 4 September and seal off Walcheren

Island and the South Beveland peninsula from the Dutch mainland. Had he done so, Fifteenth Army would have been trapped and annihilated, as von Kluge's had been in Normandy, and the seaward approaches to Antwerp could have been opened at small cost in casualties. Ultra intercepts before and after 4 September showed that Hitler was determined to deny the use of Antwerp to the Allies by holding on to both the north and south banks of the estuary leading from the city to the sea,[1] and the clearing of those banks should have been the first consideration if the newly captured port was to become operational.

What an opportunity the Allies missed! Fifteenth Army poured back across the estuary into the South Beveland peninsula to reinforce the German defence of the lower Rhine just as the Allies planned to cross it on the run. Williams's Twenty-First Army Group Intelligence Summary of 18 September reads: 'Three German Corps – 67, 86 and 89 – with probably over 100,000 men have crossed into the Scheldt peninsula since Antwerp was captured.'[2]

As we have seen, Montgomery had written to the CIGS that he intended to advance upon Wesel and Arnhem, and that he wanted a drop of 1st Airborne Division and the Polish Parachute Brigade on the evening of 8 September to secure a bridge over the Rhine between the two towns. The increased German resistance made the timing of such an operation impossible, and instead Montgomery opted for a better-prepared plan for the Airborne Army to put down a carpet through hostile territory, providing a safe corridor for Second Army tanks to drive at great speed to the Rhine.

According to Williams, Montgomery felt that if he could use the airborne troops to force a crossing of the Rhine, Eisenhower would be bound to reinforce success and that this

> would tilt the centre of gravity and give the British priority of supplies before the US armies. Probably Monty thought then it was just a question of who put in the final punch against a defeated enemy before a final victory. If this airborne drop succeeded in front of his Second Army drive his punch, not Patton's, would be the triumphal road to final victory.

For Montgomery, the choice quickly became not whether to

refuse the Airborne Army and instead concentrate on clearing the port of Antwerp, but only whether he preferred Arnhem or Wesel as dropping zones for a Rhine crossing. To clear the low-lying Breskens area, with all its hundreds of drainage canals and ditches, and then make an amphibious assault on the island of Walcheren was bound to be a long, unglamorous campaign. Originally he had suggested that First Airborne Army should plan a drop on Walcheren Island, and Eisenhower had backed him. Brereton, however, had refused, saying that such an operation would not be suitable for airborne troops[3] – at this date Eisenhower had not yet definitely put the Airborne Army at Montgomery's disposal. Now, on 4 September, the Supreme Commander ordered Brereton to support Twenty-First Army Group with his airborne forces. Montgomery was going to make full use of them.

Ever since he had crossed the Seine, Montgomery had been considering plans for airborne assaults, but had discarded them as his chosen dropping zones were overrun too quickly by his armour. Eisenhower had suggested to Bradley that the Airborne Army should instead be dropped in the Maastricht-Aachen area to help US First Army through the Siegfried Line, but Bradley had refused. He was never enthusiastic about airborne operations, and in any case he had blind faith that Patton could win all his battles provided he had enough petrol. So Eisenhower's directive of 4 September definitely placed the Airborne Army at Montgomery's disposal, and the latter embarked upon his plan of dropping three airborne divisions in front of Second Army to clear the way for a swift armoured advance over the Maas and the Rhine. He would then have outflanked the defences of the Siegfried Line, which ended at Aachen, and would be poised to end the war with a thrust into the north German plain.

In the end, Montgomery decided on Arnhem, not Wesel, for his air landings on the banks of the Rhine. The Allied air forces also favoured Arnhem because there seemed to be fewer German anti-aircraft defences there than at Wesel. This argument had, however, been heard before in connection with the US air landings in the Cherbourg peninsula, when Leigh-Mallory had been overruled to good purpose. Brigadier Williams, however, considers that Montgomery was against landing at Wesel because he would have had to share the follow-up assaults by the land forces with the Americans on his right flank.

By 9th September Montgomery knew, from Dempsey's latest sitreps, that he must pierce a tough cordon of German troops before he reached the Rhine. It was particularly galling to him that Bradley's US XIX Corps (Maj-Gen Corlett) had not been able to keep pace with Horrocks's advance through Belgium, since its leading formation, US 2nd Armoured Division, ran out of petrol, halted for three days and only reached the Albert Canal on 12 September. As a result, XXX Corps' right flank was unprotected, and although on the 8th Guards Armoured secured an important bridgehead over the Albert Canal, Student's newly arrived parachutists began to counter-attack in strength. Only on the 10th did XXX Corps capture a canal bridge in sufficient strength to be in a position to line up for the full-blooded offensive on which Montgomery's heart was set.

Dempsey and 'Boy' Browning, the two key commanders for the proposed operation, met Montgomery at his Tac HQ on the morning of 10 September. Dempsey had telephoned Montgomery earlier in the day to say that he favoured Wesel, and had thought that his superior agreed with him.

Also on the same morning, a War Office telegram arrived at Twenty-First Army Group announcing that the first V2 had fallen on London.[4] It has been said that this influenced Montgomery in his choice of Arnhem, which was nearer to the rocket launching sites than the German town of Wesel, forty-odd miles to the south-east, but this is almost certainly not the case. Churchill and Brooke were abroad, and it is unlikely that the Home Secretary, Herbert Morrison, tried to exert any pressure because he never interfered in military matters. There is no mention of Holland being given priority in the Chiefs of Staff Minutes, and General Simpson told me categorically that no pressure was put on Montgomery to opt for Holland. Clearly the capture of Arnhem would make it easier for Second Army to advance to the Zuider Zee, thus cutting off Germany from Holland and eliminating the threat from the V2s. But once over the Rhine in strength at Wesel, Montgomery could have dropped another airborne division to close the Arnhem-Zuider Zee gap.

After the war David Belchem took part in a series of French television programmes with the German Generals Siegfried

Westphal and Hasso-Eccard von Manteuffel, respectively von Rundstedt's Chief of Staff and the GOC Fifth Panzer Army. They agreed that on 10 September, in Belchem's words, '21 Army Group could have cycled to Wesel', and General Günther Blumentritt, whom Westphal succeeded, also confirmed this. There was, too, one less river crossing towards Wesel than towards Arnhem, which reduced the need for bridging equipment,[5] and lessened the chances of being held back by demolitions.

At the Tac HQ conference on 10 September Dempsey told Montgomery that Ultra had mentioned the presence of tanks at Arnhem, and that the Dutch Resistance had reported 'battered Panzer Divisions had been sent to Holland to refit near Arnhem'. Williams had already told his chief that Ultra showed tanks in reception areas near Eindhoven and Nijmegen, although there was no indication of the number. Dempsey also said that the unexpectedly tough resistance on the Albert Canal made him doubt whether he could advance north fast enough to link up with a drop at Arnhem, and added that his right flank would be exposed because the Americans were by now heading east, not north. He emphasised to Montgomery that he would like to hold a firm flank along the Dutch border and turn east against the lighter opposition to cross the Rhine, in partnership with the Americans, at Wesel.

Unfortunately de Guingand was in hospital in Aldershot with one of his periodic bouts of exhaustion, and was thus unable to take a hand in these arguments; Dempsey himself had little influence on Montgomery. Williams told me that 'Monty treated Dempsey more as a Corps Commander than an Army Commander, and although he would discuss a lot with Dempsey, in the end Monty held to his own line.' Moreover, Montgomery's hand was strengthened because Browning was itching to see his beloved airborne soldiers in action once more, and did not care whether it was at Arnhem or Wesel; besides, elements of I Airborne Corps had been training in England for some considerable time, without action, and were thought to be going 'stale'. After talking to his two generals, therefore, Montgomery declared for Arnhem. Brigadier Williams thought that:

It was an appalling decision to go for an airborne operation instead of clearing the banks of the Scheldt to open up Antwerp. Monty impulsively decided to go for Arnhem, not Wesel, and I was shocked by the sheer wilfulness of the decision. At that time Monty had the psychology of pursuit with the elation of the advance, and I had it too, and found it difficult to keep my Intelligence reports and judgements completely free from the heady feeling that we had won the war. During these few days it was difficult to be dispassionate. If Ike had preferred the Scheldt option he should have imposed his will on Monty. But you must remember at that time Ike was in no position to contradict Monty, because the incredible victory in Normandy and the swift advance had established Monty as a brilliantly successful commander in the field.

So, on the morning of 10 September 1944, Field-Marshal Sir Bernard Montgomery made the two worst military decisions of his career — having decided upon an airborne operation to secure a Rhine bridgehead instead of opening up Antwerp, he compounded the error by going for Arnhem instead of Wesel. Eisenhower backed the two wrong decisions.

That afternoon, Montgomery conferred with Eisenhower at Brussels aerodrome, for the latter was too lame to leave his aeroplane. The conference started badly. Eisenhower had brought with him Lt-Gen Humfrey Gale, head of SHAEF Administration, in order to discuss Twenty-First Army Group's supplies, but Montgomery, made arrogant by the prospect of another world-shaking victory, objected to his being present. Gale withdrew, although Tedder remained. Montgomery then took Eisenhower's directive of 4 September out of his pocket and began to condemn it roundly, for all the world as though he was addressing his Staff College pupils. As the tirade gathered fury Eisenhower stayed silent, but as soon as Montgomery stopped for breath, he leaned forward, put his hand on the other's knee, and said: 'Steady Monty. You cannot talk to me like this. I am your boss.' Montgomery mumbled an apology, but relations between him and Eisenhower had reached new depths.[6]

Montgomery suggested that he should use his hoped-for bridgehead over the Rhine to make a single thrust to Berlin, arguing excitedly that once the Ruhr was encircled from the north the Nazis would lose its vast output of iron and steel—the war could not then last long. According to Tedder, Eisenhower thought that it was 'fantastic' for Montgomery to talk of marching to Berlin with an army still drawing its supplies from the Normandy beaches. He turned down the proposal out of hand and, when he got back to Granville, noted in his office diary: 'Monty's suggestion is simple: give him everything, which is crazy.'[7]

On the day before the meeting at Brussels airport Montgomery had signalled Eisenhower: 'Providing we have the ports of Dieppe, Boulogne, Dunkirk and Calais, and in addition 3,000 tons per day through Le Havre WE CAN ADVANCE TO BERLIN. In order to reach the Munster Triangle we require one good Pas de Calais port, 1,000 tons per day air lift, plus additional allotment of motor transport.'[8] This signal, designed to discourage Eisenhower from supporting the American southern drive, shows how optimistic Montgomery was at that moment, and how much he had underestimated Hitler's power of recovery.

As soon as Montgomery realised that he would get nowhere with his Berlin argument, he explained to Eisenhower the details of his Arnhem plan. The latter was keen to use the Airborne Army to secure a bridgehead over the Rhine, and felt that at last Montgomery had found a bold plan which suited his own strategy as Supreme Commander, as well as matching Patton's and Bradley's ambitions for the southern drive. He eagerly endorsed the Arnhem drop, promising Montgomery extra supplies, but he firmly refused to order Bradley to carry out a supporting operation on Dempsey's right flank at the expense of Patton's drive through the Siegfried Line.

Eisenhower, at that time misinformed by his Intelligence staff about the speed of arrival of German reinforcements in front of Twenty-First Group, specifically authorised Montgomery to defer clearing the Scheldt until after Arnhem, and emphasised that he wanted the airborne attack, now called 'Market Garden', to be launched before the Germans reinforced Holland. Montgomery explained that his chief difficulty lay in the need to bring up the halted British VIII Corps from the Seine to cover his right flank, since Bradley would continue to operate eastwards. Eisenhower clearly hoped that the drop at Arnhem would win a Rhine bridgehead without there being any need to halt Patton, but it was important in the Supreme Commander's eyes that, in the end, the American armies should be seen to be at least equal victors with the British. The two Allied commanders now agreed on 17 September as D-day for 'Market-Garden'.

At I Airborne Corps HQ at Moor Park, rushed plans were made for the Arnhem drop, while Dempsey and Horrocks conferred about the operations for the link-up. Liaison between Second Army and XXX Corps and the Airborne Headquarters was, however, unsatisfactory, for neither Horrocks nor Dempsey sent a sufficiently senior or experienced representative to the Arnhem planning conferences. And there was, in any case, an even greater urgency than that imposed by the 17 September deadline, for it would take five days to brief the necessary aircrew, which were dispersed on twenty-two different airfields.[9]

Allied First Airborne Army HQ, situated at Ascot, was a new joint British-US creation, bristling with teething problems and equipped with few trained planners. There were problems with the commanders as well, for Browning never managed to establish close relations with his American opposite numbers, while Brereton, in the words of David Belchem, 'was pleasant and kind, but never came alight until after half a bottle of Scotch'. The American historian Russell Weigley is less generous, writing that Brereton was 'perpetually discontented and querulous' because of his ill luck in the Far East[10] (when commanding the US Far East Air Forces in the Philippines in December 1941, his bombing strike force had been destroyed in a surprise attack on Clark Field by Japanese aircraft).

Unfortunately, the problems did not end at Airborne HQ. There were not enough transport aircraft available to carry more than half the Airborne Army in one lift, so that instead of three divisions landing on D-day, as Montgomery anticipated, only three half-divisions could be dropped. When Montgomery heard this he sent Belchem to see Brereton at Ascot, to try and persuade him to find the aircraft for at least a partial 'double-run' by 1st Airborne Division, which was to take and hold Arnhem bridge. However, Maj-Gen Paul Williams, head of US Troop Carrier Command, firmly turned this suggestion down, saying that it would be impossible because of 'the strain on the aircrews'. Maj-Gen Roy Urquhart, commanding British 1st

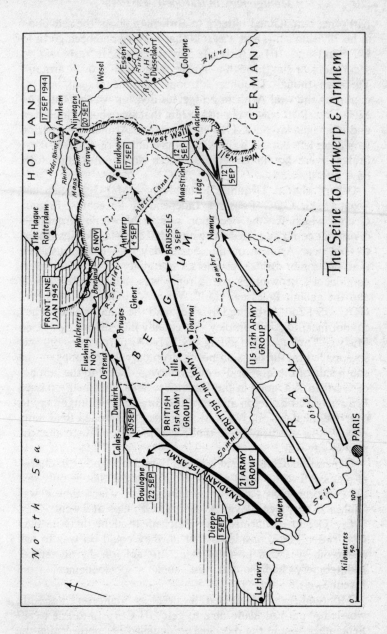

The Seine to Antwerp & Arnhem.

Airborne, complained bitterly to Browning about the reduction in his division's lift, and was told that priority had been given to US 82nd and 101st Airborne Divisions, whose task was to secure a clear run through to Arnhem for XXX Corps' armour. Yet even though Urquhart's troops had the crucial task of capturing the vital Arnhem bridge, his division was allocated no extra aircraft. It was explained to him that since both Eindhoven and Nijmegen lay on XXX Corps' route to Arnhem his division would be left out on a limb, without chance of relief, if these bridges were not taken—the southern drops must, therefore, have priority.

Others shared Urquhart's misgivings. Maj-Gen Stanislaw Sosabowski, GOC Polish 1 Independent Parachute Brigade Group, which for the operation was to be within Urquhart's divisional command, told Browning that the plan for his troops to land near Arnhem on the second day was 'disastrous', and that the senior British planners were guilty of 'reckless over-confidence'. Browning's poetic reply was that 'the Red Devils and the gallant Poles can do it'. When Maj-Gen James Gavin, GOC US 82nd Airborne Division, read the plan he said: 'They cannot mean it', and Bradley was equally incredulous. Maj-Gen Maxwell Taylor, commanding US 101st Airborne Division, was so appalled by the decision not to drop parachute troops on the south side of the Zon bridge at Eindhoven, owing to the number of German AA guns in the Eindhoven area, that he by-passed Browning and Brereton and appealed directly to Montgomery to overrule the decision. When Montgomery telephoned Browning, however, he was firmly told that it was much too late to alter the plan in any way.[11]

General Sir Charles Richardson, then the brigadier in charge of plans at Twenty-First Army Group, told me that he only saw the Airborne Corps plan on D-minus-2, by which time it was final, and Maj-Gen David Belchem (BGS, Ops at Twenty-First Army Group) confirmed this. Belchem thought that the plan was 'rotten', but considered that all they could do was to ask Montgomery for a postponement. In fact, on 11 September Montgomery had sought just such a postponement from Eisenhower.

Montgomery had passed a sleepless night on the 10th, worried about not being able to get VIII Corps into line by 17 September, and in the morning he signalled Eisenhower that the

23rd, or possible even the 26th, were the earliest dates possible for D-day. The signal galvanised Eisenhower into sending Bedell Smith on 12 September from Granville to Montgomery's HQ. There, to Montgomery's delight, Bedell Smith promised an extra 1,000 tons of supplies per day by air or road for Twenty-First Army Group; he also said that Patton's southern drive would he halted so that the bulk of American supplies could go to US First Army for operations on Montgomery's eastern flank. In addition, three US divisions would be grounded and their transport assigned to Twenty-First Army Group. Montgomery felt that he had won his battle, and reinstated 17 September as D-day for 'Market-Garden', declaring that he hoped 'the war would soon be won'. He was deaf to warnings from his staff.

Bedell Smith also gave Montgomery a verbal assurance that US First Army would operate on the British eastern flank, and that petrol earmarked for American forces would be provided in order to bring up British VIII Corps to Holland, together with its non-divisional artillery – the last was still immobilised in the Seine valley because of lack of fuel.

Unhappily, Bedell Smith's promises were not fulfilled. Elements of VIII Corps and the non-divisional artillery did not reach the Meuse-Escaut Canal until D-plus-2. The three US divisions to be grounded were not in the line, as Montgomery had thought, but had just landed in Normandy – they had no transport. American Red Ball* convoys did start running to Brussels from Normandy on 16 September, but Montgomery's supply airlift was only slightly increased, from 400 tons a day to 500. Montgomery was forced, therefore, to rely on his own resources for his build-up. He had to choose between supplies and extra troops, and decided to dispense with VIII Corps. As a result, during the advance to Arnhem XXX Corps' right flank became dangerously exposed – US First Army was by then deeply involved around Aachen against tough opposition, and thus was unable to conduct an offensive in support of 'Market-Garden' on XXX Corps' right.

This was not Eisenhower's fault. On 16 September he had asked Bradley to halt Patton and to give priority in everything to US First Army, so that it could support Montgomery. Patton

---

*The Red Ball Express was a one-way truck transport supply system, improvised by the Americans in order to keep up with the sudden swift Allied advance in the late summer of 1944.

disobeyed Bradley's instructions and, in order to prevent American help going to the British, immediately involved Third Army in an assault on Metz which required yet more supplies; when this failed he sent an unauthorised spearhead on to the Rhine. Bradley connived in this disobedience.

By 15 September the Airborne Corps' plan was complete – and unalterable – in every interlocking detail. With only two days remaining to D-day, Montgomery either had to accept the whole package or call the operation off. He chose to go ahead, despite the forebodings of his staff.

During the week 10-17 September, more and more evidence was found of German tanks in the Arnhem area. Colonel Tony Tasker, in charge of land intelligence at Airborne Army HQ, and Major Brian Urquhart at Airborne Corps HQ, became convinced that air reconnaissance photographs showed tanks around Arnhem. This was confirmed by Ultra signals, which showed II SS Panzer Corps HQ to be there, and which also positively identified 9th and 11th SS Panzer Divisions in the area. Of course, no one was able to assess how many tanks these divisions had left after their battering in Normandy but, since German tank production was in full swing, these crack formations would obviously have priority with new tanks.

Bill Williams told me that:

Boy Browning knew that the morale of his airborne troops was still high, in spite of seventeen cancelled operations, and he was determined to go on with Arnhem, ignoring the alarming reports of tanks. Morale is terribly important in airborne operations. Browning was good-looking and brave, but not willing to listen. Both Tasker and Urquhart told him an appreciable number of tanks had shown up on air pictures of the Arnhem area. I was horrified when I heard later that Browning had got rid of Brian Urquhart just as he was being awkward about Arnhem by alleging he was having a nervous breakdown.

Brian Urquhart wrote to me that he remembers Brereton as 'an extremely unimpressive and somewhat bewildered American general', and that US Maj-Gen Floyd Parks, Brereton's Chief of Staff, was the dominant figure at Airborne Army HQ. His letter continues, very fairly:

Montgomery comes ashore in Sicily, 12 July 1943.

On the road to Catania, sharing a brew-up with his staff.

Patton (left), Eisenhower and Montgomery in Palermo, captured by Patton's US Seventh Army on 22 July.

Mark Clark (second from right) with Montgomery after the link-up with the Salerno beach-head—one of the rare occasions on which the two men met. The Americans thought Eighth Army had moved with 'reprehensible slowness'.

Montgomery, with Dempsey in the background, congratulating RM Commandos after their successful landing at Termoli, October 1943.

The CIGS, Brooke, with Montgomery during the former's visit to Italy in December 1943—'Frankly, I am rather depressed . . . Monty is tired out'.

Montgomery's popularity with ordinary people, and with soldiers, was enormous—unofficial messages were sent asking him to stop his tours. He refused. Cheering factory workers and a guard of honour from the Home Guard here confirm his belief in morale building, March 1944.

German prisoners taken on the Normandy beaches: many were of poor physical quality or very young, and a great number were from countries other than Germany.

Infantry coming out of the line on D-plus-5. Many are tired out, but plainly delighted by Montgomery's gift of cigarettes.

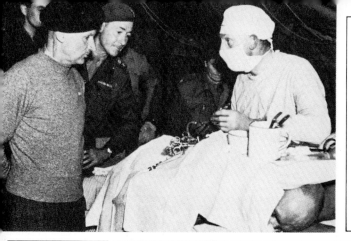

Patton, wearing his famous pearl-handled Colt, with Bradley and Montgomery after the Avranches break-out, August 1944.

Montgomery in a Field General Hospital near Caen, watching an operation to remove a bullet from a soldier's spine. He is horrified.

King George VI studying the situation with Montgomery in the map caravan at Tac HQ, June 1944.

20 July 1944. Churchill, in dour mood, at Tac HQ, despite Montgomery's tactless attempts to keep him away—'I have both a right and a duty to acquaint myself with the facts.'

Two days later, and Montgomery's charm had softened the Prime Minister, who was impressed. Montgomery did not understand how close he had come to the loss of his command.

Lt-Gen Bucknall (second from left), commanding XXX Corps, with Eisenhower, Dempsey and Tedder. A few days later, on 2 August, Montgomery dismissed Bucknall for dilatoriness during the 'Bluecoat' attack—he was replaced by Horrocks.

De Guingand, Montgomery, Horrocks and Coningham at the Alamein reunion dinner in Brussels, October 1944. The city had been liberated in early September.

Some of Montgomery's brilliant staff: Brigadier 'Bill' Williams (left), Lt Col L. M. Murphy, and Brigadier 'David' Belchem.

Montgomery with Crerar, GOC First Canadian Army. The two men frequently clashed.

Montgomery with Hodges, after the former had taken over a part of Bradley's army, November 1944. Hodges was shattered when he learned this.

Montgomery with the US Generals Collins (left) and Ridgway during the Ardennes offensive, December 1944. He greatly admired Collins.

Montgomery explains his plan for the advance on Berlin to Eisenhower and Bradley. Eisenhower, however, had already decided that he was not to go—Montgomery said to Simpson that this was evidence of double-crossing —'all very dirty work'.

Churchill on the German bank of the Rhine, March 1945—he told Eden that he had had 'a jolly day'. In the background are Bradley and Brooke.

It was not such a jolly day for these Airborne Forces casualties, being evacuated by jeep ambulance.

The Canadian Lt-Gen Simonds, Churchill, and Montgomery, with Dempsey in the background, on the German bank of the Rhine.

I used to believe that Boy Browning was the villain of the piece, but have since concluded that I was wrong and that he was obeying, against his better judgement, orders from much higher up designed to give the British the last victory of the war (you will remember the publicity that Patton's Third Army got was extremely unpopular with Montgomery). Of course, Browning was extremely ambitious, but my correspondence with his wife and my look at the papers of Cornelius Ryan have shown me that he was in fact extremely uneasy about the task he had been given at Arnhem. Actually, I liked Browning very much and feel that he has been unnecessarily made the scapegoat for this disgraceful disaster. The film of *A Bridge Too Far* is a travesty on this score, as on many others.[12]

Neither General Sir Nigel Poett nor Field-Marshal Lord Carver hold to this opinion of Browning, however. Lord Carver told me that:

The pressure to do 'Market-Garden' came from Airborne Corps. They were a very expensive organisation and had to be used. At that time Monty had two priorities:

1. To break his image of being over-cautious.
2. To make sure he did the main attack over the Rhine himself.

Of course there was a shortage of experienced planners; at that stage not many people had any experience of air operations. Until D-Day there had only been one real airborne operation in the British Army – Sicily.

This view is supported by General Poett:

Monty alone was responsible for the Arnhem decision, but he was pushed into it by Browning. Boy Browning was too anxious to deploy 1st Airborne Division at Arnhem. He was itching to do it because 1st Airborne, the veterans of airborne landings, were so eager to go and prove that they were as good as we new boys in the 6th Airborne Division who had been so completely successful in Normandy. They were jealous of us.

If the gliders had crash-landed close to Nijmegen and Arnhem bridges [as proposed in 'Market-Garden I'] they would have been successful in capturing the bridges, and there is no reason why the ground troops should not have linked up with them in time. It is always a disaster to make the dropping zone too far from the bridge.

During the week before D-day, Belchem and Richardson briefed Montgomery about the flaws in the Airborne Army plans of operations, and Williams repeatedly warned him of the unexpected armoured strength in the Arnhem area.

The weakness [Williams told me] was that no one could tell Monty not to go, and it was unfortunate that de Guingand was away ill. Without him the only operations officer with much influence on Monty was David Belchem. Belchem was opposed to Arnhem, but he was acquiescent ...

Monty preferred Arnhem or Wesel to opening Antwerp, and during their talk in Ike's aeroplane at Brussels Ike promised him extra supplies and eventual support of US troops if he did the Arnhem drop. Monty knew if he made the Rhine crossing at Wesel he would have had to share it with the Americans.

Both he and Dempsey knew of the reported Panzer strength at Arnhem on the morning of 10 September.

In the evening of 10 September I briefed Monty about the ominous German strength at Arnhem. I could not get him to change his mind. This was out of character as he was usually so careful to minimise casualties with his 'metal not flesh' philosophy.

With de Guingand away there was no one to argue the toss with Monty in that fatal week except myself and Oliver Poole, a 21 Army Group Colonel Q who was the brain tank of General Miles Graham, in charge of 21 Army Group administration. Unfortunately Graham would never contradict Monty.

I sat up late one night that week arguing with Poole how we could stop Monty doing Arnhem. My second in command was Joe Ewart. He lived at Tac HQ with Monty while I worked at Main. I remember him saying to me one morning: 'He is determined to go to Arnhem. I have told him all I can about the strength of the Germans. See what you can do to stop him.'

As Monty's Head of Intelligence it was my job to tell him all about the enemy. I could always contradict Monty if I said 'Sir' at the end of the sentence. Graham and Belchem were both Regular soldiers and they had to think of their careers in peace-time after the war when Monty was sure to be all-powerful. As temporary soldiers this was not a factor with Oliver Poole or myself. We could tell Monty he was wrong.

At first our knowledge of the enemy at Arnhem was flimsy, but it built up during the week. I forecast the enemy's strength at Arnhem reasonably accurately, but 10th and 9th SS Panzer had survived [the defeat in Normandy] and had refitted, so they were stronger than I had expected, and General Student with his Para Corps also reacted more quickly than I had forecast. Student was a very intelligent reptile.

Wing-Commander Asher Lee, an expert in reading Ultra signals, was lent by the Air Ministry to Allied Airborne Army HQ as Air Intelligence Officer for the duration of 'Market-Garden'. He became so concerned at the Ultra evidence of a strong Panzer presence in the Arnhem area that he began to 'badger' Brereton, who in turn told him to pay a visit to Twenty-First Army Group in Brussels. Asher Lee told me:

I wanted to emphasise to Monty's HQ the importance of having enough anti-tank weapons. From Ultra signals it was impossible to estimate the number of German tanks there. I had a long interview at 21 Army Group HQ but I did not see a very high-ranking officer. Brereton himself at my HQ was remote from the detailed planning and I had no contact with General Browning at Corps. 1st Allied Airborne Army HQ had been hastily slammed together.

I was good friends with Colonel Tony Tasker at Corps HQ who had a parallel job to mine, but he never showed me any air pics. So fed up was Tasker at the seventeen postponements of operations since D-Day that he put up a notice: 'D-Day is any day from Monday to Sunday and you must choose your own bloody dropping zone.' Definitely at that point airborne troops were itching to have a go.[13]

On 15 September Maj-Gen Kenneth Strong, Eisenhower's British Chief of Intelligence at SHAEF, received confirmed reports from the Dutch underground that 9th and 10th SS Panzer Divisions were refitting in the Arnhem area. Strong reported this to Bedell Smith, who was so worried by the reports that he went straight to the Supreme Commander. Eisenhower told Strong and Bedell Smith: 'I cannot tell Monty how to deploy his troops. You must fly to 21 Army Group immediately and argue it out with Monty. I cannot order Monty to call Market Garden off when I have already given it the green light.' Bedell Smith flew at once to Brussels and saw Montgomery, who ridiculed the idea that, merely because of reports about German tank strength at Arnhem, he should revise the 'Market-Garden' plan. And he added: 'Market-Garden will go alright provided you at SHAEF honour your commitment to me made on 11 September to divert supplies to me.' Smith remarked afterwards: 'I tried to stop him but I got nowhere.'[14]

Montgomery had decided on 'Market-Garden' entirely on his own, but because Allied First Airborne Army was the SHAEF strategic reserve, and not part of Twenty-First Army Group, he had little influence on its detailed operation plan. He could, however, have sent more senior staff officers from Twenty-First Army Group, Second Army or XXX Corps to take part in the planning. This he failed to do, and the inexperienced airborne planners let him down badly.

Belchem felt strongly that it was a major mistake not to send a senior planner from Twenty-First Group, but even after he and Richardson, in Brussels, had gone through the detailed plan with a fine-toothed comb, and found it to be sadly wanting, Montgomery refused to cancel 'Market-Garden', preferring to go through with his gamble. General Richardson informed me that 'By the time I saw the plan for Market-Garden it was a *fait accompli*.' 'The Lord God Almighty in Battle', to whom Montgomery liked to refer so often, had smiled on him from Alamein to Antwerp – with only a few setbacks – and he could not believe that, this time, he was pushing his luck too far.

On 10 September Montgomery's state of mind might have been put, in his own style of language, thus:

I have three alternatives, all equal militarily:

1   to clear the Isle of Walcheren and the South Beveland isthmus.

2   to use airborne troops to obtain a bridgehead over the Rhine at Wesel.

3   to do ditto at Arnhem.

If I do 1, I shall be involved in an unrewarding hard slog not likely to enhance my reputation; once Antwerp is open the supplies landed there will probably be used to support a triumphant USA drive to Berlin, and the 21 Army Group part in the final stages of the war will be unglamorous.

If I do 2, I will have to share the Rhine bridgehead with the Americans who, because of their greater numbers, will get most of the glory for the final battles of the war on German soil.

If I do 3, successfully, it will be hailed as a dazzling and daring operation and Ike will be forced to give me all the help in troops and supplies I need for a drive to Berlin. Also 3, if successful, will mean that British troops will save London by capturing the V2 launching-sites in Holland. This will put the seal on my reputation.

From the very moment that his troops reached Antwerp, Montgomery failed to appreciate the absolute necessity of capturing the port – from this single error stems a host of others. He instructed Dawnay to write in the Log:

From a purely British point of view Antwerp had never been a vital necessity; the Pas de Calais ports provided all that we required. But to the Americans it had become vital and for the British armies it would be very convenient and would save a long haul over bad roads. American maintenance difficulties were responsible for creating the urgency to open the port of Antwerp.

At the time he was seeking excuses for his strategic error, although he was to admit the mistake after the war.

Montgomery's decision to take the Arnhem option, in despite of warnings from his staff and of evidence of enemy strength, resulted in resounding defeat. He wasted the Allies' strategic reserve, a force which could have brought victory in 1944, and sacrificed the cream of the British Army – the young airborne volunteers of whom over 1,000 died and more than 7,000 were casualties or POWs. After the disastrous Arnhem drop British 1st Airborne Division could not be re-formed for future operations.

8

Arnhem

On 17 September, as the air armada presaging 'Market-Garden' flew out from England, Montgomery could only await events. The detailed airborne plans had been made in England in compliance with his overall directive, but the airborne divisions would only come under his orders once they had landed in Holland.

XXX Corps's plan for the link-up had been agreed with Montgomery and his staff at Twenty-First Army Group, but it was ambitious to the point of recklessness. Against mounting German opposition, the Corps would have to fight its way across water obstacles whose average widths were: Wilhelmina Canal at Zon – 80 to 100 feet; Willems Canal at Veghel – 80 feet; River Maas at Grave – 800 feet; River Waal at Nijmegen – 850 feet; Lower Rhine at Arnhem – 300 feet. Behind the tanks pushing up the narrow, exposed road were 2,300 lorries carrying a massive amount of bridging equipment, together with some 9,000 Sappers and battalions of Pioneers. The road congestion was bound to be appalling.[1]

XXX Corps' task was to reach Arnhem Bridge in forty-eight hours; indeed, Montgomery even over-optimistically suggested to Browning that they might link up on D-plus-1. The whole operation was a daunting enough task for I Airborne Corps, particularly since XXX and VIII Corps had taken four days to cross the defended Albert Canal at Beeringen and win the small bridgehead over the Meuse-Escaut Canal, only fifteen miles further on. Of course, the road in front of XXX Corps was to be cleared by the two American airborne divisions, but it was sixty-five miles to Arnhem from the start-line.[2]

On 14 September, three days before D-day, Montgomery's

directive had stated that Twenty-First Army Group's objective was to secure crossings over the Rhine and Maas in the general area Arnhem-Nijmegen-Grave, by the use of airborne troops combined with a rapid and violent thrust by British Second Army. That army was to establish itself on a line between Zwolle on the Zuider Zee and Arnhem, facing east and with deep bridgeheads east of the Ijssel River. Then, in conjunction with US First Army, the entire force would surround the Ruhr.

Browning's I Airborne Corps contained three airborne divisions, British 1st, and US 82nd and 101st. These were to land in three areas: US 101st to seize bridges and defiles on XXX Corps' main axis at Eindhoven, Zon and Veghel; US 82nd to seize and hold the bridges at Nijmegen and Grave and to 'capture and retain the high ground' around Groesbeek; while British 1st Airborne Division had to capture the Arnhem bridges,* and establish sufficient bridgeheads to pass through formations from XXX Corps on the latter's arrival. In addition, 52nd (Lowland) Division, designated 'airportable', was to be flown in as soon as Deelen airfield, north of Arnhem, was captured. (In the event 52nd Division was never used in the operation, although its commander, Maj-Gen Edmund Hakewill Smith, volunteered to fly one brigade in.) To comply with Montgomery's directive, Guards Armoured Division, the XXX Corps vanguard, would have to advance sixty-five miles in forty-eight hours and mostly on a single elevated road through boggy country – thus the advance effectively had a one-tank front.

Horrocks already had a bridgehead over the Meuse-Escaut Canal. On 10 September the Irish Guards had surprised the Germans defending the canal and captured a road bridge intact. The Coldstream and Grenadiers had enlarged the bridgehead after heavy fighting against counter-attacks on the following day, and this bridgehead was now the break-out base for XXX Corps.

XXX Corps was to follow the main road through Eindhoven, Grave and Nijmegen, linking up with the US airborne divisions on the way. Then, after relieving British 1st Airborne Division at Arnhem, they would push on to the Zuider Zee, and wait for the rest of the Second Army to catch up with them before advancing

---

* There were three bridges over the Lower Rhine at Arnhem – a railway bridge to the west of the town, a pontoon bridge, and the main road bridge.

to the North German Plains, thus outflanking the Siegfried Line. In fact, such a plan was never really feasible – the timing was too optimistic.

Guards Armoured Division was to punch a hole in the German defences, through which 43rd Division was to follow, while 50th Division was to hold the flank. All the leading units were told that they had just two days in which to reach Arnhem.

Tanks of the Irish Guards were to lead the attack at 1435 on 17 September, against opposition identified by Second Army Intelligence as six infantry battalions, supported by twenty tanks and twenty-five guns, including twelve 88-mms. It was plain that if there were many more German anti-tank guns than had been forecast, the whole effort would be a disaster from the start.

At 1400 the artillery bombardment started as the gigantic air armada swished through the blue sky overhead. The artillery fired a narrow rolling barrage up the single road front, while a 'cab rank' of Typhoons surged overhead, waiting for the ground troops to identify their targets. For the first three miles ahead to the Dutch frontier all went well, but once over the frontier there came stiff opposition from Germans concealed in woods. There had unfortunately been no air reconnaisance photographs of the area, with the result that enemy anti-tank guns had not been pinpointed. Nine Irish Guards tanks in a row were knocked out before a single German self-propelled anti-tank gun was identified and destroyed by the Typhoons, which, directed from the ground, fired at enemy targets and enabled the tanks to advance. Soon 250 German prisoners were being escorted to the rear.

At 1730 the leading Irish Guards had advanced seven miles, and had reached the bridge south of Valkenswaard and found it intact. German resistance inside the town and in the surrounding woods was tough, however. When the Irish Guards finally battered their way in it was '... a complete shambles with three or four really big fires burning. Germans still firing; other Germans milling about trying to find their way back to Germany ... all the inhabitants in the streets yelling themselves hoarse and getting in the way of the fighting.' The Mayor's clerk came running into Battalion HQ with a telephone message intercepted from the German commander in Eindhoven that Valkenswaard must be defended to the last man.

The capture of Valkenswaard was good news, but now the

first day was gone and the leading troops of XXX Corps were still fifty miles from Arnhem, which Montgomery had promised would be relieved by the end of the next day. In Arnhem, British 1st Airborne was already suffering grave problems.

On the 18th, however, the Guards' advance was slowed because the Typhoons were no longer available – no satisfactory reason for their absence has ever been given. The tanks had to make flanking movements in difficult ground to pass 88-mm guns and Spandaus concealed behind concrete walls. But once Aalst, a dormitory town for Eindhoven, was taken, the managing director of the Phillips Electrical Works there produced a sketch map of the German positions, marked with crosses to show the gun pits. His map was completely accurate, and of incalculable value to the British armour.

During the afternoon the leading Irish Guards were halted yet again by German 88-mm guns, and spirits fell. Then suddenly there came a telephone message from Zon that Eindhoven had fallen to the airborne troops. Soon the tanks were rolling past abandoned German 88s, and they entered Eindhoven amidst cheers from the Dutch and from US 101st Airborne's parachutists – orange banners and flags, flowers and fruit were everywhere.

Unfortunately, the bridge at Zon had been blown because no airborne troops had been dropped to the north of it. Sappers built a new bridge, and the armoured advance began again at 0600 the next morning, 19 September. Messages came through that US 82nd Division held the Grave bridge, the Maas-Waal Canal bridges, and were heavily engaged 300 yards south of the Nijmegen bridge. There are two bridges over the Waal at Nijmegen – a road bridge 1200 yards long and, downstream, a railway bridge. Both were still intact, although prepared for demolition.

Cheered on by Dutch civilians and the American parachutists at every crossroad and village, the 1st Grenadier Guards, now leading, drove their tanks flat out along the highway, and at 1200 on Tuesday 19 September – a fine, sunny day – they linked up with the US forward units locked in fierce battle with German SS troops in the streets of Nijmegen. Lt-Col E.H. Goulburn, CO of the Grenadiers, held a hurried conference with Gavin, and learnt that 1st Airborne Division still held the north end of Arnhem bridge although they were by now in dire straits.

Goulburn then dashed forward to the old monastery of Marienboom in the suburbs of Nijmegen, where he issued orders for one of the most dramatic attacks of the Second World War.

Capture of the bridge intact was a glittering prize, for it promised not only the salvation of thousands of men of 1st Airborne from otherwise inevitable disaster, but also the end of the war within a few weeks. At any moment the Germans might blow the huge bridge, but here was British armour within a few hundred yards of it, and all the Americans, Dutch and British concerned were seized with an unparalleled feeling of urgency.

Goulburn made his HQ in a café in Marienboom. Groups of wildly excited civilians rushed in and out; it was full of Dutch liaison officers and underground fighters; just outside, American 75-mm guns blazed away as hard as they could at the German positions. The café's owners did a roaring trade.

Typhoons pounded the German positions inside Nijmegen at 1530, as the Grenadiers, with some platoons of American parachutists, advanced into the stricken town, where the Germans had wantonly burnt countless houses. At first there was no opposition, and a few leading tanks and armoured cars safely crossed the wide square of Maria Plein. For a moment the British thought the Germans were waiting for the tanks to get on to the bridge before blowing it. But suddenly intense anti-tank and small-arms fire pinned down the follow-up troops on the large open space of Maria Plein, and the frenzied rush to the bridge ground to an abrupt halt.

A maze of streets made the tanks highly vulnerable to German anti-tank guns, and as daylight disappeared it became clear that the bridge would not be taken without much more hard fighting; indeed, Browning planned to drop another whole parachute brigade to capture the bridge next morning. His gamble was never put to the test because the weather suddenly became bad, and at 0200 on 20 September Goulburn was told that his Grenadiers would have the sole glory of assaulting the bridge, on whose capture the Allied Command was pinning all its hopes.

At 0530 the Grenadiers attacked, painfully edging their way through the small streets towards the bridge. After five hours of slow advance Goulburn felt he held a position from which he could plan the eagerly awaited assault on the bridge.

At 1530 US 82nd Airborne troops crossed the Waal in British

assault boats, supported by the guns of 100 Guards' tanks, and secured a toe-hold on the north bank of the 400-yard-wide, swiftly running river, west of Nijmegen railway bridge. By dusk a few Americans reached Lent, a mile inland, where the railway crosses the main road. Casualties during the crossing were savage, but it was undoubtedly one of the finest feats of arms of the Second World War.

Simultaneously with the American river crossing, Goulburn sent his Grenadiers, still accompanied by a few American paratroopers, to take Huner Park and the Valkhof, a large wooded mound, well tunnelled and trenched, to the north of which there was a fort overlooking the bridge. British casualties were heavy, but at 1800 German resistance surprisingly cracked after 150 Germans had been burnt alive in a large house set on fire by phosphorus grenades.

From the Valkhof the Grenadier tanks continuously pumped shells into the enemy positions on the southern approaches to the bridge; a patrol found the southern end clear of Germans, except for a number of shell-shocked soldiers who were soon made prisoner. At 1830 a troop of tanks moved towards the bridge, but fell back as anti-tank fire proved too strong. As dark fell, hopes of reaching Arnhem in time dimmed. Another day had been lost.

The situation was suddenly transformed. At 1900 Sergeants Robinson and Pacey of the Grenadiers saved the day for the Allies by a desperate but successful rush across the 1200-yard bridge in their tanks. They braved bazookas and anti-tank guns, and although two of their comrades' tanks were knocked out, they skidded broadside through the road block at the north end of the bridge and knocked out the devastating German anti-tank guns. A third tank, Sergeant Knight's, followed, and the three bravely went on north to link up with the Americans in a dangerous position one mile up the road to Arnhem at Lent. Here they held on all night.

The first officer to cross the bridge was Captain the Lord Carrington (later Foreign Secretary from 1979-1982), and other tanks followed to consolidate the bridgehead. By the grace of God the Germans did not counter-attack during the night, and their attempts to blow the bridge failed.

A Sapper officer, Lieutenant Jones, ran behind the tanks, to cut any wires leading to the demolition charges. His men then went out to search for the explosives, but German snipers, who had lashed themselves to the iron girders, shot at them. Eventually, a German POW offered to show the Sappers where the demolition charges were: they were laid across the whole width of the bridge, each explosive securely fastened, numbered, and painted green to merge with the girders. If the bridge had been blown up there would have been a gap 200 feet long – too wide for a Bailey bridge.

Why did the Germans not blow the bridge? A citizen of Nijmegen called van Hoof claimed that on the night of 20 September he swam the river and climbed the pillars to tamper with the charges and make them safe. Van Hoof was killed the next day, but his claim can be dismissed because the pillars were unclimbable. The likely answer is that Field-Marshal Model, commanding Army Group B, thought that he had sufficient armour to throw back the Guards and fight on south of the Waal. For this he needed the bridge intact in order to supply his Panzers, and when the Grenadiers' surprisingly successful attack brought them on to the Valkhof no German officer had the courage to order the bridge to be blown without authority from a higher command.

If Nijmegen had been the ultimate target, then Montgomery's airborne operation was a tremendous success. But, now, after three days, XXX Corps was still ten miles from Arnhem, and a steel cordon of the élite Frundsberg Panzer Division, together with fresh tank reinforcements from Germany, barred the Corps' advance up the main road, now known as 'Hell's Highway'.

During the morning of 21 September (D-plus-4) the Irish Guards formed up in the bridgehead over the Waal at Lent for a final effort to reach their comrades at Arnhem. Their assault started at 1330, four and a half hours after the remnants of the British 2nd Parachute Regiment at Arnhem Bridge had surrendered. For two miles all went well, but when they reached Bessen, halfway from Nijmegen to Elst, they ran into severe trouble. Here the Germans had prepared strong defensive positions with machine-guns, anti-tank guns and Tiger tanks.

British tanks had to travel on the main road, elevated some six feet above the surrounding countryside with deep drainage ditches on both sides. At Bessen, Frundsberg Division Tigers brewed up the leading three tanks, and the road which comprised the single-tank front was completely blocked. An Irish Guardsman later remarked: 'Our tanks were like coconuts at a cockshy for the Germans to shoot down. We could never understand why the Tigers did not knock out our remaining forty-nine tanks in a row.' Typhoons were in the air and on call, but the wireless link failed and they were never called down.

At 1900 the stationary Irish Guards were ordered back to clear the road, so that the whole of 43rd Infantry Division could come up to try and resume the advance. They attacked again and again all the next day, 22 September (D-plus-5), but could make no progress up the highway to Arnhem. Montgomery's plan to reach the Zuider Zee via Arnhem had foundered, and 1st Airborne had now been isolated for five days, far too long.

Luckily, on 23 September 130 Infantry Brigade succeeded, after heavy fighting, in manoeuvring westwards down side roads, by-passing the western flank of the Frundsberg Division, and at dusk they reached the south bank of the Rhine to link up with the Polish Parachute Brigade near Driel, six miles west of Arnhem.

It is necessary now to consider what befell British 1st Airborne Division in Arnhem from the beginning of the operation.

Maj-Gen Urquhart landed his troops at Arnhem in five zones – three to the north of the Arnhem-Utrecht railway line at Ginkel Heath, and two south of the railway at Renkum Heath. At 1330 on 17 September the occupying German troops and the Dutch population were enjoying their Sunday lunch. Suddenly at Renkum and Ginkel parachutists dropped like confetti out of a clear sky, and gliders swooped in to land.

The astonished Dutch watched the liberating army descend on them. Jeeps and light guns came out of the gliders, and the jeeps were driven straight through hedges and barbed-wire fences. Parachutists helped farmers to catch terrified horses and to tether cows and put them in the farm buildings. British officers commandeered farm carts and horses to take scattered ammunition to a central depot. The Dutch were asked: 'Does anyone speak English?' 'Are the Germans around?' 'Where am I on the map?' 'Where is Arnhem?' Cups of tea and congratulations were showered on the British as they collected their weapons for an immediate advance.

Already there had been a hitch. The plan was that the

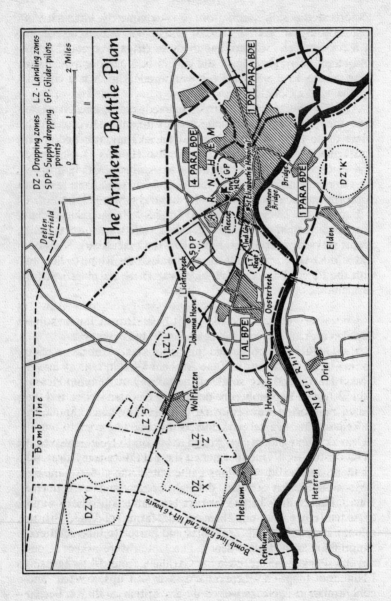

The Arnhem Battle Plan

DZ - Dropping zones   LZ - Landing zones
SDP- Supply dropping   GP- Glider pilots
points

0   1   2 Miles

Bomb line

Deelen Airfield

1 POL PARA BDE

4 PARA BDE

A R N H E M

DZ 'K'

GP
Div HQ
St Elizabeth's Hospital
Pontoon Bridge
Bridge

Recce

SDP 'V'

1 PARA BDE

Lichtenbeek

Johanna Hoeve

LT Regt

Elden

LZ 'L'

Oosterbeek

Wolfhezen

1 AL BDE

LZ 'S'

Heveadorp

Neder Rhine

Driel

LZ 'Z'

DZ 'X'

Heelsum

Bomb line from 2nd lift +6 hours

DZ 'Y'

Renkum

Heteren

Reconnaisance Squadron of 1st Airborne should drive off immediately to capture Arnhem bridge in a surprise attack, and hold it until the rest of 1 Parachute Brigade arrived. Unfortunately, although only a few gliders had gone astray, hardly any of the Recce Squadron's armoured jeeps had arrived on the landing ground.

The German High Command reacted spontaneously. Almost incredibly, Field-Marshal Model was sitting down to lunch in his HQ at the Taffelberg Hotel at Oosterbeek, only two miles to the east of Renkum Heath. Had the British been luckier, he would have fallen into their hands like a ripe plum, but within minutes of seeing the British parachutists Model's car was speeding to Area Command HQ in Arnhem, where he radioed news of the landings to Hitler at the Wolf's Lair, adding, 'I have escaped through the eye of a needle.' Hitler's reaction, typically selfish, was: 'Everyone must understand the deadly danger in which I stand. The enemy would not hesitate to risk two parachute divisions if at one blow they could get their hands on me and the whole German command.'

The Dutch Resistance had passed news to the Allies of Model's whereabouts, but why this vital information was never used remains a mystery. Had 1st Airborne known where he was, he would almost certainly have fallen into their hands – a very valuable prize indeed. Model was the most efficient of the pro-Nazi generals. Always well briefed, up to date and modern in his thinking, Hitler relied on him whenever the front line was crumbling or needed restoring. If Model had been captured on 17 September the war would have been shortened.

After contacting Hitler, Model drove on to Deetinchem to the HQ of Lt-Gen Willi Bittrich, the GOC, II SS Panzer Corps, who had 9th and 10th SS Panzer Divisions under his command. Model and Bittrich conferred at 1430, and within five minutes of the landings Bittrich had alerted Harzer, commanding 9th SS Panzer (Hohenstaufen) Division at Beeksbergen, and Harmel, commanding 10th SS Panzer (Frundsberg) Division in Ruurlo, together with the Luftwaffe.

9th Panzer was ordered to Arnhem, and 10th Panzer to Nijmegen to defend the bridgeheads south of the Waal. These SS armoured divisions were only at one-third strength, but they were still far too formidable opposition for lightly equipped airborne troops.

By 1500 three battalions of 1 Parachute Brigade were ready to move off from Renkum Heath, each following a different route into Arnhem. Lt-Col John Frost's 2nd Battalion, the Parachute Regiment, left first, meeting little opposition in Oosterbeek, where it turned immediately right for Arnhem, following the most southerly road. The streets were deserted except for a few exultant Dutch policemen. By dark Frost and 600 men had reached the north end of the road bridge at Arnhem, and had thus sealed off the shortest route to Nijmegen from German Panzer reinforcements. Without Frost's success Nijmegen bridge could not have been taken.

Lt-Col J.A.C. Fitch's 3rd Battalion and Lt-Col David Dobie's 1st Battalion were brought to a standstill within a few hours of leaving the landing zone. Dobie was stopped on the railway line by German infantry, and on the Ede-Arnhem road by armoured vehicles. B Company of the 1st Battalion suffered 50 per cent casualties fighting in a wood, and at 1930 Dobie went to ground for the night. They had run against the formidable strength of Harzer's 9th SS Panzer.

Fitch's 3rd Battalion also failed to reach Arnhem bridge, and again it was Harzer's tanks that kept them out—neither Fitch nor Dobie had expected, or been led to expect, armour. Only C Company of Fitch's battalion reached the Arnhem bridge to link up with Frost's men.

Meanwhile, the air-landing zone at Renkum Heath was being guarded by the 1st Battalion, the Border Regiment, in order to protect the landings planned for 18 September. The Dutch Resistance lent them as many vehicles as possible and collected the scattered ammunition containers. The leader of the Renkum Resistance acted as guide to the British and set up his headquarters in a café opposite the British forward position in Renkum. The people of the village thought that liberation had arrived. They flew forbidden Dutch flags, and the members of the Resistance movement put on their official armbands. When a Border patrol went out on reconnaisance half the population of Renkum marched with them. The Resistance also sent out patrols, but after dusk the British company commander forbade them to do so. For the rest of the night, whenever British patrols appeared in the café where the Resistance group had its HQ they were given beer and the latest telephoned news about German troop movements. To the east, pilots from the Glider

Pilot Regiment formed themselves into a battalion under Lt-Col J.W. Place and tried to occupy Wolfhezen, which became a no-man's-land.

During the night, German Panzers sealed off the southern end of the Arnhem bridge, and Frost's position became precarious. Neither Fitch's nor Dobie's battalions could reach him because the town was full of élite German troops, and XXX Corps' tanks were still far away at Valkenswaard. All that Frost could do was to fortify the northern end of the bridge and occupy the buildings around it. He ordered two infantry attacks towards the southern end of the bridge, carried out with great courage, but these were easily beaten back by Harzer's Panzers.

For two days Dobie and Fitch tried to break through to the bridge, but by the 20th they had run up against an impenetrable wall of mortars, armoured cars and tanks near the railway station: 'The Germans had hundreds of tanks,' said one British soldier.

On the evening of 17 September, Urquhart became detached from his HQ, and was forced to hide from the Germans for several vital hours. To make matters worse, most of the Division's wirelesses had failed; without its commander, and with only limited communications, 1st Airborne strove in vain to control the battle. Reinforcements duly arrived on 18 September, however. The landings took place in comparative quietness, although elements of an SS battalion had tried an attack on the landing grounds. Brigadier J.W. (Shan) Hackett, commanding 4 Parachute Brigade, found what he called 'a grossly untidy situation' as he sorted out the inevitable confusions of landing.

Brigadier P.H.W. (Pip) Hicks, commanding 1 Airlanding Brigade, took over as divisional commander in Urquhart's absence, and immediately had a flaming row with Hackett. After a nasty argument Hicks instructed Hackett to capture the high ground to the north of Arnhem. Within an hour and a half of landing on the 18th, the 10th Battalion was ready to march off, and was quickly followed by the 156th Parachute Battalion, 2nd Battalion, South Staffordshires, and the 7th King's Own Scottish Borderers; the last two had landed the previous day and were now attached to 4 Parachute Brigade. Only the South Staffords reached Arnhem, however. The other battalions did not get far, for, as they marched parallel with the Amsterdam road, they ran up against German self-propelled guns and tanks.

On Tuesday, 19 September, Frost's battalion was still isolated and being attacked continuously by German forces, who were becoming stronger and stronger every hour as they were continually reinforced from Germany with tanks, including some of the latest Tiger type. The 2nd Battalion succeeded in repelling German armoured cars and half-tracks, with their accompanying SS infantry, and knocked out several tanks. But on the same day the Germans renewed their attack east of the bridge, and at midday three tanks got into position near the river and wrought havoc amongst Frost's men, preventing them from manning their anti-tank guns.

St Elisabeth's Hospital, to the western end of the town, and near the pontoon bridge, was in the heart of the fighting. Around the hospital Fitch and Dobie, now joined by the South Staffords, suffered appalling casualties as they made one confused assault after another, trying to break through to Frost. Dobie's 1st Battalion actually succeeded in capturing several German guns and taking some prisoners in the early hours of Tuesday morning, but from then on the battle developed into a massacre. German artillery and tanks pounded the British infantry positions. Dobie himself was taken prisoner at 1730 on the 19th after being badly wounded, but soon after arriving at the hospital he made off and took refuge in a civilian house. For all Tuesday and Wednesday the four attacking British battalions* fought in Arnhem against German armour in desperate efforts to reach Frost. The town became a blazing mass of rubble.

Early on Wednesday (D-plus-3) German tanks and infantry broke through the British lines. Battered remains of the 1st, 3rd and 11th Parachute Battalions and the South Staffords were ordered by Urquhart to Westerbouwing, west of Oosterbeek. They straggled back, harried by German tanks, and, with Hackett's brigade, joined up with the remnants of the Division, making a total of only 3,000 fighting men. These remnants dug in and prepared to defend one small area, which became known to the Germans as 'The Cauldron'.

---

* 1st, 3rd and 11th Parachute Battalions, and 2nd South Staffords. On the afternoon of the 18th Hicks had sent Lt-Col G.H. Lea's 11th Parachute from Hackett's Brigade to support the South Staffords. Urquhart was still missing, and did not reappear until the following morning.

Frost's battalion fought on through the night and into the early hours of Thursday, but at 0900 on that day, 21 September (D-plus-4), they were over-run, with more than half their number dead or wounded. The route was now open for German tanks to drive south towards Nijmegen and hold up XXX Corps' advance.

On the afternoon of Friday, 22 September, Sosabowski's Polish 1 Independent Parachute Brigade landed south of the Rhine near Driel, as XXX Corps stood stationary at Bessen. But by then the ferry over the river at Driel had been lost and all the crossings were dominated by German guns. The Poles had lost all their transport (landed by glider on D-plus-2), and enemy preparedness now meant that there were far heavier casualties on landing than in the previous two drops. Worst of all, many of the gliders were attacked by German fighters. For the German pilots flying time from their aerodromes to the Arnhem landing grounds was only twenty minutes, and with Dunkirk still in German hands the Luftwaffe were told the exact numbers and direction of the Polish transport aircraft. On 23 September, however the Poles were fortunately able to link up with the 4th Dorsetshire Regiment from 43rd Division (the latter was now leading XXX Corps' advance), and one troop of Household Cavalry armoured cars from the same division also got through to them.

But now it was only a question of what Montgomery could save from the wreck. On 22 September a few Poles managed to cross the river by boat to the British perimeter at Westerbouwing, but their presence made no significant difference. The ground left to the besieged British was a long narrow corridor, only a few hundred yards wide in places, backing on to the Lower Rhine just to the east of the Driel ferry. It was under very heavy all-round German assault from Thursday onwards, but, inspired by Urquhart's outstanding resolution and courage, 1st Airborne troops withstood attack after attack by superior forces.

Even so, XXX Corps had at last reached the Rhine at Driel – albeit through a wretched, precarious, narrow corridor of bad roads. Here, however, was a route which could link up with Urquhart's hard-pressed troops within their small perimeter; through this corridor survivors of British 1st Airborne Division were to escape to fight again. But

Montgomery's bridgehead over the Rhine was lost.

Horrocks remained optimistic about exploiting the bridgehead over the Rhine gained by Urquhart's men. His hopes seem still to have been high – on the morning of 23 September he paid a flying visit to the Guards and told them that the taking of Nijmegen bridge was a feat 'which deserved champagne all round'; he then produced some of the wine from his jeep. On the same day he signalled Dempsey: 'As more troops become available will when road open pass up to two brigades of 43 Division into north of river. For subsequent exploitation an additional infantry division required.' And later on the 23rd another signal to Dempsey read: 'Considerable opposition between Nijmegen and Arnhem but have broken through west of main road. Leading elements 43 Division with Recce well out on left flank are approaching Neder Rijn in close contact Poles in loose contact 1 Airborne Div.' Unhappily, 'loose contact' with 1st Airborne was wishful thinking. There was no contact, not even by wireless.

Dempsey was more realistic, and in the afternoon of 23 September he signalled Horrocks: 'If you consider establishing a bridgehead in Arnhem area too difficult you may withdraw 1 Airborne without consulting me.' The road had been temporarily cut by the Germans behind XXX Corps, and Dempsey knew that as a result it would be difficult for him to rendezvous with Horrocks.

In the event, Dempsey and Horrocks met at St Odenrode on the 24th (D-plus-7). At the meeting Dempsey ordered Horrocks to see how the planned night operations over the Lower Rhine fared, when he could either pass a complete brigade of 43rd Division across the river to support Urquhart's perimeter, or give up the 'existing slender bridgehead and withdraw 1 Airborne south of the river'. He added that he would give Horrocks his own decision by 1200 on the next day. During the night, 24/25 September, the Dorsets and Poles tried, and after heavy casualties failed, to cross the river to reinforce Urquhart.

On Monday, 25 September, Montgomery and Dempsey met and agreed that British 1st Airborne Division – such as it now was – should be withdrawn south of the river that night. The Arnhem gamble had failed.

Soon after nightfall on the 25th all 43rd Divisional artillery opened up on the German positions around the Westerbouwing perimeter. Evacuation had been ordered, and during the early hours of 26 September, under heavy German artillery and machine-gun fire, boats manned by 43rd Division infantry and Canadian sappers ferried Urquhart and what was left of his division, together with a few Poles and Dorsets, to the south bank of the Rhine at Driel and safety. Out of 11,000 of Urquhart's men who had landed, more than 8,000 were killed, wounded, missing or made prisoner.

On 'Market-Garden' D-day, Browning and the staff of 1 Airborne Corps flew in gliders and landed, safely and unopposed, in the US 101st Airborne Division dropping zone. Browning established his HQ near Groesbeek, a small height to the east of the main axis of advance. Here he was twenty miles from 1st Airborne at Arnhem, and he never established any communication with the beleaguered division at all, although contact was made both with Second Army and with his HQ in England. Worse, transporting Browning and his staff had squandered airlift that could have carried an extra combat unit to 1st Airborne.

When I spoke to John Frost (now Major-General) he was scathing about Browning, and told me that the latter should have either stayed in England, gone in with 1st Airborne at Arnhem, or have flown in an aeroplane above them to observe and take action as necessary. He considers that the presence of the Corps HQ was 'nothing more than a nuisance'. In his memoirs, General Frost declares that the worst mistake of the 'Market-Garden' plan was the failure to give priority to capturing Nijmegen Bridge: 'The capture of this bridge would have been a walk-over on D-day, yet the American 82nd Airborne Division could spare only one battalion as they must at all costs secure a feature called Groesbeek Heights, where ... the HQ of Airborne Corps was to be sited.'[3]

According to Twenty-First Army Group's rather defensive official account, issued a few weeks after the operation, the Groesbeek Heights had to be captured in order to prevent German armour from the east from cutting the highway. Neither Frost nor the American historian Russell Weigley agree, however.[4] Certainly XXX Corps' east flank had to be defended, but on 17 September enemy forces there were weak. Even so, Montgomery vitally needed US VIII Corps as a guard for his east flank, and this was denied him because Eisenhower, badgered by Bradley and Patton, had failed to give VIII Corps priority in supplies.

The main task for Gavin's US 82nd Division was to capture the nine-span, 350-yard-long road bridge at Grave and the massive 1200-yard-long highway bridge over the Maas at Nijmegen. These bridges had to be kept open and usable, so that the Guards' tanks could advance unchecked to Arnhem — otherwise British 1st Airborne Division was doomed. Unfortunately, however, Gavin and Browning, instead of giving absolute priority to Nijmegen after taking the Grave bridge, concentrated instead on defending the Groesbeek Ridge between Beek, east of Nijmegen, and Mook, on the Waal east of Grave, fearing counter-attacks from German armour hidden in the Reichswald Forest. In fact, this enemy armour did not exist; US 508th Parachute Battalion found no tanks in the area, and were told by many civilians that the reports of armour in the Reichswald were false. Troops occupied in this fruitless search should have been ordered at once to Nijmegen, when it became clear that there was no Panzer threat.

Before take-off from England, Gavin and Browning had decided on the following priorities: first, Groesbeek Ridge; second, Grave Bridge; and third, Nijmegen Bridge. Gavin himself placed greater importance on Nijmegen than did Browning, and in his memoirs recorded that, seventy-two hours before take-off, he had decided that 'If I could possibly spare a battalion I knew I had to commit it to the Nijmegen [road] bridge as quickly as I could send it in that direction.' He added that he gave a verbal order to US 508th and 1st Parachute Battalions to attack Nijmegen on the evening of D-day if the situation at Groesbeek was quiet. In the event, a fatal misunderstanding occurred. The situation at Groesbeek was indeed quiet by the evening of the 17th, but Colonel Lindquist, commanding US 508th Parachute, did not obey this order, and later testified that he understood his orders were to send no troops to Nijmegen until all other objectives were secured. Nor did Colonel Warren's US 1st Parachute Battalion attack the bridge as Gavin had anticipated, assuming instead a defensive position on the outskirts of Nijmegen. In actual fact, when Warren's battalion reached the town the bridge was defended by only eighteen men, although German reinforcements soon arrived.[5]

Certainly Gavin showed more concern about the delay in capturing Nijmegen bridge than Browning. As late as the afternoon of D-plus-1 Browning rejected a plan for a strong effort against the town's rail and road bridges, instead instructing 82nd Airborne to concentrate on holding the Groesbeek Ridge. By adopting the wrong priorities, Browning sealed the fate of 'Market-Garden', but it is surprising that neither Horrocks nor Montgomery insisted before D-day that Nijmegen bridge should be the prime objective. Browning obviously interpreted his orders as being that he need not order an attack on Nijmegen bridge until XXX Corps' tanks arrived, but it is strange that Montgomery condoned this obvious error. Frost wrote:

> The Guards had expected to be able to motor on and over, but when they arrived, late as it was, the bridge was still firmly in German hands. Now the 82nd, trained at vast trouble and expense to drop by parachute over obstacles, had to cross the river in the teeth of intense opposition in flimsy canvas folding boats that they had never seen before. When so bravely it was done, it was too late.[6]

Frost also complains that although Browning continually stressed to Urquhart the imperative need to capture 'Arnhem Bridge. And hold it', he never stressed to Gavin in the same way the vital need to secure Nijmegen bridge.

The official Twenty-First Army Group report on 'Market-Garden' bears signs of having been heavily doctored by Montgomery. In the section entitled 'Important Lessons' there is this statement: 'If the weather had been good the operation would have been 100% success instead of 90% because the Poles would have dropped on D-plus-2 and 352 Glider Regiment on D-plus-2 as planned and normal scale of air supply would have been available.'[7] That Arnhem was 90 per cent successful is a theme reiterated by Montgomery in his memoirs and in talks he gave: such a view is, however, both wrong and unworthy of him. British 1st Airborne Division casualties were appalling; the Nijmegen bridgehead gained could not be exploited until March of 1945; and the Allies were left with a deep salient to defend. Meanwhile, because of 'Market Garden' the opportunity to clear swiftly the Scheldt and open up

Antwerp was irrevocably lost. Montgomery himself admitted that failing to clear the Scheldt was a bad mistake on his part – the corollary is that his Arnhem decision was also wrong.

What is unquestionably false is the statement in the Twenty-First Army Group report that if the weather had been good enough to allow Polish 1 Parachute Brigade to land on D-plus-2, then a complete victory would have been assured. In fact, by D-plus-2 the German armour dominated the Poles' designated DZs south of Arnhem Bridge; if the planned drop had been executed it would have been catastrophic. At the time there was insufficient news of German troops and movements to warrant changing the plan, and it was therefore a happy accident that the drop was cancelled on D-plus-2 because of bad weather. Instead, the Poles landed at Driel on the afternoon of D-plus-4, and their arrival was fiercely contested by the Germans. Frost wrote that if the Polish drop had taken place on D-plus-2, as planned, he was ready to send a suicide squad to rush the south end of the bridge, but that he 'dreaded to think of the reception they [the Poles] would have'. Sosabowski himself was highly critical of the lack of drive shown by both Horrocks and Browning. He pointed out in his memoirs that the road from Nijmegen to the banks of the Rhine where his brigade was deployed was open, but that no large body of troops was moved up it for an assault, and gave as his view that if Montgomery had been on the spot then a final, and possibly successful, attack over the river would almost certainly have been mounted.

In his report to the US Chiefs of Staff, Brereton stated that 'It was the breakdown of 2nd Army's timetable on the first day – their failure to reach Eindhoven in 6 to 8 hours as planned – that caused the delay in taking Nijmegen Bridge and the failure of Arnhem.'[8] Here, however, he is wrong, while Frost's cogent views are clearly right. By the end of D-day XXX Corps was thirty-three miles behind according to its planned timetable. If the leading Guards' tanks had found Nijmegen Bridge in the hands of 82nd Airborne Division when they arrived, then they could have pushed straight on and reached Frost on D-plus-2, and the whole course of the tragedy would have been altered. But the XXX Corps vanguard could not have advanced from Eindhoven on the evening of D-day, as Brereton claimed, because the Zon bridge was down and was not repaired until 0615 on D-plus-1. This delay was entirely

Brereton's fault for refusing Montgomery's request to allow US
101st Airborne to drop on both sides of the Zon bridge, in which
case it would almost certainly have been captured intact. At
Grave, in contrast to Eindhoven, the US paratroopers dropped
on both sides of the river and captured the bridge there before it
could be demolished. Brereton, like Montgomery, refused to
admit any mistakes in planning.

General Frost told me that: 'Parachutists should always land
behind the enemy and not be forced to cross rivers in the face of
intense fire. Rivers and defiles are always considered vital and are
heavily defended. You need to be on both sides. We wanted to
drop on both sides of the river at Arnhem, but the air forces would
not comply', and these views are echoed in his book.

Frost added that one glaring snag about the Arnhem
operation was that the DZs, selected by the air forces, were
several miles from the objective, and all on the north side of the
great main river obstacle. During the planning for 'Market-
Garden' the air force staff had claimed that the polder nearer
Arnhem was unsuitable for glider landings, as it was too soft.
This was not, in fact, the case. I Airborne Corps' After Action
Report stated: 'The difficulty of selecting DZs and LZs was
greatly over-estimated. Landings could have been made almost
anywhere as far as the terrain was concerned.' [9] It is quite clear
that, had the air forces agreed, 1st Airborne could have landed
south of the river close to Arnhem Bridge, as well as to the
north.

Chester Wilmot exculpates Montgomery, and claims that
where XXX Corps failed was in their drive forward from
Nijmegen on D-plus-5.[10] When I put this to General Frost he
scoffed and said: 'It did not matter in the least what XXX Corps
did on Friday [D-plus-5] We were bound to have been out of
ammunition long before then, and you cannot fight tanks and
armoured cars without plenty of that. If it had been Wednesday,
that would have been another matter.'

How far Browning was out of touch with the battle is shown
by his reaction to Maj-Gen Hakewill Smith, GOC 52nd
(Lowland) Division, when, on D-plus-2, the latter offered to take
one of his brigades by glider to Urquhart's rescue. Browning
replied: 'Thanks for message. Offer not, repeat not, required as
situation better than you think.'[11]

General Belchem considered that 'Browning had no idea

about whether or where his troops landed, and relied on me at 21 Army Group HQ for information.' He made the point that '1st Airborne Divisions's communications systems remained dead, and no one has found out what their senior signals director was doing from D-day until D-plus-4'; his conclusion was that Urquhart failed to appreciate the over-riding importance of radio communications, and 'lacked expert professional signal advice'. He maintained that Urquhart understood neither the importance of, nor what top priority had to be given to, radio and WT communications in air landings, although he had been a 'splendid infantry commander' – but Belchem thought that artillery or tank units understood the need for radio links far better than the infantry, even at this late stage of the war. And shortly before his death Belchem wrote to General Richardson: 'Can you imagine that you or I would have conceived a seaborne or airborne operation without insisting on a deputy for all key commanders?'[12]

General Poett disagrees strongly with Belchem about the need for a deputy, however. He told me that it was just a waste of a good man and 'a rotten frustrating job': 'For the D-Day landings I refused a Deputy Brigade Commander and I was sorry for the Deputy Commander of the other Brigade in 6th Airborne Division who had no real job on D-Day.'

After the war, Montgomery always claimed that 'full success' at Arnhem was denied to him because of bad weather preventing the planned build-up of forces. Belchem and others who helped Montgomery with the writing of his reminiscences found that he would never discuss the rights and wrongs of the Arnhem operation.

In his books and post-war lectures Montgomery overlooked the fact that neither he, nor anyone else at Twenty-First Army Group, realised in time that, by sending 1st Airborne in two drops to DZs eight miles from the objective, not only was the fighting force halved on landing, but it was in fact reduced to a quarter because half of the initial force successfully landed had to stay eight miles from the Arnhem bridge to guard DZs for the second lift. Once Montgomery had agreed to two lifts on successive days, instead of all on D-day, he ruined his chances of victory. Ronald Lewin rightly points out that out of some 10,000 men of 1st Airborne Division landed near Arnhem, only about 700 reached the bridge, the focus of the whole operation.[13]

The same handicap was an important factor in preventing US 82nd Airborne from capturing the Nijmegen Bridge before Guards Armoured arrived.

Belchem, in a correspondence with Williams, contradicted and effectively demolished Montgomery's assertion that the weather can be blamed for the failure:

> Weather conditions greatly hampered air co-operation and air delivery, but this was not the principal shortcoming. On some occasions when the Allied tactical air force was standing by to take off to support the land troops, it remained grounded because the air force ground controller accompanying the foremost elements lost radio contact with his air force base.
>
> This was an additional planning failure. The possibility that air supply drops might have to be changed in the course of operations was overlooked. An experienced planning staff would have organised a ground signal procedure indicating the change of dropping zone. These procedures would, of course, be independent of radio or WT failures. No such arrangements were considered, and much of the drops fell behind German lines and many air crew were lost trying to supply 1st Airborne.[14]

Another major, avoidable, problem noted both by Belchem and by Chester Wilmot was that, for XXX Corps, the traffic congestion was much worse than it need have been because it was never realised that the road verges were not mined by the Germans – two additional traffic lanes could have been in use if the verges had been driven over. No mine clearance notices were put up, and bottlenecks would have been avoided if the drivers had known they could use the verges. On one afternoon Chester Wilmot drove for miles on the verge past stationary traffic in order to file his copy, yet it took 43rd Division seventy-two hours to drive fifty-five miles in trucks to reach Nijmegen on Wednesday. They were better off on foot. No blame can be put on Montgomery for the failure to fix 'mines swept' notices on the verges, which was a matter for divisional staff, and the signals' failure, the choice of dropping zones, and the failure to give priority to Nijmegen bridge are indictments of Allied First Airborne Army, not Montgomery's Twenty-First Army Group. Similarly, the blame for the failure to react correctly to available intelligence rests with First Airborne Army. In a letter to the official historian in 1966, Williams wrote that 'You should be tougher about the Intelligence failure re Arnhem; of the many errors that, together, ensured the disaster, this was one of the greatest.'

Montgomery was reluctant to admit to the CIGS and the Prime Minister that his Arnhem adventure had failed. Even on the last day, 24 September, he sent this signal to the CIGS:

> If we suffer heavy casualties tonight in trying to get across (tricky business because we have not got a wide front or sufficient troops) I shall probably give it up and withdraw 1AB. Decision will be taken tomorrow morning. It may well be that we can attain our object equally if not better by developing thrust from lines eastwards. And we shall have greater resources for these if we abandon attempt to cross the Neder Rijn west of Arnhem.

For once Montgomery was wide of the mark. The airborne troops were the Allies' only strategical reserve, and they had been largely wasted; his own troops had shot their bolt; and his intelligence had told him that new German armies were forming to the east, while the unbeaten Fifteenth Army was pouring back from South Beveland to strengthen the enemy forces on the Lower Rhine.

Did the Field-Marshal try to find a scapegoat for the disaster? He refused to criticise his favourite corps commander, Horrocks, although I have found a strong feeling amongst some of the more senior survivors of XXX Corps that the latter was not well during those fateful days, and that this detracted from the dash of his corps' advance from the Dutch frontier to Arnhem. Not long afterwards Montgomery sent Horrocks home on compulsory sick leave, and on 27 December he wrote to Brooke: 'Am sending Horrocks home on leave tomorrow. During the past ten days he has been very nervy and difficult with his staff and has attempted to act foolishly with his Corps. He is definitely in need of rest, and I want him to have 3 to 4 weeks quietly in UK.'

Montgomery was not so kind about the Poles, however, nor about Brigadier Hicks, the 1 Airlanding Brigade commander who had taken over 1st Airborne during Urquhart's enforced absence. He wrote to the CIGS that Hicks was not fit for further promotion: 'Too old ... not now fit to fight again in battle in this war in his present rank. No doubt that he did extremely well at Arnhem, but no doubt that it has been too much for him.'

Of the Poles, Montgomery wrote to Brooke on 17 October: 'Polish Para Bde fought very badly here, and the men showed no keenness to fight if it meant risking their own lives. I do not want this Bde here again, and possibly you may like to send it to join other Poles in Italy.' This was a harsh judgement, taking into account the appallingly difficult landings, the language problem, and the XXX Corps failure to link up with Sosabowski's force satisfactorily.

Certainly both in its conception and in its execution 'Market-Garden' was the greatest military mistake of Montgomery's career, a defeat that prolonged the war. Montgomery's strategy was risky and, when put into effect on the ground as a joint Anglo-American operation, showed terrible flaws in planning and execution. It was unreasonable to expect British 1st Airborne Division to hold out until XXX Corps could reach it, but when, early in the operation, it was known that 1st Airborne was *in extremis*, Montgomery was unable to speed up its relief. Many people, including both Belchem and Chester Wilmot, have commented on how different might have been the result if Maj-Gen Matthew Ridgway of US XVIII Airborne Corps had commanded at Nijmegen in place of Boy Browning.

In his memoirs Montgomery wrote: 'I remain an unrepentant advocate of "Market-Garden".'[15] The verdict of history must be that he was wrong.

9

The Canadians on the Coast

When Twenty-First Army Group crossed the Seine on 30 August, Canadian First Army, reinforced by British I Corps, began mopping up German resistance on the coast with considerable élan. In his directive M520 of 26 August, Montgomery showed a deep understanding of Canadian and Scottish feeling, writing: 'All Scotland will be grateful if the Commander Canadian Army can arrange that the Highland Division can capture St Valery. I have no doubt that the Canadian Second Division will capture Dieppe.'

Montgomery's message was greatly appreciated by both the Scots and the Canadians, for both divisions would now have the chance to even the scores. The first-line 51st (Highland) Division had been captured almost intact by Rommel at St Valéry in June 1940, chiefly because Churchill, in a vain bid to boost French morale, had insisted that the division stayed in France when all was lost. The Canadians, during their disastrous raid on Dieppe on 19 August 1942, had lost almost 1,000 dead, with total casualties of nearly 3,500, in nine bloody hours. Now St Valéry quickly fell to the Scots, Dieppe to the Canadians, and the inhabitants of both towns gave their liberators enthusiastic receptions, in which they paid tribute to their predecessors.[1]

In his personal relations with the Canadians, however, Montgomery often made mistakes. In 1942, for instance, he was barracked while addressing a Canadian unit – he had picked his moment badly, too near to the troops' mealtime. A few days later the Canadian I Corps GOC, Lt-Gen Henry Crerar, travelling in Montgomery's car, got out his cigarettes and offered one to the British general. Montgomery refused, and ordered the driver to stop, saying, 'Smoke if you have to, but if you do I will get out of the car.' The two men clashed later in Italy, when Crerar informed Montgomery that he would be visiting the Canadian Division from time to time and wanted to leave batmen, drivers and vehicles at Eighth Army Main HQ – Montgomery refused to let the Canadian 'clutter up' Eighth Army Main. On another occasion Crerar sent a signal stating that he wanted to visit Montgomery, who replied that he did not want to see Crerar. Montgomery's Canadian liaison officer had a most difficult job in soothing over a potentially dangerous international incident.

Again, in Sicily Montgomery refused to allow the GOC-in-C, Canadian First Army, Lt-Gen Andrew McNaughton, to visit Canadian 1st Division. As has been said earlier, this was ill received; plainly Montgomery, brought up in the days of colonialism, did not appreciate the emergence of the Commonwealth. While in Normandy, he told the War Office firmly that he would not accept Canadian Army HQ 'with all its troops' into the narrow bridgehead and, despite protests, Crerar's HQ only became operational on 31 July, even though Crerar himself had been in France for weeks.

Bill Williams told me:

> Monty's handling of the Canadians was strange ... [He] did not like Crerar, whom he used to describe, correctly, in my view, as more of a Quartermaster-General than a Field Commander. With hindsight, I feel Monty was astonishing in his relationship with all the Dominion troops. He ordered them around like British troops, ignoring the devolution of the British Empire ... he was completely out of date. Still, he handled them well in battle. He liked the Canadian General Guy Simonds very much and he respected Simonds's qualities as a soldier greatly, but he was far too grand in his attitude to their commanders and could never understand they were allies, not subordinates. Because he admired Simonds so much he frequently bypassed Crerar and dealt with him direct. The best way to describe Monty's manner with Crerar is *de haut en bas*.

Maj-Gen Guy Simonds commanded Canadian 1st Division, part of Eighth Army, under Montgomery in Sicily in 1943. In contrast to his opinion of Crerar, Montgomery thought Simonds's performance in battle was exceptional, describing him after the war as 'the best product of the Allied side'. But just after Dieppe was taken by the Canadians on 1 September there occurred a bizarre incident between Crerar and Montgomery, involving Simonds, which revealed the British commander at his arrogant worst, although in the end he showed his resilience by rescuing himself from a dangerous quicksand. On 2 September, Montgomery took exception to an order issued by Simonds, as Canadian II Corps commander, which allowed a period of rest to his Canadian 2nd and 3rd Divisions in the Dieppe and Abbeville areas respectively. Simonds had obviously agreed this with Crerar, but his order produced from Montgomery, late on the same day, this testy signal to Crerar:

> Personal for Army Commander from C-in-C
> Second Army are now positioned on the Belgian frontier and will go through towards Brussels tomorrow. *It is very necessary* that your two Armoured Divisions should push forward with all speed towards St Omer and beyond. Not repeat not consider this time for any div to halt for maintenance. Push on quickly.

Crerar, nettled by this signal, and also by the failure of Second Army troops to support his flank at Abbeville, where the Germans were resisting on the Seine, replied:

> Personal for C-in-C from CDN Army Commander
> ... 2 Cdn Inf Div bns down to average of strength 525 and in my opinion a 48 hour halt essential in order it can absorb approx one thousand reinforcements arriving today. You can be assured there is no lack of push or rational speed Cdn Army. St Omer and beyond will be reached without any avoidable delay.

Montgomery's attitude, and Crerar's response, now started a flaming row, almost without reason. On 3 September a moving and politically charged religious service was to be held in the cemetery at Dieppe, where over 800 Canadians killed in the 1942 raid lay buried. There was to be a formal march-past of Canadian 2nd Infantry Division units, and Crerar had an obvious duty both to his government and to his men to be present and take the salute. But on 2 September Montgomery ordered Crerar to meet him at Second Army Tac HQ at 1300 on the 3rd, the day of the parade. Crerar replied:

Unless operational situation requires me request meeting at 1700 not 1300. At noon have arranged to be present formal religious service and parade and from Canadian point of view desirable I should be there. Will conform to your wishes. Advice required.

At 1440, just before the Dieppe march-past started, a dispatch rider brought Crerar a signal from Montgomery saying that it was essential that he should be at the meeting. As soon as he could decently depart, therefore, Crerar flew to Second Army HQ, where Dempsey told him that it was quite unimportant whether he had been present at the meeting or not, since no urgent operations had been discussed. Montgomery's Tac HQ was two miles away, so Crerar drove there. He described the interview:

On reaching the caravan, the Field-Marshal addressed me abruptly, asking me why I had not turned up at the meeting, in accordance with his instructions. I kept myself under control and briefly, with occasional interruptions, gave him the explanation ... The C-in-C intimated that he was not interested in my explanation – that the Canadian aspect of the Dieppe ceremonial was of no importance compared to getting on with the war, that he had checked through his signals and determined that my Tac HQ had received a message from him at 0615 hrs that morning, instructing me to keep the appointment and that, even if I had not received it, then in default of other agreed arrangements, I should have made it my business to be present.

I replied to the C-in-C that I could not accept this ... I had carried out my responsibilities ... as the Cdn Army Comd in what I considered to be a reasonable and intelligent way ... I had found him, in the past, reasonable in his treatment of me and I had assumed that this situation would continue to prevail. The request in my message, for the postponement of the hour of our meeting, had been fully explanatory and, I thought, tactful, ... I had ... a definite responsibility to my Government and country which, at times, might run counter to his own wishes. There was a powerful Canadian reason why I should have been present with 2 Cdn Inf Div at Dieppe that day. In fact, there were 800 reasons – the Canadian dead buried at Dieppe cemetery. I went on to say that he should realise, by our considerable association, that I was neither self-opinionated, nor unreasonable, but that, also, I would never consent to be 'pushed about' by anyone, in a manner, or direction, which I knew to be wrong.

The Field-Marshal reiterated that I had failed to comply with an instruction issued by him and that such situation could only result in his decision that our ways must part. I replied that I assumed he would at once take this up through higher channels and that, I, in turn, would at once report the situation to my Government.

At this point Montgomery, to Crerar's surprise, suddenly said that the incident was closed. The Canadian replied that he did not want it closed, and 'desired that it be properly ventilated through official channels.' After further discussion, Montgomery again said that he wanted the matter closed, and went on to give Crerar the gist of what had happened at the conference.

At the time, Montgomery had just given up overall command of the ground forces, and he was desperately anxious to have that command given back to him. He had always found it hard to prevent himself from treating both the Canadians and the Poles (as has been shown earlier) as subordinates and not allies, but as soon as the Crerar stood up to him, refusing to be bullied, Montgomery became cautious. He knew that his chances of becoming overall commander again would be ruined if he started a row over a triviality with the Canadian Government, which undoubtedly would back Crerar. Dieppe was an emotive word in Canada, and Montgomery himself was blamed by many Canadians for his part in that disaster.

Crerar recorded his conviction that the row was started in an attempt to rub in the fact that he was a subordinate, and had no duty to anyone except Montgomery, and certainly the Canadian emerges from the incident with greater dignity than his C-in-C. Thwarted by his failure either to humiliate or to sack Crerar, Montgomery vented his irritation that night by writing to the

CIGS in his daily signal: 'Canadian operations since crossing the Seine have been badly handled and very slow.' At that time he wanted to replace Crerar with Simonds, but had no power to do so.

In fact, Montgomery soon made amends. Crerar gave him details showing how the signal calling him to the meeting had been delayed, and Montgomery wrote him a pleasant note dated 5 September: 'I am sorry I was a bit rude the other day, and somewhat outspoken. I was annoyed that no one came to a very important conference. But forget about it – and let us get on with the war. It was my fault.' But unfortunately the incident served to heighten the tension between the two men.

In a directive given out on 3 September Montgomery wrote: '5 Canadian Armoured will clear the coastal belt and will then remain in the general area Bruges-Calais until the maintenance situation allows of its employment further forward.' When he issued this, however, he did not realise that the Germans intended to fight for the Channel ports, for when Hitler ordered them to be defended as 'fortresses' the Nazi commanders obeyed his instructions to the letter. On 4 September Simonds's corps directive ordered his divisions to advance to the Scheldt and destroy or capture all the enemy south of it within the Canadian Army boundary. Alas, this was quite impossible. Boulogne, Dunkirk, Calais and Le Havre were all strongly defended, and the German Fifteenth Army held the south bank of the Scheldt in great strength.

On 9 September Crerar attended a conference at Twenty-First Army Group with Montgomery, Dempsey and Hodges. There it was decided that the Canadian Army was to take over Ghent and the south bank of the Scheldt as far east as the point where the Dutch border crosses the river north-west of Antwerp, but that the first priority was to capture the Channel ports. On 12 September, after three days of fighting, Le Havre fell to British I Corps. But then, in a letter to Crerar on the 13th, Montgomery ordered priority to be given to 'setting in motion operations designed to enable us to use the port of Antwerp'. Later in the day he signalled 'Early use of Antwerp so urgent that I am prepared to give up operations against Calais and Dunkirk and be content with Boulogne.' Boulogne did not fall to the Canadians until 22 September, and Calais until 1 October, but the sea approaches to Antwerp remained obstinately in

German hands. Worse, these operations against the Channel ports consumed valuable time, and tied up troops that might otherwise have been used to free Antwerp. Montgomery said later that he regretted that, in his 3 September directive, he had initially put clearing the channel to Antwerp at the bottom of the agenda for the Canadian troops, although the Channel ports captured paid some slow dividends in terms of supplies landed while Antwerp was closed. Dunkirk, however, held out until after Hitler's death in April 1945.

The task which Montgomery had given Crerar was beyond the power of his army. Ostend, Bruges and Ghent fell to the Canadians and the Poles, but German Fifteenth Army obeyed Hitler's orders and put up a ferocious resistance behind the two canals (the Leopold and the Derivation de Lys) which protect Breskens and the mouth of the Scheldt. In the middle of September the Germans still held the coast east from Zeebruge to the port of Breskens, together with all the southern bank of the Scheldt estuary. Plainly Montgomery's hopes that Crerar could open Antwerp on his own were a hollow dream, for General von Zangen, commanding Fifteenth Army, followed Hitler's instruction literally, obstinately defending his strong points and turning them into 'fortresses'.

On 27 September, after the failure of 'Market-Garden' at Arnhem, Montgomery issued a fresh directive to Crerar to obtain 'the free use of the Port of Antwerp', while Second Army was to 'operate strongly against the Ruhr'. This was merely reiterating the impossible objective he had given Canadian First Army on 13 September, for opening Antwerp meant not only clearing the Germans out of the mainland Breskens pocket on the south bank of the Scheldt estuary, but would involve a seaborne assault on Walcheren Island, together with a land attack from north of Antwerp westwards against the South Beveland peninsula.

Obviously Montgomery, even as late as 27 September, still hoped for a German collapse before Antwerp was open, for on 28 September he declared: 'I cannot see how D-Day for the Walcheren-South Beveland assault can be before 15 October.' It is difficult to understand how such a realist could still have been sufficiently optimistic to believe that he could carry out the double task of clearing the Scheldt and capturing the Ruhr with the limited number of troops within Twenty-First Army Group.

Certainly Montgomery, with his eyes fixed on the more exciting target of the Ruhr, grossly underestimated the time and effort needed to open up the approaches to Antwerp.

To defend the Breskens pocket on the mainland, Model left his crack 64th Division behind the Leopold Canal – 14,000 men reinforced by much artillery from Fifteenth Army, which was being steadily evacuated from the port of Breskens to Flushing on Walcheren Island. Although completely trapped in the Breskens pocket, around 65,000 men of German Fifteenth Army crossed the estuary to fight again, reinforcing the German right flank opposing Montgomery's drive to the Rhine. The Breskens pocket was christened 'Scheldt Fortress South' by Hitler, a grandiloquent name which, he thought, would encourage his soldiers to realise that it had to be held to the last man.

By the end of September Montgomery was so heavily involved in the Nijmegen bridgehead that he just could not spare extra divisions to enable Crerar to carry out the Antwerp clearance. Some of the blame must also lie with Eisenhower, for in spite of his acknowledging the paramount importance of the Scheldt he sent extra supplies and troops to Patton in the south, while Crerar's Canadians were starved of their vital requirements. For instance, for a fortnight after the fall of Le Havre on 12 September 51st (Highland) Division was grounded for lack of transport, although it was urgently needed by the Canadians for the attack on the Leopold Canal.

The Canadian Corps Commander, Simonds, originally thought that he could take the Breskens pocket in three days; it took three weeks. So stiff was the enemy's resistance that the German coastal battery near Breskens was not captured until 2 November, although Breskens itself fell on 21 October. In the end 12,700 German prisoners were taken by the Canadians in the Breskens pocket. Total Canadian Army casualties from 1 October to 8 November 1944 amounted to 12,813 officers and men, of whom 6,357 were Canadians.

Eventually, Canadian 2nd Division, advancing from northeast of Antwerp on 31 October, reached the causeway from South Beveland to Walcheren, and on the following day a seaborne assault against Walcheren was made by 4 Commando Brigade and Royal Navy Force 'T'. On 6 November the German troops in Middelburg, the principle town, finally surrendered, and on the 8th all resistance in the Walcheren Islands ceased — at last it was possible for the Royal Navy to start clearing the Scheldt. It took 100 minesweepers three weeks to clear the mines, and the first Allied merchant ship convoy did not reach Antwerp until 28 November. When Walcheren was captured it was found to be bristling with heavy calibre coastal batteries encased in impregnable thicknesses of concrete; if the Allies had sought to use Antwerp before the Scheldt was cleared the results would have been catastrophic.

Both Montgomery and the Canadians wanted to use airborne troops in the Scheldt battle. As we have seen, Montgomery's first request to the Airborne Army for a drop on Walcheren — Operation 'Infatuate' — was turned down by Brereton, but would an airborne operation have made much difference? Simonds certainly thought so, and in a letter to Crerar, dated 13 September, Montgomery wrote: 'The whole energies of the Army will be directed towards operations designed to enable full use to be made of the port of Antwerp. Airborne troops are available to co-operate.' In his diary for 11 September, however, Brereton listed ten possible airborne operations which had been under consideration, and added: 'I refused Operation Infatuate because of intense flak on Walcheren; difficult terrain which would prevent glider landings; excessive losses because of drowning.'

On 17 September General Cutler, a senior staff officer from Allied First Airborne Army, discussed a possible airborne operation on Walcheren and South Beveland with Crerar. The former's view was that, since such an operation was now planned to assist a ground assault, it had become more attractive, and he added that two parachute regiments of US 17th Airborne Division were available. Three days later Montgomery asked Eisenhower for a decision about employing these airborne troops. The Supreme Commander telephoned Brereton, and then, with Leigh-Mallory opposing it, turned the proposition down because of 'terrain factors and types of targets'. Nevertheless, at his conference on 22 September Eisenhower told de Guingand that he would ask Allied First Airborne Army to reconsider the operation. The answer was again a refusal, to Simonds's disappointment. On 21 October Crerar once more requested an air drop, this time to be at the west end of South Beveland on the 29th in order to seize the

Walcheren causeway. But on the day after his request Crerar was firmly told that the Airborne Army was no longer at Twenty-First Army Group's disposal.

Any air drop on Walcheren or South Beveland must have been highly expensive in casualties, given the German troop concentrations, and not even Montgomery seriously argued that employing airborne forces would have significantly altered either the casualties suffered in, or the time taken up by, the Scheldt campaign.

In the general euphoria that followed the capture of Brussels and the planning for 'Market-Garden', with its attendant chance of securing a Rhine crossing, Montgomery failed either to appreciate or to heed the intelligence reports about German Fifteenth Army's strength on both banks of the Scheldt – in this lies his chief error. As soon as the Allies took Antwerp land telephone lines between Hitler and Fifteenth Army HQ were cut – as a result there was a sudden increase in the number of German radio signals deciphered by Ultra at Bletchley. These disclosed not only the enemy's strength, but also his plans. Within twenty-four hours of the fall of Antwerp, Twenty-First Army Group knew from Ultra that Hitler had sent two signals ordering his troops to hold both banks of the Scheldt, and each day more signals gave news of the substantial ferryings of troops across the estuary to Walcheren and South Beveland. For the first three days these movements could have signified a German evacuation of the southern shore of the Scheldt, but Hitler's signal to Army Group B on 7 September gave the firmest possible evidence that the Breskens pocket on the south bank would be 'obstinately defended'. An Army Group B order of 4 September had ordered Fifteenth Army units which could not fight their way through by Louvain to go back via Flushing and Breda, and further series of signals revealed to Twenty-First Army Group the enemy's corps and divisional locations; these indicated considerable strength in front of the Canadians both on the mainland and on South Beveland.[2] Montgomery ought to have known that, once the initial opportunity had been lost on 4 September, the clearing of the Scheldt must be a massive, long and costly operation.

During the seven days before 'Market-Garden', Ultra revealed the daily performance of the Breskens ferries from Terneuzen to Flushing and inland; it was reliably estimated that by 17 September 25,000 men and 550 vehicles had crossed from the mainland to the north bank. Montgomery failed to interpret this intelligence as evidence that these escaping troops would be ideally placed to attack the left flank of his XXX Corps as they advanced towards Arnhem. During the Arnhem operation itself, Ultra signals showed that 82,000 men, 530 guns and 46,000 vehicles had been ferried north over the Scheldt, which in the end meant that German Fifteenth Army was able to make strong attacks on both XXX Corps and the airborne troops from the south-west.

Neither Montgomery nor Eisenhower showed a proper understanding of the true significance of the escape of Fifteenth Army and of the threat it posed to any further Allied advance through Holland to the Rhine. Throughout September SHAEF intelligence reports were over-optimistic about the end of the war, and gave no prominence to the menace of Fifteenth Army in Holland, nor to the impossibility of opening Antwerp unless more divisions were diverted to the battle of the Scheldt. Bill Williams at Twenty-First Army Group understood the situation perfectly, and insisted again and again to Montgomery that clearing the Scheldt must have priority over an air drop and a Rhine crossing.

His general, however, would not listen, being too intent on persuading Eisenhower to pursue a strategy which would enable him (Montgomery) to command a powerful force in a drive over the Rhine into Germany. Eisenhower was only concerned about balancing the conflicting claims of the Americans and the British to priority in what he expected to be the final victorious thrust. Thus, in the first weeks of September the overriding importance of dealing with German Fifteenth Army on the Scheldt was overlooked by both commanders. As far as Montgomery is concerned, the only possible verdict is that the prospect of an immediate, complete victory in Europe blinded him to the threat on his left flank, of which normally, with his usual caution and professionalism, he would have been completely aware.

Montgomery wrote in his memoirs: 'I admit a bad mistake. I underestimated the difficulties of opening up the approaches to Antwerp. I reckoned the Canadian Army could do it while we were going for the Ruhr. I was wrong.'[3]

10

After Arnhem

Montgomery found it hard to accept that withdrawing from the bridgehead over the Rhine meant that he must abandon his cherished plan for a drive into Germany, a drive backed by the US troops which Eisenhower had only assigned to him after so much argument. Once the withdrawal from Arnhem was completed, Montgomery immediately signalled the CIGS: 'A fine division has been practically wiped out in sacrifice but it has ensured operations succeeding elsewhere.' This statement was misleading, but it was part of his philosophy of never admitting defeat. General Simpson told me that 'Monty felt it was his duty to exude confidence in front of his subordinates, and inside himself too he always felt cocksure,' although David Belchem wrote that: 'After the Arnhem setback Monty was quiet and withdrawn, usually a sign of anger.'[1] Brigadier Williams, however, told me that:

> The failure of Arnhem did not make Monty despondent. He was as cocky as ever. In his mind it was essential to pretend it was not a major defeat in order to keep up morale and deceive the enemy. He found no difficulty in doing precisely that because of his peacock vanity. His reaction was: 'It is no good pining – as a good soldier I must get on with the next move.'
> This fitted both his moods, eg one, that as the best general in the world he must plan his next operation, and two, his peacock vanity, which would not let him admit defeat.

When 'Market-Garden' began, both Montgomery and

Eisenhower were euphoric about an early end to the war. On 15 September, for instance, Eisenhower wrote a circular letter to army, naval and air commanders stating that, as the Allied armies were about to close up on the Rhine, it was 'time to plan the final offensive.'[2] This, too, was unrealistic. In the south, Patton had been checked at Metz, the Germans were counter-attacking strongly at Nancy, and Bradley was halted in the narrow Aachen corridor – all SHAEF hopes were therefore pinned on Montgomery, for only if 'Market-Garden' succeeded could there be a rapid victory. Unfortunately, and unknown to the Allies, Hitler had staged a lightning recovery among his forces.

At the beginning of September, Student's parachute regiments were training and re-equipping in Germany. On the 4th of that month Hitler ordered Student to establish a new army – First Parachute Army – along the Albert Canal in Belgium, with its western flank held by those elements of Fifteenth Army already emerging from the north Scheldt peninsula; it was this hastily assembled force that robbed Montgomery of success at Arnhem. To the south, along the Siegfried Line, Hitler had also concentrated a new Panzer army (Fifth) under von Manteuffel, and already the Führer hoped to launch a massive counter-attack early in November through the Ardennes. On 26 September Hitler ordered the Nazi Party to raise a people's militia, the Volkssturm, to defend German soil, a force made up chiefly of men up to the age of sixty, and boys of sixteen and sometimes younger, together with a number of men classed as unfit for service in the armed forces proper. At the same time, over a million workers set about erecting tank obstacles, bunkers and fortifications to defend Germany's western borders, under the direction of Martin Bormann, Hitler's deputy. The remaining fifty-five German divisions in the west were quickly reinforced by conscripts, mostly ardent young supporters of Hitler, dedicated Nazis ready to fight frenziedly in defence of their homeland. Meanwhile, aircraft, tanks, guns, bazookas and arms of every description were pouring out of the factories to equip the swelling numbers of new Nazi soldiers. Germany's power of recovery had been badly underestimated by the Allies.

On 14 September Eisenhower had written to Marshall explaining why he had rejected Montgomery's proposal (10

September) for a single thrust to Berlin, and stating that: 'We will have to fight one more battle for Germany to break through the defences on the border.'[3] Unhappily, this view, even by then, was wishful thinking, so quick had been Hitler's reaction. But on the 15th Eisenhower wrote in a directive that 'Berlin is the main prize', and emphasised that he would give Montgomery priority in supplies, and that Bradley would support Twenty-First Army Group on the right.[4] He did, however, make it clear that he still intended to push a double-thrust advance into Germany – one in the north, the other in the centre towards Leipzig – but he was assuming that Antwerp would soon be open to supply this 'double-front strategy', and, like Montgomery, he fell into the error of believing that the numerically small Canadian First Army could clear the Scheldt estuary while Second Army was putting all its resources into the crossing of the Rhine.

On 18 September Montgomery wrote Eisenhower a long letter, emphasising that 'a concerted operation in which all the available land armies move into Germany is not possible ... it is my personal opinion that we shall not achieve what we want by going for Nuremberg, Augsburg, Munich etc. and establishing our forces in Central Germany ... the best objective is the Ruhr and then on to Berlin by the northern route.' He continued by writing that, if Eisenhower agreed, 'the northern route should be used 21 Army Group plus 9 Divisions of 1st US Army would be enough provided they had everything needed in the maintenance line ... If the proper axis is by Frankfurt and Central Germany then I suggest that 12 Army Group should be used and have all the maintenance.' Twenty-First Army Group would do the best it could with what was left over, though it was possible that British Second Army would be wanted in a secondary role on the left flank.[5] Bradley, meanwhile, had told Eisenhower that he wanted drives from both the north and south, with the main southern attack towards the Ruhr from Frankfurt.

Faced with these contradictory proposals from his Army Group commanders, Eisenhower wrote to Montgomery on 20 September declaring himself against 'a narrow front policy', and firmly rejecting Montgomery's suggestion 'that all troops except 21 Army Group should stop in place where they are, and that we can strip all these additional divisions from their transport and everything else into one single knife like drive towards Berlin.' This, Eisenhower said, did not mean that he intended an advance into Germany 'with all armies moving abreast'; instead, the crossing of the Rhine would be accomplished by a joint assault from both Montgomery's and Bradley's forces. He went on to remind Montgomery that he had given him priority in supplies while the other forces had been 'fighting with a halter around their necks.'[6]

At this stage Eisenhower was confident that Montgomery would win a bridgehead over the Rhine at Arnhem, and that this success would have to be reinforced at the expense of the US armies, despite the complaints of the American generals, who were accusing the Supreme Commander of being in Montgomery's pocket. Although the latter tactfully suggested that he would co-operate if Eisenhower gave the US armies the main drive, he was supremely confident that he would win his bridgehead over the Rhine, in which event he would have an unanswerable case for priority in supplies.

In his letter, Eisenhower told Montgomery that: 'Generally speaking I find myself so completely in agreement ... that I cannot believe there is any difference in our concepts,' and added that he had never intended to advance into Germany with all armies moving abreast, and that he would give priority to the British northern thrust.

Montgomery replied on the 21st: 'Our concepts are not the same, and I am sure you would want me to be quite frank.' He emphasised that he definitely wanted Eisenhower 'to stop by binding orders the advance of the 12 Army Group's southern drive', and to 'put everything into the left hook. If this is not done you will not get the Ruhr.'[7]

The Supreme Commander realised at once that he would get nowhere by continuing this argument in writing, so he called a top-level conference at Versailles (the new site of his HQ since 15 September) for 22 September. This was the most important SHAEF conference since D-Day, and Eisenhower hoped that it would produce agreement over major decisions for a swift ending of the war. He wrote to Marshall saying that he still hoped for a quick breakthrough by the British to Arnhem, although by then the attempt was doomed.

The Versailles conference was the first full SHAEF meeting since the conference at St Paul's School in May. But, to Eisenhower's fury, Montgomery refused to attend, sending de Guingand in his place. Eisenhower's reaction was mild enough, under the circumstances: 'It is a great pity all of us cannot keep in closer touch because without exception when all of us get together and look at our various problems squarely in the face the answers usually become obvious.'

Although Montgomery signalled Eisenhower that he was too busy with thê critical Arnhem battle to come to Versailles, this was not in fact true. Control on the ground lay perforce with Horrocks and Browning, and in any case Montgomery had great difficulty in keeping in touch with his forward formations since his front was now a salient fifty miles deep. John Henderson told me that his general only once got as far as Nijmegen bridge between 17 and 24 September, but even then did not cross the Waal, for he stuck resolutely to his routine of being back at his HQ early each evening, relying on his liaison officers' contacts with his commanders. He himself had little contact with his troops at the time, and his claim that he was closely involved at the front was specious, to say the least.

Probably Montgomery's main reason for not going to Versailles was that he knew that Simpson would be there on that day – he knew also that he could rely on the latter to put his point of view more persuasively than he could himself. What was more, Simpson, an exceptionally charming, able and tactful man, was on excellent terms with Morgan and Whiteley, the British generals at SHAEF, whereas Montgomery was not. Montgomery also knew that Bedell Smith would listen more sympathetically to Simpson than to himself, for the two men were friends. Simpson was devoted to Montgomery (Brooke used to tell him 'You worship Monty'), and Montgomery was convinced that at Versailles on 22 September Simpson would be the best advocate for his ambitious plans, with the loyal de Guingand in support.

Even on D-plus-4, 21 September, Montgomery was still optimistic about 'Market-Garden', and was most anxious that the conference should agree to Bradley's Twelfth Army Group covering Twenty-First Army Group's right flank during the Rhine crossing. Still expecting the establishment of a strong bridgehead over the Rhine, he wanted to get Hodges's US First Army to turn north to join him, since the gap between the US and British armies was now nearly 100 kilometres. To a certain extent Montgomery ignored the strength of Student's reinforced army and the dire plight of British 1st Airborne Division when, on 21 September, he sent the following signal to Eisenhower:

> If we are to take quick advantage of our favourable situation
> in the NIJMEGEN area it is essential that the right Corps of
> Second Army should develop at once a strong thrust on the
> axis GENNEP – CLEVE – EMMERICH. In order to do this
> the inter-Army Group boundary would have to be adjusted to
> read all incl 12 Army Group HASSELT – WEERT –
> ASTEN – DEURNE – VENRAY – MAASHEES. I
> recommend this adjustment to be made at once so that
> Second Army can develop a strong left hook against the
> RUHR. FREDDIE [de Guingand] will explain full details at
> conference tomorrow and will show you some notes on the
> problem which I have sent him.[8]

The signal, in cipher, was marked 'Top Secret', 'Most
Immediate', and 'Personal for Eisenhower from Montgomery'.
Its main purpose was to get Bradley to turn left to cover
Montgomery's exposed right flank, and the 'notes' to be shown
to Eisenhower reveal that the British commander, against all
odds, still expected to win the battle for Arnhem. De Guingand's
instructions for the Versailles Conference read:

Notes for Chief of Staff

1. If we are to take quick advantage of the good situation we
   have achieved in the general area GRAVE-NIJMEGEN-
   ARNHEM, it will be necessary for the right Corps of
   Second Army to develop a strong thrust on the axis
   GENNEP-CLEVE-EMMERICH.
2. Having established itself in the CLEVE area, this Corps
   would operate in a S.E. direction between the RHINE and
   the MEUSE, directed on the N.W. corner of the RUHR.
3. The remainder of Second Army would move on HAMM.
4. But the right Corps of Second Army is at present holding a
   front facing east through DEURNE and WEERT, so as to
   protect the right flank of the Army. It cannot take on the
   task outlined in para 1 unless it is relieved from this
   protective role.
5. The task is to isolate and capture the RUHR. The best
   way to do this is to take quick advantage of our favourable

situation and deliver a strong left hook with Second Army. First US Army should use its left wing in holding role. so that Second Army can develop its full potential.

6. I consider that the inter-Army Group boundary should be adjusted *at once* as follows:

All incl 12 Army Group:

HASSELT - WEERT - ASTEN - DEURNE - VENRAY - MAASHEES

Exact and detailed boundary to be settled between Second British and First US Armies.

7. If I were in full command and control of the operations to capture the RUHR, I would at once order the above adjustment of boundary.

8. As things stand at present, the command set-up is such that I can only recommend it.

But I have been directed to co-ordinate the action on the Northern route.

Therefore I definitely recommend this new boundary.

9. I have cabled my recommendation to the Supreme Commander.

Bring the matter up at the conference tomorrow.

21.9.44   Signed B.L. Montgomery[9]

This was more than optimistic: Cleve is south-west of the Rhine, Emmerich is on the Rhine, and Hamm is well inside Germany, to the east of the Rhine and beyond the Dortmund-Ems Canal. Plainly, achieving these objectives was a pipedream unless Arnhem Bridge was taken and held. But, even as the Versailles conference was taking place, Twenty-First Army Group was bogged down between Nijmegen and Arnhem and had lost any chance of mounting an immediate offensive beyond the Rhine. Montgomery's notes for de Guingand proposed operations which could not possibly be carried out without victory at Arnhem.

Before he left his office for the conference room, Eisenhower had written to Montgomery confirming his decision to make the main drive in the north, with Twelfth Army Group in support of Twenty-First. American generals at the conference, under the mistaken impression that Montgomery was about to obtain a bridgehead over the Rhine at Arnhem, were in no position to disagree with the Supreme Commander when he said that the

main Allied operations for the present were to be those of
Twenty-First Army Group, which would both free Antwerp and
attack the Ruhr from the north.

Both Alanbrooke and Churchill were away in Quebec,
attending the 'Octagon' Conference, and Simpson flew out to
Brussels on 20 September in Montgomery's personal Dakota,
which had brought back to England the artist James Gunn, who
was working on Montgomery's portrait at the time. Simpson
spent the night of the 20th and 21st at Twenty-First Army
Group Tac HQ,* where Montgomery immediately, and
emphatically, briefed him about the non-arrival of the extra
supplies promised by Bedell Smith on 12 September. Simpson
undertook to raise this subject in the strongest terms when he
got to SHAEF HQ at Versailles on 22 September. While at
Versailles, he made a note in detail of his talks (chiefly, as he
says, for Montgomery's benefit), which gives an authentic
picture of the atmosphere at SHAEF, and demonstrates what
united support Montgomery would have received if 'Market-
Garden' had succeeded.[10]

Morgan was waiting to meet Simpson at Paris aerodrome on
the 22nd, and took him directly to the luxurious Hotel Trianon
at Versailles, where SHAEF had its HQ. Simpson found it all
extremely imposing and comfortable: 'Masses of officers and
other ranks, both sexes and all nationalities, moving around with
determined faces ... Smartly dressed sentries everywhere,
including two very well dressed, curious hybrids from the RAF
Regiment, outside the beautiful château where Eisenhower had
his living quarters.' He thought the large organisation was
impressive, but noted that he could not find out what it was
producing, and also that there was 'certainly little thought of any
critical battle being fought on the frontiers of the same country.
Everyone was living in luxury.'

On arrival, Simpson immediately pitched in with the
complaint about the non-arrival of the promised supplies, telling
Morgan, as nearly as possible in Montgomery's own words, just
what Twenty-First Army Group's commander thought about

---

* On 21 September Montgomery lent Simpson a jeep to go forward to
Eindhoven. There, crowds in the streets cheered him as a senior British
general and threw flowers into his jeep. Modestly, Simpson says that he felt
'phoney', because he did not think that a 'War Office warrior' should receive
the applause due to fighting troops.

the British staff at SHAEF. The views he expressed were certainly not very complimentary – Morgan was 'hit hard', and at a loss for an answer. Simpson went on to tell Morgan that he wanted to make the same complaint to Gale* but did not know him quite well enough. At that moment Gale came into the room, and Morgan repeated Simpson's remarks to him. Gale listened, and then replied: 'I was expecting this. You may not know it, but I had an extremely awkward interview with Monty yesterday. He cannot understand my difficulties and that I really have no control over administrative questions, which are run by the War Office for 21 Army Group and by General Lee's HQ [Lt-Gen J.C.H. Lee, commanding the US Services of Supply for the theatre; his HQ was then still in England] for the Americans.'

Morgan commented: 'Yes, you certainly came back with your tail between your legs from that interview with Monty,' to which Gale replied: 'Yes I did, and today I find Monty has followed up the interview with a telegram to Ike accusing me of being responsible for the non-arrival of the extra supplies promised to him.'

On 16 September Eisenhower had sent an apologetic signal to Twenty-First Army Group, just as the struggle for Arnhem began to get under way:

> I hear that our frantic efforts to scratch together ad hoc companies to deliver you 500 tons a day did not get the supplies flowing on September 15. However I assure you that the first batch will arrive there to-morrow morning 17 September. Bradley's left is striking hard to support you.

Montgomery's signal of 21 September to Eisenhower, complaining of Gale, is tough, even for him, and demonstrates that he looked upon Gale as an enemy:

> Have seen Gale. Since the change in command on 1 September I have not been in touch with the supply situation in 12 Army Group. From what Gale tells me it seems clear that 12 Army Group has been allowed to outstrip its

---

* Lt-Gen Sir Humfrey Gale, Eisenhower's chief Administrative Officer, and not Maj-Gen Richard Gale, GOC British 6th Airborne Division.

maintenance and as a result we have lost flexibility throughout the battle area as a whole. From my talk with Gale it seems to me he is greatly to blame for not keeping in touch with the situation and ensuring things were in hand. My own admin situation is not in blooming health but I can quite well continue the battle and am doing so.

In fact, Simpson had read this outspoken signal on the day before at Montgomery's Tac HQ, though he did not tell Gale and Morgan this. He did, however, tell them that Montgomery felt very strongly that the senior British staff at SHAEF were not representing fully and accurately to Eisenhower the position regarding Twenty-First Army Group's supplies. At that moment, word came that Bedell Smith was free, and Morgan took Simpson along to his room. Bradley was also there, but as soon as Simpson pointed out that he had a personal message from Montgomery for Bedell Smith, the latter at once asked Bradley to excuse him. Simpson went with Bedell Smith to his private room, and there told the American that Montgomery hoped that he would not be asked to any more conferences like the one on that day at Versailles, since he was too busy running the battle 'up forward'. He had no intention of attending the conference – Paris was a long way from the actual battle, and the weather at that time of the year was unreliable, and might prevent him from getting back quickly to his own HQ after a conference. In reply, Bedell Smith said: 'I am glad to have this message because we were feeling it very much that the Field-Marshal could not manage to come. Now we know the reasons, and I will tell Ike at once what you have said.'

If, as seems to be the case, this explanation of Montgomery's refusal to attend the Versailles conference mollified Eisenhower and Bedell Smith, then it says a great deal for Simpson's tact and charm, for on paper his excuse appears very thin. But the spoken word and the speaker's personality can sometimes make a considerable difference, and the likeable Simpson was always persona grata with Bedell Smith and Eisenhower, although both men well knew that he frequently disagreed with them, supporting Montgomery utterly at all times and in all circumstances.

Simpson continued by explaining to Bedell Smith Montgomery's belief that he had an unlimited opportunity to advance to the east, where the Germans were weak (although German Fifteenth Army had up to 150,000 men on its west flank), but that he would not be able to take full advantage of this magnificent opportunity unless all the Allied resources were put behind him. The American general assured Simpson that both he and Eisenhower understood this, and that they fully intended all resources to go to Montgomery. All that worried Eisenhower, said Bedell Smith, was that Montgomery must not try to go straight off to Berlin on a narrow front, to which Simpson replied: 'An advance to Berlin may come later. Monty's present intention is to capture the Ruhr. This is what Eisenhower has ordered him to do and SHAEF ought to give him logistic resources for it.'

According to Simpson, Bedell Smith repeated most emphatically that Montgomery could rest assured that SHAEF would do everything possible to support Twenty-First Army Group in the capture of the Ruhr. He told Simpson, very frankly, that Eisenhower had given orders to Bradley and Patton to 'conserve' their administrative resources, but that they had not obeyed. 'Our trouble,' he continued, 'is that Ike, instead of giving direct and clear orders, dresses them up in polite language and this is why our senior American commanders take advantage. However, Ike has given me full authority to make it clear to them today that they must obey orders.'

Bedell Smith went on to say that he had considered asking Simpson to the top-level conference that afternoon, but had decided not to because 'so much dirty linen is going to be washed that it would be better if an outsider was not present'; Simpson got the impression that Eisenhower intended to savage Bradley and Patton. Then, for a second time, Bedell Smith promised Simpson that Eisenhower fully intended to support Montgomery's major thrust to the Ruhr, and that he, Bedell Smith, would advise the Supreme Commander at the conference to put US First Army under Montgomery's command, although he realised that this decision would not be well received in the United States. He added, in confidence, that when the American chiefs had discussed the command set-up a month before, Roosevelt had instructed Stimson to tell Eisenhower categorically that all the American troops must be kept under Bradley's command. But, he continued, 'I think Ike is quite prepared now to disobey this instruction and to put Hodges's 1st

American Army under Monty. If it is the best way to get the Ruhr and thus win the war, the chips can then fall as they will.'

On the day before, 21 September, Montgomery had sent this personal note to Bedell Smith:

> I consider the organisation for command control of the operation to capture the Ruhr is not satisfactory. It is a task for one man and he should have the operational control and direction of all the forces involved. To achieve success the tactical battle will require very tight control and very careful handling. I recommend the Supreme Commander hands the job over to me and gives me operational control over First US Army.[11]

It says a great deal for Bedell Smith's tolerance of Montgomery at this time that he took this arrogant message so well, and was himself prepared to agree to an extension of Montgomery's command to include US First Army.

Thanks either to Simpson's or to de Guingand's persuasiveness, the conference decided exactly as Montgomery had hoped. That evening (22 September) a happy de Guingand signalled his chief that the conference 'had given 100% support'.

Paragraph IV of the minutes of the Versailles conference shows how completely Eisenhower endorsed Montgomery's plans:

Minutes of Meeting held in the War Room
SHAEF Forward at 14.30 22nd September 1944.
IV – *ADJUSTMENT OF THE BOUNDARY BETWEEN 21ST AND 12TH ARMY GROUPS*

General de Guingand outlined the 21st Army Group plan for attacking the RUHR from the north and pointed out the necessity for employing three Corps in that effort. He inquired into the practicability of the 12th Army Group taking over the sector occupied by the BRITISH 8th Corps. General Bradley outlined his views as to various solutions which were practicable.

The Supreme Commander approved the following:

a. The envelopment of the RUHR from the north by 21st Army Group, supported by 1st Army, is the main effort of the present phase of operations.

b. The boundary between 21st and 12th Army Groups to be HASSELT - WEERT - ASTEN - DEURNE - VENRAY - MAASHEES, all inclusive to 12th Army Group. Effective date of alteration and detailed boundary to be settled between 12th and 21st Army Groups.

c. General Bradley to bring up two divisions as quickly as possible to take over the sector now held by 8th Corps. General Bradley hoped to complete this in about ten (10) days.

d. (1) 12th Army Group to continue its thrust so far as current resources permit towards COLOGNE and 12th Army Group will be prepared to seize any favourable opportunity of crossing the RHINE and attacking the RUHR from the south in concert with 21st Army Group's attack on the RUHR from the north when the maintenance situation permits.

(2) The commander of 12th Army Group will take no more aggressive action than is permitted by the maintenance situation after the full requirements of the main effort have been met.

Next morning, Bedell Smith handed de Guingand a copy of the minutes for him to take back to Twenty-First Army Group, but the latter responded by telling the American that, in his view, the instructions in IV d. were not strong enough to stop Bradley indulging in further attacks in order to consume resources, and thus force Eisenhower to support the American front. The original draft of IV d. (2) read: '... 12th Army Group to remain on the defensive on the remainder of the front [that is, apart from aiding Twenty-First Army Group] until logistical considerations permit a more active policy.' In his own handwriting de Guingand reworded the clause to read: '... no more aggressive action than is permitted by the maintenance situation after the full requirements of the main effort have been met.'[12] This amendment is incorporated in the official record (now in the National Archives, Washington), and provides evidence of the close co-operation between Bedell Smith and de Guingand.

Unhappily for Montgomery, just when he had manoeuvred Eisenhower into accepting his cherished plan he was unable to provide the key to the whole scheme — the bridge over the Rhine at Arnhem. On that day Urquhart was preparing to evacuate his besieged positions over the river.

At the conference, US First Army was not officially placed under Montgomery, but Bradley was given the clearest possible orders that he was to put his full weight on the left to support Twenty-First Army Group, even if that meant grounding his right flank. In all probability Eisenhower wanted to put US First Army under Montgomery's command, but was worried by the inevitability of opposition from Bradley and Patton. What is certain, however, is that the Supreme Commander's generous support for Twenty-First Army Group's proposed drive into the Ruhr, clearly demonstrated at the Versailles conference, frees him of the charge of being biased against Montgomery. Among the officers at SHAEF, however, the story was different.

Three and a half weeks previously, Simpson had spent the day at SHAEF HQ in Portsmouth, just before it moved over to France. Morgan had invited him down since he felt that SHAEF staff were under the impression that the War Office was hostile to their organisation – this 'hostile tone', Morgan said, permeated the War Office from Brooke himself downwards. Simpson did his best to pour oil on the troubled waters, agreeing that War Office staff had not visited SHAEF sufficiently, and adding his view that some senior War Office staff officers feared that there might be an anti-British attitude in SHAEF. Simpson asked the SHAEF officers how often any of them had visited Montgomery's own Twenty-First Army Group HQ, and they admitted that in this respect they had been at fault. At Versailles on 22 September, however, senior SHAEF officers still displayed an 'anti-Montgomery' attitude, while the War Office supported him strongly.

At lunch on the 22nd, Morgan and Gale defended themselves to Simpson against a charge that the senior British staff officers at SHAEF were not supporting Montgomery. Morgan said: 'We do not look on ourselves as British staff officers responsible for the British point of view. We are Allied staff officers serving Ike, who is the Allied Commander.' To this, Simpson replied:

All I want is that you should try to find out what Monty wants, just as the American staff officers find out what Bradley and Patton want, and then put it to Ike in terms that Ike can understand. Have you ever tried to find out what Monty wants by going to see him? Gale saw him yesterday for the first time since coming to France and you, Freddie Morgan, have not seen him yet. From the War Office point of view we feel you are not doing your duty in representing British interests. It can be done in a perfectly fair manner without prejudicing the Allied cause.

Both Gale and Morgan were on the defensive, replying: 'We know well that we are looked on by everybody as having sold ourselves to the Americans, but we know also that we have no future in the British Army once Ike has finished with us.' Simpson replied that this was nonsense, and that unless they 'pulled their socks up' they would be regarded by everyone as being 'completely gutless' – whether as British staff officers, Allied staff officers, or anything else. Simpson felt that what he said left Gale quite unmoved, but that it distressed Freddie Morgan, and might therefore make him more co-operative with Montgomery in future. And, naturally, he reported his conversation with the two generals to Montgomery.

General Simpson told me that, with hindsight, his considered opinion of the senior British officers at SHAEF – Morgan, Gale, Whiteley, Strong and Tedder – was that they had fallen under Eisenhower's spell; he had noticed that the American nearly always inspired a genuine affection in those who served him. For instance, according to Simpson, Morgan was not malicious, as Montgomery believed him to be; it was just that he doted on Eisenhower, although undoubtedly Tedder, for one, was at times moved by a 'sharply critical' view of, and a 'distaste' for, Montgomery.[*]

Whatever the views of Eisenhower's British staff officers, however, Montgomery was not without powerful support. For not only were Churchill and Brooke backing him to the utmost in his demand for overwhelming strength for his northern thrust, but the Secretary of State for War, Grigg, was also strongly on his side. Grigg wrote to Montgomery on 25 September: 'I should like to know how much you are being injured by what I assume to be a fact that although Ike has assured you that your thrust gets priority, his staff, ably assisted by Gale, are in practice disregarding this pledge.'[13]

---

[*] Tedder's views are given in Lewin, *Montgomery as Military Commander*, and, more forcefully, in his own memoirs, *With Prejudice*.

With such influential backing from home, Montgomery should perhaps be excused some of the arrogance and lack of tact which he displayed in his dealings with Eisenhower during the controversies over strategy that ensued.

When all the surviving British troops over the Rhine had been withdrawn, Montgomery, bluffing that 'Market-Garden' had been '90% successful', continued his attacks towards Arnhem in a futile effort to salvage his Ruhr plan. Eisenhower at first endorsed his efforts, and Montgomery gave Second Army complete priority in supplies, starving the Canadians for their attack along the Scheldt, and even ordering them at one point to cover Second Army's left flank.

For a few days more Eisenhower blithely continued to believe that Twenty-First Army Group could both force a Rhine crossing and clear the port of Antwerp. He ordered Bradley to take over even more of Twenty-First Army Group's front, and as late as 8 October declared that the Allies 'must retain as first mission the gaining of the line north of Bonn as quickly as humanly possible,' a view to which Montgomery undoubtedly subscribed. Brigadier Williams told me that:

> Monty was reluctant to start the Battle of the Scheldt. Antwerp was fifty-five miles inland, and he knew that one fine day he must clear the banks of the estuary, which could so easily have been taken immediately after Antwerp fell. To him it was not an interesting military operation ... it lacked glamour from his point of view and so did not appeal to his vanity. He knew it would be a battle of attrition with very heavy casualties [in the end nearly 13,000, mainly Canadians] and whatever the result the Scheldt attack could not fit into the series of victories on which his reputation was based at that moment. His attitude was: 'If you finished the war, the Scheldt operation would be unnecessary since the Germans would soon capitulate without further casualties.' It wasn't just vanity – it was because of the feeling that the war was nearly over and it would be a pity to get any more people killed in the doing of it – all part of his 'economical' generalship psychology.

In September, Montgomery's judgement may have been clouded by euphoria, given the extent of the Normandy victory.

If that was the case, however, the scales quickly fell from his eyes during the first few days of October. Williams's intelligence reports showed Montgomery the extent of the German recovery, and he was too intelligent and too clear-minded not to understand that he had insufficient troops both to clear Antwerp and to continue with offensive operations from the Nijmegen salient. Dempsey recorded that on the morning of 7 October, at a conference at Second Army HQ, he gave Montgomery the unwelcome news:

> I have not enough divisions to carry out at one and the same time
> (a) a successful defence of the Nijmegen bridgehead.
> (b) the elimination of the enemy on my right flank west of the River Meuse.
> (c) an attack south east between River Rhine and River Meuse.

Montgomery accepted Dempsey's judgement and that afternoon sent out the following situation report to SHAEF and his army commanders, revealing a cold professionalism in the face of a bitter disappointment.

TOP SECRET

1. I am not happy about the overall battle situation in the northern part of the Allied front. The enemy has re-acted very violently to our threat to the RUHR and has concentrated strong forces against Second Army. I have three commitments which could become very awkward and unbalance the whole business in the north:

   A. *The opening of ANTWERP*
      We must get that place going and I must have reserves of ammunition ready to throw in; I may need fresh divisions.

   B. *The bridgehead north of NIJMEGEN*
      This is daily threatened by the enemy and is none too strong. The US Airborne Divisions alone cannot hold it; I must reinforce them by two Inf divisions.

   C. *The enemy situation west of the MEUSE*
      There is considerable enemy strength south of the line MAASHEES-DEURNE. It was thought that 7 US

Armd Div could clean it up; but it cannot. First US Army is very involved about AACHEN.

Therefore I must use 8 Corps to clean up this area and push the enemy back of the MEUSE.

2. I could possibly carry ANTWERP, plus B; but I definitely cannot carry all three, *and also launch Second Army towards KREFELD.*

3. If I carry on as we are now, and launch Second Army towards KREFELD on 10 October, that Army will have two hostile flanks – as well as strong frontal opposition. A German threat north of NIJMEGEN, with possibly danger of some enemy success, would unbalance me completely and my thrust towards KREFELD would cease.

I would then find myself very stretched, and possibly unable to hold all my gains.

I might then find that Canadian Army wanted more help to open up ANTWERP; and I would not be able to supply this help.

4. I therefore consider that I cannot launch Second Army towards the RUHR until I have eliminated the following commitments:

Para 1 (A). Finished the operations for opening ANTWERP.

Para 1 (C). Pushed the enemy back over the MEUSE.

5. I have decided to act as in para 4. I have ordered that the attack of Second Army toward KREFELD and the RUHR be postponed.[14]

7-10-44   B.L. Montgomery
                                                    Field-Marshal

The opening paragraph is an understatement. 1A. and B. are together a desperate cry to Eisenhower for more American divisions, and 1A. is also an admission that too much ammunition had been going to Second Army and not enough to the Canadians. Montgomery had also been unable to release US 82nd and 101st Airborne Divisions – without them he could not have held the Nijmegen bridgehead, let alone attacked again.

Until he received this very clear statement, Eisenhower had maintained his faith in Montgomery's promise both to force a Rhine crossing and, simultaneously, to clear the Scheldt estuary and free Antwerp. As a result, he had allowed the US airborne divisions to stay in the line with Twenty-First Army Group, despite frantic protests from Brereton that it was a 'useless waste of trained paratroops'; he had ordered Bradley to take over more of Twenty-First Army Group's front; and, an hour before Montgomery's statement arrived, he had dictated that 'the Allies must retain as first mission the gaining of the line north of Bonn as quickly as humanly possible.' All this he had done while continuing to emphasise to Montgomery that Antwerp must be speedily opened up.

Eisenhower was gravely disappointed by the 7 October situation report; worse, he was extremely angry, and his anger was fanned by Tedder, Morgan and the American generals at Versailles, all of whom opposed Montgomery in greater or lesser degrees. They felt, and Eisenhower shared that feeling, that Montgomery had let down SHAEF by his over-optimism both about 'Market-Garden' and the subsequent fighting in the Nijmegen area, and that they had been persuaded at the Versailles conference to divert supplies from Patton to Montgomery under false pretences. More than this, Montgomery had disobeyed Eisenhower's order to clear the Scheldt and open Antwerp.

The Supreme Commander now regretted that he had not backed the southern thrusts by Bradley and Patton instead of concentrating, at their expense, on Montgomery's northern drive to the Ruhr, which he and his Versailles colleagues now suddenly realised was a 'shocking failure'. Montgomery would never see his dream of leading a massive Anglo-American army to Berlin, because Eisenhower would never again trust his promises, nor would he ever receive the support held out to him at the Versailles conference. In Holland, as in Normandy, Montgomery's performance had fallen too far short of his promises – but in Holland there was no overwhelming Allied victory in which to hide the failures.

The following letter, written to Grigg on 10 October, demonstrates once more Montgomery's conviction that he could advance into Germany and finish off the war in 1944, provided that he was given command of enough American divisions and had supplies diverted to him from the other American armies. It is surprising that he really considered that he could achieve this without first liberating the approaches to Antwerp – plainly his judgement must have been clouded by his anger with the command set-up and his frustration at being denied extra resources.

Personal and Top Secret	TAC HQ
	21 Army Group
	10-10-44
	Most Important

My dear P.J.

1. I am glad it is to be Hughes. I have been turning over in my mind the problem of his successor.*

2. I cannot feel happy about things out here. The two big points that require a very sound solution and plan have always been:

(a) the thrust line.

(b) the command set-up.

The Thrust Line

3. Eisenhower's idea has always been for the *whole line* to go forward, to capture the Ruhr *and* the Saar *and* the Frankfurt area, line up the armies on the Rhine, and then decide what to do next.

4. I have always said that this is not possible, because our maintenance situation would not allow of it.

My idea has been to hold back on the right, and to swing hard with our left against the Ruhr and right through to Berlin. All resources to be put into the left hook.

5. My plan was not approved. We worked on Para 3 above. The American armies have outstripped their maintenance, and as a result we have lost flexibility on the front as a whole. We are now unlikely to get the Ruhr, *or* the Saar, *or* Frankfurt. In fact it is my opinion that we have 'mucked' the whole show, and we have only ourselves to blame. It is a great tragedy. I did what I could; I have always taken my stand by my cable to Eisenhower of 4th September, in which I said we must concentrate everying in one terrific blow.

---

* Canon Frederick Hughes, the newly appointed Chaplain-General to the Forces. Montgomery had taken a keen interest in Hughes's appointment, preferring him to the other candidate for the post, the Bishop of Maidstone. Hughes had been Deputy Chaplain-General at Twenty-First Army Group.

I said that if we attempted a compromise solution and split our maintenance resources so that neither thrust is full blooded, we would prolong the war. You have that telegram in the War Office.

The Command Set-up

8. All our troubles can be traced basically to the fact that there is no one commander in charge of the land battle. The Supreme Commander runs it himself from SHAEF by means of long telegrams. SHAEF is not an operational HQ and never can be.

9. General Marshall came to see me on Sunday last, 8 October, and I gave him my views on the present organisation for command. I think it did good.

Tedder, Deputy Supreme Commander, came to see me also; I gave *him* my views. Then I wrote a paper on it and I have sent it to Eisenhower; I enclose you a copy herewith; it explains itself.

Yrs ever,

Monty

Will you get Simbo to send me a wire to say you have got this letter; I do not want it to go astray!!!

P.S. If the business is properly handled now, we could get away with it I believe and could finish the business this year — or as near as matters.

But unless it is so handled, and a very firm grip is taken, I fear we shall have only ourselves to blame if it goes on.

B.L.M.

10-10-44

P.P.S. I think I have let off a good bit of steam in this letter and you had better burn it.

B.L.M.[15]

This letter perfectly reveals Montgomery's attitude of mind at the time, and it is most fortunate that Grigg did not burn it as requested. It is also interesting that Montgomery refers to Marshall's visit, which he mistakenly thought 'did good'. It is quite clear from American sources that there was no meeting of minds at all during their interview.

Before writing to Grigg, Montgomery had again irritated Eisenhower by suggesting that US First Army would be put under his command. In accordance with the decisions made at the Versailles conference, Eisenhower had ordered Hodges to send part of US First Army to help Montgomery east of Eindhoven, where Student's Parachute Army was both uncomfortably close and unexpectedly strong. Instead of there being 3,000 Germans, as Allied intelligence had supposed, Student had deployed over 20,000 in the Peel marshes west of Eindhoven. Accordingly Eisenhower lent Montgomery two American divisions, hoping that once the British general had this help he would detach part of Second Army for the clearance of Antwerp.

Unfortunately, Montgomery's impression of what had been agreed did not tally with Eisenhower's, and the breaking point came on 9 October, when Montgomery issued his General Operational Situation and Directive M530, which emphasised the stronger-than-expected German 'reaction' and contained the words: 'The use of Antwerp is vital ... operations to open the port must have priority as regards troops, ammunition and so on.' At the same time, he wanted the Peel marshes swept clear of Germans in preparation for a new attack, writing: 'Second Army will immediately develop operations designed to drive the enemy back to the east side of the Meuse between Gennep and Roermond with a view to an offensive towards Krefeld.' The directive promised no help to the badly overtaxed Canadians.

At SHAEF, this was correctly held to be paying 'only lip service to Ike's insistence that Antwerp must be cleared'; indeed the arrival of the directive coincided with reports from impatient Royal Navy officers that the Canadians would not be able to launch their main attack on the Scheldt until 1 November, because of shortage of ammunition. Eisenhower at last braced himself to take a really strong line with his unruly subordinate. During the afternoon of 9 October, angry and frustrated, he sent Montgomery the most imperative order, and snub, of the whole campaign:

Unless we have Antwerp producing by the middle of November our entire operations will come to a standstill. I must emphasise that of all our operations on the entire front from Switzerland to the Channel I consider Antwerp of first importance, and I believe that the operations designed to clear up the entrance require your personal attention.[16]

Receiving this, Montgomery was angry in his turn. He felt that Ramsay had gone behind his back* in telling Eisenhower about the Canadians' ammunition shortage, and wired back indignantly: 'Request you will ask Ramsay from me by what authority he makes wild statements to you concerning my operations about which he can know nothing repeat nothing. Canadians already attacking; there is no repeat no shortage of ammunition.'[17]

He continued by reminding Eisenhower that the Versailles conference had made the attack against the Ruhr the 'main effort', although he promised to open Antwerp as early as possible, concluding 'The operations are receiving my personal attention.' Eisenhower replied on the 10th, saying that he was glad that the news about an ammunition shortage was false, and reminding Montgomery that 'the possession of the approaches to Antwerp remains with us an objective of vital importance ... Nothing I may ever say or write with respect to future plans in our advance eastward is meant to indicate any lessening of the need for Antwerp.'[18]

Shortly after Eisenhower's reply was sent, Bedell Smith called Montgomery on the telephone and demanded to know when SHAEF could expect some action around Antwerp. Heated words followed, until finally Smith, 'purple with rage,' turned to Morgan and thrust the telephone into his hand – 'Here,' he said, 'you tell your countryman what to do.' Morgan, convinced that Montgomery would be CIGS after the war, immediately thought to himself, 'Well, that's the end of my career.' He then told Montgomery that unless Antwerp was opened soon his supplies would be cut off.[19]

When Eisenhower's abrupt and categorical order to concentrate on Antwerp arrived, Montgomery's thoughts were still focused upon the Peel marshes, so vital to his east flank if ever he was to launch an offensive over the Rhine into the Ruhr. But Lt-Gen Sir Richard O'Connor's VIII Corps, helped by US 7th Armoured Division, was finding Student's army in the marshes a hard nut to crack. Reluctantly, Montgomery decided that he must temporarily give up his ambitions to cross

---

* In fact, the report, made to Eisenhower by the Navy on 9 October, came not from Ramsay but as a result of a Royal Navy/Canadian Army Planning Conference, although it may well have been inspired by him.

the Rhine, and he issued a directive (M532) on 16 October giving, in the clearest possible terms, absolute priority to freeing the approaches to Antwerp.

21 Army Group
GENERAL OPERATIONAL SITUATION AND DIRECTIVE
General Situation

1. The free use of the port of ANTWERP is vital to the Allied cause, and we must be able to use the port soon.
2. Operations designed to open the port will therefore be given complete priority over all other offensive operations in 21 Army Group, without any qualification whatsoever.
3. The immediate task of opening up the approaches to the port of ANTWERP is already being undertaken by Canadian Army and good progress has been made.
   The whole of the available offensive power of Second Army will now be brought to bear also.

In addition, the Canadians were to be relieved of all responsibility for holding Second Army's eastern flank. Instead, the Canadian right wing was to attack the South Beveland peninsula, with US 104th Infantry and 52nd (Lowland) Divisions assigned to Crerar's army for the purpose. Previously, Montgomery had intended to use these two divisions for Second Army attacks. All 'large scale offensives' by Second Army towards the Peel marshes were to be 'closed down' – the battle for the marshes would not be won until 3 December.

So instead of driving the enemy back from the east flank of Nijmegen and out of the salient over the Meuse, as ordered in M530 on 9 October, Montgomery directed in M532 a week later that: 'The whole available offensive power of Second Army will be employed in a strong thrust westwards on the general axis Hertogenbosch-Breda with the right flank on the Meuse'; in other words, to clear the north bank of the Scheldt. This was a complete change of direction. Montgomery had shelved for the time being any thoughts of crossing the Rhine, while he himself moved from his Tac HQ at Eindhoven to Main HQ at Brussels, in order to be nearer 'the vital point of Antwerp.' Belatedly, he had come to see the crucial necessity of clearing the Scheldt estuary. The Directive went on to state: 'I must impress on my

Army Commanders the early use of Antwerp is absolutely vital. The operations now ordered by me must be begun at the earliest possible moment; they must be pressed with the greatest energy and determination; and we must accept heavy casualties to get quick success.'

Impulsively, Montgomery now abandoned operations on his right flank where, in co-operation with the Americans, he had almost cleared three German divisions out of their bridgehead over the River Roer. As a result of attacks by VIII Corps these Germans were in a hopeless position, and on 17 October the corps commander was planning to throw in a fresh division (15th Infantry) to finish the job. On that day, however, orders came suddenly from Montgomery that 15th Division was not to be used for this attack, but would instead be sent north to help with the attack on German Fifteenth Army in the operations to clear Antwerp. After 20 October VIII Corps made no further progress against the Germans in the Roer bridgehead, and suffered heavy casualties in enemy counter-attacks a few weeks later.

General Roberts feels strongly that weakening VIII Corps' offensive capability at this time was a mistake, and that Montgomery threw away an important tactical advantage during a moment of tension caused by Eisenhower's firm orders to concentrate on clearing Antwerp. General Roberts wrote to me:

Another example of Monty's inflexibility was on 17th October 1944. Then the Operation 'Constellation' carried out by VIII Corps to clear up what was known as the Maas pocket around Venlo was suddenly discontinued by Monty at the very moment when it could have cleaned up the whole pocket within forty-eight hours.

No doubt this was to meet Eisenhower's demand to open up the port of Antwerp, but forty-eight hours' delay was nothing compared with the advantage of folding up the Maas pocket, where later we had fairly heavy casualties.

I cannot believe that Monty was misinformed about the dominating position of VIII Corps, and he missed grasping a splendid opportunity.

Eisenhower had at last got his way, although Montgomery

was not ashamed. With grave lack of tact, he had chosen to raise again the question of command, and in a letter to Bedell Smith on 10 October (the day of 'heated words' between the two) had stated that one of the troubles with 'Market-Garden' had been 'lack of co-ordination' between his forces and Bradley's; he had suggested that therefore he should have command of US Twelfth Army Group. This letter had confirmed Eisenhower in his decision to assert his authority as Supreme Commander over Montgomery.[20]

For if Montgomery would not accept that authority, then Eisenhower would try and get him sacked. In a surprisingly strong reply, dated 13 October, the American wrote:

> The Antwerp operation does not involve the question of command ... If you as Senior Commander in this theatre of one of the great Allies feel that my conceptions and directives are such as to endanger the success of operations it is your duty to refer the matter to higher authority for any action they may choose to take however drastic.[21]

He added that Twenty-First Army Group's current commitments would leave it with such depleted forces facing eastwards that Montgomery could not be expected to carry out anything more than supporting movements in the attack on the Ruhr. Originally, in September, Eisenhower had written that he hoped Montgomery could take Antwerp and clear the west coast of Holland rapidly, and therefore be in a position to make a major attack on the Ruhr, an operation for which US units would have been made available to Twenty-First Army Group. He had, however, gathered from the Versailles conference that Montgomery agreed that 'the British Army Group could not produce the bulk of the forces required for the direct Ruhr attack.'

Montgomery knew that the American armies, and not his, must now take on the push to the Rhine. He decided therefore to play down his more extravagant demands and to talk sensibly, replying to Eisenhower:

> You will hear no more from me on the question of command. I have given you my views and you have given your answer. I, and all of us, will weigh in 100% to do what you want, and

we will pull it through without a doubt. I have given Antwerp top priority in all operations in 21 Army Group and all energies and efforts will now be devoted towards opening up the place.[22]

The letter was signed 'Your very devoted loyal subordinate'.

Sadly Montgomery, aided and abetted by Brooke and Grigg (and at times even by Churchill), was to raise again, and repeatedly (though always unsuccessfully), not only the question of command, but also that of priority for a northern thrust. But Eisenhower now knew that he had the support of Marshall, Roosevelt and the US Chiefs of Staff, and was determined never again to give in to Montgomery. For the time being, however, Montgomery had to concentrate on the long battle of attrition to clear the Scheldt estuary and free Antwerp.

11

The Dreary Autumn

For Montgomery, the autumn of 1944 became increasingly dreary. Twenty-First Army Group attacks from the Nijmegen bridgehead achieved nothing, and the main bulk of his forces was bogged down in the long and costly battle to open the port of Antwerp. The contrast between this and the euphoria of early September was sharp, and Montgomery felt intensely that the chance to obtain a quick victory over Hitler had been wantonly thrown away by Eisenhower's refusal to concentrate all resources on a single drive.

Whether a southern drive by the American armies would have had a better chance of success than Montgomery's pencil-like northern thrust is debatable. What is indisputable, however, is that Eisenhower, by dissipating his supplies between the two army groups, achieved the worst of both worlds, and literally threw away his chance of ending the war in 1944.

By the middle of October there was no short-cut to victory, and in matters of strategy Montgomery and Eisenhower were as far apart as ever; worse, Eisenhower had now set his face against Montgomery, although the latter did not realise this. This setback, this blow to the Allies' hopes, was even worse for the people of Britain than for the Americans. In the United States there were fresh divisions and reserves of trained men; in Britain, on the other hand, after five years of austerity and complete mobilisation, the people were sick and tired of war, and it was a bitter blow to their morale that the high hopes raised after the liberation of France could not now be realised. There was, moreover, a drastic shortage of manpower both for the British factories and for trained reinforcements in North-West Europe, Italy and the Far East, and losses were high. The wastage of infantrymen in Twenty-First Army Group was higher than estimated by the War Office; some divisions were up to 2,000 men under strength, and the reinforcements pool was nearly dry. Only by breaking up existing divisions and other units could reinforcements be found.

Hitler, on the other hand, had found extra manpower for the war and for the manufacture of arms by an intensive combing-out of all able-bodied Germans, and by an unscrupulous use of slave labour from occupied countries. Even twelve- to fourteen-year-olds were taken out of school to dig fortifications, and his new battalions contained an almost sacrilegious proportion of schoolboys. By mid-October twelve new German divisions had been formed. Morale was surprisingly high, even in the newly raised Volkssturm and Volksgrenadier divisions of factory workers, shopkeepers and petty officials. Schoolboys, transformed overnight into fighting soldiers, had known no government or faith other than Nazism, and fighting for Hitler was considered romantic by many of these fresh youths. And, moreover, the efforts of Hitler and the Nazi Party received a considerable boost at this time by the publication of details of the ill-conceived American Morgenthau Plan.

In September 1944 the US Treasury Department under its Secretary, Henry Morgenthau, prepared an economic plan for Germany after her defeat. The plan called for a policy of 'pastoralisation', that is, to deprive Germany for ever of her power to build armaments by stripping the industrial regions of the Ruhr and the Saar of their factories, either by destruction or by removing their machinery as war reparations. Instead Germany was to become mainly an agricultural nation, and one in which rearmament would be impossible. Morgenthau presented the plan to Roosevelt and Churchill at the Quebec Conference ('Octagon', 12-16 September); impulsively, and without consultation or proper consideration, the two leaders immediately initialled their agreement to a statement endorsing Morgenthau's principle. In the next few weeks Henry Stimson, US Secretary of War, Harry Hopkins, Roosevelt's most trusted adviser and his personal link with the US Chiefs of Staff, Anthony Eden, the British Foreign Secretary, and Cordell Hull, US Secretary of State, persuaded Churchill and Roosevelt that the plan was dangerous and unworkable, and it died a natural death.

By then, however, the damage was done. On 24 September the essential details of the Morgenthau Plan appeared in the American press, to Roosevelt's fury, since he now rued his ever having approved it. Goebbels and Hitler, on the other hand, were delighted.

Goebbels's propaganda throughout the summer of 1944 had consistently stated that the Allies 'intend to exterminate us root and branch as a nation and a people', and on 21 October, for instance, German national newspapers proclaimed that their country's enemies 'want to exterminate 30 to 40 million Germans'. Unhappily, the published details of the Morgenthau Plan supported this propaganda, for besides outlining the intention to destroy German industry, it stated that any people trying to leave Germany would be shot by armed guards, and included a long list of categories of officials to be executed. Goebbels was swift to point out that the author of the plan was a Jew. Nazi propaganda about the Morgenthau Plan, coupled with the publicity given to Roosevelt's and Churchill's commitments to indiscriminate bombing and unconditional surrender, produced in Germany a revival of enthusiasm for the Nazi Party almost unbelievable in the light of the military collapse in Normandy.

Indiscriminate area bombing undoubtedly stiffened the German population's will to resist, for it was widely believed that the resultant appalling damage and casualties were an integral part of the Morgenthau Plan for 'extermination'. Furthermore, the dislocation and destruction of cities caused the population to become more and more dependent on the Nazi Party for even the bare essentials of life. During the autumn any German generals willing to 'stab Hitler in the back' were discouraged by the fear that his death would be followed by the collapse and destruction of Germany. By subtle propaganda Goebbels convinced the majority of the people that their only hope of survival lay in complete obedience to the Führer.

There were, of course, desertions and breakdowns of morale in the German forces, but rabid Nazis predominated more often than not in most units and, by dint of threats, forced the unwilling to go on fighting. More and more units came under SS command, and one famous order issued by Heinrich Himmler, the leader of the SS and one of the chief architects of genocide, undoubtedly kept many would-be deserters at their posts:

Reichsfuhrer SS

10 September 1944

Certain unreliable elements appear to believe the war will be over for them as soon as they surrender to the enemy.

I want to contradict this belief and emphasise that every deserter will be prosecuted and will find his just punishment. What is more his ignominious conduct will entail the most severe consequences for his family. Upon exposure of the circumstances of desertion they will be shot.

Signed: HIMMLER

Reinforced and re-equipped, the German armies offered stubborn resistance to the Allied attacks during October, and Eisenhower felt that it was his duty to make it clear that the war was far from won. He wrote to an American friend on 20 October: 'We have chased the Hun out of France, but he is fighting bitterly on his own frontiers and there is a lot of suffering and sacrificing for thousands of Americans and their Allies before the thing is finally over.' In this same mood he called a conference with Montgomery and Bradley at Brussels on 18 October – this time Montgomery, his HQ being so close, had to come in person. At the conference Eisenhower decided that as the bulk of Twenty-First Army Group, now backed by two US divisions, was fully engaged in clearing the Scheldt (a subsidiary operation), US Twelfth Army Group must take the main offensive action in November. Accordingly, Bradley was ordered to drive east and to try and obtain a Rhine bridgehead south of Cologne. Nettled by the Americans being given the main offensive role, Montgomery succeeded in persuading Eisenhower to agree that, once Antwerp was open, the main effort would switch back to Twenty-First Army Group's offensive towards the Ruhr, and Bradley agreed that, even in November, the main effort should be north of the Ardennes, with US Ninth Army filling the dangerous gap on the right flank of Montgomery's salient beyond Nijmegen. Eisenhower's orders resulting from the conference read: '12th Army Group will have charge of the operations for the capture or encirclement of the Ruhr. 9th US Army will operate north of the Ruhr and 1st US Army south of the Ruhr.'[1]

It did not suit Montgomery's temperament to have his army group mainly confined to the Scheldt, without any involvement in the capture of the Ruhr. And, as Williams fed him accurate – and depressing – information about the German build-up and restored morale, he became more and more disturbed at the flaws in Eisenhower's strategic plan. Twenty-First Army Group's Intelligence Review for the middle of October stated that 'the enemy has effected comparative stabilisation with formation of a crust thicker than had been thought possible in previous issues of this Review.'[2] German morale on the Canadian front was reported to be high, and there was a confirmed report of fresh German armoured reserves in Westphalia, close to the Ruhr. There had accumulated by now overwhelming evidence that the soldiers and people of Germany would not revolt against the Nazi régime, and Montgomery, always a realist, saw that the only way to win the war was to defeat the enemy military machine in battle. But as the American attacks on a wide front ground to their inevitable halt, both he and Brooke became almost desperate about the way Eisenhower was conducting operations. Brooke had complete faith in Montgomery, and both men felt that the Supreme Commander was making a mess of things.

Early in November, Montgomery had a 'heart-to-heart' talk with Cyril Falls, military correspondent of *The Times*, during which he emphasised that Eisenhower was only pretending to command the land forces, and added his own views about the proposed American attacks towards the Rhine. Falls reported the conversation to Brooke, who recorded in his diary on 8 November: 'I do not like the lay out of the coming offensive. I doubt whether we shall even reach the Rhine. It is highly improbable that we should cross before the end of the year.'

On 9 November Montgomery came to London, and there poured out his heart to Brooke. The latter remarked in his diary:

Monty goes on harping over the system of command in France which prolongs the war. He has got this on the brain as it affects his own personal position and he cannot put up with not being in sole command of land operations. I agreed the set up is bad but it cannot easily be altered as USA are preponderate and consider they have a major share in the running of the war. Perhaps after they see results of dispersing their strength all along the front it may be easier to convince them some drastic change is desirable leading to a concentration of forces at some vital part.

This extract demonstrates how completely the CIGS endorsed Montgomery's views, and how willing he was to back Montgomery to the hilt in challenging Eisenhower.

On 14 November, Churchill and Brooke met Eisenhower at the SHAEF advance HQ near Rheims. Brooke, often critical of the Americans, noted in his diary that Eisenhower had made a most unfavourable impression because his pretty private secretary, Kay Summersby,* had acted as hostess at the luncheon, and Churchill was put to sit on her right. 'This has done Ike no good with a lot of undesirable gossip ... Ike completely fails as Supreme Commander. He does nothing and lives in Paris out of touch. The war is drifting in rudderless condition. Long and despondent letter from Monty. I am preparing case as we shall have to take it up with Americans.'

With this solid support from Brooke both about command and the single-thrust strategy, Montgomery was encouraged to badger Eisenhower to change his plans and the command structure. Surprisingly Brooke, in touch with American opinion in London, never saw the hopelessness of his cause, for with the United States providing so much in the way of men and resources it was politically impossible to make Montgomery overall land commander. Yet the CIGS encouraged the latter in his fruitless argument with Eisenhower — as a result, relations between Montgomery and the Supreme Commander, already strained, became disagreeable and damaging to the Allied cause, and remained so for the rest of the war.

On 24 November Brooke put before the COS Committee his views on the 'very unsatisfactory state of affairs in France', that is, his opinion that no one was running the land battle. He wrote in his diary: 'Ike supposed to do so is detached with his lady chauffeur on the golf links at Rheims. Matters got so bad that a deputation of Whiteley, Bedell Smith, etc. told him he must get down to it and run it the way in which he said he would.' And he recorded his view that the only satisfactory solution would be:

Bradley - Land Commander
Tedder - Air Commander

---

* Formerly she had been Eisenhower's driver.

Montgomery - North of Ardennes
Patton - South of Ardennes

Montgomery had written to Brooke on 17 November, voicing more complaints about Eisenhower, and saying that he had neither seen nor spoken to the Supreme Commander since the meeting in Brussels on 18 October, and had only met him four times since the end of the Normandy campaign.

The Directives he issues have no relation to the necessities of the battle. It is quite impossible for me to carry out my present order ... He has never commanded anything before in his whole career and now for the first time he has elected to take direct command of very large scale operations and he does not know how to do it ... the urgency to finish the German war is very great. The only way is to concentrate strength at some selected place and hit the Germans a colossal crack. I would be grateful for your advice whether you think I ought to take the initiative.

Brooke replied sensibly on 20 November:

Without hesitation I would advise you: a) Not to approach Eisenhower for the present; b) To remain silent now unless Eisenhower opens the subject. We will make strongest representations in Washington ... I feel certain that in view of American preponderance in strength they will insist on any Land Commander being American. Do you consider Bradley fit for the job? Will he be able to control Patton and Devers [General Jacob L. Devers, commanding US Sixth Army Group]? I won't conceal I anticipate the greatest difficulty lies in getting the Americans to agree to any change in the set up.

If this was Brooke's considered view, then it is strange that he went on making such efforts to change Eisenhower's mind.

Montgomery replied: 'I have offered in writing to serve under Bradley but it is no use,' and suggested that the front should be divided in two, with himself commanding north of the Ardennes and Bradley south, the CIGS's own solution. But Brooke immediately saw the flaw in this plan, and told Montgomery, in a letter dated 24 November, that:

This will not get at the root of the matter and the same evils will persist ... You are asking for command of the northern group, and therefore proposing yourself for the one and only front that can play any major part. Have you considered if you are likely to be very acceptable in American eyes for this command? I have grave doubts.

He also again strongly advised Montgomery not to raise the matter with Eisenhower, and in order to make doubly sure that the restive Field-Marshal did not do so, he also cabled him to the same effect.

Montgomery replied that he would do nothing without authority, and flew back to London for consultation about the line he should take when he met Eisenhower on 28 November. The two friends agreed that Montgomery would tell the Supreme Commander that they wanted Bradley as Commander, Land Forces, and Montgomery in charge of the northern army group with Patton with him, and Devers commanding the southern group. They all also decided to oppose strongly what they termed 'the pernicious USA strategy of attacking all along the line.' Brooke told Montgomery that he would raise this matter of reorganising the command structure with the Prime Minister, and would suggest that Marshall be asked to come over; he noted in his diary that: 'Without some such change we shall just drift on and God knows when the war will end.'

The same argument had already been put to Eisenhower, and lost, in September, and Brooke ought to have known that if Marshall came over he would be sure to back the Supreme Commander to the hilt. Nevertheless Brooke saw Churchill, who agreed to ask Marshall to come after they had heard the outcome of the Eisenhower/Montgomery meeting.

In the event, the encounter between the two commanders on 28 November went badly. Brooke's enthusiastic support had boosted Montgomery's ego, making him more arrogant and cocksure than ever. With the CIGS's adulation and praises ringing in his ears, Montgomery had difficulty in hiding his contempt for the Supreme Commander. The latter, however, had decided in advance that he would not be drawn into an argument with his subordinate, and listened quietly while becoming more and more nettled as Montgomery postulated, again and again, that 'We must have a single Commander and concentrate our forces on a selected vital thrust instead of dissipating them all along the front.'

Montgomery took Eisenhower's silence for acquiescence, and reported to Brooke, with considerable self-satisfaction, that the Supreme Commander had accepted his arguments. In this, however, he was quite wrong. Montgomery went to bed as usual at 2130, leaving the Supreme Commander to be looked after by Dawnay. On the following day Montgomery remarked that 'He agreed to everything last night', to which Dawnay replied that, from what Eisenhower had said after Montgomery had retired, he very much doubted it. The Field-Marshal overruled Dawnay, however, and to make sure that Eisenhower had understood all his points, followed the meeting up two days later with a well-written letter, clearly reiterating all the arguments he had made in conversation. The letter demonstrates a gross misjudgement of Eisenhower's character:

> We have failed and suffered a strategic reverse. We require a new plan. And this time we must not fail ... Bradley and I make a good team ... things have not gone well since you separated us ... to be certain of success you want to bring us together and one of us should have full operational control north of the Ardennes AND IF YOU DECIDE I SHOULD DO THE WORK THAT IS O.K. BY ME.[3]

Brooke's encouragement of his friend and protégé caused incalculable harm to Anglo-American relations, and Eisenhower never forgave Montgomery for the tone of his 30 November letter. The Supreme Commander, said an ADC, was 'hot under the collar'; in fact, Eisenhower was extremely angry. He managed to write a controlled letter which gave his view that the only thing achieved by Montgomery's letter was to put in writing 'your conceptions and opinions as presented to me the other evening,' and went on to say that he did not know what Montgomery meant by 'strategic reverse', since they had gained a great victory in Normandy. To emphasise his annoyance, however, Eisenhower, administered a snub by hinting that he thought Montgomery had failed in Normandy: 'If we had advanced from the beginning [that is, at Caen] as we had hoped our maintenance services would have been in a position to supply us during the critical September days'.[4] And, referring to the immediate situation, the Supereme Commander stressed that he wanted the dividing line to be the Ruhr, not the Ardennes, and that he had 'no intention' of stopping Devers and Patton.

Montgomery was shaken by this tough letter, and sensibly saw that he must mend his bridges with his superior. He replied, humbly enough, that he had never intended to give the impression that the performance of the Allied Army had been an overall failure, and that his letter was only referring to the failure of the November offensive. In reply to this, Eisenhower displayed that quality of tact and magnanimity which was eventually to bring him to the Presidency of the United States: 'You have my prompt and abject apologies ... I do not want to put words or meaning into your mouth that upsets our close relationship.'[5]

Here was an opportunity for Montgomery to establish a better working relationship with the Supreme Commander, but in the event he threw it away. First, he signalled Brooke on 4 December and asked him not to take up the reorganisation of the command with Washington, but to leave it to him. 'There is a sporting chance we may pull it off. But any outside interference at this juncture might be fatal.'

Then, on 7 December, Montgomery met Eisenhower at Maastricht. Tedder, Bradley and Bedell Smith were also present, although Montgomery had originally suggested that no one should be present except Chiefs of Staff, who should not speak. But Eisenhower now snubbed the Twenty-First Army Group commander again by saying that he insisted on taking Bedell Smith: 'I will not by any means insult him by telling him he should remain mute at any conference both he and I attend.'

There were other clashes at Maastricht between Montgomery and Eisenhower. Montgomery harangued the conference, arguing that the main battlefield must be 'north of the Ruhr', the only terrain suitable for mobile warfare, and that therefore everything must be put into a concentrated offensive across the Rhine north of the Ruhr. All this the Supreme Commander had heard before, finding it merely a dreary repetition of the September arguments; the difference now, however, was that he was even more hostile to Montgomery.

Eisenhower argued that 'there were no fundamental differences'. He believed that the area further south, around Frankfurt and Cassel, was suitable for armour. He still favoured the northern advance, but he wanted to make two thrusts to exploit the Germans' great weakness – immobility. Montgomery interrupted, declaring emphatically that a thrust from Frankfurt had no chance of success and would only mean that his drive north of the Ruhr would not be strong enough. But Eisenhower brought the argument to an end by categorically refusing to stop Patton. Nettled by this, Montgomery rashly jumped again into the old argument about command. In vain he said that he 'would willingly serve under Bradley', after reiterating his view that he must have command of all operations north of the Ardennes. Testily Eisenhower once more refused to give up the land command.

Tedder, Bradley and Bedell Smith said little, but Montgomery was only too aware they sided with the Supreme Commander, and this added to his frustration. An artificially cheery lunch followed the meeting and, with a wry face, Montgomery watched the other four drive off together. At the lunch he had emphasised to Eisenhower that although, as commander of the armies of one of the principal allies, he disagreed with the existing strategy he would stand by Eisenhower's decisions. According to Montgomery 'We parted good friends', but this was untrue. The two men were no longer friends, although neither was prepared to force their quarrel to breaking point. Moreover, Montgomery now knew that Marshall and Roosevelt would never agree to Eisenhower's replacement, and that he, Montgomery, must lose if the dispute ever went to government level. Eisenhower, true to his temperament, was prepared to paper over the cracks.

Montgomery vented his frustration during the afternoon of 7 December, writing letters of complaint both to Brooke and to Grigg. To the CIGS he wrote:

> I played a lone hand against the three of them ... any points I made which caused Eisenhower to wobble would have been put right by Bradley and Tedder on the three hour drive back to Luxemburg ... If you want the war to end within a reasonable period you have to get Eisenhower's hand off the tiller. I regret to say he just does not know what he is doing. And you will have to see Bradley's influence is curbed.

And to Grigg:

I have returned from my conference with Ike at Maastricht. The result was complete failure, and he went back on all the points he had agreed to when alone with me. Bradley and Tedder were there too; I played a lone hand against the whole three. *That Tedder should take their side is too dreadful.*

I have written the whole thing in a long letter to the C.I.G.S, and he will doubtless show it to you.

The American plan for winning the war is quite dreadful; it will not succeed, and the war will go on. If you want to end the war in any reasonable time you will have to remove Ike's hand from the control of the land battle; and Bradley's hand also. How you will do this I do not know; but unless you do so, the war will go on. I hope the American public will realise that, owing to the handling of the campaign in western Europe from 1 Sept. onwards, the German war will now go on during 1945. And they should realise very clearly that the handling of the campaign is entirely in American hands.

We did quite reasonably well when it was in British hands.

One must just keep on plugging away at it; possibly some miracle will happen. But the experience of war is that you pay dearly for mistakes; no one knows that better than we British.

We must keep on fighting all through the winter, and one would not mind if success came at the end of it. But success will not come.

Come and see me sometime. I will send my aeroplane for you at any time.

> Yrs ever,
> Monty[6]

In both letters Montgomery enclosed a long memorandum of complaint against Eisenhower, which is reproduced in the Appendix to this book.

During this period of wrangling, Roosevelt had informed Churchill, in response to a preparatory request for a meeting of the Joint Chiefs of Staff to discuss the stalemate in France and Belgium, that he considered that the agreed broad front strategy was going according to plan. Frustrated by this reply from Washington, Churchill, at Brooke's request, asked Eisenhower to London to discuss the front.

The two men met at 1800 on 10 December in Churchill's map room — all the British Chief of Staff were also present, together with Tedder. Eisenhower reiterated his plan for a double advance into Germany, and Brooke immediately took up Montgomery's argument, telling the American that he was violating the most sacred principle of warfare – the need to concentrate forces – and that this had caused the present failure. Later, at dinner at 10 Downing Street that night, Brooke kept returning to Montgomery's theme. The Prime Minister kept Eisenhower up until 0135, but to Brooke's disappointment failed to support the arguments about the need for concentration. During these meetings Eisenhower, to everyone's horror, gave the impression that he did not expect to cross the Rhine until May, although later he corrected this view, declaring that all he had meant was that his staff feared a major crossing might not be possible until May because of the threat of floods.

On the next day Churchill told Brooke, somewhat disingenuously, that he had been unable to argue with Eisenhower because the American general was his guest at Downing Street. Instead, the CIGS was asked to prepare a Chiefs of Staff paper for the War Cabinet to be presented at a Cabinet meeting on 18 December. When finished, the paper pursued the same old Montgomery line that victory was being frittered away because of failure to concentrate 'on one major thrust in the north'. Brooke hoped that, after the Cabinet meeting, the paper would go before a special Joint Chiefs of Staff meeting in Washington, and that its effect would be to 'bulldoze' Eisenhower into changing his plan. However, after the Downing Street meeting, the Supreme Commander wrote complacently to Marshall that Brooke had been disturbed but, after hearing Eisenhower's explanation, had 'understood the situation better'. He added that despite the pressure from Montgomery and Brooke he still felt that 'it was important when the time comes that we should be on the Rhine at Frankfurt.'[7] Brooke would have been both annoyed and disturbed by this letter, so at variance with his own views, but in fact he never saw it.

Marshall and Eisenhower were determined that the Americans should play the dominating part in the final victorious campaign. Roosevelt too insisted upon this, and thus any change of command or strategy which gave Montgomery and Twenty-First Army Group the major role was politically impossible. As soldiers, both Brooke and Montgomery can be excused for their failure to realise this fact of life, but it is strange that Churchill, with his far greater political acumen, never understood it. The simple truth was that the badgering of Eisenhower, and the British appeal to the Joint Chiefs of Staff, could not be successful; all that such ploys could produce was a further deterioration in Anglo-American relations.

Two days before Brooke's paper could be discussed by the Cabinet, the stalemate on the front ended. On 16 December, Hitler unexpectedly launched two giant Panzer armies, comprising over half a million men, at the weakest point in the Allied line in the Ardennes.

12

Ardennes

At dawn on 16 December 1944 von Rundstedt and Model, on Hitler's direct orders, launched Fifth Panzer and Sixth SS Panzer Armies across five-inch deep snow against the American forces in the Ardennes. They struck at the thinnest point in the defensive line, held by only two inexperienced infantry divisions since the terrain was considered by the Allies to be unsuitable for this type of warfare. Now, however, German tanks and armoured cars quickly drove deep into the US lines, creating havoc.

Hitler had ordered von Rundstedt in September to build up reserves of petrol and ammunition for the attack, but it was expected that the Panzers would advance far and fast enough to capture sufficient petrol from American dumps to fuel their onward progress. The German plan was to crash the two well-equipped tank armies, with Seventh Army providing flank protection in the south, through the weakest American divisions and then turn west and north towards the Meuse. The assault depended upon cloud cover to ground the dominant Allied air forces and, luckily for the Panzers, low cloud and fog, with rain or snow, prevailed in the Ardennes for over a week. Soon the Germans had driven a wedge between US First and Third Armies, and within five days were closing up to the Meuse.

Montgomery, like the Americans, was caught completely by surprise. The day before the attack started he had written to Eisenhower saying that he wanted to go to England on 23 December to spend Christmas with his son, and on the morning of 16 December he sent out this report, contained within Directive M538:

3. The enemy is at present fighting a defensive campaign on all fronts; his situation is such that he cannot stage major offensive operations. Furthermore at all costs he has to prevent the war from entering on a mobile phase; he has not the transport or the petrol that would be necessary for mobile operations, nor could his tanks compete with ours in the mobile battle.

4. The enemy is in a bad way; he has had a tremendous battering and lost heavily in men and equipment. On no account can we relax or have a 'stand still' in the winter months; it is vital that we keep going, so as not to allow him time to recover and so as to wear down his strength still further. There will be difficulties caused by mud, cold, lack of air support during periods of bad weather, and so on. But we must continue to fight the enemy hard during the winter months.

5. The main objective of the Allies on the western front is the RUHR; if we can cut it off from the rest of Germany the enemy capacity to continue the struggle must gradually peter out.

A further, and very important, object of our operations must be to force mobile war on the Germans.

Paradoxically, as the report was being signed Hitler himself had already forced mobile war upon the Allies; Montgomery can seldom have been so far astray in his appreciation of a battle situation. Having signed this statement and dealt with other business at his Tac HQ, a relaxed and confident Field-Marshal flew to Eindhoven for golf with the professional, Dai Rees. Before he had played many holes, however, he received an urgent message which sent him hurrying back to his HQ.

I showed Montgomery's Directive M538 of 16 December to Brigadier Williams, who told me that he could not recall ever having seen it before and that paragraph 4 was typical of his chief. He added:

Monty ignored my Intelligence Summary of 3 December, which made it clear Sixth Panzer [Army] was waiting in reserve intact. Monty never showed his draft orders to anyone. He just wrote them. On this occasion he ignored my briefing about Rundstedt's Sixth Panzer Army. He was always inclined to be euphoric, and if you gave him news he did not want to hear he would switch off. That is what had happened to him on 16 December, and it has a trace of pig-headedness about it.

In his Intelligence Report of 3 December, Williams had reported the existence of Sixth SS Panzer Army, uncommitted in reserve, but he added that he was positive that it was being held back for a counter-attack when the Allies advanced further.[1] In compiling his report Williams had taken Ultra evidence into account, and part of the summary reads:

The bruited German drive on Antwerp is just not within his [von Rundstedt's] potential ... he needs more infantry of better quality. Although von Rundstedt has 6 Panzer Army in reserve he, at the age of 69, will wait to use it to smash our bridgeheads over the Roer ... 6 Panzer Army may contain 1, 2, 9, and 12 SS Panzer Divisions west of the Rhine forward of Cologne.

Williams emphasised that the strategic reserve, that is, Sepp Dietrich's Sixth SS Panzer Army, had not been committed at this date, and that to have a Panzer army in reserve was 'a luxury not known to von Rundstedt since D-Day'. The words 'bruited German drive on Antwerp' show that Montgomery and Williams had discussed the danger of an enemy counter-offensive by Sixth Panzer Army, but had dismissed it. I asked Williams why he had thought that von Rundstedt's age was relevant, to which he replied:

At that stage we knew the German plans came from Hitler's sick bed and not from von Rundstedt, and although I have now reached the age of 69, I still think von Rundstedt's age was relevant because it meant he would be set in his ways and inflexible, and as it was Hitler's plan and not his own he would let it take its course, willy-nilly. But in fact Model led the offensive, not von Rundstedt himself.

US First Army's Intelligence Report of 9 December was nearer the mark than Twenty-First Army Group's, and stated that Sixth SS Panzer Army had high morale and that the Germans might soon be ready 'for an all-out offensive'.[2] About this Brigadier Williams commented: 'Colonel Mark Dickson, G2 Intelligence, US First Army, went on leave to Paris just after he had written the 9 December report. This is scarcely the behaviour of an officer agog about an enemy offensive. In fact he always prophesied every sort of woe about an enemy offensive'. Dickson was indeed treated as an alarmist by the senior American commanders who, from Eisenhower downwards, continued with their preparations for a festive Christmas.

In mid-November Ultra had revealed that there was a concentration of enemy fighter aircraft in the central Rhineland, described by the Germans with the word *Jägeraufmarsch* (fighter assembly or deployment) – significantly, the Allies had seen that word used on other occasions only before a major attack. On 2 December Model's Army Group B was reported by Ultra to be asking urgently for fighter cover to protect 200 trainloads of troops, including the Führer Escort Brigade, Hitler's dedicated personal guard. Other messages showed that thousands of trucks were being collected for Sixth Panzer Army. So what had gone wrong with Allied intelligence?

Brigadier Williams told me that:

As far as we were concerned every item of information fitted the picture, whereas we should have rethought the picture itself, as events made us do speedily enough.

There was a curious wireless silence before the attack. This put Ultra at Bletchley on the *qui vive* (so I gathered after the war). Their traffic analysis made them think something was on. At 21 Army Group we were too near the battle to be alerted in the same way.

Bad intelligence brought about the attack; good intelligence defeated it. Once the balloon went up we shaped our reactions correctly, based on our information from German wireless messages. Joe Ewart said to me two days after the attack: 'Have you seen the German Air Force signals? They reveal the intentions of the German Air Force.' When I plotted them [the target names given in the signals] on the map I realised, as Joe had already done, that they disclosed the line of thrust from the list of bridges to be attacked and not attacked; the omissions were significant. And shortly after the attack began

Ultra intercepts became good. Hitler had amazing luck because all our aircraft were grounded when his Ardennes offensive began.

By 2240 on 16 December Ultra had confirmed to Twenty-First Army Group that on the next day German fighter aircraft would support the assault by the two Panzer armies. No one on the Allied side, however, appears to have been unduly troubled, although at first Montgomery took the German attack more seriously than did the Americans or the staff at SHAEF. For instance, Strong's weekly SHAEF Intelligence Summary of 17 December (alleged by one historian to have been later doctored*) dismissed the enemy offensive as 'a diversionary attack on a fair scale', and declared that it was too early to say much about it, insisting it was designed only 'to relieve pressure from the Cologne, Dusseldorf and Saar sectors.'

On the same day Montgomery, not over-worried by the situation south of his army group, presented medals to the Canadian troops, and held a conference to discuss 'Veritable', the proposed combined British-Canadian attack to close up on the Rhine. But on the following day, 18 December, there came the alarming news that 1st SS Panzer Division was within a few miles of Stavelot, where there was a giant American petrol dump containing two million gallons, and almost no troops to defend it. Fortunately, the Panzer columns turned away three miles from the dump, but there were other German gains. The Panzers were pouring through a fifty-mile gap in the line, and the American forces were scattering in front of them. By nightfall German forward troops were some twenty miles over the Belgian frontier.

Montgomery, well briefed, but still effectively out of the battle, signalled Brooke on 20 December:

Situation in American area is not *not* good ... great confusion and all signs of full scale withdrawal. There is definite lack of grip and control ... and atmosphere of great pessimism in First and Ninth Armies. Bradley is still at Luxemburg but I understand he is moving as his HQ are in danger ... I have heard nothing from Ike or Bradley and had no orders or requests of any sort. My own opinion is the American forces have been cut in half and the Germans can reach the Meuse

* David Irving, *Hitler's War*, p.342.

at Namur without opposition. The Command set up always faulty is now futile. I have told Whiteley that Ike ought to place me in operational command of all troops on northern half of the front. He should be given a direct order by someone to do so. The situation needs to be handled very firmly and with a tight grip.

Brooke, fearing that Montgomery would upset Eisenhower by badgering him for command of the northern sector, included the following in his reply:

5. Agree would be a great advantage to have one Commander (preferably yourself) for all troops on northern half of front. But only authority which can order Eisenhower to do so is Combined Chiefs of Staff, and I see no chance of our being able to convince US Chiefs of Staff at present that necessity exists for Combined Chiefs of Staff to take the drastic step of instructing Eisenhower on his conduct of the battle.
6. Be careful what you say to Eisenhower himself on subject of command set up as it may do much more harm than good especially as he is now probably very worried about whole situation. It is a different thing to make suggestions to Whiteley as you have done and this may bear fruit.
7. I have sent the P.M. copy of your telegram.

Fortunately Eisenhower, supported by Bedell Smith, had already decided that he had no option but to put Montgomery in charge of all the northern sector, where a great number of troops from US First and Ninth Armies had been cut off from Bradley by the 'bulge' of the German attack. On the morning of the 20th Eisenhower telephoned Montgomery from Rheims, and told him: 'We now have two fronts and I want you to assume command of the northern front.' The Supreme Commander went on talking, but Montgomery paid no attention (the line was in any case very bad). He had got what he wanted, though under much less happy circumstances than would have prevailed at the end of September, when he would have had virtually the same command of the northern sector if only Twenty-First Army Group had succeeded in crossing the Rhine at Arnhem.

As soon as Churchill received from the CIGS a copy of

Montgomery's signal of 20 December he began to work himself up into a state of excitement and, according to General Simpson, started to draft a telegram ordering Montgomery to take action at once 'with XXX Corps on some thrust line or other'. Both Simpson and Brooke were appalled to find that the Prime Minister was in effect attempting to order about formations that came under Montgomery. Brooke pointed out to Churchill that any orders to Montgomery could only come from Eisenhower, and also that it was impossible for anyone in London to say at that time how Montgomery could act, because the circumstances on the ground were not known in London. Reluctantly, the Prime Minister agreed not to signal orders to Montgomery, and asked Brooke what he should do instead to help. The CIGS recommended that Churchill should telephone Eisenhower and ask him about the situation, and if possible suggest that the whole of the northern half of the front should be under one commander, preferably Montgomery.

At 1615 on the 20th Churchill telephoned Eisenhower with the delicate objective of getting command transferred to Montgomery. He started tactlessly, telling the Supreme Commander that he ought to work 'on a pincer nip from the north and south upon the German offensive bulge', and going on to say that Montgomery should be put in charge of the northern effort, to which Eisenhower replied testily that he had already asked Montgomery to take over. The CIGS, in the Prime Minister's room at the time, was greatly relieved.

Brooke went back to the War Office and gave Simpson the good news. As generals, the two men were worried when Churchill, a keen amateur strategist, involved himself in operations, and the CIGS was moved to remark to Simpson:

> Even I never give Monty advice on tactics. All the advice I send him is on major strategy and especially relations with the Americans. Monty is my tactical master and again and again he has been right and I have been wrong. But Monty never lets you forget this, and my heart bleeds for poor Ike now because of what Monty will hint at concerning what Eisenhower ought to have done. It will be 'I told you so'.[3]

Within a few hours of Eisenhower's call, Montgomery had visited Lt-Gen William Simpson, GOC US Ninth Army, and

Hodges, GOC US First Army. According to one British officer, his visit to Chaudfontaine at 1330, where Hodges had his HQ in a sports field hut, was 'like Christ come to cleanse the temple', and David Belchem, who accompanied Montgomery, thought that 'Hodges and his senior staff officers looked as if they had seen a ghost'.[4] Montgomery could not believe that Hodges was correct in saying that two of his divisions had been overwhelmed so quickly, and decided to send out his own liaison officers, who crossed no-man's-land to visit the troops in question. They found the Americans withdrawing successfully, although they had taken severe casualties.

Brigadier Williams also accompanied Montgomery, and commented to me:

> After Monty, Belchem and I had talked to him [Hodges] Monty said 'He is so shaken he needs a pause to recover his calm'. So we went to another room to discuss the situation. Thoughtfully Monty wanted to nurse him back into a state of resolution.
>
> Hodges looked ashen to me. He looked as if somebody had punched him in the tummy, or indeed kicked him in the crutch. Years older than when last I'd seen him; you must remember he'd only been sitting under Bradley until the change of ground-force command and this was his first experience of 'independent' command. He wasn't either intellectually or morally fit for bearing responsibility, which requires, from my observation, a special sort of guts which Bradley had, Monty had, Mike Carver has, Shan Hackett has, but I haven't, because I've been trained or have grown up to see both sides of every question and that makes for hesitation, ie irresolution.
>
> I don't think Hodges knew quite what to do or quite what had hit him. He was mightily relieved to find a father-figure showing up to sort it all out for him. The Chief of Staff, Bill Keen, brought up with Bradley, was, however, resolute and steady and an excellent soldier. Hodges was an example, even a victim, of the seniority principle, which to the Americans (like ourselves earlier) had got to work itself out of the system.

Montgomery immediately placed some British divisions under Simpson's command, and ordered the latter to take over part of

Hodges's front – he also ordered XXX Corps to station divisions behind the Americans in case they collapsed. Montgomery then asked Hodges who he considered to be the most aggressive general in First Army, and the American singled out Maj-Gen Lawton Collins, whose US VIII Corps had captured Cherbourg and had been spectacularly successful in the St Lô break-out. Now two of Collins's divisions, together with British 51st (Highland) Division, were held as strategic reserve for US Ninth Army, with orders to prepare for a counter-attack as soon as Montgomery was ready.

On the night of the 20th Montgomery sent this tale of woe to Brooke:

> Neither Army Commander had seen Bradley or any of 15 Army Group staff since the battle began ... no reserves behind front ... morale very low. They seemed delighted to have someone to give them firm orders ... All bridges over the Meuse from south east of Liege to north east of Givet are now held by British garrisons ...* I have every hope that the situation can be put right now that we have a properly organised set up for command and proper supervision and control can be kept over the battle. It will take a day or two to get the American front reorganised and we may have a few more shocks ... there was literally no control or grip of any

* 3rd Royal Tank Regiment from 29 Armoured Brigade took over responsibility for the Meuse bridges at Namur, Givet and Dinant. When the 23rd Hussars arrived at Givet they found American reinforcement troops queueing for the cinema, and these told the British, quite incorrectly: 'It is OK. George Patton is coming'. 3rd RTR crossed the Meuse on Christmas Eve, and met a battle group from 2nd Panzer Division. The British force knocked out several Panthers, and on Christmas morning tanks from US 2nd Armoured Division, part of Collins's corps, appeared from the north across 3rd RTR's front. 2nd Panzer had reached the furthest limit of the German advance, but by now it was out of petrol, its supply column having been devastated from the air as it approached on 23 December. The Meuse was never crossed, and US 2nd Armoured knocked out the 2nd Panzer battle group at Celles on Boxing Day. In a café at Celles crossroads, four miles from the Meuse bridge at Dinant, is an inscription in French, Flemish and English: 'The Rundstedt offensive (Battle of the Bulge) was stopped here on 24 December 1944'. On 5 January Montgomery sent a cocky signal to the CIGS after examination of the Celles battlefield had revealed eighty-eight German tanks destroyed, and this tangible evidence of success may have contributed to his very optimistic mood at his famous press conference on 7 January.

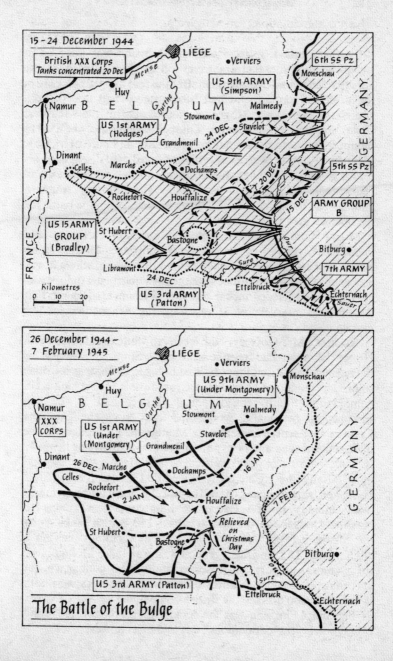

15 – 24 December 1944

British XXX Corps
Tanks concentrated 20 Dec

LIÈGE
• Verviers
Meuse

6th SS Pz
Monschau

US 9th ARMY
(Simpson)

Huy

Namur B E L G I U M

Malmedy
Stoumont
24 DEC
Stavelot

US 1st ARMY
(Hodges)

Grandmenil

GERMANY

Dinant
Celles   Marche
• Dochamps

5th SS Pz

Rochefort   Houffalize

15 DEC   7 20 DEC

ARMY GROUP
B

US 15 ARMY
GROUP
(Bradley)

St Hubert

Bastogne

FRANCE

Bitburg •

Libramont   24 DEC

Sûre

7th ARMY

Kilometres
0   10   20

Ettelbruck   Echternach
Sauer

US 3rd ARMY
(Patton)

**26 December 1944 –
7 February 1945**

LIÈGE
• Verviers

Meuse

Monschau

US 9th ARMY
(Under Montgomery)

Huy

Namur   B E L G I U M

XXX
CORPS

Malmedy
Stoumont

US 1st ARMY
(Under
Montgomery)

Grandmenil

Stavelot

GERMANY

Dinant
26 DEC   Marche
Celles   • Dochamps

16 JAN

Rochefort
2 JAN   Houffalize

7 FEB

St Hubert   Bastogne

Relieved
on
Christmas
Day

Bitburg•

Sûre

US 3rd ARMY (Patton)

Ettelbruck   Echternach

The Battle of the Bulge

sort of the situation.

To the south, US 101st Airborne Division was besieged in Bastogne, and the Panzers were still driving forward as the Americans fell back before them. But the real danger point lay in the north of the bulge where Montgomery had firmly taken control; a German tank group was in sight of the Meuse at Celles, four miles from Dinant, although Montgomery refused to mount a counter-attack until he was ready and sure of victory. Meanwhile Patton, with extraordinary speed, had disengaged his forces south of the bulge, turned them through 90 degrees, and driven them with some success against the Germans' southern flank as Montgomery was savouring his key role in the battle for Europe.

Montgomery visited Hodges and Simpson each day and undoubtedly served as a steadying influence. Hodges soon pulled his First Army HQ back behind the Meuse, where it was less exposed to capture, but Montgomery felt that Hodges was very tired and needed moral support. Williams considered that 'Monty was marvellous' in restoring the American general's morale.

At first, Montgomery had been so little impressed with Hodges that he had telephoned Bedell Smith to discuss his replacement because of his 'exhaustion', adding that, as a British soldier, he could not personally be responsible for sacking a US commander. Smith replied that if Hodges had to go, then Eisenhower personally would tell him, and the Supreme Commander sent a message to Montgomery: 'Hodges is the quiet reticent type and does not appear as aggressive as he really is. Unless he becomes exhausted he will always wage a good fight.' Montgomery generously replied that Hodges, 'originally a bit shaken, very tired and in need of moral support is improving.'[5]

By midday on 22 December Montgomery was able to reassure Hodges that he had deployed 150 British tanks along the Meuse between Namur and Givet like 'clothes pins on a clothes line'. The American general was grateful to Montgomery for his moral support, and absorbed some of his confidence, but according to Stephen Ambrose, Eisenhower's biographer, both he and Simpson disliked the British commander.

'Big Simp' Simpson was far cockier than Hodges. He found Montgomery 'rather pompous', but told Eisenhower:

I and my army are operating smoothly and cheerfully under the command of the Field Marshal Montgomery. The most cordial relations and a very high spirit of co-operation have been established between him and myself personally and between our respective staffs. You can depend on me to respond cheerfully and as efficiently as I can to every instruction he gives ... Yesterday the Field Marshal paid me a visit and at his request I took him to HQ XIX Corps where he met my Corps and Divisional Commanders. He made us a splendid talk on the present situation. Then we all had lunch together.[6]

Hodges may have felt grateful to Montgomery in his initial relief at the strong, confident handling of his worrying situation, but Chester Wilmot, who saw a lot of Montgomery and the American generals, commented that: 'Monty felt in defeat the Americans had to turn to him to extricate them from a predicament which would never have developed if he had been left in command ... [he] did not endear himself to the Americans for his confident tone seemed to carry a note of censure.'[7]

The stimulus of taking command in a crisis after everything had gone wrong was a tonic to Montgomery, and during this period he was a ball of energy, radiating confidence – exactly what the American and British commanders needed, even though his lack of tact tended to nettle the Americans. He was already looking ahead to the end of the Battle of the Bulge, and began to plan in his mind the final offensive against Germany in which, more than ever, he was anxious to have overall command of the vital northern drive. Brooke urged him to be cautious, however, and on 21 December wrote:

A word of warning. Events and enemy action have forced on Eisenhower a more satisfactory system of command. It is most important that you should not even in the slightest degree rub this undoubted fact in to anyone at SHAEF or elsewhere. Any remarks you make are bound to come to Eisenhower's ears sooner or later and that may make it more difficult to ensure that this new set up for command remains even after the present emergency has passed. I myself have felt you were right all along.

Montgomery neglected this good advice. When Bradley visited him at Zondhoven on Christmas Day he could not resist the temptation to crow, and told Bradley that he had always said that the Allies should not try two thrusts at the same time because neither would be strong enough. 'Now', he summed up, 'we are in a proper muddle.' Bradley contained his rage so well that Montgomery was unaware of it.

Tactlessly, Montgomery went on to tell the American that in future they must hold shorter fronts in the south, and withdraw units from there for an all-out attack in the north. On his return that evening Bradley, infuriated by his talk with the Field-Marshal, told Patton that if Hodges stayed under Montgomery then 'First Army would not launch their attack for three months', and, to Patton's disgust, forecast that the southern thrust would probably have to fall back to the Saar/Vosges line, or even to the Moselle.[8]

Montgomery wrote to Grigg of Bradley that 'he looked thin and worn and ill at ease', and added, incorrectly, that the American had agreed with everything he had said. He went on patronisingly: 'Poor chap, he is such a decent fellow and the whole thing is a bitter pill for him.'[9]

In fact, Bradley silently disagreed with almost everything Montgomery had said, but felt, at the moment when his divisions had been removed from his command, that he could not argue. In particular, he was cross because Montgomery wanted to retreat to shorten the front, which Bradley felt might prejudice the eventual Allied counter-attack. Hodges and Collins were also strongly opposed to Montgomery's plan for a limited withdrawal.

Eisenhower held a meeting with his staff and Bradley on Boxing Day. There Bradley said that he wanted immediately to be given back command of Seventh,* First and Ninth Armies, but the Supreme Commander refused, saying that it was logical for Montgomery to command on the northern flank of the German salient. Eisenhower added that he did not hold with Patton's demand for an immediate counter-offensive and that he

---

* US Seventh Army (Lt-Gen Alexander Patch) was normally a part of Devers's Sixth Army Group, but during the Battle of the Bulge covered much of the US Third Army's front, freeing Patton's forces for counter-offensive operations.

agreed with Montgomery that the Allied attack should not begin at once. Montgomery claimed that he had reorganised the American armies during his period of command in the Ardennes; the US generals merely said that 'interrupted communications had been restored'. The truth lies between the two claims.

On 23 December Montgomery wrote to Grigg: 'I will not write my views on what has gone on here. I do not know of any ink that would stand it. Personally I am enjoying a very interesting battle, but we ought to be in tears at the tragedy of the whole thing.' Unhappily, such talk about enjoying very interesting battles while commanding American troops was shortly to lead Montgomery into another crisis. But, having assumed command, he was cautiously optimistic about the position, despite reports received on 21 and 22 December by Twenty-First Army Group that the enemy intended to launch parachute attacks on the Brussels and Antwerp areas – the RAF advised that the Germans were capable of putting up 125 troop-carrying aircraft, enough for 1,500 men.[10] Calmly and methodically, the British commander and his staff set about restoring the situation.

Williams's Twenty-First Army Group Intelligence Report 169, dated 20 December, shows strong indications of having been written in consultation with Montgomery. It states cryptically that 'We were wrong' on 3 December in anticipating that von Rundstedt would husband Sixth SS Panzer Army 'until we crossed the Roer', and continues:

So the bruited drive for Antwerp, the dash to the wire,* is on. The next 48 hours should reveal what are the limits of his [von Rundstedt's] potential which in early December we deemed inadequate. The plan of the attack is for two drives westwards towards the Meuse between Liege and Givet made by 6 SS Panzer Army on the right and Fifth Panzer Army on the left ... Companies of paratroopers were dropped close

---

* A familiar expression to anyone who, like Williams, had served in the Western Desert. The 'Wire' was the name given to the border between Libya and Egypt, and the phrase 'dash to the wire' refers to Rommel's lightning, though eventually unsuccessful, armoured thrust westwards during the 'Crusader' battles in Cyrenaica in November 1941.

behind the Allied line to hinder the move of reinforcements from the north and confuse the issue.

Between these two powerful drives, the more northerly of which is the more formidable and evidently the main thrust, the situation is obscure ... the situation is uncertain it is clearly also serious ... it is evidently a measure of desperation for Von Rundstedt who has now committed 6 Panzer Army which we failed to force him to do a few weeks ago, and he has left the excellent defensive positions nature and sweat had given him in a prodigious effort which may prove indeed the last Blitz to disrupt our preparations for a winter assault of Germany ... Von Rundstedt is playing for high stakes, Antwerp among them.[11]

Montgomery was in no doubt that he might have to fight a desperate battle to defend Antwerp, but he was determined not to be panicked into hasty reactions, or indeed to make any move until he knew the full strength of the enemy attack.

The next Intelligence Report, 170, issued on Christmas Eve, made it clear that the threat to Antwerp had receded: 'The Allied hinge in the area Monschau-Malmedy has frustrated every enemy attempt and proved expensive for him ... 6 SS Panzer Army has abandoned its attempt to reach Liege by Verviers and instead is trying a left hook across the Salm ... The object remains Liege but now the enemy is trying to take it from the south.'

On Boxing Day, Williams's report (171) gave full credit to Patton's Third Army for relieving Bastogne, adding that US 101st Airborne Division's defence of the town was reminiscent of Alam Halfa, Montgomery's successful defence of the Alamein line in August 1942. The report continued:

The second plan for 6th SS Panzer Army to approach Liege from the south is going more slowly than the enemy had assumed for the Allied Air Forces have reduced the sting and denied impetus to 2 SS Panzer Division. 6th Panzer Army on the left has discovered that probing forward with tanks will no longer prove sufficient and that a properly co-ordinated attack is called for ... 5th Panzer Army must now consider how much help it can give to its right hand neighbour if its own underbelly is being threatened. The enemy has been trying to get his second wind.[12]

Patton noted on Christmas Day, the day before his Third Army troops relieved the key nodal point of Bastogne, that 'The German has shot his wad. We should attack,' and told his staff: 'The damn Jerries have stuck their heads in the meat grinder and I have got the handle.' Montgomery was equally confident, but he was not in a hurry to attack even the head of the 'pincer', which was now becoming inviting for him. And he still baulked altogether at a big bite across the base of the salient, although Collins was proposing a major attack southwards to drive right through to Bastogne.

Patton, irritated by Montgomery's caution in restraining Collins, commented: 'If Ike put Bradley back in command of 1st and 9th Armies we can bag the whole German Army. I wish Ike were more of a gambler, but he is certainly a lion compared with Monty.' This remark sums up the US generals' feelings about Montgomery who, oblivious of their discontent, was hoping that the Germans would attack again, and thus give him an even better opportunity to catch them on their flank.[13] Eisenhower, with his considerable experience of Montgomery's caution, feared that the British commander would delay his counter-attack and thus give the Germans a chance to consolidate their positions and bring up supplies and reinforcements – he knew from past events, however, that there was little good in giving Montgomery direct orders.

Eisenhower and Montgomery conferred at Hasselt on 28 December. The American was somewhat put out because the meeting had been planned to take place in Brussels, but when he got there he found that Montgomery had gone forward unexpectedly. This sort of thing had happened before, and it did not put the Supreme Commander in a good temper.

Montgomery was most impressed by American security arrangements when Eisenhower arrived at Hasselt in his special train on the 27th. At the time it was thought that the Germans had sent out squads of SS troops dressed in US Army uniforms to assassinate the American chiefs, and possibly Montgomery as well. Colonel Otto Skorzeny had indeed organised an operation during von Rundstedt's attack when disguised SS troops operated behind the American lines, and these caused considerable confusion, though their numbers were greatly exaggerated by the Allies. The assassination plot, however, was merely a rumour started by Skorzeny. Nevertheless, as soon as the Supreme Commander's train drew up at Hasselt station teams of machine-gunners leapt out and set up their weapons on both platforms at each end of the train, while other guards positioned themselves at all the vantage points; Montgomery commented that 'It would have been hard for Nazi assassination troops to kill Ike'. In fact there was concern in London about Montgomery's personal safety, and the Field-Marshal told Frank Simpson that, having seen Eisenhower's guard, he felt rather naked because his only protection was an armoured car travelling behind his own vehicle. When, a few days later, Simpson himself spent the night at Montgomery's HQ, now moved to a villa 'adequate but not very comfortable' because of the cold weather, he tested the security after Montgomery had gone to his usual early bed. He saw a tank outside with a couple of British soldiers looking out of the top of it, two armoured cars in the bushes on either side of the house, and similar protection at the back. On his return he was able to tell Brooke and Churchill that Montgomery was taking 'sensible precautions'.[14] No British or American commanders were assassinated,* although some risk existed.

As the Field-Marshal and the Supreme Commander talked on 28 December there was a lull in the fighting – the Germans had been stopped, at least temporarily. Hitler had in fact decided to launch a southern attack against Devers's Sixth Army Group in the Vosges on 1 January, believing that the American force had been much weakened in the initial Ardennes onslaught. Eisenhower had been briefed by General Strong that the Germans in the bulge were badly battered and short of all supplies, and he therefore wanted Montgomery to attack their exposed salient immediately. Montgomery refused. Von Rundstedt, he said, would attack again in the north, and he preferred to wait for this attack and launch a strong counter-attack as soon as the German thrust petered out. The two commanders argued but could not reach agreement, and eventually Eisenhower asked Montgomery to promise to attack on 1 January if there had been no further German attack in the

---

* It has been suggested, albeit with very little evidence, that Patton, who died as a result of a car accident in Germany in December 1945, was in fact the victim of an assassin.

north by then. The American left the meeting thinking that Montgomery had agreed to this scheme.

At the meeting, to Eisenhower's extreme irritation, Montgomery once more insisted on discussing future operations, and ploughed into another exposition of why it was essential for him to have co-ordinating powers in order to synchronise the movements of the American northern armies with his own. Then, as he saw his arguments foundering, he again offered to serve under Bradley, to which Eisenhower once again firmly replied that he had no intention of giving Bradley such a command. Even so, Montomgery wrote to the CIGS that Eisenhower had accepted his points, although the letter prompted Brooke to record in his diary:

> Monty has had another interview with Ike. I do not like the look of it. It looks to me as if Monty has been rubbing into Ike the results of not having listened to his advice ... According to Monty Ike agrees that the front should now be divided in two and that only one major offensive is possible. I expect whoever meets Ike next day may swing him to another point of view.

At this stage Montgomery was extremely patronising about the Americans, and particularly about Eisenhower. A letter he sent to Grigg on 31 December typified his attitude towards them, as well as his supreme confidence in himself:

> Simpson takes this and will tell you what I am doing. All is well and the Germans will now not get what they wanted. But they have given the Americans a colossal 'bloody nose' and mucked up all our plans; however, as we had not got a plan I suppose they will say it does not matter.[15]

Thinking that Montgomery would attack on 1 January, as Eisenhower believed he had promised, the Americans attacked the south of the salient on that day. Von Rundstedt immediately transferred Panzer divisions from the north to meet and contain this assault, something he could do with relative ease since Montgomery did not attack. Eisenhower and his colleagues were livid at the British commander's failure to fulfil what they claimed was his agreement to attack simultaneously.

Unfortunately, the British press was now interpreting Montgomery's temporary command of the north of the bulge as presaging his being put in overall command of a number of American divisions. In Washington Marshall was so angered by reports on 29 December in *The Times* and other nationals, which stated that Eisenhower would leave US First and Ninth Armies under Montgomery, that he signalled the Supreme Commander:

> They may or may not have brought to your attention articles in certain London papers proposing a British Deputy Commander for all your ground forces and implying that you have undertaken too much.
>
> Under no circumstances make any concession of any kind whatsoever. You not only have our complete confidence but there would be terrific resentment in this country following such action. I am not assuming you had in mind any such a concession. I just wish you to be sure of our attitude on this side. You are doing a grand job, and go on giving them hell.

On New Year's Eve, de Guingand had arrived at Versailles to explain to Eisenhower why Montgomery would not attack on 1 January. Montgomery, he said, felt that 'the Allies had the Germans on the run like a wet hen from one side of the salient to the other'; time was on the Allies' side, and they should let the Germans exhaust themselves before attacking.

Eisenhower, who liked de Guingand, nevertheless turned on him and said that this was a breach of faith by Montgomery, who had promised at the Hasselt conference three days before to start his attack on 1 January; he sent his staff scurrying through the files to see if the promise was in writing. De Guingand calmly said: 'Knowing Monty, I can tell you the last thing he would do would be to put a commitment to attack on paper.'

At that moment, as Eisenhower was breathing fire against Montgomery for not co-ordinating his attack with the Americans, a tactless letter for the Supreme Commander arrived from the subject of his present rage. As usual, Montgomery had decided that he must follow up his discussion with Eisenhower on the 28th at Hasselt with the usual written confirmation of his cogent arguments – plainly he believed that the Supreme Commander had swung round to his view, but this time he went too far with the written word:

My dear Ike,
It was very pleasant to see you again yesterday and to have a talk on the battle situation.

2. I would like to refer to the matter of operational control of all forces engaged in the northern thrust towards the Ruhr, i.e. 12 and 21 Army Groups.

I think we want to be careful, because we have had one very definite failure when we tried to produce a formula that would meet this case ...

3. When you and Bradley and myself met at Maastricht on 7 December, it was clear to me that Bradley opposed any idea that I should have operational control over his Army Group; so I did not then pursue the subject.

I therefore consider that it will be necessary for you to be very firm on the subject, and any loosely worded statement will be quite useless.

4. I consider that if you merely use the word 'co-ordination', it will not work. The person designated by you must have powers of operational direction and control of the operations that will follow on your directive.

5. I would say that your directive will assign tasks and objectives to the two Army Groups, allot boundaries, and so on.

Thereafter preparations are made and the battle is joined.

It is then that one commander must have powers to direct and control the operations; you cannot possibly do it yourself, and so you would have to nominate someone else.

6. I suggest that your directive should finish with this sentence:

'12 and 21 Army Groups will develop operations in accordance with the above instructions. From now onwards full operational direction, control, and co-ordination of these operations is vested in the C-in-C 21 Army Group, subject to such instructions as may be issued by the Supreme Commander from time to time.'

I put this matter up to you again only because I am so anxious not to have another failure.

I am absolutely convinced that the key to success lies in:

(a) all available offensive power being assigned to the northern line of advance to the Ruhr;

(b) a sound set-up for command, and this implies one man directing and controlling the whole tactical battle on the northern thrust.

I am certain that if we do not comply with these two basic conditions, then we will fail again ...

Yours always, and your very

devoted friend

Monty[16]

At this stage of the campaign Bradley and Patton would rather have resigned than accept Montgomery's overlordship, and this outrageous letter, coming as it did in the wake of Eisenhower's anger at the failure to attack as promised on 1 January, came close to bringing about the Field-Marshal's downfall. Like Henry II in 1170, the Supreme Commander impulsively decided that the time had come to be rid of his 'turbulent priest', and with Tedder's help he drafted a signal to Washington which, in effect, asked for Montgomery to be sacked. De Guingand, soon informed, became thoroughly alarmed by the course events were taking, and succeeded in persuading Eisenhower to hold up the signal to Washington, explaining that Montgomery did not 'understand the real situation' and promising to straighten it out with him. Both Eisenhower and Tedder were reluctant to delay, but Bedell Smith urged reconciliation. It says a great deal for Eisenhower's estimation of de Guingand that he agreed to defer sending the signal, instead giving de Guingand a letter to take to Montgomery. This read:

You know how greatly I have appreciated you and depended upon your frank and friendly counsel but in your latest letter you disturb me by predictions of 'failure' unless your exact opinions in the matter of giving you command over Bradley are met in detail. I assure you in this matter I can go no further ...

For my part I would deplore the development of such an unbridgeable gulf of convictions between us that we would have to present our difficulties to the Combined Chiefs of

Staff. The confusion and debate that would follow would certainly damage the good will and devotion to a common cause that have made this Allied Force unique in history.[17]

Eisenhower also sent a copy of the new SHAEF plan for resuming the offensive. Meanwhile, de Guingand signalled Montgomery from Versailles that he needed to talk to him urgently, and immediately set off for the latter's HQ, arriving in the afternoon of 31 December. He found Montgomery happy and relaxed, taking tea with his ADC having just written that characteristic letter to his friend Grigg, quoted above, which demonstrated his usual contempt for the Americans.

De Guingand told Montgomery that he must have a serious talk with him at once, and after tea they went to the latter's office. Years later, in a BBC interview, de Guingand described their talk. At first Montgomery could not see the danger in which he had placed himself, but the other man brutally told him that if he did not climb down pretty fast he would be sacked and replaced by Alexander. De Guingand had already drafted a letter of apology, and he argued that it was essential that it should be sent immediately if the Field-Marshal was to keep his command. Montgomery was at first amazed, but swiftly saw the light. His letter read:

31 December 1944

Dear Ike,

I have seen Freddie [de Guingand] and understand you are greatly worried by many considerations in these very difficult days. I have given you my frank views because I have felt you like this. I am sure there are many factors which have a bearing quite beyond anything I realise. Whatever your decision may be you can rely on me one hundred per cent to make it work and I know Bradley will do the same. Very distressed that my letter may have upset you and I would ask you to tear it up.

Your very devoted subordinate,
Monty[18]

This was despatched by signal, and later, at 2135, Montgomery signalled Eisenhower again, this time to say that Collins would attack at first light in three days' time. This consoled the

Supreme Commander.

Montgomery had wanted to attack at Celles and pinch out the extreme tip of the bulge, but the American Generals Hodges, Collins and Ridgway argued that he should instead lop off the German salient at its widest point, across the base. This would have necessitated US First Army converging on Patton's Third Army over sixty-five kilometres of poor hilly roads which the winter weather had made almost impassable. Montgomery therefore refused to entertain the American plan. Bradley then proposed a compromise. Third Army would drive northwards from Bastogne, and First Army south-east towards St Vith, the aim being to meet at Houffalize having pushed through the middle of the bulge; it was this proposed attack that Montgomery announced to Eisenhower in his late signal on 31 December 1944. At 1140 on 6 January elements of the two US armies met south-west of Houffalize and the Battle of the Bulge was over, although the original American positions were not restored until 7 February.

On 7 January US First Army was returned to Bradley's command, and Montgomery wrote to him: 'What a great honour to command such fine troops ... How well they have all done.' But the American generals now began to abuse Montgomery, saying that the junction at Houffalize was a compromise solution which had been forced upon them, and which had allowed a large proportion of the German armies to escape, whereas an attack across the base of the bulge would have trapped the major part of the enemy force engaged. Von Rundstedt's offensive had cost the Germans 85,000 men killed, wounded or made prisoner, and 600 tanks; the Americans lost 70,000 men and much equipment.

On 1 January, the German air force had carried out large-scale attacks on the Allied airfields in Belgium and Holland. Montgomery's Dakota, the aircraft that Eisenhower had given him in Sicily in exchange for a Flying Fortress, was shot to pieces in one of the raids. With great generosity and tact, Eisenhower replaced it at once, and, in reply, Montgomery wrote an effusive letter of thanks, concluding: 'If there is anything I can ever do for you to ease the tremendous burden that you bear you know you only have to command me. And I want you to know that I shall always stand firmly behind you in everything you do.' Sadly, Montgomery did not hold to his promise either to ease the burden or to stand firmly behind his superior. On other occasions than those cited he tried to force Eisenhower to put American troops under his command, and he continued a truculent and unruly subordinate.

As US First and Ninth Armies' attacks from the north on 2 January went well, Montgomery decided to hold a press conference. He signalled the Prime Minister that he hoped by such a conference to put an end to the 'slanging match' in the British press, which gave the impression that the Americans had got into terrible trouble in the Ardennes and had had to call in Montgomery to sort it out. Churchill was keen on the idea, as was the CIGS. The conference was therefore called for 7 January, and on that day Montgomery signalled the CIGS that 53rd (Welsh) Division had captured Grimblemont and the high ground east of it, cutting off the Germans' northern maintenance route – he had told his staff that he coveted this road, for its capture must hamstring the German communications. US 82nd Airborne was also making good progress in the south, and Montgomery's signal demonstrates that he was happy with the battle, and felt that the Germans must lose heavily if they were to hold on to the salient any longer. He considered that he personally had won the Battle of the Bulge, and was as a result even more cocky than usual.

Unfortunately, the full text of his prepared statement to the press correspondents, given out as a record of what he had said at the conference, described his own part in the battle in rather too glowing terms:

1. *Object of this talk*
   I have asked you to come here today so that I can give you some information which may be of use to you, and also to ask you to help me in a certain matter.
2. *The story of the present battle*
   Rundstedt attacked on 16 Dec.; he obtained tactical surprise. He drove a deep wedge into the centre of the First US Army and split the American forces in two. The situation looked as if it might become awkward; the Germans had broken right through a weak spot, and were heading for the Meuse.
3. As soon as I saw what was happening I took certain steps myself to ensure that *if* the Germans got to the Meuse they

would certainly not get over that river. And I carried out certain movements so as to provide balanced dispositions to meet the threatened danger; these were, at the time, merely precautions, i.e., I was thinking ahead.

4. Then the situation began to deteriorate. But the whole allied team rallied to meet the danger; national considerations were thrown overboard; General Eisenhower placed me in command of the whole Northern front.

I employed the whole available power of the British Group of Armies; this power was brought into play very gradually and in such a way that it would not interfere with the American lines of communication. Finally it was put into battle with a bang, and today British divisions are fighting hard on the right flank of First US Army. You have thus the picture of British troops fighting on both sides of American forces who have suffered a hard blow. This is a fine allied picture.

5. The battle has been most interesting; I think possibly one of the most interesting and tricky battles I have ever handled, with great issues at stake. The first thing to be done was to 'head off' the enemy from the tender spots and vital places. Having done that successfully, the next thing was to 'see him off', i.e. rope him in and make quite certain that he could not get to the places he wanted, *and also* that he was slowly but surely removed away from those places. He was therefore 'headed off', and then 'seen off'.

He is now being 'written off', and heavy toll is being taken of his divisions by ground and air action. You must not imagine that the battle is over yet; it is by no means over and a great deal still remains to be done.

The battle has some similarity to the battle that began on 31 Aug 1942 when Rommel made his last bid to capture Egypt and was 'seen off' by the Eighth Army. But actually all battles are different because the problem is different.

6. What was Rundstedt trying to achieve? No one can tell for certain. The only guide we have is the message he issued to his soldiers before the battle began; he told them it was the last great effort to try and win the war; that everything depended on it; that they must go 'all out'.

On the map you see his gains; *that* will not win the war; he is likely slowly but surely to lose it all; he must have scraped together every reserve he could lay his hands on for this job, and he has not achieved a great deal.

One must admit that he has dealt us a sharp blow and he sent us reeling back; but we recovered; he has been unable to gain any great advantage from his initial success.

He has therefore failed in his strategic purpose, unless the prize was smaller than his men were told.

He has now turned to the defensive on the ground; and he is faced by forces properly balanced to utilise the initiative which he has lost.

Another reason for his failure is that his air force, although still capable of pulling a fast one, cannot protect his army; for that army our Tactical Air Forces are the greatest terror.

7. But when all is said and done I shall always feel that Rundstedt was really beaten by the good fighting qualities of the American soldier and by the team-work of the Allies.

I would like to say a word about these two points.

8. I first saw the American soldier in battle in Sicily, and I formed then a very high opinion of him. I saw him again in Italy. And I have seen a very great deal of him in this campaign. I want to take this opportunity to pay a public tribute to him. He is a brave fighting man, steady under fire, and with that tenacity in battle which stamps the first class soldier; all these qualities have been shown in a marked degree during the present battle. I have spent my military career with the British soldier and I have come to love him with a great love; and I have now formed a very great affection and admiration for the American soldier. I salute the brave fighting men of America; I never want to fight alongside better soldiers. Just now I am seeing a great deal of the American soldiers; I have tried to feel that I am almost an American soldier myself so that I might take no unsuitable action or offend them in any way. I have been given an American identity card; I am thus identified in the Army of the United States, my fingerprints have been registered in the War Department at Washington – which is far preferable to having them registered at Scotland Yard!

9. And now I come to the last point.

   It is team-work that pulls you through dangerous times; it is team-work that wins battles; it is victories in battle that win wars. I want to put in a strong plea for Allied solidarity at this vital stage of the war; and you can all help in this greatly. Nothing must be done by anyone that tends to break down the team spirit of our Allied team; if you try and 'get at' the captain of the team you are liable to induce a loss of confidence, and this may spread and have disastrous results. I would say that anyone who tries to break up the team spirit of the Allies is definitely helping the enemy.

10. Let me tell you that the captain of our team is Eisenhower. I am absolutely devoted to Ike; we are the greatest of friends. It grieves me when I see uncomplimentary articles about him in the British Press; he bears a great burden, he needs our fullest support, he has a right to expect it, and it is up to all of us to see that he gets it.

    And so I would ask all of you to lend a hand to stop that sort of thing; let us all rally round the captain of the team and so help to win the match.

    Nobody objects to healthy and constructive criticism; it is good for us.

    But let us have done with destructive criticism that aims a blow at Allied solidarity, that tends to break up our team spirit, and that therefore helps the enemy.[19]

Although kind about US troops and about Eisenhower, the tone is patronising and self-congratulatory. And in off-the-cuff remarks, made after he had read out the press statement, Montgomery was equally rash, giving the impression that he had saved the Americans from disaster. The result was inevitable – Eisenhower and Bradley were livid, and all the American generals were up in arms at this tactless and not altogether truthful view of the battle. Certainly Montgomery had greatly helped to restore a dangerous situation, but the victory had not been achieved by his efforts alone. The Americans were perhaps being over-sensitive, but they had suffered heavily in the battles, and the Field-Marshal should have realised this.

Brigadier Williams commented to me:

I begged him not to hold the press conference. He came in wearing a purple airborne beret and was like a cock on a dunghill ... [he] loved his press conferences. The journalists liked him because he was crystal clear and they could understand exactly what had happened, or rather what Monty wanted them to understand, because he was capable of telling whopping lies. At the 7 January conference it was not so much the press release, but Monty's attitude in the discussions which did so much harm to Anglo-American relations. It was crazy of him to say that a battle which had cost so many American lives and produced the crisis of the campaign was 'one of the most interesting ... battles I have ever handled.' This was absurdly patronising.

I came away from the press conference with Alan Moorehead. We both agreed it was disastrous, and I said to Alan: 'For God's sake do something to pour oil over the waters, which are going to be very troubled.'

Chester Wilmot's radio signal to the BBC giving the gist of the conference was picked up by the Germans, who immediately rewrote his copy with an anti-American bias and then broadcast it in English from their Arnhem radio on 8 January. Picked up by an American monitoring service, the broadcast was mistaken at Bradley's HQ for a BBC transmission and 'this twisted text' started an uproar, fuelled by the fact that the *Daily Telegraph* carried the corrupt German version in full on 11 January:

Field-Marshal Montgomery came into the fight at a strategic moment. He scored a major success across the Laroche road, which American tanks cut on Saturday.

Many tanks, as well as British and American infantry, are coming up. Gains of from 1,000 to 3,000 yards were made yesterday. Our forces are not more than 12 miles apart on opposite sides of the salient. The American Third Army from the south made two and a half miles at one point.

To the south of the line at a point two miles north of Strasbourg the Germans have about 500 to 600 men and some tanks across the Rhine river. In the three weeks since Montgomery tackled the German Ardennes offensive he has transformed it into a headache for Rundstedt. It is the most brilliant and difficult task he has yet managed. He found no defence lines, the Americans somewhat bewildered, few reserves on hand and supply lines cut.

The American First Army had been completely out of contact with Gen. Bradley. He quickly studied maps and started to 'tidy up' the front. He took over scattered American forces, planned his action and stopped the German drive.

His staff, which has been with him since Alamein, deserves high praise and credit. The Battle of the Ardennes can now be written off, thanks to Field-Marshal Montgomery.[20]

It was a skilful piece of black propaganda by the Germans, and one that helped widen the growing rift between Montgomery and the Americans.

Collins, for instance, who Montgomery esteemed so highly and whose troops were fighting under him, was indignant: 'Monty got under my skin by downgrading the American troops at the time of the Battle of the Bulge ... however reassuring it was to know Brian Horrocks' XXX Corps was backing us up, only one British Division participated in the fighting. It left a sour note.'[21] And Eisenhower wrote to Marshall on 8 February that 'No single incident that I have ever encountered throughout my experience as an Allied Commander has been so difficult to combat as this particular outburst in the papers.' He repeated this remark in a letter to Brooke on 16 February, and added that 'Both the Prime Minister and I tried every device at hand to counteract this feeling but it was just one of those things that seem to cause lasting resentment due largely to the fact that American troops here have their principal sources of information through London newspapers or the BBC.'[22]

Churchill, much concerned, did his best to calm the situation and to soothe ruffled American feelings, but with little success. Eisenhower left US Ninth Army under Montgomery for the time being, but the notorious press conference was a key factor in his later decision to withdraw all American troops from Montgomery's command in the final triumphal drive to victory. In his memoirs, Montgomery agreed that he should not have held the press conference, and that the use of the word 'interesting' to describe the costly battles against the Panzer armies had been a mistake. By then, however, he had paid for his rashness.

13

Rows over Strategy

After the 7 January press conference the attacks directed by Montgomery on the German Ardennes salient from the north went well, and Patton's army in the south also made progress. Each evening, the British commander sent cheerful signals back to the CIGS, but both he and the War Office were becoming increasingly concerned about Eisenhower's plans for the advance to Germany and for dealing with the perennial problem of command. The Supreme Commander had temporarily satisfied the British by promising to put the greater weight into the northern advance, but both Brooke and Montgomery feared that Patton, Bradley and Devers would deflect Eisenhower from this course by persuading him to divert resources into their subsidiary attacks in the south.

On 31 December Eisenhower had sent Montgomery his outline plan for operations once the enemy counter-attack in the Ardennes had been defeated, which ordered the Allied armies to:

Prepare for crossing the Rhine in force with MAIN EFFORT NORTH OF THE RHINE ... 21 Army Group with 9 US Army under operational control to resume preparations for Veritable [the code-name for a Canadian Army drive to secure all the ground west of the Rhine by a push from the Reichswald Forest] ... the front south of the Moselle to be strictly defensive for the time being ... as soon as reduction of Ardennes salient permits 12 Army Group will move north in close proximity to 21 Army Group ... details of emergency co-ordination along Army Group boundaries and between the two Army Groups will be affected by the two Army Group

Commanders with power of decision vested in C.I.C. 21 Army Group.[1]

Delighted that he retained US Ninth Army under command, and had 'power of decision' over Bradley, Montgomery told Eisenhower that he agreed enthusiastically with this plan, and on 18 January he signalled Brooke that he had held 'a fine conference with Bradley. Agreement reached on every point. Veritable to start on 10 February'. But although Montgomery was content with the short-term plan, both he and Brooke were in fact at loggerheads with the Supreme Commander. The two British field-marshals were adamant that the Allies must advance into Germany on the front from Bonn northwards, leaving static the rest of the Allied line to the south. They would not entertain even a secondary thrust in the south, for they knew that if Bradley and Patton were given any leeway they would seek – and obtain – too great a proportion of the supplies, and that Eisenhower was too weak to restrain them.

Eisenhower, however, had different ideas. Backed by Marshall, he wanted to close up to the Rhine along its entire length, and then force crossings both in the south and the north. Nevertheless, he always conceded that the (predominantly British) northern crossing should have priority, although this was hotly disputed by Bradley. Marshall continued to tell Eisenhower that he must not give authority to the British, and that neither American public opinion nor the troops in the field would stomach Montgomery commanding many American divisions for long.

In discussions, SHAEF told the War Office that the Supreme Commander would try and seize the bridgeheads between Wesel and Emmerich in the north, and Mainz and Karlsruhe in the south, Eisenhower explaining that he insisted on the southern attack because if successful, it would deprive Hitler of the industrial production of the Saar. It would, moreover, give the Allies some degree of flexibility if the British attack in the north failed – since Normandy, he had viewed somewhat cynically Montgomery's promises to win battles against the Germans on schedule.

Churchill, Brooke and the British Chiefs of Staff agreed to ask the Joint Chiefs of Staff in Washington to order Eisenhower to concentrate his immense air and tank superiority upon an all-out attack on the Northern German plains north of the Ruhr, and around Hanover. At the same time, they also decided to urge a change in the command structure at SHAEF, and to seek the appointment of a single overall ground commander. Brooke was not at all confident of forcing any change out of the Americans because the US generals were still sensitive about their failure in the Ardennes, and deeply resentful of the outcome of the 7 January press conference. Furthermore, by now neither Eisenhower in Versailles nor Marshall in Washington made any secret of the fact that they both distrusted and disliked Montgomery. Brooke persuaded Churchill to reactivate the British memorandum to the Joint Chiefs of Staff which he had prepared at the Prime Minister's request, but which had been held in abeyance since the German attack on 16 December, and to request an urgent meeting of the Joint Chiefs of Staff to discuss Eisenhower's strategy. The memorandum, duly despatched to Washington, concluded with these words:

(a) All available offensive power must be allotted to the northern front i.e. from Prum northwards, and
(b) One man must have power of operational control and co-ordination of the ground forces employed on this front.[2]

With the row over Montgomery's press conference still ringing in American ears it was an unfortunate moment to raise again the question of command. The American Chiefs of Staff replied that Eisenhower should be ordered to submit a detailed appreciation of his plans, and that a tripartite summit on strategy should be held with the Russians at Yalta on 4 February, to be preceded by an Anglo-American Combined Chiefs of Staff conference in Malta. Not surprisingly, the Americans told the British that they firmly opposed any change in the system of command. Montgomery was ready to leave the subject there, at least for the time being, but not so Brooke. General Sir Frank Simpson told me that the CIGS realised that he was almost certainly banging his head against a brick wall, but he was so certain that putting Montgomery in command would shorten the war that he felt it was worthwhile forcing the issue to the limit.

The following extracts from Eisenhower's long appreciation

for the JCS illustrate the differences between his views, on the one hand, and Montgomery's and Brooke's on the other:

> The attack north of the Ruhr is definitely the one that we must hold in front of us as our principal purpose ... an advance to the Frankfurt Cassel area would secure the important industrial area around Frankfurt ... we would have less opposition to our advance than in the north ...
>
> To sum up operations across the Rhine north of the Ruhr offer the greatest strategic rewards within a short distance but this area will be most strongly held by the enemy. An advance to Frankfurt offers less favourable terrain and longer route to vital strategic objectives. Depending on the degree of enemy resistance it may be necessary to use either or both of these two avenues.
>
> The possibility of failure to secure bridgeheads in the north or in the south cannot be overlooked. I am therefore making logistical preparations to switch my main effort from the north to the south should this be forced upon me.[3]

After a conference with Eisenhower, Brooke told Simpson that the Supreme Commander had accepted Montgomery's plan for 'Veritable' and 'Grenade',* but had also given way to Bradley who, they knew, wanted an offensive in the southern sector on the axis Prum-Euskirchen and on to Frankfurt. Brooke commented on Eisenhower's plan: 'It leaves us again with a confused picture; still hankering after the Frankfurt line of advance, and in the end backing both and being insufficiently strong for either.'[4]

On the same day (22 January), Montgomery wrote to Brooke about the appreciation:

> The old snags of indecision and vacillation and refusal to consider the military problem fairly and squarely are coming to the front again. The real trouble is there is no control and the three Army Groups are each intent on their own affairs.

---

* 'Grenade' was a plan for US Ninth Army, still under Twenty-First Army Group, to attack in the southern part of the sector, closing up to the Rhine and completing an encircling movement by joining up with the Canadian 'Veritable' offensive. Both operations were to have begun at the same time, that is, early in February.

Patton today issued a stirring order to the Third Army saying the next step would be Cologne ... One has to preserve a sense of humour these days or otherwise one would go mad.

Montgomery also told the CIGS that it was clear that Bradley was being allowed to go off on his own, and that both Eisenhower and Bradley believed that no one should cross the Rhine in strength until the Allies were lined up all along its western bank.

Certainly Eisenhower's appreciation was vague and unclear, but equally it was plain that the Supreme Commander would not give up his 'broad front approach'. Montgomery came to England for a few days' leave and lunched with Brooke on 26 January. The two field-marshals complained about the same old problems of lack of strong command from Eisenhower and the failure to concentrate the Allied resources on an all-out attack at one vital point. Simpson had found out from Lt-Col Milne, a former staff officer of Simpson's at the War Office and now Military Assistant to Tedder, that nothing would shake Eisenhower's belief in the need for 'an option somewhere south'. Eisenhower had told his colleagues that he must have 'elasticity' in case Montgomery's northern thrust failed — plainly the failure to break out at Caen still rankled with the Supreme Commander.

Briefed by Milne, Simpson reported to Brooke exactly how the land lay at SHAEF, and how immovable Eisenhower was over his alternative southern thrust.[5] Churchill and Brooke therefore decided to resist the appreciation, and the Chiefs of Staff suggested to Washington an alternative directive, coupled once more with the need for 'one Land Force Commander':

In preparing your plans you should bear in mind our views as follows:
(a) All the resources which can be made available for offensive operations should be concentrated on one main thrust. This thrust should be made in the maximum possible strength with sufficient fresh formations held available to keep up the momentum of the advance. Only such forces as cannot be employed to support this main thrust should be used for subsidiary operations. Only if the main thrust is held and the subsidiary operations

prosper should the latter be exploited.

(b) If tactical considerations allow, this main thrust should be made in the north, in view of the overriding importance to the enemy of the Ruhr area.

(c) The best results will be achieved if one Land Force Commander, directly responsible to you, is given power of operational control and co-ordination of all ground forces employed in the main thrust.[6]

No government could have given fuller support to its field commander in his dispute with his allies than that given to Montgomery by London at this time. It was to no avail, however. Washington disagreed completely; the US chiefs insisted on retaining the command set-up, and endorsed to the full Eisenhower's plan for 'a strong secondary effort'.

Neither Montgomery nor Eisenhower attended the Joint Chiefs of Staff conference in Malta. Instead Montgomery briefed Brooke about his plans and intentions during his short leave in England, and Marshall met Eisenhower at Marseilles. Marshall told Eisenhower that both he and Roosevelt would back his plan to the hilt, and that he would not hear of interposing a ground force commander between the Supreme Commander and the army groups, declaring that he personally would resign rather than accept such a proposal.

Not surprisingly, the Malta conference produced long and acrimonious discussions between the British and American Chiefs of Staff – some, fortunately, held in private. On 30 January Brooke told the Americans at the conference that he would not approve Eisenhower's appreciation, and reminded them that the British were sending five divisions from Italy to strengthen Twenty-First Army Group. These reinforcements comprised three Canadian divisions together with the two British infantry divisions that had been on operations in Greece. The news of the allotment of these five extra divisions mollified the Americans somewhat, but not sufficiently.*

---

* As a result of their losses in the Ardennes the Americans were worried about manpower. When Montgomery took over command of US Ninth and First Armies he complained strongly to SHAEF that the American divisions were, on average, 2,000 men below strength. In a generous gesture, Churchill had ordered the call-up of an extra 250,000 British at the worst moment of the Battle of the Bulge, and the Americans, equally worried, speeded up the

Bedell Smith, who was at Malta as Eisenhower's representative, argued that his chief accepted the basic British contention that the main thrust should be made in the north, and that 'the southern advance was not intended to compete with the northern advance but must be of sufficient strength to draw off German forces to protect the important Frankfurt area and to provide an alternative line of attack if the main effort failed.' But Brooke wanted the appreciation reworded so that it contained a guarantee 'to deploy east of the Rhine and north of the Ruhr the maximum number of Divisions which can be maintained (estimated at 35 Divisions) and to deploy on the Frankfurt Cassel axis such forces as may be available after providing 35 Divisions for the north and essential security elsewhere.'

The Americans agreed with this, and thus went a long way towards meeting Brooke's objections, but the CIGS still baulked at Eisenhower's plan of reaching the Rhine along its full length before attempting a major crossing. Bedell Smith therefore persuaded Eisenhower to signal the conference: 'I will seize the Rhine crossings in the north immediately this is a feasible operation and without waiting to close the Rhine throughout its length ... I will advance across the Rhine in the north with maximum strength and complete determination as soon as the situation in the south allows me.'[7] The British had to be content with this somewhat loose assurance, although after the session Brooke had a row with Bedell Smith. When the CIGS ran down Eisenhower, Smith replied: 'Then you had better take this to the Joint Chiefs of Staff', and Brooke realised at once that he could go no further, since there was plainly no chance of removing Eisenhower or of promoting Montgomery now that American troops were numerically so predominant in the north-west European theatre.[8]

At Malta, Montgomery's plan for the northern thrust was accepted, but so incensed was Marshall about the British open contempt for Eisenhower as land commander that the question of Montgomery assuming that post, even for the northern

---

sending of divisions from America to Europe; four fresh divisions arrived in February to strengthen Eisenhower's forces. The latter combed out combat-trained and fit men from the base units, and risked political trouble by agreeing to ask for coloured volunteers for infantry duty in the combat zone, but the US Government told him firmly that at home the cupboard was bare, and that there were no reserves of American manpower.

operation, was never formally discussed. On 1 February Brooke had an acrimonious private session with Marshall in which the American Chief of Staff made it clear how strong was his antipathy towards, and dislike of, Montgomery. In Williams's words, 'There was no oil in Brooke'; the CIGS was possessed of a very quick brain and an equally quick temper, and for all his manifest ability he could be indiscreet 'and tactless'. One is tempted to wonder how de Guingand or Simpson would have fared in the meeting with Marshall. The conference in Malta was an unhappy one, and undoubtedly the strain of the war was telling on Brooke. Churchill would not allow him to push the issues of strategy and command too far because not only did the Americans have an enormous preponderence of troops in Europe, but also there was always the danger that the American government might decide not to give the defeat of Germany full priority, and instead switch some of their resources to the war against Japan in the Far East. Such a switch would have been disastrous for the European campaign.

Brooke had suggested to the Prime Minister, as far back as 28 November, that the best way to deal with Eisenhower's incompetence as a land commander would be for Alexander, now a Field-Marshal and the Supreme Allied Commander, Mediterranean Theatre, to replace Tedder as Deputy Supreme Commander and 'to command the land forces for him [Eisenhower] as in Tunisia'. Were Alexander to be appointed Eisenhower's deputy then Brooke was certain that Montgomery's strategy would be accepted at SHAEF – in Tunisia and Sicily Alexander had complied with everything Montgomery had wanted. Churchill had returned to this proposal and discussed it privately with Brooke on 3 January 1945, when they were staying with Eisenhower at Versailles. On the next day Churchill had suggested the proposal to Eisenhower at lunch while they were travelling up in the Supreme Commander's special train to see Montgomery at his HQ at Hasselt, and the American had replied that he would welcome Alexander as his Deputy in place of Tedder. On 5 January Brooke had put his suggestion to Montgomery, who answered that he 'was all for such a plan' as it might go some way towards putting the business of command 'straight'.

It is surprising that Brooke seriously considered this scheme for replacing Tedder, since he had a low opinion of both

Alexander and his Chief of Staff, Lt-Gen Sir John (later Field-Marshal Lord) Harding. He continually commented adversely on Alexander, stating that he was too much under the thumb of Harold Macmillan, the Minister Resident at Allied HQ, North-West Africa, in the theatre in which he commanded. Churchill's proposal that Tedder should replace Alexander in the Mediterranean would, however, have given more power to Harding, and indeed to Macmillan.

When, on 22 August 1944, Brooke had visisted Alexander in Italy, he had been contemptuous of a detailed plan, written by Harding and approved by Alexander, to make the Italian front an all-British affair by removing the American divisions and sending them to France, replacing them with British forces drawn from that theatre. Brooke thought the scheme was 'fantastic', and an example of Alexander's lack of appreciation of what he was faced with. Given the lack of shipping at the time, such a move would have taken months, during which time a large force would have been out of action on either front. When Churchill had visited Alexander the two men had indulged in pipedreams of capturing Vienna with an all-British force; Brooke had thought nothing of these plans.

At the Malta conference on 31 January Brooke informed Alexander of the possibility of his becoming Eisenhower's Deputy (and also scolded him severely for being too subservient to Macmillan in Italy) – Alexander replied that he would be happy with the change. Two days later, Churchill asked Brooke to discuss with himself, Roosevelt and Marshall the proposal for Alexander to replace Tedder. The two Americans felt that there might be repercussions in America if the change was implemented immediately, since it could be interpreted as Alexander being put in to support Eisenhower after the Ardennes failure. They were, however, prepared to accept the change in six weeks' time, after more Allied attacks had helped dispel the image of the near-defeat in the Ardennes. Marshall told Eisenhower of the proposal, and warned him that with Alexander as his Deputy he would have 'great difficulty' in offsetting the direct influence of the British Prime Minister. It at once became clear to the Supreme Commander that the mooted change was Churchill's device for ensuring that Montgomery's strategy would be dominant, and that Twenty-First Army Group would have the greater portion of the resources.

On 10 January, after Churchill had made the suggestion of a new SHAEF deputy, Eisenhower had written to Marshall that Tedder could not help him with visits and conferences with troop commanders, and had added that 'the only deputy I could think of myself would be Alexander.' At the time, however, he had not told Marshall that this had already been suggested by Churchill. Marshall had replied that Alexander's appointment would mean that the British 'had gained an important point in getting control of ground operations', in which their divisions would play a minor part while the US forces would inevitably suffer heavy casualties, and that with Alexander as his Deputy Eisenhower would have great difficulty in offsetting the direct influence of Churchill. Eisenhower's response to this had been that he had not foreseen these disadvantages, and that he had enjoyed a fine relationship with Alexander in the past but that Tedder, although equally splendid, suffered a handicap in that senior ground officers, especially the British, assumed him to be 'incapable of discussing intelligently any ground operations not in the single field of air-ground co-operation' – this was certainly Montgomery's attitude towards Tedder. At this point Eisenhower had decided to oppose Alexander's proposed appointment.

The jealousy between the Americans and the British, never far beneath the surface, was even more evident at this date because both sides wanted their troops to have the lion's share of the glamour of the final military victory. Eisenhower knew well that Alexander, if he should be appointed Deputy Supreme Commander, would try and hand as much of the glory as possible to the British, and this was Churchill's definite intention. Now, having been briefed by Marshall after Malta, the Supreme Commander determined to retain Tedder and to keep Alexander out. Accordingly, he wrote a cunningly worded letter to Brooke on 16 February in an attempt to quash the British plot. Part of the letter read:

> It is extremely important, in my view, that Alexander should understand in advance exactly how our whole set-up is working in order that later he may not feel that he has been badly used nor his great qualities as a soldier ignored. There can be no question whatsoever of placing between me and my Army Group Commanders any intermediary headquarters,

either official or unofficial in character. For many weeks we have been working on future plans of operations and keeping them constantly revised in accordance with changes in the local and the general situation. Day before yesterday I saw Montgomery for the second time since his return from leave and he was most emphatic in insisting that the command arrangements I have made are as nearly perfect as circumstances, including diverse nationalities, will permit. He asserted with particular emphasis that any thought of an intermediate ground command, or of any interference with the clear line of authority extending from me to him, should be carefully avoided. All measures to implement his plans for the Northern operations (except possibly for some small shortage in bridging equipment) have been met, and the projected timing of our several operations to secure the lines west of the Rhine that will permit the greatest possible concentration North of the Ruhr, are agreed upon. If any other view reaches you, through any channel, I'm certain such view is not shared by Montgomery.

No fundamental change in plans or command organization is contemplated, and unless Alexander is clearly informed of all these things, he may feel that his new position is one of less influence than he should properly have.

Another factor that has entered the picture is the extent to which U.S. forces, including relatively high commanders, feel themselves aggrieved by the unfortunate burst of publicity in the London papers following upon my placing of Montgomery in temporary command of the First and Ninth Armies during the Ardennes battle ... The upshot is that should there be any attempt on the part of any newspaper to interpret Alexander's appointment here as the establishment of a ground headquarters or the interposition of any kind of intermediate control between myself and my Army Group Commanders, I would find it immediately necessary to make a formal announcement setting forth the facts. I trust the newspapers won't cause us any more trouble, but their interpretation of events is often faulty. Such an announcement on my part might hurt Alexander's feelings, and, in addition, might give the British and American papers another opportunity to indulge in futile but nevertheless disturbing argument.

There is no question, of course, as to the good work that Alexander could do. I admire him and regard him as a great friend. One of the things that has caused me some concern is to provide for all of the liberated countries and people of Western Europe a decent living standard, and, where this is not possible, to keep them convinced that we are doing everything humanly possible to meet their requirements. Many of our current problems in liberated manpower, relief, rearmament, and so on, will influence Allied relationships, far into the future. As the Prime Minister brought out when we had our great struggle concerning the bombing of French communication systems, Great Britain is much more closely concerned, at least geographically, than is the United States in the development and maintenance of friendly relations with the peoples of Western Europe.

Because of these reasons I have recently directed that my present Deputy be brought into these matters more and more closely and to examine carefully everything that is done currently, and with respect to future plans, to assure these things are handled sanely and skilfully. This is a job for the senior British Officer present in my headquarters, and I shall expect Alexander to concern himself in them very intimately.

Naturally, it will be a great pleasure to me to discuss every type of problem I have with a man of his stature and experience. I do not want this letter to be interpreted as a protest against any arrangements my superiors may find it necessary to make. But it is one of my principal jobs to see that nothing occurs that may tend to create misunderstandings within my own command, or to mar the generally splendid British-American relationships that we try to promote. Unless all concerned, including Alexander, are perfectly aware of these implications, difficulties of this nature may arise. Consequently, I will be very glad if you will make certain that both the Prime Minister and Alexander are informed as to my views and intentions so that the perfection of cooperation, which is the secret of every success we have had, may be fully preserved.

If you think it advisable, either or both of them may read this letter, since I am certain that both will understand it merely represents on my part an attempt to be perfectly straightforward in a matter which is almost certain to have its delicate aspects.

With personal regard.
Sincerely,
Dwight D. Eisenhower[9]

Brooke immediately showed this letter to Churchill, who was annoyed by it, and especially by the suggestion that Alexander would be chiefly concerned with the living standards of the people of the liberated countries, rather than with the conduct of the battle against Nazism. Eisenhower's reference to possibly damaging newspaper reaction also disturbed the Prime Minister, although he probably did not realise that bringing up again the question of Montgomery's injudicious 7 January press conference was a measure of how upset the Supreme Commander was. Churchill immediately dictated an irate letter to Eisenhower, in which he said:

> ... In that spirit I placed Alexander under you in the Tunisia operations although I think we had four times as many troops engaged as the Americans. Similarly I was delighted to propose the appointment of General Mark Clark to the Command of the 15th Army Group where we also had a large preponderance of British or British controlled troops.[10]

In the letter he actually sent two days later, on 22 February, the Prime Minister cut out these phrases as being too strong, but made it clear that he would not abandon the proposal even though he was shocked at the idea of Alexander being used for 'non-military functions'. The letter also gives the impression that Churchill was prepared to railroad the change through, in spite of Eisenhower's objections (General Simpson told me that the latter admitted to him more than once that he was frightened of Churchill). The Prime Minister followed up the letter with a signal saying that he would personally use his influence with the Fleet Street newspaper proprietors to prevent any news of the changeover in command or of the five divisions coming from Italy to North-West Europe from being published for six weeks, the period set by Marshall and Roosevelt before Alexander could assume his new post. The signal read:

Personal from Prime Minister to General Eisenhower. Not

only will I look after the press myself through their
proprietors, but also I consider it may well be necessary to
impose an absolute blot out on the change for at least a
month after it has taken place to cover the movement of
troops from Italy by which you are receiving five British
Divisions [in fact, three of these divisions were Canadian].

Plainly Churchill was determined to do all in his power to
smooth Alexander's path to the post of Deputy Supreme
Commander, for the signal assumes a *fait accompli*. His letter of
22 February had been even more definite:

> ### Private and Confidential
> 22 February, 1945
>
> Brooke has shown me as you wished your letter about the
> proposed change and I take the first opportunity on my
> return to let you know how matters stand.
>
> I had a long talk with General Marshall at Malta, and on
> February 2 I had a conference with the President at which
> General Marshall and also Field Marshal Brooke were
> present. It was agreed that this change should take place in a
> month or six weeks' time, that is to say, about the middle of
> March. No question has ever been raised by me of any
> change in the system by which you exercise your Command,
> nor any proposal made to set up an Intermediate Staff or
> Intermediate Authority between yourself and your Army
> Group Commanders. On the contrary, I have always, as I
> thought you knew, been opposed to such a needless
> complication. I felt however that there would be a great
> advantage, now that the passage of the Channel is over, in
> filling the post of Deputy, which belongs to us, by a
> professional soldier. I have also high employment in view for
> Air Chief Marshal Tedder. Your reception of the suggestion
> when I made it to you at Versailles, gave me great pleasure,
> and I understood from General Marshall that you had
> expressed the same opinions to him.
>
> I have asked Brooke not to send your letter to Alexander. I
> have no doubt what his reactions would be, namely, that he is
> always ready to serve wherever he is told, and to do his best
> to discharge such duties as are assigned to him. If however I
> am to gather from your letter that the British Deputy to the

Supreme Commander would not be concerned with military matters except in an informal way, and would be principally responsible for dealing with the supplies of food and setting up a decent living standard in liberated and conquered territories, I must say quite frankly that I consider this would be a waste of Field Marshal Alexander's military gifts and experience. I thought he would be a help to you in all your cares and burdens, and that the change would be personally agreeable to you.

I was not aware that your British Deputy was relegated to such non-military functions. The Deputy is the second in the Army, and the trusted confidant of the Supreme Commander. This is the way the office has always been interpreted in the Mediterranean and we never doubted it was the position in North West Europe. Although our Army in France is much smaller than the United States Army, it nevertheless amounts to about a million men, before whom much heavy fighting lies, and therefore I am sure you would not wish to deny us the kind of representation on your Staff in respect of military matters which is our due.

Neither you nor I have ever taken a narrow or nationalistic point of view in regard to the High Commands and I feel sure that you will approach the matter in that spirit of true comradeship of which you are the outstanding exemplar.

With all good wishes,

Believe me,

Yours very sincerely[11]

W.S.C.

General Dwight D. Eisenhower, G.C.B.

P.S. I am hoping to see you soon. W.S.C.

Eisenhower replied swiftly, stressing that Alexander would be consulted on 'everything we do including military briefings', and that the intent of his previous letter had been 'to point out the tendency of the press over the delicate question of command to give its own interpretation and this might injure Alexander's feelings.' Churchill, however, was so ready to ride roughshod over the Supreme Commander's clear dislike of the change that he signalled Alexander on 1 March that he was to replace Tedder by the middle of the month, but that news of the change would be 'blocked by D Notices for a few more weeks.'[12] The

Prime Minister's perseverance, against the more-or-less declared wishes of Eisenhower, Marshall and Roosevelt, was a measure of his certainty that, once Alexander was installed, Montgomery's views and aims would prevail, and that British troops would be given their righteous, glamorous role in the final battle.

But even as Churchill gained his point and Alexander prepared to come to SHAEF, the unpredictable Montgomery had changed his mind. In his memoirs he wrote that he advised Brooke and Churchill that: 'There would be storms both in the press and with the American Generals and [he] was happy with the present set up.' He and Eisenhower had held a friendly conference at Namur on 5 February, where the Supreme Commander falsely gave Montgomery the impression 'that he had swung over to his side'. Montgomery told Dawnay that he felt that 'Bradley was playing the lone hand', for Eisenhower now agreed with the British view, which Bradley did not share, that the Allies should not close up to the Rhine along its length. At this period the influential Hearst press in America had become critical of the US generals, and had stated several times that Eisenhower did not have the time to act as land commander, and that Montgomery should do the job under his direction. The British field-marshal gave too much weight to these press articles and misinterpreted the American view, believing that Marshall and Eisenhower were in favour of the British plan for strong thrusts in the north. In this he proved to be wrong.

On 14 February Eisenhower and Montgomery had met again, this time at Zondhoven. For once the meeting had been harmonious. Eisenhower promised Montgomery that he would leave US Ninth Army, with its twelve divisions, attached to Twenty-First Army Group, and Montgomery reported this to Nye, the Deputy CIGS, saying in a letter written that evening that 'the sky is now clear'. Eisenhower did, however, complain to Montgomery that at the Malta conference Churchill had told either the President or Marshall that he (Eisenhower) did not visit Montgomery enough, and had also implied that the British side of operations was being neglected. This, Montgomery's letter to Nye continued:

Hurt him a great deal, and he went on to say he was always being bullied by Marshall and the U.S. Chiefs of Staff for being too British or by the P.M. and the British Chiefs of Staff for being too American and neglecting to visit me. I am sorry this was said at Malta; it got back to Ike very quickly and was no doubt attributed to me and he is such an awfully decent chap that I hate to see him upset. It may not have improved my stock in SHAEF circles.[13]

Eisenhower had put not only US Ninth Army under Twenty-First Army Group but also one British and two US airborne divisions. Montgomery now had all that he could realistically hope for, and thought that this advantageous state of affairs would continue. So when Eisenhower mentioned the command situation during their meeting, Montgomery agreed with him that it was unnecessary to have Alexander interposed as a land commander between the Supreme Command and the army groups, and went on to express the hope that the present command set-up would remain unchanged until the end of the war, which, he said, would be in the spring. Montgomery wrote in his letter to Nye that:

Eisenhower was delighted that I was happy about the present command situation. There is no doubt that he was worried about something when he arrived at Zondhoven and appeared so during our talks.

I have even now no idea what is at the bottom of this worry. But it was very obvious that as soon as I had said I was very well satisfied with the present situation about command he became a different man; he drove away beaming all over his face.[14]

The Field-Marshal had miscalculated badly, however. Eisenhower was in fact worried about Alexander becoming his deputy, and had only wanted to persuade Montgomery to tell Churchill that he too was opposed to the change in command.

On 16 February, clearly relieved by Montgomery's friendliness, and by his agreement that it was unnecessary to appoint a land commander, Eisenhower wrote to Brooke. This is the letter, quoted earlier, in which the Supreme Commander sought to set aside any idea of there being a land commander, and to diminish Alexander's role to that of dealing primarily with 'non-military functions'. Brooke showed the letter to

Churchill who, as has been said, worked desperately to obtain
Alexander's new appointment, while the CIGS had reason to
believe that the letter showed that Eisenhower had decided to
leave Montgomery in charge of major Allied operations –
certainly the latter thought so. In view of the Supreme
Commander's later change of plan, the letter may almost be
considered as evidence of bad faith, since, in his attempt to
prevent Alexander's appointment, Eisenhower had virtually
promised Montgomery that the northern front would be the
'main effort'. The deployment of US Ninth Army and the three
airborne divisions under Twenty-First Army Group seemed to
support this promise.

Brooke and Montgomery were wrong in their views about
Eisenhower's intentions, however, while Churchill, the only
person who might have forced through Alexander's
appointment, had had the ground cut from beneath him by
Montgomery's sudden *volte-face*. Eisenhower, with a
combination of charm and tact (and a certain amount of 'red
herring' about his being 'bullied' by Marshall and Churchill),
had convinced Montgomery that he had been forgiven for his
past truculence, and that American troops would be left under
his command for the rest of the war. The Supreme Commander
had no such intention, however. Within himself Eisenhower
concealed that he was still fuming with rage at Montgomery's
arrogance; he also knew that his American generals hated
serving under the British field-marshal. He therefore planned to
withdraw the US troops from Montgomery's command as soon
as the battle situation made this convenient – with Alexander as
Deputy Supreme Commander, however, this would have been
difficult, if not impossible, to achieve. As will be seen, in the
absence of a pro-Montgomery faction at SHAEF – Alexander –
Eisenhower removed all American troops from Montgomery's
command, and allotted to Twenty-First Army Group a minor
and unglamorous role in the last few weeks of the war. This was
precisely what Churchill had most feared, foreseeing that
Alexander's presence at SHAEF would have prevented such a
course from being adopted, let alone implemented.

Although Montgomery now believed that Eisenhower would
be permanently well disposed towards him, and attentive to his
demands, Brooke was under no such illusion. On 6 March, after
seeing Eisenhower in Rheims, Brooke noted in his diary that

'... his relations with Monty are quite insoluble; he only sees the worst side of Monty and cannot appreciate the better. Things are running smoothly for the present but this cannot last.' He added that: 'to insert Alex now is only likely to lead to immediate trouble for all, I gather.'

When, on 2 March, Churchill visited Montgomery, the latter told him emphatically that he did not want Alexander at SHAEF, and that he had told Eisenhower so on the previous day. The Prime Minister was displeased. Brooke arranged for Churchill to see the Supreme Commander alone on his train on the 5th, and there Eisenhower stated that replacing Tedder with Alexander would cause undesirable publicity and 'upset the apple cart'. Churchill caved in, albeit reluctantly, remarking that he would leave the decision about Alexander to Eisenhower, who immediately said 'no change'. Returning to London, Churchill signalled Alexander that, after passing three days with Montgomery and Eisenhower he had found Montgomery to be 'in perfect accord with SHAEF and happy about his affairs and relations ... at the eleventh hour on the western front you would not obtain the scope appropriate to your military standing ... and it would be wise not to disturb the existing harmony.'[15] The Prime Minister was frustrated after wasting much time on the abortive Alexander plan, and, alas, the 'harmony' which he described was not to last for long.

14

Eisenhower's Revenge

The two operations begun in February 1945, 'Veritable' and 'Grenade', had by early March pushed the Germans back to the east bank of the Rhine. Montgomery's plan had been for a double envelopment of the Germans once the 'bulge' in the Ardennes had been eliminated, with Canadian First Army conducting 'Veritable' from the north and linking up on the Rhine with US Ninth Army executing 'Grenade'; this was achieved by 3 March. Unfortunately the Germans opened the dams in the River Roer, with the result that 'Grenade' could not be begun until 23 February ('Veritable' had jumped off on schedule on 10 February); both operations, however, proved to be long and hard, and Allied casualties were high, although 'Grenade', once started, produced surprisingly swift results. On 10 March the Germans finally withdrew, in remarkably good order, from their last bridgehead over the Rhine at Wesel, blowing both the bridges there – the battle for the Rhineland was at last over, and Montgomery could now prepare for his set-piece crossing. In 'Veritable', a month's fighting had cost 15,500 British and Canadian casualties (XXX Corps had been placed under Canadian First Army for the duration of the operation), against 44,000 German casualties, of which about half were taken as prisoners. During the seventeen days of 'Grenade' the US Army had suffered 7,300 casualties, taking 29,000 German POWs and killing or seriously wounding another 16,000. But Hitler's efforts to save the Fatherland were daily becoming more apparent, for the Allies had encountered battalion after battalion of fanatical young Nazis, including schoolboys in uniforms.

German resistance during 'Veritable' was stronger than

Montgomery had expected. On 13 February 1945 he had written to Grigg that:

> The battle up in the Reichswald goes well; the problem is the mud and the floods and not the enemy. The German soldiers are not fighting well; they surrender freely given a suitable opportunity. Yesterday all that was left of a Para Bn — six officers and 200 men surrendered en masse without firing a shot; they walked over to our lines south of Gleve.

Three and a half weeks later, however, he admitted, again to Grigg, that 'The Germans seem determined to hold on in the Wesel area to the last and are causing us some trouble.'[1] As in September, Montgomery had underestimated enemy morale. The German soldiers' devotion to Hitler, and their will to defend their homeland, made them formidable opponents still, despite the Allied supremacy in the air and superiority in equipment and supplies. On 7 March, as the Germans prepared to give up their last foothold in the Rhineland, Hitler retired von Rundstedt, and on the 10th brought in Field-Marshal Albert Kesselring from Italy to take over command of the last, desperate, defence in the west. To the south, however, in an operation code-named 'Lumberjack' and begun on 5 March, US First and Third Armies were closing up to the Rhine, with Devers's Sixth Army Group undertaking an operation ('Undertone') that completed a front that extended all the way to the Swiss border.

On 7 March came the dramatic news that US 9th Armoured Division, part of Hodges's First Army, had captured intact the Ludendorff railway bridge at Remagen, which the Germans had mistakenly failed to destroy. In taking the bridge US 9th Armoured Division's casualties were unbelievably light, and almost at once First Army troops poured across the Rhine to make a consolidated bridgehead. The bridge itself collapsed ten days later, after repeated German air raids, but by then pontoon bridges had been built, and the Americans were well established on the far bank. The capture of the bridge had a decisive impact on the Germans' power to defend their home territory and on 8 March, after tactfully consulting with Montgomery, Eisenhower ordered Bradley to put at least six divisions into the bridgehead.

The capture of Remagen bridge and the successful

establishment of a bridgehead across the Rhine decided the
Supreme Commander in his course; he would make Bradley's
thrust into Germany 'equal in scope and importance' to
Montgomery's. On 21 March SHAEF issued a directive which
instructed Bradley to use Patton's Third Army to establish a
firm bridgehead over the Rhine in the Frankfurt area south of
Remagen, and then 'make an advance in strength' towards
Cassel. If successful, this would lead to a link-up between
Hodges's First Army advancing east from Remagen and
Patton's coming up from Frankfurt – the two armies had
already (9 March) joined forces on the west bank. Eisenhower
signalled the Chiefs of Staff in Washington that, if successful,
this plan would give him a force south of the Ruhr at least equal
in strength to Montgomery's Twenty-First Group in the north.[2]
That order sounded, irrevocably, the death knell for
Montgomery's ambition to lead the Allied armies in their
triumphal march on Berlin.

Montgomery had ordered Twenty-First Army Group to begin
its planning for a Rhine crossing early in October, once it had
become plain that 'Market-Garden' would not snatch a bridge
intact. Besides the troops necessary to force an opposed
crossing, 37,000 British and 22,000 American engineers were
involved, while both the Royal and the US Navies supplied
ocean-going assault boats. In all, Twenty-First Army Group
built up 250,000 tons of material and supplies for the Rhine
assault, codenamed 'Plunder'. As soon as the Wesel pocket was
eliminated on 10 March, Montgomery fixed the 24th for his set-
piece attack, although the first troops would start crossing on
the evening of the day before, 23 March. With full air and
artillery support, Twenty-First Army Group, aided by US Ninth
Army and a massive airborne drop over the river, would storm
across the Rhine at Wesel. The American generals, basking in
the reflected glory of the capture of the Remagen bridge, scoffed
at Montgomery for his ponderous build-up, and were jealous of
his retaining US Ninth Army under his command.

To Montgomery's horror, Churchill insisted on being present
for D-day of 'Plunder'. The Prime Minister had visited
Montgomery on 2 March when it was becoming clear that
'Veritable' and 'Grenade' were drawing to successful
conclusions, and had asked both him and de Guingand to dinner
on his special train. Montgomery went early to bed, and

Churchill then told de Guingand that he intended to come over to watch the Rhine crossing on 24 March, asserting belligerently that he had discussed this idea with Eisenhower, who had said: 'You will be alright if you go forward in a tank'. De Guingand annoyed Churchill by failing to take the suggestion seriously, and Montgomery also viewed it light-heartedly, telling Simpson that 'It just was not on as he could not have the Prime Minister wandering about in the middle of the battle disturbing the commanders who were running it.'

Churchill became angry at being fobbed off, and made his wishes clear to Brooke. On 7 March the CIGS wrote to Montgomery: 'If the Prime Minister is not allowed to come you have the seeds of serious trouble ahead. When the P.M. gets such ideas in his head nothing will stop him.' In his own diary Brooke noted: 'I am not happy with this trip. He will be difficult to manage and has no business to be going. All he will do is to endanger his life unnecessarily and get in everyone's way and be a damned nuisance to everybody. However nothing can stop him.' When, on 8 March, Simpson went out to see Montgomery, he had been instructed by Brooke to insist that Churchill was invited to see the start of 'Plunder'.[3] Making the best of a bad job, Montgomery wrote to Brooke: 'If the P.M. is determined to come out for the battle of the Rhine there is only one course of action and that is to ask him to stay at my camp. Then I can keep an eye on him and see he goes only where he will bother no-one. I have written him a letter which should please the old boy. Simpson will show you the copy.'

The Prime Minister was indeed pleased by the letter. His happy reply demonstrates the difficulties facing commanders who have to entertain heads of government during a major battle, and also both his schoolboy delight in the trip and his disregard of any inconvenience that he might cause:

TOP SECRET

10, Downing Street.
March 11, 1945.

My dear Field Marshal,

I was delighted to receive your letter, which reached me at 2 a.m. this morning. I am resolved to be no hindrance to you, and you must consider yourself absolutely free from any obligation during this important battle. I would not come if I thought there was the slightest chance of my getting in your way or making inroads on your time and thought. I will come on D minus one with only the C.I.G.S., Tommy* and my valet, four in all.

However it would be necessary for me to have somewhere 20 or 30 miles farther back a train, or perhaps a railway coach, where I can keep a Private Secretary and Mr. Rinna, who deals with facilities for scrambling messages. Probably one or two detectives will be there; I do not need them at the front. You must remember I have to keep in touch with events, which sometimes move very quickly indeed. A motor-cyclist or two would keep me in contact with this 'base', which I would drop wherever you say on my way out and pick up on my way back. The nearer to an airfield the better. I shall most certainly come in a Dakota as my Skymaster is taking Clemmie on her mission to Russia.

I may add that General Eisenhower suggested to me when I talked my wishes over with him that a tank would be the best way of seeing things, and would give protection in the forward areas from stray airplane attacks. Perhaps this has already occurred to you.

Any details about my visit which you may like to give can be sent to Ismay† by your staff.

> Yours very sincerely,
> Winston S. Churchill[4]

Montgomery wrote to Grigg on 16 March: 'The following weekend the P.M. will be here; I did not want him so I invited him to keep the peace.' And in another letter to Grigg four days later, he wrote:

I am expecting the P.M. here on 23. He seems to be getting restless and querulous. Why he wants to go about in dangerous places I cannot imagine. He may quite likely get shot up. However it is his own affair. I shall make it quite clear to him that he goes to these dangerous places

---

* Commander C.R. Thompson, RN, Personal Assistant to the Minister of Defence.

† General Sir Hastings Ismay, Chief of Staff to the Minister of Defence. Churchill held this last post as well as that of Prime Minister throughout his wartime period in office.

against my definite advice, and then leave it to him. I shall be far too busy to attend him.[5]

The preparations for the Rhine crossing were ponderous and deliberate, and received much publicity from the BBC, while the British press billed 'Plunder' as a spectacular assault over the widest river in Europe. This glamour, however, had been severely dented by US First Army's capture of the Remagen bridge, intact, a fortnight earlier; then, on 22 March, one day before Montgomery's attack was due to start, US Third Army captured the Rhine bridge at Oppenheim, south of Mainz, 'on the run'. Patton's press statement, issued on the 23rd, pointedly emphasised that 'Without benefit of aerial bombing artillery preparation and airborne assistance the Third Army at 2200 Thursday evening March 22 crossed the Rhine.' Bradley told journalists that 'American troops are capable of crossing the Rhine without aerial bombardent or airborne assistance, and on March 22 had done it',[6] his implication clearly being that Montgomery was incapable of achieving the same results without a massive build-up.

On 17 March Montgomery had written to Simpson, saying that 'conditions are excellent for Plunder; the banks quite easy and the approaches in good order.' He emphasised that the roads on the Allied side were in good condition and had carried no heavy traffic, and continued:

Operation Plunder as planned is a very good operation ['very good' was underlined twice], and has every chance of being a great success. I have therefore decided to wait for good weather; the decision will be taken at 1700 on 23 March as to whether I launch Plunder on 24 March. If the weather is bad it will be postponed 24 hours. The decision will be taken again at 1700 on 24 March and so on. The operation is so good that I shall wait if necessary four or five days.

There is still the possibility that I decide to launch the operation and the troops of assaulting divisions start off at 2100. The weather then plays tricks on us and the operation of launching the airborne force has to be cancelled. If the airborne troops can be dropped at all on D Day the drop will be in the planned area. If this is not possible they will be dropped on D plus 1 in some other area. This other area will be that between the Lippe River and the road Wesel, Brunen, Raesfeld, Erle, Schermbeck; in reading this you should note that D Day is March 24. The assaulting divisions begin to go over at 2100 23 March i.e. on D Day minus 1, hence the need for a decision by 1700 on D minus 1.

I consider that the Prime Minister and the CIGS would be well advised not to leave England until they hear that the operation has actually been launched. If they come on D minus one they may have to hang about for anything up to four or five days if we have bad weather. I hope the above is clear.[7]

This letter is, as usual, perfectly clear, but the inclusion of the postponement options is evidence of Montgomery's extreme caution, even at this stage of the war – quite simply, he was not going to risk a failure like Arnhem. Needless to say he had not consulted with Eisenhower about postponing the assault if the weather was bad; the Supreme Commander would almost certainly not have agreed, and the American generals would have jeered even more at Montgomery if 'Plunder' was put off. US Third Army's capture on the run of the Oppenheim bridge between the despatch of the letter quoted above and D-day for 'Plunder' must have caused Montgomery to have second thoughts about postponement, especially since he knew that he was under criticism both for his avowed need to employ airborne forces and for his slow build-up to the operation. Churchill, regardless of the risk of postponement, had decided to come to Twenty-First Army Group Tac HQ on D-minus-1. The problem of entertaining the Prime Minister, and of 'putting on a good show' before him, must have increased Montgomery's reluctance to put off the assault, even if the weather was bad. Churchill himself was so taken with the romance of a British Rhine crossing that he pre-recorded a BBC message in London before he flew to Tac HQ. The recording, scheduled for transmission at 1800 on D-day, focused upon the drama of the set-piece attack, referring to it as the 'first modern assault crossing of the Rhine'. Patton's success on 22 March had made this remark out of date, but the BBC put out the Prime Minister's broadcast nevertheless.

Although Montgomery had always insisted to Eisenhower that he needed US Ninth Army to give him sufficient strength for 'Plunder', he had originally decided, in fact, to put Dempsey at Second Army in full command of the whole operation, leaving Lt-Gen William Simpson's Ninth Army HQ out of it, although the latter was contributing at least a corps to the assault. Simpson objected strongly to this, and Dempsey sensibly backed him. In addition, the two army commanders urged Montgomery to split the assault area in order to give equal frontage to both armies on the far, enemy-held, bank of the Rhine. Montgomery insisted, however, that Simpson's crossing should be restricted to a single corps, but he did concede that this force should operate under Ninth Army command, and thus averted a potentially dangerous inter-Allied quarrel.[8]

With a marked lack of consistency, given his reluctance to use US Ninth Army, Montgomery also badgered Eisenhower for an additional ten American divisions in order to guarantee success. The Supreme Commander said that he would agree to this only on condition that Bradley's Twelfth Army Group HQ moved north to command all the American troops during the crossing; Montgomery immediately answered that he did not want the US troops on these terms. His desire to employ extra American forces only if they came under his own direct command, coupled with his unwillingness to allow Simpson's Ninth Army HQ a part in 'Plunder', implies that Montgomery's mind was occupied to some extent by the glamour and prestige attached to the Rhine crossing. This was certainly the view of the American commanders at the time, a view enhanced by their jubilation at their earlier successes at Remagen and Oppenheim – Montgomery, they felt, was determined to achieve a similar triumph. When US Ninth Army reached the Rhine at Neuss on 2 March, Simpson reported that seven of his twelve divisions had nothing to do. He suggested to Montgomery trying a surprise assault over the river, but got the reply that the Field-Marshal preferred to wait for his prepared assault on 24 March.[9]

Given the enormous build-up for the crossing, the time spent in preparation, and the use of American and airborne troops, the question is raised, did Montgomery over-insure for 'Plunder'? General Sir Charles Richardson told me:

> Monty really left the supply build-up to Miles Graham, who was not the sort of character to over-insure. You must remember we needed our supplies not only for the Rhine

crossing, but also for the long advance over many rivers in the German plain to the Elbe and beyond, including, we thought, to Berlin. Monty would have left all that to Graham. Personally I was amazed at the amount of geological data we had about the Rhine river, sub-strata, soil, depth of mud, etc. That was all very thorough, and as a sapper I liked it.

250,000 men were lined up for the assault; thirty divisions together with army troops and independent brigades made up British Second, US Ninth and Canadian First Armies. 7,311 air sorties were flown against any targets which might conceivably cause trouble to the attacking troops, and 50,000 tons of bombs were dropped — Wesel itself was all but destroyed. Montgomery's exhortation to his forces ended with the words: 'Having crossed the Rhine we will crack about in the plains of northern German chasing the enemy from pillar to post.'

Operation 'Plunder' started at 1700 on 23 March with a massive artillery bombardment, and at 2100 the first troops began to cross, arriving safely on the far bank a few minutes later. Initial German opposition was scattered and poorly organised, and casualties among the leading Allied divisions were consequently light. On the following day the main weight of Montgomery's forces went in, and all went according to plan, including 'Varsity', the airborne drop, by both parachute and gliders, of British 6th Airborne and US 17th Airborne Divisions. That evening Montgomery signalled the War Office, drafting the message after the CIGS and the Prime Minister, present since the start of the operation, had listened to the reports of the day's fighting from his liaison officers: 'First day's operations in Plunder have been most successful. We have got six Divisions over the Rhine including the two Airborne. Our casualties about 1200.'[10]

His signal on the next evening, however, reported (provisionally) heavy airborne casualties. Although the two airborne divisions had captured all of their first day's objectives, together with 3,500 POWs, British 6th Airborne had lost 30 per cent of its personnel killed or wounded: the Airlanding Brigade, which came in gliders, had lost 70 per cent of its equipment: and US 17th Airborne had suffered 500 casualties. On the first day of 'Plunder' Simpson's divisions had lost only 41 men killed and 450 wounded; by comparison, after three days the US airborne troops had lost 1,544 total casualties, and British 6th Airborne Division 1,344. Many historians (especially American ones) have been critical of 'Varsity'[11], and it is necessary now to consider whether Montgomery was justified in his use of airborne troops for 'Plunder'.

Conscious of the planning failures of 'Market-Garden', Montgomery made sure that there was plenty of time for detailed planning of the air drops, and for their co-ordination with the 'Plunder' ground operations. A planning conference for the airborne operation had been held at Twenty-First Army Group Main HQ as early as 9 February, with David Belchem as its Chairman – Richardson, Parks, Maj-Gen Richard Gale, commanding British Airborne Corps, and Ridgway, now GOC, US XVIII Airborne Corps, also attended. At this conference Montgomery had insisted that the airborne troops should be 'concentrated and in strength'; they were to drop 'within range of artillery, at least of medium artillery'; there should be 'a quick line up between the ground and airborne troops,' and all these criteria were met. Ridgway, however, stated that the earliest possible date for such an operation would be 1 April, because US 17th Airborne Division was still in the line, and had suffered 4,000 casualties, but he later agreed to 24 March. The conference had paid great attention to communications, so deficient at Arnhem, and elaborate signal diagrams for radio nets were prepared. With the basis of 'Varsity' laid, the airborne planners had gone on to attend two other 'Plunder' conferences at British Second Army HQ in Brussels on 27 February and 9 March.[12]

Montgomery's insistence that the drop should be close enough for a quick link-up was militarily sound, but as a result the airborne troops landed in the German gun area. In consequence, the enemy was able to rush light anti-aircraft guns to the dropping zones, and these contributed greatly to the high Allied casualties. The Allied First Airborne Army report on the operations states that zero hour for 'Varsity' was 1000 on 24 March, and that 6th Airborne Division began landing at 0952, achieving complete tactical surprise in 'timing and locations'. The report continues:

Initial losses were light but hostile mobile AA guns of 20mm batteries were quickly moved to the threatened areas by the

Germans. The incendiaries used by this lethal weapon began to take its toll of low flying parachute aircraft at 600 feet, and the glider aircraft and the resupply aircraft which flew at 200 feet. This occurred during the early stages of the drop. Approximately 75% of the losses occurred during the first 30 minutes of the battle; the remaining were sustained in the next two hours.

The report also said the operation demonstrated the successful use of double tow gliders.[13]

Final casualty lists for the first day showed that US 17th Airborne Division had lost 921 killed and wounded, whereas the two land-assaulting US divisions (30th and 79th) had together lost only 500 men, and only 41 killed in the actual crossing. In addition, the American airmen suffered 350 casualties, while total British and American aircraft losses amounted to 50 gliders destroyed; 44 transport aircraft were also destroyed, and 332 damaged.

Several of those who took part in the land assault have commented to me that the airborne operation made the crossing of the Rhine easier, but the conclusion must be that Montgomery was not justified in employing the two airborne divisions because their contribution to the advance was quite out of proportion to the casualties they suffered, and land troops could have achieved the same results with fewer losses. Field-Marshal Lord Carver said to me that:

It was not essential to employ airborne troops for the Rhine crossing. It would have succeeded without. You could say it was a superfluous effort.

I crossed the Rhine early on March 24 as Commander of 4 Independent Brigade supporting the 15th Scottish Division. At 1000 when the paratroopers started dropping on the German gun positions the German artillery fire on my troops stopped. They had to pull back hurriedly and did not harass us again seriously.

Probably it hurried up the whole operation by 24 hours and possibly 48. I doubt if this was sufficient compensation for the heavier casualties amongst the airborne troops. They lost considerably more than land troops would have done. There were nasty casualties amongst the second wave. I could see the German 20-mm guns shooting them down. Personally I am deeply sceptical about the value of airborne operations.

General Sir Nigel Poett commanded 5 Parachute Brigade, which dropped over the Rhine on 24 March in Operation 'Varsity'. Not unnaturally, his view is rather different:

> We had the hell of a lot of casualties, as we expected. I parachuted down with my HQ staff, and within five minutes of jumping I had lost my Brigade Major, Signals Officer and Administrative Officer. We landed behind the front in the gun areas and quickly mopped up the resistance. They could not concentrate against us. At that time there was no technique for dropping jeeps and anti-tank guns by parachute, and they had to come in the second wave by gliders. I do not think the German moved in any 20-mm guns. They were there already.
>
> I rate the operations as very successful. We captured all our objectives, and without us the Rhine crossing would have been held up considerably. We saved the ground troops at least a whole day. It was costly, but then we knew that beforehand.

And the late General Sir Richard Gale remarked:

> I have never stopped to wonder if the use of airborne troops for the Rhine crossing was justified. I was asked to do the job, and I did it. 'Varsity' was well planned and successful. We swamped the Germans in the landing zones. Someone had to do the attack, and there were bound to be casualties whether it was done by air or land. As Corps Commander I watched it from our bank of the Rhine and I was proud of my chaps, who did a marvellous job.

Whatever the verdict on the use of airborne troops during 'Plunder', history must salute Poett and Gale as two gallant airborne commanders whose operations in the Second World War were entirely successful. Montgomery was fortunate in having such men to serve him.

The British encountered stronger German resistance in their sector of the Rhine crossing than had the Americans, but Horrocks's XXX Corps and Lt-Gen Neil Ritchie's XII Corps reached all their objectives on D-day. (Like Horrocks, Ritchie had served with Montgomery in the desert – indeed, he had for a time commanded Eighth Army there until the reverses of May and June 1942 caused Auchinleck to relieve him.) The Second Army War Diary says of the action: 'Speaking generally early opposition was not particularly severe, and the enemy appeared overwhelmed by the weight of the assault. POWs said our attack came out of the middle of the barrage. Any stubborn resistance was due to determination by particular groups rather than a concerted effort.'[14] By evening Wesel was cleared, but it was several days before nearby Rees was subdued. Unlike Wesel, Rees had not been bombed, and this was later to have a profound effect. In the closing stages of the war Dempsey, with Montgomery's approval and with the lesson of Rees still clear in his mind, insisted on heavy bombing before he would attack Bremen and Hamburg. The result, for German civilians, was tragic.

Despite some setbacks, Montgomery's meticulous planning, coupled with the skilful use of his immense resources in artillery and bomber aircraft, secured a bridgehead over the Rhine with a bare minimum of casualties, excepting the airborne operation. In 'Plunder', his philosophy of 'wasting metal, not flesh' paid dividends, and the low casualty figures of the ground-assaulting troops are an answer to critics who complain of his over-caution and slowness. By the evening of 28 March his Rhine bridgehead was twenty-five miles wide and had an average depth of twenty-eight miles; Twenty-First Army Group's front line ran from Emmerich through Ralstern and south-west to Duisberg. Total Allied casualties, killed, wounded and made prisoner, amounted to 5,800 men. It was an exciting victory.

On 16 and 17 March, Frank Simpson had gone to stay at the SHAEF headquarters in Rheims.* He was told nothing important by Eisenhower while he was there, but in talks with Bedell Smith, Tedder, and the British generals Morgan and Whiteley, he had become alarmed, since they had made it apparent that the Supreme Commander had decided to clip Montgomery's wings, giving to Bradley the lion's share of the last

---

* At Rheims, Simpson found Marlene Dietrich entertaining American troops. Seeing her with another good-looking girl he asked 'Is that Myrna Loy as well?' He was immediately told to be quiet, for the other beauty was Kay Summersby, Eisenhower's confidante and former chauffeuse.

battle. Simpson was asked by Smith what Montgomery's reaction would be if US Ninth Army was removed from his command, to which he had given a non-committal reply, although he knew well that Montgomery would be furious. Simpson had, however, made it as plain to Smith as he could that the CIGS would consider any change in command as 'unfortunate', and had added that his own strongly-held view was that one man ought to be in command of all operations north of the Ruhr.

The British general had found, in fact, that the SHAEF planners had clearly decided that ten divisions of US First Army would move north of the Ruhr after 'Plunder' to link up with US Ninth Army. This would mean a force of twenty-two American divisions in the centre of the Allied front, and plainly there would have to be an American army group commander in charge of them. Simpson emphasised to the senior SHAEF officers that he quite agreed with this, and said that it would be acceptable to the British if Bradley was put in overall charge of all post-Rhine-crossing operations, including those conducted by Montgomery's Twenty-First Army Group.

Bedell Smith had replied: 'That would never do. The Supreme Commander could never face the howl there would be in the British press if Bradley was put over Monty.' Simpson had countered by remarking that this was nonsense, and that if the British press had the facts put to them properly there would be no howl, except perhaps from one or two of the 'gutter press'. 'Anyhow', he had added, 'if that is your trouble, why not put Monty in command?' to which the American had answered: 'Then we could not face the American press.' Simpson had finished by saying, reasonably, that 'The Supreme Commander ought to leave the press out of all this.' In spite of the disagreement the two men remained friendly, but there were to be other, more worrying, developments.

According to Simpson, Tedder carried no weight at SHAEF except in air matters, despite being Deputy Supreme Commander. During this visit Tedder had complained to Simpson that the Chiefs of Staff in London did not keep him informed of their views, and, with Morgan and Whiteley, had grumbled that Montgomery continually communicated directly with Brooke, and through him with the Prime Minister, with no one at SHAEF having any idea of what he might be saying. On·

the other hand, Bedell Smith had told Simpson that he saw nothing undesirable in this, for he knew that Patton and Bradley continually wrote to Washington. To Simpson, however, the complaints had indicated more trouble for Montgomery.

Simpson had realised that Eisenhower was considering removing US Ninth Army from Montgomery's command as soon as the Rhine was crossed, and that not only Bedell Smith but also the British at SHAEF – Tedder, Whiteley and Morgan – were involved in writing a detailed plan for a main thrust into Germany by Bradley's army group, which might leave Montgomery with the minor role in the north of liberating Holland and sealing off Denmark from the approaching Russians.[15]

As has been said, both Roosevelt and Churchill were seeking as glamorous a role as possible for their respective nations' armies in the final victory, since those roles would be of great importance to them in gaining votes in the post-war elections. During 1945 Churchill had become anxious to hold a General Election as soon as possible once peace was declared; his government was doing badly in by-elections and he hoped to capitalise on his reputation as the architect of victory in a snap election. This, he felt, could repeat Lloyd George's steamroller victory in the 'Khaki Election' of December 1918, achieved in the after-glow of the defeat of the Kaiser.

Marshall, however, was encouraging Eisenhower to give the more important part to the Americans, and Simpson had been shocked to find out at Rheims that the senior British service chiefs at SHAEF were conniving in the American plans to deprive the British Army of its full share of glory. This anti-Montgomery attitude may be seen in Whiteley's remark to Cornelius Ryan: 'Monty wants to ride into Berlin on a white charger wearing two hats',[16] and according to Professor Ambrose the feeling at SHAEF in March 1945 was that the principal British concern was not to finish the war, but to make a hero out of Montgomery.[17] On 24 March Eisenhower had written to Marshall: 'When operations carried out under his [Montgomery's] direction are of considerably less magnitude than those in other parts of the front and even though large American forces cooperate there is some influence at work that insists on giving Montgomery credit that belongs to other commanders ... I will continue to give attention to this matter.'[18]

Simpson had finally obtained confirmation from Whiteley and Morgan that the SHAEF plan was to put US Ninth Army under Bradley on or around 15 April, as soon as US First and Ninth Armies had encircled the Ruhr. Simpson had decided not to tell Montgomery, since he did not want to give him distracting news on the eve of 'Plunder'; he had, however, told Brooke as soon as he got back to the War Office on 19 March. The CIGS, now almost euphoric about an early end to the war, had said in answer that he was strongly opposed to the suggested SHAEF shift in command, but as the battle situation was so fluid he was not going to worry about anything as far away as 15 April. In his turn, however, Brooke had decided not to warn Churchill of the likely *volte-face* at SHAEF.[19] On 21 March, two days before 'Plunder' started, Montgomery had told Whiteley: 'In the north 21 Army Group must secure a bridgehead over the Rhine and then impose mobile warfare on the Germans in the plains of north Germany,' and it seems reasonable to assume that he felt that he would still have US Ninth Army under command for these operations. According to Montgomery, Whiteley had agreed, after some discussion, to put up this plan to Eisenhower, together with the recommendations of the operations section at SHAEF, even though he knew by then of the SHAEF plan and of the intention to hand the American army back to Bradley.[20]

On 18 March Eisenhower had sent Montgomery a further ominous warning that a change in the command structure might occur, and that US Ninth Army might revert to Bradley's command:

Dear Monty,

In considering future situations which might involve some changes in present command relationships, the one that looms most importantly is the possibility that we may be able, and may desire, to employ at least two Army Groups in a deep thrust eastward from the lower RHINE.

So long as the requirements of the North can be fully met by the 21st Army Group, plus the Divisions it is getting from the Mediterranean, reinforced by not more than one U.S. Army, we will stick to present arrangements. If it becomes necessary to employ a full U.S. Army Group of the First and Ninth Armies north of the RUHR, each Group will then naturally operate under its own commander in a suitable zone of operation.

Should this situation actually eventuate, it will likewise create a change in the command arrangements for the secondary effort. This burden will be borne principally by the U.S. Third and Seventh Armies and since Bradley, under this assumption, will be actively engaged in the north, Devers will be in command of the southern operations. His forces will be those that can be spared from the requirements of the north.

A further factor of this particular plan would be the bringing up of Fifteenth Army on a defensive role on the RHINE as part of Twelfth Army Group.

One eventuality that must be constantly borne in mind by the 21st Army Group is that of the possible necessity, on orders from the Combined Chiefs of Staff, of moving into Holland before strictly military considerations might dictate such an operation.

Sincerely,
IKE

Ten weeks before this would have evoked a petulant, if well argued, response from Montgomery. With the showdown with Eisenhower on 1 January still much in his mind, however, the Field-Marshal had decided to remain silent, and to concentrate instead on the Rhine crossing. On 20 March he sent the letter on to de Guingand, with this terse minute in his own handwriting: 'I shall make no comment to Ike. The employment of two Army Groups *north* of the Ruhr is unsound tactically, and is impossible administratively.'[21] He knew that Eisenhower had fired a warning shot across his bows, but he had decided, for the time being at least, to ignore it.

At Twenty-First Army Group Tac HQ on 24 March Eisenhower had shown Montgomery a draft report prepared by the SHAEF planners for the Combined Chiefs of Staff – this was the document in preparation the previous week which had so alarmed Simpson after his talks with Whiteley and Morgan. The Supreme Commander had pointed out to Montgomery that the planners considered an advance north of the Ruhr only had 'limited possibilities until railway bridges had been built over the Rhine,' and that this would take two months. Instead the SHAEF document recommended that the Allies 'should widen the base of the operations to isolate the Ruhr by also advancing in force from the south [the old broad-front pincer plan to envelop the Ruhr]', which, according to the planners, would greatly increase the speed of 'deployment of offensive forces against the enemy.' Eisenhower said that in principle he agreed with the plan, but that he wanted to hear Montgomery's reaction to it.[22]

Montgomery read the document. He did not like the tone, for it implied what he considered was a vague, rather than an immediate, threat to his retaining US Ninth Army under his command. Eisenhower deceitfully promised that he would 'broaden the report' so that it could still be read as meaning that the Twenty-First Army Group attack would be the major one, but in fact this was most definitely not the Supreme Commander's intention, though he flinched from telling Montgomery so. Eisenhower decided to use the lack of a railway bridge over the Rhine at Wesel as an excuse for revenging himself on Montgomery for his arrogance and lack of consultation in the earlier stages of the campaign, and to carry out Marshall's and Roosevelt's wishes for the American armies to win the greatest glory in the final victory. That night SHAEF wired the document to Washington but not to London, and Eisenhower added to it: 'The enemy strength on the western front is becoming so stretched that penetrations and advances will soon only be limited by our own maintenance. I intend to reinforce every success with utmost speed.'[23]

After his visit to Montgomery, Eisenhower went on to stay with Bradley. The two American generals made firm plans to withdraw US Ninth Army from Twenty-First Army Group as soon as the latter had linked up with Hodges's US First Army coming up to encircle the Ruhr from the south.[24] On the following day, 25 March, Eisenhower, with Bradley in tow, met Montgomery again, at a small house overlooking the Rhine where US XV Corps had its HQ. Churchill and Brooke were also present. Much of the time was taken up with Churchill explaining to Eisenhower the enormity of a signal from the Soviet Foreign Minister, V.M. Molotov, in which the Russian complained bitterly and unreasonably about Alexander's handling of the possible surrender of the German army in Italy. Eisenhower too waxed hot about Molotov's rudeness, and Churchill formed the impression that the Supreme Commander was as keen as himself to take Berlin before the Russians; that night the Prime Minister minuted Eden: 'Eisenhower much upset about Molotov's letter. We had a jolly day yesterday* and crossed the Rhine.'[25]

Churchill and Montgomery did most of the talking at the 25 March meeting. Once the Prime Minister had finished his tirade against the Russians, Montgomery took over, demonstrating on maps how he would direct his advance out of the Rhine bridgehead which, even as he spoke, was expanding spectacularly. But Eisenhower, when his turn came, was far from frank. He failed to mention that he was on the brink of shifting his main advance from the north to the centre under Bradley, and of removing US Ninth Army from Montgomery's command, and, further, that he had virtually decided *not* to capture Berlin.

We shall never know with certainty whether Eisenhower had not finally made up his mind, or whether he just jibbed at telling Churchill that he was shifting his main attack away from Montgomery in the north to Bradley in the centre, and that he wanted to leave Berlin to the Russians. The most favourable interpretation one can put on the Supreme Commander's deceit is that he was still undecided, but the evidence is that he *had* already made up his mind, but had baulked at incurring the spontaneous rage of the Prime Minister and an unpleasant and acrimonious discussion.

Eisenhower may be justly criticised for his silence on 24 and 25 March. He owed a definite duty to Churchill, as head of the British Government, and to Montgomery, as commander of the army of his principal ally, to discuss his plans with them before changing his main strategy. But even more serious was his failure to mention that he no longer wanted to capture Berlin, but was instead ready to leave that city to the Russians.

When he became Supreme Commander in December 1943, Eisenhower's brief was to 'undertake operations aimed at the heart of Germany and the destruction of her armed forces.' This directive imposed upon him no specific obligation to give priority to the capture of Berlin, but it had always been

---

* This was a most callous remark. From the west bank of the Rhine Churchill had witnessed through his binoculars the destruction of many gliders and tow-planes, a great number being shot down in flames. He wrote about this in his memoirs with scant feeling for the airborne losses.

considered by Churchill that the instructions encompassed the taking of the German capital – indeed, in September 1944, as we have seen, Eisenhower had told Montgomery that 'Berlin [was] the main prize'. If it was wrong of the Supreme Commander to deceive the British on 24 and 25 March about removing US Ninth Army from Twenty-First Army Group, it was an even greater breach of faith not to tell the Prime Minister that he had abandoned Berlin as a target, a breach that Churchill never forgave. In the earlier stages of the campaign Eisenhower had made every effort not to be over-nationalistic in matters of command, but by March 1945 he had become anti-British and, prodded by Marshall, was ready to snub both Churchill and Montgomery. Patton and Bradley, the Supreme Commander's close friends (Bradley and Eisenhower had been at West Point together), had frequently chided him for being too pro-British; at one point in the campaign Patton had made the typical remark: 'Ike is the best God-damn general the British have got'. But it cannot be denied that much of the blame for Eisenhower's developing feeling of antagonism towards his allies rests squarely with Montgomery, whose actions and personality, coupled with his occasionally extreme caution, had so often provoked American resentment.

By 27 March, Montgomery's advance beyond the Rhine was rolling away, meeting little serious German resistance. Given the swiftness of the advance and his comparatively light casualties, his appreciation of the agreed plan, even after his talk with Eisenhower on the 24th, was that once well into the plains of north Germany he would send his armour at top speed towards both the Baltic and Berlin. Montgomery looked on Berlin as a 'priority objective', and had become convinced that the city would play an important part in the peace if the Allies were to occupy it before the Russians, something which Churchill had made clear to him. Late on the 27th, relaxed and confident after hearing encouraging reports from his liaison officers, Montgomery signalled Eisenhower:

Today I issued orders to Army Commanders for the operations about to begin ... My intention is to drive hard for the line of the Elbe using the [US] ninth and [British] second armies. The right of the ninth army will be directed on Magdeburg and the left of the second army on Hamburg ...

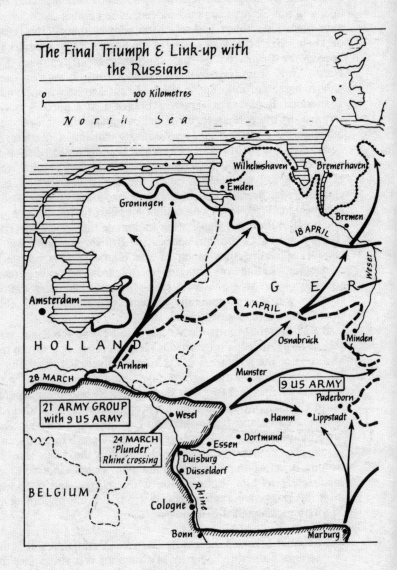

The Final Triumph & Link-up with the Russians

0 — 100 Kilometres

North Sea

Wilhelmshaven
Bremerhaven
Emden
Bremen
Groningen
18 APRIL
Weser
4 APRIL
G E R
Amsterdam
Osnabrück
Minden
HOLLAND
Arnhem
Munster
28 MARCH
9 US ARMY
21 ARMY GROUP
with 9 US ARMY
Paderborn
Wesel
Hamm
Lippstadt
24 MARCH
'Plunder'
Rhine crossing
Essen
Dortmund
Duisburg
Düsseldorf
BELGIUM
Rhine
Cologne
Bonn
Marburg

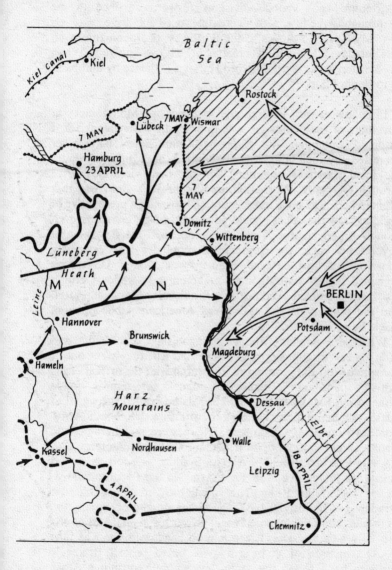

I have ordered ninth and second armies to move their armoured and mobile divisions forward at once to get through to the Elbe with all possible speed and drive ...

My Tac HQ moves to the northwest of Bonninghardt on Thursday, 29 March. Thereafter my HQ will move to Wesel Munster Widenbruck Herford Hanover – thence by autobahn to Berlin I hope.[26]

Eisenhower, with little enough patience for Montgomery at this stage of the campaign, was infuriated by the signal, for it assumed (although the Supreme Commander had never promised any such thing) that US Ninth Army would stay under the Field-Marshal's command for the final victorious drive through Germany. Worse still, in Eisenhower's view, was that Montgomery was once more usurping his senior's prerogative of deciding how the Allies should advance through Germany even though American troops vastly outnumbered the British. And beyond his rage, the Supreme Commander was extremely conscious of how enraged Bradley would be if US troops remained under Montgomery's command while German resistance crumbled. And not only Bradley, for Marshall, Patton and the other generals, as well as American public opinion, would be equally outraged.

Whatever qualms about antagonising Churchill and Mongomery Eisenhower might have had left, they went out of the window on the morning of 28 March with the arrival of his British subordinate's imperious signal. Ill temper made Eisenhower, for once, curt and clear as he drafted the signal to quash the Berlin proposal and to withdraw US Ninth Army from Montgomery's command. There were no characteristic woolly compromises now. First he informed Montgomery that US Ninth Army would revert to Bradley as soon as it had 'joined up hands' with US First Army in the Paderborn area, having ringed the Ruhr. The signal then continued bluntly: 'Bradley will be responsible for mopping up and occupying the Ruhr and with minimum delay will deliver his main thrust on the axis Erfurt-Leipzig-Dresden to join up hands with the Russians ... The mission of your army will be to protect Bradley's northern flank.'[27] On the same day, without consulting either London or Washington, Eisenhower signalled directly to Stalin that his plan was for the Allied armies to link up at Dresden, thus making it plain that Berlin would be left to the Russians.[28] He also made it clear to Marshall (in a signal copied to London 'for information') that he did not intend to capture Berlin.[29] Tedder, Eisenhower's deputy, was not even informed until after the signals had gone, and staff at SHAEF felt that the Supreme Commander was so angry with Montgomery that he was determined to carry out his own plan, willy-nilly, and would brook no argument.

Montgomery was appalled to find his role so suddenly downgraded after what he considered to be his Rhine triumph. As we have seen, Simpson had given Brooke a fair idea on 19 March that something like this might come from Eisenhower at any moment, but neither Montgomery nor Churchill had been aware that such a turn of events was likely, or even possible. It had, in any case, been thought that such changes would come about later, in mid-April, and no one could have foreseen that Montgomery would precipitate his own downfall. But it was humiliating now for him to be forced to rewrite his army commanders' orders in the light of Eisenhower's signal, the more so since, on the day before, he had issued a directive telling them to go 'flat out' – their advance had already begun. A downcast Montgomery signalled the Supreme Commander back: 'I note from your FWD 18272 that you intend to change the command set up. If you feel this is necessary I pray that you do not do so until we reach the Elbe as such action would not help the great movement which is now beginning to develop.'[30]

Eisenhower had no sympathy for Montgomery's disappointment, however, and signalled that he had chosen the Kassel-Leipzig axis for the advance, and that his main strength would be concentrated in the centre, and not on Twenty-First Army Group's front in the north. He promised to give twenty-four hours' notice before Ninth Army reverted to Bradley after the junction at Paderborn, and slightly sugared the pill by suggesting that an American formation might come under Montgomery's command 'for operations beyond the Elbe'. There was, however, another shock for the British commander: 'You will see that in none of this do I mention Berlin. So far as I am concerned that place has become nothing but a geographical location; I have never been interested in these. My purpose is to destroy the enemy.'[31] More bitter still, the signal's last paragraph indicated that the final role for Montgomery and Twenty-First

Army Group in the liberation of Europe would be modest. The Supreme Commander's intention was that they should: 'cross the Elbe without delay, drive to the Baltic coast at Lubeck and seal off the Danish Peninsula.'

Learning of these events, both Churchill and Brooke were surprised and horrified at what they looked upon as Eisenhower's bloody-mindedness. Throughout the campaign the American had pandered to the British, and Churchill, in particular, found it hard to believe that, suddenly and without consultation, Eisenhower would make a fundamental change in the agreed strategy, and would not only downgrade the British forces to the minor role of occupying Holland and Denmark, but would also forego the coveted prize of Berlin. The Supreme Commander's real antipathy towards Montgomery had started with the latter's disastrous press conference of 7 January, and had been fanned by Marshall, among others. But a clue to Eisenhower's sudden firmness on 28 March can be found in a statement he made to Cornelius Ryan: 'Montgomery had become so personal in his efforts to make sure the Americans and me in particular got no credit, that in fact we hardly had anything to do with the war, that I finally stopped talking to him.'[32] Certainly Montgomery had misjudged Eisenhower's attitude towards him at Zondhoven in mid-February, and as a consequence he had lightly thrown away the opportunity of bringing Alexander to SHAEF, and thus of strengthening British influence over strategy. At the time Montgomery had had no idea of the depth of Eisenhower's dislike for him, but on 1 April when he wrote this bitter letter (published here for the first time) to his friend Frank Simpson, his eyes had at last been opened:

It has occured to me that Ike may be saying that I set my forces in motion for the Elbe without consulting him. The true facts are that on March 25 when I took the Prime Minister and the CIGS to meet Ike and Bradley at 15 US Corps HQ, I got hold of Ike and Bradley and had a talk with them round the map.

I explained my plan of moving up to the Elbe line and drew on the map the right boundary that I suggested for 21 Army Group: i.e. between me and Bradley. The only comment made by Ike was that he thought Magdeburg, which is on the Elbe, should be inclusive to Bradley. I had drawn it as inclusive to me. I at once agreed and Bradley agreed also. No other comment was made, though on that day Ike must have known that he was going to take the 9th Army away from me, and that he intended the main thrust to be south-east towards Dresden so as to join up with the Russians in that area.

I went away, thought out my plans, and issued my order. On March 27 I sent these plans to you and to Ike. On March 28 I issued my written directive to my armies. On the same day I received the blow from Ike in his directive in which he agrees with my plan and removes 9th Army from me. A very good counter-attack.

All very dirty work, I fear.

It is useless to deny the events of March 25 as I have described them above. It was photographed and I enclose a copy. From the look on Bradley's face* there is obviously trouble ahead.[33]

'Very dirty work' is a harsh condemnation, even for Montgomery, but it is justified when one considers the underhand way in which the cup had been dashed from his lips. His bitterness was scarcely contained, and on 2 April he signalled Brooke:

We are about to make a terrible mistake. The great point now is speed of action so that we can finish off the German war in the shortest possible time. SHAEF do not understand if you make big changes in Army Groups you create confusion in signal arrangements and communications. My communications have been built up on the assumption that 9th Army would remain in 21 Army Group until we cleared northern Germany, and this was the declared intention of Eisenhower. My Main HQ is moving this week to a site which will now be well inside 12th Army Group. It seems the doctrine that public opinion wins wars is coming to the fore again.

---

* According to Brooke, Churchill had told him that 'Bradley was a sour faced bugger who would not listen', a picture of the American general that does not always fit the accepted image.

The CIGS remained sympathetic towards his protégé in the hour of his disappointment. The Chiefs of Staff met with the Prime Minister on 1 April, and cabled the Joint Chiefs of Staff in Washington that London was opposed to the shift in command proposed for US Ninth Army, and asked for the decision to be reconsidered. To console Montgomery, Brooke wired him on 3 April that he was disputing the change with Washington, although he considered that Eisenhower would be left a completely free hand. The CIGS expressed his full sympathy with the difficulties in which Montgomery had been placed, but advised him that, since he had made his views clear to Eisenhower, he should take no further action..

Kit Dawnay told me that at this time Montgomery would frequently ask him 'Why are they so hostile to me at SHAEF? Who are my enemies?' and Brigadier Williams provided me with a plausible answer. He told me that Strong, the British major-general in charge of SHAEF Intelligence, together with Major-Generals Humfrey Gale, Whiteley and Morgan, had developed considerable loyalty for, and bias towards, that largely American organisation. Williams continued: 'Montgomery continually rubbed them up the wrong way. Morgan and Whiteley were always under suspicion at SHAEF which was dominantly an American HQ because they were 'limeys'. Therefore they had to over-work their passages to be accepted properly, and latterly this meant being anti-Monty and anti-21 Army Group.'

General Sir Charles Richardson told me that he never went to visit SHAEF if he could possibly avoid it, and this typified the Twenty-First Army Group approach. SHAEF had become too large and impersonal. It was remote from the fighting and its atmosphere was alien to the British-trained staff officers at Twenty-First Army Group and in the War Office, and without a doubt these attitudes, and the frequent quarrels, were not altogether of Montgomery's making.

On 6 April, Montgomery made another effort to persuade Eisenhower to let him go on to Berlin. He wrote to the Supreme Commander, saying that if British Second Army was over the Elbe and captured Hamburg it should advance towards Lübeck and south-east to Berlin, and that 'this should be comparatively easy ... I consider Berlin has definite value as an objective and I have no doubt the Russians feel the same; but they may well pretend this is not the case.' The letter drew a dusty response from his superior, who replied on the 8th: 'Berlin has political and psychological significance, but of far greater importance will be the location of the remaining German forces ... on them I am going to concentrate my attention ... it is not Bradley's role to protect your southern flank. My Directive is quite clear on this point.' He did, however, add that if he had a chance to take Berlin cheaply he would do so. Montgomery's last chance to deliver the final blow had gone, and Eisenhower's phrase 'it is not Bradley's role to protect your southern flank' was plainly intended as a snub.[34]

Montgomery instructed Dawnay to write an interim view of the controversy in the Log:

At this moment of swift advance following the victory in the battle for the Rhine crossings a cloud suddenly appeared which threatened the prospect of reaping to the full the fruits of the victory which had been gained ...

The Field-Marshal moreover had heard privately that there had been great political pressure, from the staff at SHAEF and from General Bradley, to get Ninth US Army back under command of 12 US Army Group. And with victory in sight, the violent anti-British element at SHAEF was pressing for a set-up which would clip the wings of the British Group of Armies, and would relegate it to an unimportant role on the flank, while the Americans finished off the campaign alone ...

... He [the Field-Marshal] considered that the Allies were now repeating the mistake they had made in September, 1944. Then, having won a great victory south of the SEINE, the Allied armies advanced to the RHINE on a broad front; they were nowhere strong enough to get decisive results *quickly*. And so the war dragged on through the winter of 1944-45.

In April, 1945, the Allies had achieved a very favourable position; they had won the battles for the Rhineland and the battle of the RHINE, inflicting smashing defeats on the German Army; now once again the Allied armies were to advance on a wide front, nowhere strong enough to get decisive results *quickly*. And so the war would drag on longer than otherwise would be the case.

The Field-Marshal had always considered that the correct strategy for the campaign in north-western Europe was to be strong in the north. From September, 1944, to January, 1945, the Allies were never strong enough in the north to achieve decisive results ...

However, the Field-Marshal considered that it was useless to continue to argue with the American Generals as to what the correct strategy should be. They were unable to see his point of view, and were in any case determined to finish off the war in their own way.

He therefore decided to make no comments of any kind on the American plan, and to adopt a policy of complete silence while he did as much as he could in the north with the strength available.

The final end of the war was now certain, though the American strategy would make the war last longer than might otherwise have been the case; for quick victory could be achieved only by the concentration of great strength in the north. But as the end approached, the great point was to remain good friends with the Americans. Any further argument with them on their strategy would only exacerbate relations, and had no chance of achieving any results.

He therefore decided to get on with his own job on the northern touchline, from which point of vantage many an international match has been won.[35]

It is perhaps surprising that, in all his attempts at this time to reverse Eisenhower's decisions about command or strategy, Montgomery presented a case that was fair, reasonable, and truthful. His letters, notes and signals imply his bitterness, but there is no trace of self-pity, only a strong and honest belief in his own views. Now he decided 'to get on with his own job', as he put it. Nothing could have been more statesmanlike than the Twenty-First Army Group commander's reply, dated 9 April, to Eisenhower's letter of the 8th:

Dear Ike,
    Have received your letter dated 8 April. It is quite clear to me what you want. I will crack along on the northern flank one hundred per cent and will do all I can to draw the enemy forces away from the main effort being made by Bradley.
                                        Yours ever,
                                        Monty[36]

In the meantime, Montgomery's ever loyal friend, Simpson, was beavering away at Whiteley on the telephone, in the vain hope that the staff at SHAEF might change their minds about US Ninth Army. Although he had had his suspicions, Simpson had not realised until then how strong were Whiteley's anti-Montgomery feelings. Eventually, after several calls, Simpson said: 'Can you imagine Monty's feeling when he finds out how his most promising plan has been whittled down? Do you ever talk to him yourself?' to which Whiteley replied: 'Oh Simbo – be fair. Bradley has feelings too, and he must be allowed to have US Ninth Army for a bit.' At that point Simpson finally realised that Whiteley's loyalties lay entirely with the Americans, and in a letter to Montgomery he told him of this conversation, adding: 'There you have the whole matter in a nutshell. Further comment would be useless.' Montgomery at last understood that his long battle for command and priority was lost.[37]

On 3 April Tedder, in his capacity as Deputy Supreme Commander, was summoned to the meeting of the Chiefs of Staff in London. Churchill was unable to attend on that day, but Brooke, supported by Ismay and Cunningham, gave the Air Marshal a difficult time, although the official record merely states that there was 'an informal discussion with Air Marshal Tedder'. Apart from the four officers mentioned everyone else was turned out of the room, and the CIGS then cross-examined Tedder about the SHAEF changes to plans and command. Tedder told the meeting that the SHAEF planners had had to change the command 'because Monty had suddenly declared he was going off on his own plans for a thrust to the north,' to which Brooke replied, referring to the Supreme Commander's actions on 28 March: 'It is most unsatisfactory when Ike has to appeal to Stalin to help him to control Monty.' Tedder answered by saying that Eisenhower neither showed him the signal to Stalin, nor consulted him about sending it.[38]

Eisenhower's deputy left the meeting feeling somewhat aggrieved, but London had not yet done with him. On the next day Churchill sent for him, and immediately blamed him for allowing Eisenhower to send the telegram to the Soviet leader. This was unfair, for not only had Eisenhower acted without consulting his Deputy, but the Prime Minister had himself continually undermined Tedder's position at SHAEF by cutting him out of decisions, and by dealing directly with Eisenhower.

According to Simpson, Tedder went back to Rheims 'not only confused, but battered'; the Air Chief Marshal made no reference to these incidents in his autobiography, despite its title – *With Prejudice*

Churchill now vigorously took up the cudgels for Montgomery. Worried by Russian intentions, the Prime Minister desperately wanted Allied troops to take Berlin, and knew that the logical advance upon the German capital was by Twenty-First Army Group from the north. On 29 March he had telephoned Eisenhower and emphasised the political importance of Allied troops taking Berlin as a counter-balance to the imminent Russian occupation of Vienna (although that city was not eventually captured until 13 April). On the next day he followed up his telephone call with a signal:

> Withdrawal of 9th US Army from 21 Army Group may stretch Montgomery's front so widely that his offensive role may peter out ... I do not consider myself Berlin has lost its military and certainly not its political significance ... While Berlin remains under German flag it is the most decisive point in Germany ... I prefer the plan on which we crossed the Rhine, namely that the 9th US Army should march with 21 Army Group to the Elbe and beyond to Berlin.

Churchill had sent a similar message to Roosevelt. The American President had been gravely ill and exhausted since the Yalta Conference in February, and as a result Marshall had taken over the reins of military affairs. The latter was backing Eisenhower to the hilt, and Churchill was therefore rebuffed. But on 2 April the Prime Minister had tried again with Eisenhower, writing: 'I deem it highly important that we should shake hands with the Russians as far east as possible,' and reminding the Supreme Commander that Tedder, the senior British officer at SHAEF, had neither been informed of, nor consulted about, the signal to Stalin.[39] Eisenhower had made his decision, however, and would not yield an inch, even to the sometimes domineering and intimidating Churchill.

This last rebuff tipped the balance. With the American forces in Europe outnumbering the British by almost two to one, Churchill sensibly realised that, in this hour of victory, he had fired his last shot in defence of Montgomery. He therefore wrote to Eisenhower, concluding his letter: 'All this business is settling down quite satisfactorily,' and added in a letter to Roosevelt: 'Changes have turned out to be very much less than we first supposed. My relations with General Eisenhower are of the most friendly character.'

In the meantime Bradley had been urging Eisenhower to withdraw US Ninth Army from Montgomery as soon as was practicable, rather than desirable. Bradley was also strongly opposed to capturing Berlin, for he knew that if the Allies adopted such a plan, then Montgomery would need US Ninth Army, and that in turn would mean halting Patton at Leipzig. Alone amongst the Americans Lt-Gen Bill Simpson, whose army was the subject of the controversy, wanted to go to Berlin, and he was in any case less 'anti-Monty' than the other US commanders. Simpson's view, expressed later, was that when his Ninth Army crossed the Elbe on 12 April, forty-eight miles from Berlin, he could have been in Berlin in a day and a half because 'German resistance was non-existent. There was none.'[40]

An important factor in the decision to leave Berlin to the Russians was that SHAEF had become obsessed by intelligence (false, as it turned out) that Hitler was preparing a last-stand redoubt in the Alps, on the Italian-Austrian frontier. A SHAEF Intelligence Report of 10 March 1945 read:

> There have been numerous reports that Hitler and his Nazi leaders supported by SS units, young Nazi fanatics and Quislings, are planning to make a last stand in the so-called redoubt in western Austria ... it is unlikely that large scale preparations for organised military resistance are being made.
>
> We should therefore be prepared to undertake operations in southern Germany in order to overcome rapidly any organised resistance by the German armed forces or by guerilla movements which have retreated to the inner zone and to this redoubt.

And on 25 March the G2 sections of US Seventh Army had concluded that there was hard evidence that Hitler intended a final stand in an Alpine redoubt.[41] Even the shrewd Kenneth Strong, sceptical about the strength of the redoubt, nevertheless believed that Hitler would try to create the legend of a fighting, unconquered, immortal Nazism, a legend that would one day plant the seeds of the Reich's reincarnation.

So Eisenhower decided to give the non-existent redoubt priority over Berlin, influenced by Bradley, who claimed that taking Berlin 'might cost the Allies 10,000 casualties ... a pretty stiff price to pay for a prestige objective.'[42] This was a false appreciation in the light of US Lt-Gen Simpson's reports, and besides, to Stalin's anger the Germans were already withdrawing troops from the west to fight the Russians in the east. The western approaches to Berlin lay almost open, and many German generals were prepared to surrender to the Western Allies rather than to the Russians. Doubtless when Hitler realised that the Allies were approaching Berlin from the west he would have tried to concentrate divisions for its defence, but this might have precipitated an earlier break-up of the Nazi regime.

On 7 April Eisenhower signalled Marshall: 'If the CCOS consider that the Allied effort to take Berlin should outweigh purely military considerations I would cheerfully adjust my plans,'[43] but he was given no orders to make such an adjustment, nor did he expect any. Stalin, immediately on receiving Eisenhower's signal saying that the main Allied thrust would be towards Dresden, had redeployed the Red Army to make Berlin its main objective. The Supreme Commander had no worries about the political controversy caused by his unprecedented signal to the Soviet leader, for Marshall had made it plain that both he and the US Government approved. Berlin fell to Marshal Georgi Zhukov's Russian forces on 2 May.

Eisenhower's three signals of 28 March – to Montgomery, to withdraw US Ninth Army; to Stalin, to tell him that the western Allies would not capture Berlin; and to Marshall, to say that his main effort would be to the south – have been in the American archives and available to historians for years. These three cables should be read by future historians in the context of Montgomery's exasperated letter to Simpson, which has already been quoted on pp 376-7, for their military, economic, political and even social effects upon present-day Europe cannot be underestimated. In the first week of April Churchill abandoned his arguments for capturing Berlin and the controversy was ended. Eisenhower had his way, and Montgomery philosophically got on with his job; as he wrote in his memoirs: 'It was useless for me to pursue the matter further. We had had so much argument on great issues; anyhow it was almost too late.'[44]

After his 'dirty work' tirade to Simpson on the subject of Eisenhower's duplicity, Montgomery settled down to organise the final defeat of the Germans in his now-reduced sector. While he had a job to do he was not one to worry for long about past grievances, and his daily signals to Brooke were cheerful and optimistic. He was plainly elated by the rapid advance of his divisions, and by the coming defeat of Germany. He was not to enjoy his long-planned advance over the Hanover plains to Berlin, but he happily pushed his divisions forward via Bremen and Hamburg, and on towards the Elbe. His main objective was to reach the neck of the Danish peninsula before the Russians, since the occupation of Denmark by Soviet troops would produce dire political consequences, and his targets were Lübeck and Wismar, with Hamburg as his intermediate objective.

Montgomery's advance would cut off a large enemy army in Holland on his west flank, but these German troops had little appetite for fighting by now, and the main problem there was the lack of food supplies, which was causing grave distress to the Dutch people. Montgomery told the War Office that he could clear Holland with two divisions, but that he rated this job 'the lowest as regards priority,' and Simpson replied by warning him that feeding the people of Holland would be a heavy strain on his lines of communication and on the Rhine bridges once the country was freed from the Germans. Eisenhower, in consultation with Montgomery, agreed that Twenty-First Army Group should clear Holland as far west as the line running north and south through Utrecht, and that only then would it be decided whether to go further west or not.

In the event German opposition to the advance was slight, and on 8 April Montgomery signalled Brooke: 'We now control country west of Ems River with armoured cars and SAS troops. A great deal of shooting up of enemy is going on. The whole area is covered with small bodies of enemy trying to get away.' He continued by saying that he expected heavy resistance at Bremen, and that he would therefore cross the Weser River well to the east, at Verden, and then send back one division west towards Bremen. Montgomery was encountering trouble from small German units which had been by-passed by his advance, and he reported to the War Office that officers and ORs, especially despatch riders, were being murdered or simply disappearing, and also that at Second Army Tac HQ a bomb had been thrown into a tent, wounding six men. These instances served only to underline the lack of serious opposition, however, and General Pip Roberts told me that his 11th Armoured Division met only slight resistance after they had crossed the Rhine, except for a difficult and hard-fought battle near Osnabrück. By 27 March the Germans had been in many cases reduced to using oxen to draw their guns, and a captured artillery officer told his interrogators: 'What is the use of having a battery if you have neither petrol nor ammunition?'[45] while German staff officers argued whether farm carts should be used for barricades or for transport. The Wehrmacht in the west was up against the best-equipped army that an industrial nation could produce, and Montgomery, to use a favourite metaphor, was now batting on the easiest of wickets.

Worried about the German strength in Bremen, Montgomery went forward to see Horrocks towards the middle of April, remarking, 'Jorrocks, I am not happy about Bremen'. The two men made detailed plans on a large-scale map, and Montgomery told the XXX Corps commander: 'I will give you two extra divisions and you must use four infantry divisions'.[46] The main assault on Bremen started on 24 April, and the greater part of the city was captured by the 26th. Unhappily, by then much of Bremen had been reduced to rubble by heavy RAF bomber attacks, but Second Army had firmly told 83 RAF HQ 'Delayed action bombs not acceptable'.[47]

Given his reduced role, Montgomery had displayed no pettiness or rancour, or at least, not openly. As we have seen, he had replied meekly to Eisenhower on 9 April that he would 'crack along on the northern flank one hundred per cent and will do all I can to draw away the enemy forces from the main effort,' and on the same day he had written to Simpson: 'All is now clear as regards what Ike is trying to do. I shall play my part to the best of my ability'.[48] But long before Bremen fell, Eisenhower had started to nag him about going too slowly towards Lübeck. On 8 April the Supreme Commander had asked Montgomery what logistical help he would need from the Americans, to which the Field-Marshal had replied 'nothing', and Bradley, visiting Montgomery on the 10th, had got the same answer.

Eisenhower was not reassured, however. Declaring to his SHAEF colleagues that he was unhappy with Twenty-First Army Group's rate of advance, he went to see Montgomery on 20 April. This time Montgomery said that he wanted part-time use of the railway bridge at Wesel built by American engineers, and that he would like an American corps to help with the Elbe assault. Eisenhower immediately responded by assigning him Ridgway's XVIII Airborne Corps, to the disgust of Bradley, who still had to keep that force supplied.

Of these attempts to hurry him, Montgomery himself commented that both Churchill and Eisenhower sent him messages prodding him on faster, and 'I fear I got somewhat irritated and my replies possibly showed it.'[49] Then, on 26 April, the Supreme Commander delivered his final pinprick, ordering his SHAEF staff to telephone Montgomery and emphasise to him the urgent need to get to Lübeck before the Russians, in order to seal off the Denmark peninsula. Montgomery wrote to Simpson on the following day:

My dear Simbo,

The Bremen battle went well and quickly and the whole city is now in our hands. We go over the Elbe tonight. The technique is the same as in the Rhine crossing. The Commando Brigade crosses first at 0200 hours and secures Lauenberg; 15 Division then goes over.

Yesterday I had a telephone enquiry from Supreme HQ to say they hoped I realised the urgent need to get to Lubeck before the Russians. This is adding insult to injury and made me very angry. I told Freddie [de Guingand] to get on to Whiteley and inform him as follows:

(1) I have always been very well aware of the urgent need to reach and cross the Elbe quickly. See my signal of March 28.

(2) It was Supreme HQ which prevented this plan being implemented. They removed the 9th Army from me and left 21 Army Group so weak that the tempo of the operations became slowed down.

(3) If the Russians should get to Lübeck and on up to Kiel and Denmark before we can do so I would suggest that Supreme HQ should accept the full blame. I trust I shall have

no more enquiries on that line.

After a spell of lovely weather it is now cold and wet and altogether very unpleasant. I hope it will clear up before tonight.

Yours ever,
B.L. Montgomery

P.S. Since writing the above I have had a wire from Ike about Lubeck. I enclose his wire and my answer.[50]

Eisenhower's wire, passed on to Simpson, took the form of a letter, and was copied to Brooke at the War Office. It read:

Dear Monty,

All our plans have agreed on the tremendous importance of anchoring our flank on Lubeck as quickly as possible. I know that you fully appreciate the importance of this matter in the mind of the Prime Minister. I note in this morning's briefing that the front around Stettin is, as we anticipated, growing fluid. This re-emphasizes the need for rapidity. While I realize that you are straining every nerve to move as quickly as you can, I want you to let me know instantly if any slowness on the part of the U.S. corps assigned to your command might hold up your plans for a day or even an hour. I am informed here that additional logistic support promised your army group is fully forthcoming. This headquarters will do anything at all that is possible to help you insure the speed and the success of the operation.

As ever,
Ike

Montgomery replied on the same day with a letter marked 'Top Secret', 'Personal', and 'Eyes Only for Eisenhower':

Dear Ike,

I have your signal of today's date. I have always realised the great importance of getting quickly up to the Elbe and crossing it without delay, and it was for this purpose that I issued my signal of March 28.

That plan could not be implemented quickly as you took the 9th Army away from me on April 1 and left me very weak in the north. The whole tempo of operations in the north slowed down after that and I did the best I could with what I had left.

We have had some heavy fighting against some fanatical resistance. It is not easy to recover lost time. You can rely on me and my troops to do everything that is possible to get to Lubeck as quickly as we can.

Yours ever,
Monty.[51]

Having written this relatively mild reply to Eisenhower, Montgomery let off steam by dictating a note for the Log full of resentment at Eisenhower's behaviour. The following is an extract:

Note by the Field-Marshal
on 27th April 1945

1. This has been a very difficult period.
2. The ship very nearly went on the rocks ...

The reason for Eisenhower's plan was the old business of command; Bradley did not want the Ninth Army to stay under me; the anti-British party at SHAEF felt the same; they were all quite prepared to adopt an unsound plan in order to satsify national considerations and public opinion ...

3. ... Eisenhower gave way to pressure from Bradley and the SHAEF party, and he removed the Ninth Army from 21 Army Group. The plan adopted was issued without consulting me, and the staff at SHAEF had not considered the repercussions of the plan on operations in the north. The British Group of Armies struggled on with what it had got, but the whole tempo of the operations became slowed up ...

4. ... Eisenhower produced a new plan [15 April 1945] ... again I was not consulted, and again the Staff at SHAEF had not considered the repercussions on my operations in the North.

I immediately had to represent to SHAEF that I would be able to carry out my task with great difficulty and very slowly.

The only alternative was to give me less frontage on the ELBE, and at once to give me some American divisions. SHAEF became very alarmed and gave me what I asked ...

5. The net result of all this was a definite danger that the

Russians might get to LUBECK and up towards KIEL and DENMARK before we did.

6. Such is the way we run the war. We would do much better, and finish off the war far quicker, if Eisenhower could be made to understand that public opinion does not win wars. Wars are won by victories in battle, and these require sound military plans unfettered by political or national considerations.

7. This afternoon (27th April) the Operations Branch at SHAEF spoke to my Chief of Staff and said they hoped I realised the need to get over the ELBE quickly and to reach LUBECK before the Russians.

This is adding insult to injury.

I told my Chief of Staff to inform SHAEF as follows:

(a) I have always been very well aware of the urgent need to reach and cross the ELBE quickly ...

(b) It was SHAEF that had stopped this.

(c) If the Russians should get to LUBECK, and up to KIEL, and DENMARK, before we can stop it, I trust that SHAEF will declare openly that no blame is attached to 21 Army Group. The sole blame will rest with SHAEF ...[52]

The entry was initialled 'B.L.M.'

Simpson tried to console Montgomery in a letter written on 30 April, saying that the War Office sympathised greatly with his feelings on the subject of these messages from Eisenhower, and that it was 'quite needlessly irritating of the Supreme Commander to point out what had already been obvious for some time'. Simpson had shown Montgomery's letter to him of 27 April to Nye, the VCIGS, who had commented: 'It was incredible that SHAEF and the Supreme Commander should rub this point in to Monty'. But Simpson told Montgomery that he had not, however, shown the letter to Brooke, who was deeply immersed in 'other horrors', chiefly with the problems of Burma, the Far East, and Greece. By now the CIGS felt that the campaign in Europe was as good as over, and therefore wanted to concentrate on the difficulties raised in other theatres.

To add to the Field-Marshal's irritation, however, the Prime Minister, having read Eisenhower's message of 27 April, telephoned Montgomery himself and emphasised the vital need to push on to take Lübeck. These prods were timely. Montgomery had made his plans to cross the Elbe on 1 May, but after receiving Churchill's and Eisenhower's messages he advanced the date to 29 April. Even then, he only reached Lübeck a few hours ahead of the Russians.

After 27 April, Montgomery no longer had any need to write more querulous letters about Eisenhower's behaviour to his friends, Brooke and Simpson, at the War Office, for there were to be no more incidents. The war was won. The last exchange with Eisenhower at the end of April showed both commanders to be feeling the strain of the war. The Supreme Commander, egged on by his colleagues at SHAEF, did not care any longer about Montgomery's feelings, and neither was he frightened of Churchill any more, now that the latter had climbed down over the capture of Berlin and over the removal of US Ninth Army from Twenty-First Army Group. Montgomery had been so rude and abrasive with Eisenhower throughout the whole campaign that the iron had entered the American's soul. For his part, Montgomery despised Eisenhower, and resented his own minor role in the final victory.

Twenty-First Army Group, with US XVIII Airborne Corps on its right flank, crossed the Elbe against light opposition, and once they were over that river German resistance collapsed altogether. On 24 April Jodl had told the German commanders in the west that the fight against the Bolsheviks was now the only thing that mattered, and that loss of territory to the Western Allies was of secondary importance to Soviet encroachment.[53] The effect of this order was to produce immediate surrender negotiations from the German commander of the Hamburg garrison, and the city was given up to the British without a fight on 3 May. On the day before a British armoured column had entered Lübeck without opposition, and, also on the 2nd, another such column, with US troops in support, entered Wismar a few hours before the Russians. Montgomery had saved Denmark from Soviet occupation, but only in the nick of time.

On 3 May a delegation of senior German officers arrived at Montgomery's Tac HQ on Lüneburg Heath to ask for surrender terms. The envoys were Admiral von Friedenburg, on the staff of Field-Marshal Wilhelm Keitel, and General Kinsel, Chief of Staff to Field-Marshal Ernst Busch, and they were accompanied by Rear-Admiral Wagen and Major Friede, the last two described by Montgomery as 'G2s' (Staff Officers, Grade 2).

The Germans lined up outside Montgomery's caravan, their jackboots and waisted overcoats contrasting ludicrously with the workaday battledress of the British officers and men. Montgomery's first remark was 'Who are these people?' adding, 'What do they want?', although he knew perfectly well the purpose of the visit. (General Ferdinand Foch had made almost the same remark, under the same circumstances, in the Forêt de Compiègne in November 1918.) The Germans said that they had been sent by Keitel, who had given them written authority, and that they wanted to surrender to Field-Marshal Montgomery three German armies withdrawing in front of the Russians. They also wanted the Field-Marshal 'to take action to prevent the civilians in that area from falling into the hands of the Russians,' to which Montgomery replied: 'No, certainly not. Nothing to do with me – they must surrender to the Russians.'

At 1630 Montgomery telephoned Simpson at the War Office, in a 'very jaunty mood', and said that he had refused to accept the surrender, and had replied to the Germans that they must surrender to the Russians, but that if any German soldiers came into the British lines with their hands up they would be made prisoners of the British. Simpson's minute of the call goes on: 'The Germans then asked what could be done about the civilians for the "Russians would kill them all". FM Montgomery says that his only reply was "I hope so".' This sounds harsh, but General Sir Frank Simpson assures me that Montgomery did not mean it: 'Monty knew he had "finished his business" but wanted to hurry up the Germans and put an end to any argy-bargy.'[54]

During these preliminary surrender negotiations on 3 May, Montgomery asked the Germans if Keitel would surrender all his forces on the northern and western flanks of Twenty-First Army Group. The enemy officers replied that they had no authority to do so, but that they were very worried about the fate of civilians in the battle area, and were thus prepared to withdraw German forces slowly in front of a British advance so that the civilians could be spared. Montgomery then said that if that was all they had to say he must bid them 'Good morning' and get on with the battle. As they did not seem anxious to go, he showed them the battle maps – the Germans were horrified and looked 'completely collapsed'. Montgomery then said that he wanted to make three points: first, if they wanted to save German lives they must surrender unconditionally all German forces in Holland, Denmark and Schleswig-Holstein; second, once such surrender was agreed unconditionally he would discuss the best way of occupying the areas in question and of dealing with the civilians; and third, if the Germans did not agree he would continue fighting, with all the consequences that this course would have for German soldiers and civilians.

Von Friedenberg said that Keitel was in an HQ south of Kiel, and that Doenitz, C-in-C of the German Navy and acting head of the Government since Hitler's suicide on 30 April, was also there. Montgomery told Simpson that he thought that Doenitz was party to the surrender talks, and added that von Friedenberg had given his personal opinion that Doenitz and Keitel would agree to unconditional surrender. The German envoys now left, having said: 'We will try and get fresh authority and return at 1700 tomorrow', although Kinsel and Wagen asked (and were allowed) to stay behind – solitary and alien figures in the cheerful British camp.[55]

At 1600 on the next day, 4 May, Montgomery, certain of the result, assembled the war correspondents. Twenty-First Army Group had hurriedly obtained a copy of the document by which the Germans troops in Italy had surrendered (signed on 29th April and effective from 2 May), and from this a document was prepared to conclude the unconditional surrender of all enemy forces in north-east Germany, Holland and Denmark. Montgomery told the journalists: 'I am demanding they sign this piece of paper and surrender all forces facing me'; then, chuckling like a schoolboy, he added: 'If that piece of paper is signed over a million chaps will have surrendered to me. Not so bad – a million chaps. Good egg.'

A little later the German delegation arrived. The envoys filed into a tent, equipped with a single wooden table, and all sat down, together with their British counterparts. The instrument of surrender was placed before them on the table. Montgomery, enjoying himself hugely, said, like a schoolmaster, 'The German delegation will now sign in order of seniority.' The cameras clicked, and Montgomery finally said: 'I will now sign on behalf of the Supreme Commander'; then, removing his tortoiseshell spectacles, he stated: 'That concludes the surrender.' He had loved the moment; indeed, so great was his excitement that he fluffed the date while signing.

On the following day Bill Williams escorted Jodl to SHAEF HQ at Rheims, where he remarked to Bedell Smith: 'We have finished our war. If you want to finish yours, here is Jodl.' At 2.41 on 7 May, in a schoolroom in Rheims, General Alfred Jodl signed the unconditional surrender of all German armed forces to the Allies, and on the 8th he repeated the signature at Zhukov's HQ in Berlin.

On 12 May Montgomery wrote the following note for the Log:

And so the campaign in North West Europe is finished. I am glad. It has been a tough business. When I review the campaign as a whole I am amazed at the mistakes we made.

The organization for command was always faulty. The Supreme Commander [Eisenhower] had no firm ideas as to how to conduct the war, and 'was blown about by the wind' all over the place; at that particular business he was quite useless.

The Deputy Supreme Commander [Tedder] was completely ineffective; none of the Army Commanders would see him and they growled if ever he appeared on the horizon.

The staff at SHAEF were completely out of their depth all the time.

And yet we won.

The point to understand is that if we had run the show properly the war could have been finished by Xmas 1944. The blame for this must rest with the Americans.

To balance this it is merely necessary to say one thing, i.e. if the Americans had not come along and lent a hand we would never have won the war at all.

B.L.M.[56]

Montgomery knew that he would have no more battlefield triumphs, but he was content. His reputation was at its peak, and he was immensely popular. He had no intention of relaxing, wallowing in the glory of the victory he had won, although he admitted that he broke his teetotal habit on the night of 4 May and drank a sip of champagne. But on the next day his disciplined brain was grappling with the problems following the surrender – the alleviation of the suffering of the people of the occupied countries, and of displaced persons, and, above all, the well-being of the Allied POWs now being released. Demobilisation and the occupation of Germany followed, and for the remainder of his time in that country he worked ceaselessly to make the British Army happier and more efficient. Unfortunately, when later he went up the ladder to be CIGS in peacetime, the character defects which had, among other things, wrecked his relations with Eisenhower, reasserted themselves, to bring sorrow upon himself and upon his masters, the post-war Labour Government.

Conclusion

What are we to make of this remarkable man? History will record that he performed an enormous service to his country by his strong and intelligent command in the field, and by raising the nation's morale in the hour of its greatest need. Certainly he had greater qualities of leadership, and greater confidence, than any other British general, and these elements combined in him to produce the victories that were so badly needed. He possessed, too, outstanding skills in organising armies and in co-operating with the air and naval arms, and no other general had as complete a knowledge of battle techniques and of the latest weapons and equipment.

In years to come, Montgomery will be compared with the great generals of the past, a process already under way by the beginning of 1943, by which time he had become the most acclaimed British general since the Duke of Wellington. There is, too, a marked parallel with Napoleon, who with his 'ragged army' delivered to the French Republic its first military victories, the fruit of his lightning Italian campaign of 1796. During his desert campaigns Montgomery maintained direct touch with the Prime Minister, and, during his short visit to Britain in the spring of 1943, became a national hero as suddenly as had Napoleon in 1796. General Sir James Marshall-Cornwall, himself a Napoleonic as well as a modern military historian, wrote to me:

> I do not consider Montgomery just as a *bon général ordinaire*. He was more than that. In some ways he was Napoleonic and shared Napoleon's ambition, egotism and ruthlessness. He aped Napoleon's method of gaining the admiration and the affection of those serving under him.

Napoleon in later life admitted that he was never liked by any officer above the rank of captain.

It is almost certainly true that Montgomery, like Napoleon, was more popular with younger officers than with his own contemporaries.

I have relied largely upon quotations from his own writings, in all their many forms, to give a picture of Montgomery as a man. What he wrote spontaneously during the war reveals far more about his character and decisions than do his memoirs and his other books, which tend to show history as he would have liked it to be written rather than as it actually was. He had, for instance, almost a fetish for stating of an operation that everything had gone completely as he had planned, which was not always the case. Happily I have been lucky enough to unearth many hitherto unpublished letters and other documents which illuminate Montgomery's state of mind at the time, and which fill in the background to his important decisions during the campaigns.

Montgomery's letters clearly demonstrate that he always possessed complete faith in himself, and this faith seems never to have wavered. He felt that he could accomplish almost anything provided that he was given time to plan it and that he was allowed to execute it in his own way. The extreme clarity of his brain and his singleness of purpose shine through everything he wrote during the campaigns – he was completely absorbed in his work, and would not be distracted. He had, too, a great sense of the right priorities, and that single-mindedness which is the hallmark of a great man. And he had an enormous enthusiasm for defeating the Germans, an enthusiasm which he could communicate so well that it became infectious.

The exceptional harmony of Montgomery's relationship with Grigg, Brooke and Simpson shows that he possessed the ability to get on well with people of his own age provided that he had faith in them – indeed, at times this axis operated almost as a mutual admiration society. Montgomery knew that he owed his career to Brooke, and only Brooke's views would make him change his own.

When, in the course of writing this book, I met the survivors of Montgomery's close personal staff, I was impressed by their ability, integrity, good manners and obvious power to get on

well with others. I was intrigued by their accounts of the
pleasant atmosphere at Twenty-First Army Group Tac HQ, and
by their nostalgia for happy days spent working with
Montgomery. The Field-Marshal was a good chooser of men,
and had, after all, a whole army from which to pick his young
officers; naturally, anyone at all abrasive or petty-minded was
quickly weeded out of the inner circle. Those who were close to
him have emphasised to me his charm, good humour and
kindliness – in short, they did not find him a difficult 'Master', as
they affectionately called him.

Above all, Montgomery aroused devotion and loyalty
amongst those working for him, and generated efficiency. He
was, too, fortunate in Dempsey,* that most unselfish of generals,
forever prepared to accept Montgomery's views, even when they
overrode his own. General Sir Charles Richardson underlined to
me that: 'Montgomery's own staff work was so good that he
made our own job easy. No-one could pull the wool over
Monty's eyes and his orders were scrupulously obeyed.'
Retribution would undoubtedly follow for anyone who bungled
or who failed to comply. But in return, his officers knew that
they could count upon his support, and his sympathy, as just
one example illustrates. On 23 April 1945, tragically near the
German surrender, Montgomery's favourite liaison officer, John
Poston, was killed in one of the pockets of resistance already by-
passed by Twenty-First Army Group's advance. Poston,
twenty-five years old, had been with Montgomery since
Alamein, and the Field-Marshal valued his friendship and his
work highly. German youths in uniform had ambushed the
young officer's jeep while he was taking, as usual, a short cut
back to Tac HQ to report to his chief; Montgomery, learning the
news, immediately asked Simpson to get in touch with Poston's
father in England. Simpson found the latter to be greatly
distressed, the more so, rather illogically, because his other son

---

* An interesting sidelight on Montgomery's character is that he gave so
little credit to Dempsey for his part in the victories of 1944 and 1945. As
GOC, British Second Army, Dempsey played a vital part in the defeat of
Germany, but Montgomery invariably sought to give the impression, both at
the time and in his post-war writing, that he had 'done it all himself'. I found a
number of friends and former colleagues of General Sir Miles Dempsey who
resented Montgomery's failure to pay adequate tribute to his principal army
commander.

had been conscripted to the coal mines. Churchill himself had been so impressed by Montgomery's liaison officers during his visit to the Rhine that he had asked to be informed personally about any casualties, and as a result the King wrote to Poston's father, expressing regret at his loss. Montgomery himself paid a tribute to his friend in *The Times*, as he was to do for Charles Sweeney, another valued liaison officer killed soon afterwards.

At Tac HQ, Montgomery's personal accommodation consisted of three large caravans, one serving as his bedroom, another his office, and a third his map room. As accommodation the set-up was not luxurious (German and American commanders tended to prefer well-appointed châteaux) but it was convenient and fairly comfortable, and it also had a great practical advantage in that it could be moved quickly, and was easily camouflaged in woods or orchards or olive groves so as to be virtually invisible to hostile aircraft. But though Montgomery was ascetic, preferring simplicity in his surroundings and disliking alcohol and tobacco, he could enjoy luxury. In 1943 John Henderson had difficulty in persuading him to live in the beautiful villa at Taormina, on the east coast of Sicily, but once he had moved in the Field-Marshal enjoyed the surroundings. Again, Henderson booked him a suite at Claridges when he returned to London in January 1944, and he much appreciated both the comfort and the opportunity to entertain his friends. He himself, however, would never have chosen Claridges, nor the villa at Taormina.

Life at Tac HQ was happy and light-hearted, and both Henderson and Dawnay emphasised to me the 'jollity' in Montgomery's tiny mess, which echoed every evening to jokes and roars of laughter. Montgomery liked to throw out provocative remarks and then to mock his younger companions for their replies, resembling, perhaps, an unmarried Edwardian schoolmaster in his treatment of his close staff. All of them, Montgomery included, greatly enjoyed the atmosphere at Tac HQ, and the Warrant Officers, NCOs and ORs appreciated the close relationships with their commander. And, whatever rumours have been given currency, John Henderson emphasised to me that in all the time he was Montgomery's aide, from Alamein until after the end of the war, he never perceived a trace of homosexuality.

Montgomery invariably went to bed at 2130 – even when the

King or the Prime Minister were staying at Tac HQ – leaving his visitors to be looked after by his ADCs. If there were no distinguished guests once 'Master' had gone to his caravan the aides usually adjourned to the liaison officers' separate mess. Dempsey was a frequent visitor there, but only de Guingand, Graham and Williams were members of the commander's intimate mess, with its family atmosphere and its pets such as dogs, and even at one time a peacock. Montgomery always made his guests welcome, and he was an excellent host once he had relaxed after finishing his work.

Given this atmosphere of hard work, friendliness and trust, it seems grotesque that, because of his isolation, there were no regular conferences between Montgomery and Bradley and Eisenhower during the crucial moments of the campaign.

Thus we have a picture of a dedicated field commander, completely absorbed in dealing with the day-to-day problems of his armies, and reporting back to London and to SHAEF on his operations and plans. His responsibilities were awesome, yet working seven days a week over long periods, and continually having to deal with horrifying and harrowing situations, never shook his composure nor put him under strain, because each evening he relaxed in the company of his hand-picked staff, retiring at 2130 to sleep soundly until the morning. His way of life in the field resembled that of Napoleon, who also possessed a gift for relaxing and putting problems out of his head when the day's work was over, and for sleeping well.

Unfortunately, this picture of a gifted commander, working at problems and making his decisions unworried by distractions and distress, has another side. Montgomery had his defects.

He was vain, and could never bear to admit that he had been wrong. Up to a point he liked opposition to his ideas, as long as he could overcome it. He would sometimes take an impish pleasure in making mischief and sailing impudently close to the wind, although he usually knew when to call a halt to his more extreme behaviour.* He was ruthless with inefficient officers, and could suffer neither fools nor muddled thinking.

There can be no doubt that, after his desert victories, the fame

---

*A good example of this was his effort to get the Canadian General Crerar sacked in September 1944, because he wanted to replace him with Simonds, whom he liked and admired.

went to Montgomery's head. He despised the American generals, who at that time had no battle experience, and he expected them to bow to his superior expertise. At first they were ready to do so, but not for long once they had fought and won their own battles. Montgomery found it hard to realise how critical the US commanders became of him, since he was so sure that he was the best Allied general.

Given his strong individualism, the desert campaigns of 1942-43 had suited him ideally, for there he had been fighting what amounted to his own private war, with the almost nominal C-in-C, Alexander, complying with his every demand. Once the US Army arrived upon the scene, however, there was to be no possibility of Montgomery exercising sole command in the same way in subsequent campaigns. He found this hard to accept, and it galled him further that Eighth Army was relegated to parity with the Americans for the invasions of Sicily and Italy. He made a revealing remark in his memoirs about this parity: 'It was no longer to be a private war.' He knew that he was at his best in 'private wars', but from then on he was to become part of a team of commanders, and this exposed his weakness at co-operating.

Once it had become clear that the Axis forces would be thrown out of North Africa, Montgomery's eyes turned towards the major task of defeating the German armies in North-West Europe, knowing that this was essential for final victory. General Sir Charles Richardson told me that in the spring of 1943 all those with major responsibility for the desert victory felt that Eighth Army must automatically become the *corps d'élite* for the coming cross-Channel invasion. They could not believe, after the honours Eighth Army had gained since 1940, that it would be cut down in size and condemned to the relatively unimportant and profitless struggle up Sicily and Italy, a struggle which could never pay worthwhile dividends. At the time, of course (late 1943), few of those involved had any idea that the cross-Channel invasion would be delayed until the summer of 1944.

At the Casablanca conference in January 1943 Churchill and Roosevelt decided to invade Sicily and to postpone the cross-Channel attack until the summer of 1944. As we have seen, the first Allied plans for the Sicilian attack were poorly conceived, having been entrusted to staffs in widely separated centres and with little experience of the latest developments in warfare — Montgomery knew that his own planners were much more competent. The original plan was for Eighth Army to land on the south-east corner of the island, and for US Seventh Army to assault the extreme north-east tip. Montgomery demanded that this plan be torn up, and insisted that instead the British and American armies should land side by side. Given the uncertainty about the likely strength of the Italian and German resistance this was wise, although Captain Sir Basil Liddell Hart argued that if Patton's US Seventh Army had landed at Palermo in the north-west 'all the German forces in Sicily would have been trapped'.[1]

In a post-war paper on the use of Ultra by the British Army, Brigadier Williams revealed that just before the landings in Sicily Ultra had disclosed that 'the Germans had gone to the wrong side of the island.'[2] Williams told me that once the invasion armada had put to sea no alterations to the plan were possible, but he was horrified at how little information the Allies had about German troops in Sicily, except that the Hermann Goering Division was definitely there. There were no spies amongst the Sicilian population, whereas in Tunisia the Allies had learnt a great deal about German dispositions from the French living there. Brigadier Williams also doubts whether it would have been possible to provide effective air cover for a landing at Palermo.

It is a tribute to Montgomery's strength of character and to his clarity of thought that he was able to railroad Alexander and Eisenhower into accepting his plan to land the two armies side by side, despite Patton's frenzied opposition. He was, of course, a 'winning general', whereas Patton had yet to prove his prowess, and this must have weighed in the balance.

Montgomery's Sicily invasion plan worked. More troops put to sea for the invasion of Sicily than for 'Overlord', and the seaborne landings were a considerable success; indeed they were one of the greatest successes of Montgomery's career, and to him belongs the credit for their planning and execution.

The same cannot be said, however, of the airborne landings in Sicily, the first joint Allied operation with such forces. The outcome was largely disastrous, mainly because of the poor navigation of the American pilots, and many gliders were dropped in the sea or scattered over the island. Even after this failure Montgomery was considering the use of airborne troops for another drop, but Alexander, firm for once, vetoed this, signalling: 'Not prepared to sanction further use of airborne troops until training of pilots improved. Do not contemplate further use.'³

In the end, Montgomery's hopes for a quick victory in Sicily were thwarted, and when his advance along the eastern coastal route was halted, he made the mistake of refusing to allow Patton to attack to the west of Mount Etna. This infuriated the Americans, and sowed the seeds of the suspicion that was to flower in North-West Europe. When the whole of Sicily had been occupied by the Allies, after the Germans had successfully withdrawn to the mainland, the principal laurels had been won by Patton, not Montgomery.

As soon as Mussolini had been overthrown, on 25 July 1943, and Italian surrender negotiations had begun, hurried plans were made in Algiers for an invasion of the mainland of Italy. Eighth Army was to be reduced to four divisions landing in the south, with the main invasion being entrusted to Clark's US Fifth Army landing at Salerno. The scheme enraged Montgomery, for he felt that he had earned the right to be given full charge of this first invasion of the continent of Europe. Unhappily for him, he had blotted his copybook with the Americans, and as a result neither Eisenhower nor Alexander were prepared to put him in command of US divisions; instead, his favourite X Corps was taken away from him and added to Clark's forces for the Salerno landings.

Montgomery's behaviour during the Italian invasion was somewhat cynical. He knew from Ultra that the German armour was present in dangerous strength on the mainland, and he was not optimistic about the Italian army fighting effectively for the Allies if it changed sides. He would probably have been proved wrong in this last view if the planned American airborne landings on the Rome airfields had taken place, but they were unfortunately cancelled at the eleventh hour when one of the Italian generals involved panicked. After the war both American and German generals recorded that in their views the operation ('Giant II') would have succeeded, forcing the enemy to withdraw to north Italy, and this was echoed by Strong, Head of Eisenhower's Intelligence Staff,⁴ and by the German C-in-C in Italy, Kesselring, who said some years later: 'An air landing on

Rome and a sea landing nearby would have automatically caused us to evacuate all the southern half of Italy.'[5]

When Eighth Army crossed the Messina Straits unopposed and found no enemy, Montgomery made little effort to push north quickly. He felt his role to be an anti-climax, and he saw little future in the operations of his drastically reduced army at the base of the continent of Europe, faced by a strong enemy installed behind range after range of high mountains. He magnified the difficulties posed by the roads and by demolitions, and alleged that he feared a strong German armoured counter-attack, although he knew that any help Eighth Army could give to the embattled Allied beach-head at Salerno would be invaluable. During this period, as his army slowly moved north, he virtually ignored some of Alexander's instructions, yet he sent a bombastic signal to Churchill claiming to have cleared a large part of Italy, although his forces had seen very little fighting. But while he had been annoyed by his reduced role, he was not sulky. He enjoyed looking after the well-being of his troops and building up a strong base on the mainland of Europe.

When the Germans retreated from Salerno, Montgomery had no enthusiasm for Eighth Army's hard slog up Italy parallel with Clark, whose generalship he despised. The glittering prize of Rome lay on the American route, and Montgomery, after one bold and successful amphibious operation at Termoli, became resigned to unrewarding battles in the mountains and on the Adriatic coast. Again he signalled direct to Churchill, this time hoping soon 'to meet him in Rome'.

He wanted to keep his claims for command of the Second Front in front of the Prime Minister, but when the CIGS visited him in October 1943 he found him tired and pessimistic, and 'in need of a change'. Churchill himself was deeply critical of Eighth Army's slow progress, and became scathing about the stagnation of the Italian campaign and about Montgomery's failure to carry out amphibious landings on his front.[6] He considered that Alexander and Montgomery had failed to exploit the great opportunity that the possession of large numbers of landing-craft, combined with air and sea superiority, gave them to deal the Germans deadly blows in Italy[7] (Brooke had reported this failure to Churchill on his return to London).

As a result, it was touch-and-go whether Montgomery would be given command of the Second Front. Churchill's enthusiasm for his general was waning, and Eisenhower had a strong preference for Alexander. Montgomery was nearly left to kick his heels in Italy, where his full potential would never have been realised, although his expertise might have made a success of the attack on the Gothic Line in August 1944, which would have opened up Austria to the Allies. Instead, the attack on the Gothic Line became a costly failure under Alexander and General Sir Oliver Leese, who had replaced Montgomery as GOC, Eighth Army.

When, in December 1943, he was appointed C-in-C, British Group of Armies and Allied Armies, Northern France, Montgomery knew that his moment had come. He believed — correctly — that no one else in the British Army (except Brooke) was so well qualified for the job, and he had supreme confidence not only in his organisational ability and knowledge of modern weapons, but also in his power to enthuse the troops.

In addition, his health was superb, and in this perhaps lies a mystery. While in Palestine in 1939 he became seriously ill with pleurisy and suspected TB, and had had to be carried as a stretcher case aboard the boat taking him home. Yet he made a spectacular recovery while on board ship, and as soon as he was given command of a division, shortly after his return, he never looked back. John Henderson told me that he never knew Montgomery to be ill in all the time from Alamein to Lüneburg Heath, and that although he occasionally suffered from colds his staff took it for granted that he was always well. But within a few weeks of the German surrender he was ill in bed with tonsillitis, and he was never to be so fit again after the war. It seems likely that there was a psychological link between his good health and his intense involvement in all-absorbing work.

Montgomery's arrival in London in the first days of 1944 proved to be a tonic for the entire Allied invasion organisation, which until then had suffered from nervousness and from conflicting views about how to carry out the cross-Channel assault. His clear, well thought-out plans removed doubts and created unity and confidence in a confused and jealous command. At this stage Eisenhower had complete faith in his subordinate and delegated the bulk of the planning to him; Montgomery rightly insisted on widening the invasion front and increasing the number of ships to be used. During the planning, surprisingly, in view of what happened later, the Americans were content for Montgomery to command their troops during the assault phase, for they admired his battle successes and found his confidence infectious.

In early 1944 morale was low in the British Army in the UK, and few troops had done any previous fighting. Montgomery's technique of addressing personally all the fighting units worked wonders for the confidence of these troops. Of course, not every soldier fell for his somewhat bombastic approach, but there is undeniable evidence of how greatly he improved morale by his visits. With the Poles and Canadians, however, he was less successful.

D-Day vindicated Montgomery's judgements and planning, although early enemy opposition was weaker than had been anticipated. He proved to have been right about the need for the Hobart tank gadgets to avoid the disasters of the Dieppe raid, and floating DD tanks and flail attachments for clearing minefields undoubtedly made a considerable contribution to the success of the landings. Afterwards the Americans bitterly regretted that they had not taken up his generous offer of a much larger share of these adapted tanks.

From the start of the planning Montgomery had formulated his plan for the British to attract Rommel's armour to the east and for the Americans to break through in the west. Unfortunately, he gave perhaps too many hostages to fortune by promising the British air marshals that he would capture the airfields south of Caen, although he knew that this would be difficult, and was himself perfectly happy to have the RAF operating from England. The failure to take these airfields led to quarrels with the RAF chiefs.

The Deputy Supreme Commander, Air Chief Marshal Tedder, became hostile. He never forgave Montgomery for stating that he was prepared to go on with the invasion on the orginal planned date in atrocious weather when the other leaders were voting for postponement. In his memoirs, Tedder recorded that he took this to mean that Montgomery despised the support of the RAF, which could not operate in the forecast cloud cover. Montgomery never explained his vote, but it is probable that he was very conscious of the fact that his troops had already embarked, and also that the vital surprise could so easily have been lost. But, as with the Americans, his alienation of Tedder would bring him problems later.

Montgomery definitely underestimated the difficulties of the Normandy bocage in the American sector, while the Americans were very conscious that the British armour at Caen faced perfect tank country whereas, until the adoption of the Rhinoceros tank attachment, US tanks could only move on the roads. Montgomery's dilemma was that, although he had plenty of tanks, he was constantly being reminded by the War Office that the British Army was so short of reinforcements that he must not risk really heavy manpower casualties. In consequence he had to be careful not to risk too many British lives in an all-out attack to the south of Caen. The Americans, on the other hand, had many fresh divisions on the other side of the Atlantic, and Montgomery knew that in the Allied interest the US Army ought to bear the brunt of the fighting in the crucial break-out. Yet it was almost impossible to explain this to an ally, and in any case Montgomery was not temperamentally suited to so delicate a task. Not surprisingly, there were quarrels and tensions during the twelve weeks of stalemate.

At the outset, Eisenhower accepted Montgomery's master plan for the British to hold Rommel's tanks in the east while Bradley's US First Army broke out in the west. The Supreme Commander soon became restive, however, as the British attacks around Caen failed, and he disapproved of the Americans having to make the main attack with the handicap of the bocage country. His letters to Montgomery, whom he seldom saw, became progressively more hectoring in their tone. In addition, Eisenhower's HQ held four Montgomery opponents – Tedder, the Depty Supreme Commander, and the British generals Gale, Morgan and Whiteley; Strong, a late arrival, also turned anti-Montgomery. These senior officers owed their chief allegiance to Eisenhower, who possessed a charm which threw a 'spell' over those who worked with him. It was fortunate for Montgomery that the CIGS, Brooke, and the Secretary of State for War, Grigg, were his devoted admirers. These two were well aware of Montgomery's capacity for rubbing the Americans the wrong way, but they were so sure that his strategy was right that they backed him to the hilt, and the two were nearly always in agreement themselves. Brooke wrote of Grigg in his diary: 'P.J. is a wonderful help. The more I saw of him the more I liked him, respected him and admired him. He had one of the quickest brains that I had ever met and a character based on the highest ideals. Thank heaven I had him as S of S during all my difficult times with the P.M.' Grigg admired Montgomery (they became such firm friends that after the war he advised Montgomery on his personal finances), but although he gave his friend unstinted support in the controversies, this signal, dated 31 May 1945, demonstrates that he understood the Field-Marshal's failings: 'I beseech you in the bowels of Christ to watch your step or at any rate your loud speaker so long as SHAEF exists. I have quite enough quarrels to cope with.'[8]

As the Normandy campaign proceeded SHAEF became more and more hostile to the War Office and to Twenty-First Army Group. As Eisenhower began to express concern at this rift, Brooke sent the ever-tactful Simpson several times to SHAEF to try and pour oil on the troubled waters. But anti-Montgomery feeling continued amongst the British senior officers on Eisenhower's staff, an attitude described graphically by Williams:

> I knew Jock Whiteley well as BGS, Eighth Army and I liked him very much. He, Kenneth Strong and Freddie Morgan, who I also liked, developed a tremendous pro-SHAEF bias. Whiteley's loyalty to Ike started with 'Torch' [the North African landings], and he became progressively more and more anti-Monty. Pinky Bull was joint Operations Officer with Whiteley and, being American, had the lion's share of the responsibility. Whiteley was frustrated alongside Pinky Bull because he had no proper role.
>
> Morgan and Whiteley (despite having no satisfactory role) felt SHAEF was running the war, and they got fed up with 21 Army Group's independence of view. Monty continually rubbed them up the wrong way.
>
> Morgan and Whiteley were always under suspicion at SHAEF, which was dominantly an American HQ, because they were 'limeys'. Therefore they had to over-work their passages to be accepted properly, and latterly this meant being anti-Monty and anti-21 Army Group.

The American historian Forrest C. Pogue has written to me that Brigadier Williams has 'one of the most balanced views on the British-American relationship' that he has seen. If, as seems highly likely, Williams is correct about the prejudices at

SHAEF, then Montgomery was faced with an impossible task in trying to keep on the best of terms with such a set-up. Given his temperament, it is perhaps no wonder that he failed. Pogue also admits in this letter that Bedell Smith could be 'very nasty and brutal but also could be very understanding', and the first-mentioned failings cannot have helped relations between SHAEF and Twenty-First Army Group and its commander.

In the middle of July 1944 arguments from within SHAEF that Montgomery should be sacked erupted as the enemy held firm at Caen. Eisenhower, who still admired his subordinate to a certain extent, reluctantly yielded to his colleagues and prepared to ask Churchill to replace Montgomery. At this difficult stage of the Normandy campaign, following the unsatisfactory performance of Eighth Army in Italy, the Prime Minister was, in Brooke's words, 'not always too fond of Montgomery', and for a short period in July the latter's command was in jeopardy. But if he had been recalled he would have been replaced by Alexander, and this would undoubtedly have been a setback for the Allied cause.

At the same time Montgomery made a dangerous error in letting it be known that he did not wish Churchill to visit his HQ when the latter was to be in France on 20 July. Brooke, at that particular moment very anti-Churchill himself, forced Montgomery in the nick of time to send the Prime Minister a warm invitation to come and stay at his Tac HQ. The visit was a great success, for Montgomery mended his bridges with the Prime Minister and kept them in good repair for the rest of the campaign. This personal success with Churchill is evidence of Montgomery's considerable charm and personal magnetism. The campaign in Normandy had at that time the appearance of having reached a stalemate, yet Montgomery succeeded in convincing his visitor (who was not without a reputation for sacking generals) that all was well and that victory was around the corner.

Fortunately for Montgomery, it was. Within a few days the Americans were sweeping all before them towards Brittany and the Seine, although Twenty-First Army Group made disappointing progress towards Falaise and Argentan. But it was a strategic error to permit some of the American divisions to 'turn their backs' on the defeated Germans in an effort to overrun the Brittany ports instead. This was rigid adherence to the by-now out-of-date pre-invasion plan, which had laid down the next step as being the capture of the Brittany ports for the build-up of reinforcements and supplies direct from America. On 20 July Montgomery had told Eisenhower that 'We must get the Brittany peninsula. From an administrative point of view it is essential,'[9] and the two commanders had no further discussions about it, although Eisenhower echoed this in a letter on the following day: 'Time is vital. We must not only have the Brittany peninsula. We must have it quickly.'[10] It is strange that neither general, then or later, queried the wisdom of detaching so many American troops and sending them towards Brest, when an entire German army lay within their grasp.

When, on 31 July, the Americans broke out at Avranches, there were only a few German battalions defending the ninety-mile corridor between that point and the Loire, and US 4th Armoured Division, which had spearheaded the Avranches break-out, could have advanced east towards Paris almost without opposition. Instead, it was halted and the German forces, battered but still coherent, pulled back to the Seine, although most of their tanks and equipment were lost in the Falaise Gap and they suffered some 400,000 casualties killed, wounded, missing or made prisoner.

According to Liddell Hart, after the breakthrough at Avranches on 31 July 'American spearheads could have driven eastwards unopposed ... the Allied High Command threw away the best chance of exploiting this great opportunity by sticking to the outdated pre-invasion programme in which a westward move to capture the Britanny Ports was to be the next step.'[11]

In the event, Montgomery decided to send only one of Patton's corps towards Brest although the original 'Overlord' plan involved all US Third Army going into Brittany. This was sensible, and probably as much as he could do under the circumstances, since Eisenhower had divided the British and Americans into two groups with effect from 1 August. Montgomery was to retain operational control and 'tactical co-ordination of both Army Groups' until SHAEF, under Eisenhower, became operational as an HQ in France on 1 September. Thus on 31 July Montgomery could hardly, on his own initiative, have ordered the Americans to abandon the entire preconceived plan to capture the Brittany ports. Unfortunately, and largely because of Montgomery's aloofness, no conferences were held between him, Eisenhower and Bradley to consider how best to exploit the heaven-sent opportunity provided by the near-collapse of the German forces facing them.

Whatever the rights and wrongs of the controversy over closing the Falaise Gap, in the final battle for Normandy Twenty-First Army Group's progress towards Argentan was undoubtedly slow, and the American sweep into Brittany and drive towards the Seine stole the headlines. Montgomery, impervious to the criticism of slowness, felt strongly that it was his victory because his own master plan was responsible for the success. He felt that he deserved to continue in sole command and, according to Bill Williams, hoped against hope that Eisenhower would not take away his overall command on 1 September. He could not realise that politically this was impossible as 'it had to be an American victory', although Brigadier Williams told me that he had emphasised this point to his chief. Brooke and Grigg foolishly encouraged Montgomery to believe that he ought to retain overall command, ignoring the fact that Marshall had firmly told Eisenhower that for political reasons he must immediately assume the land command. Not unnaturally, Eisenhower deeply resented Montgomery's opposition to his taking over command.

Montgomery despised Eisenhower as a field commander, and made no secret of this contempt, which was echoed by Brooke. There can be no doubt, however, that if Grigg and Brooke had firmly told Montgomery to keep his peace and to accept the Supreme Commander's authority then the hideous internecine quarrels between the two commanders would have been avoided.

In the middle of August, Montgomery conceived a plan whereby, after crossing the Seine, the British and US forces should keep together as a solid mass of forty divisions, a mass so strong that it need fear nothing and which should advance northwards to Antwerp and Aachen with its right flank on the Ardennes.

The Americans would not hear of this, however. Twenty-First Army Group had crossed the Seine well behind the Americans, and Bradley and Patton were eager for the US armies to make the main thrust past the Saar to the Rhine, south of Frankfurt, with the British northern thrust reduced to a secondary role. Here began the controversy over the northern ('narrow front') thrust which was to bedevil Montgomery's relations with his allies for the rest of the war.

Was Montgomery's plan to use forty divisions in the north sound? Not in Field-Marshal Lord Carver's opinion. He told me that:

> Montgomery's single pencil-like thrust into Germany was never on. Montgomery would have run into dead trouble when he got over the Ijssel River, if not before, no matter how many divisions Ike had given him. He was dependent on the road bridges; we could not use railways, and only a few of his divisions could have been deployed against the reorganised German armies on the German plain.

De Guingand held the same view.

Liddell Hart felt that Montgomery's single concentrated thrust was better in principle than Eisenhower's broad-front advance to the Rhine, but that it foundered because Twenty-First Army Group did not keep up the pace after Brussels and Antwerp were taken, and because supplies did not arrive fast enough. Liddell Hart's view was that in the event 'the best chance of a quick finish was lost when the gas was turned off from Patton's tanks in the last week of August, when they were 100 miles nearer to the Rhine than the British.'[12] It is doubtful, however, whether Patton's fuel supplies were actually 'turned off'.

Montgomery, to his credit, given his keenness on the northern thrust, nevertheless argued with Eisenhower that as long as the supplies were concentrated on one or other of the advances, it did not matter if it was an American southern thrust or a British northern one. What frustrated him was dissipating the Allied resources on more than one major assault over the German frontier.

After Brussels and Antwerp had fallen, early in September 1944, Montgomery made a fatal mistake by failing to seal off immediately the large German army in the South Beveland peninsula, at the eastern base of which, a bare twenty miles north-west of Antwerp, there is a bottleneck only a few hundred yards wide. Through that bottleneck a large part of German Fifteenth Army escaped. He compounded this mistake, against the strong advice both of Dempsey and of his own staff, by opting for the disastrous airborne landings at Arnhem. Eisenhower weakly accepted Montgomery's Arnhem gamble against his better judgement, although he himself was convinced that without the port of Antwerp in operation the Allies would be in difficulties, even if the attempt to seize the Rhine bridge at Arnhem had succeeded.

Three days before the Arnhem drop Eisenhower had written in a letter to Marshall that 'Montgomery suddenly became obsessed with the idea that his Army Group could rush right on into Berlin provided we gave him all the maintenance that was in the theatre ... Examination of this scheme exposes is as a fantastic idea.'[13] But if the Supreme Commander thought so strongly that Montgomery's northern thrust through Arnhem into the plains of north-west Germany could not succeed, then it is extraordinary that he should have endorsed the risky 'Market-Garden' operation, which put at risk – and all but destroyed – virtually the entire SHAEF strategic reserve. This letter (reproduced in full in the Appendix) must bring into question Eisenhower's reputation and performance as a commander.

Euphoria prevailed amongst the Allies in early September. Like almost everyone else Montgomery believed that the war was over, that it was merely a matter of inflicting the *coup de grâce*. After all, in 1918 the Kaiser had been deposed and the Germans had surrendered when their armies had suffered a far less severe defeat in the west. However, none of the planners had conceived of – nor dared hope for – such a total defeat of the Germans in Normandy, and in consequence there was no plan to exploit the opportunities thus afforded.

Montgomery can perhaps be pardoned for mistakes made in the euphoria of the early days of September 1944, when he believed that his task was almost accomplished. Few people could have believed that the German nation could be so blind as to follow, devotedly, a megalomaniac prepared to devastate his country and to squander his nation's blood, continuing a hopeless defensive war with the sole object of preserving his personal power. Nor could anyone have foreseen that schoolboys would take up arms and fight, courageously and with a fanatical devotion to Hitlerism, so that the new German armies, hurriedly raised in the autumn of 1944, were almost as enthusiastic as those raised in the early stages of the war.

The German will to resist was further stiffened by the Allied policies of unconditional surrender, indiscriminate bombing, and the threat of wholesale trials of German military leaders as war criminals. The formulation of this policy had been nothing to do with Montgomery and when, towards the end of the war, he was consulted by Eisenhower as to whether German generals willing to surrender* should be offered immunity from war crimes trials, he sensibly favoured immunity.[14]

Unperturbed by his failures at Antwerp and Arnhem, Montgomery conducted the rest of a difficult campaign skilfully. Unhappily, however, his intelligent and restrained command of American troops during the Ardennes crisis was overshadowed by his unfortunate press conference, which intensified sharply Eisenhower's hostility. Montgomery displayed considerable naivety over this press conference, telling Dawnay to write in the Log: 'These remarks had a very good reception in the press in America and did a great deal towards calming the anti-British campaign in the country.'[15] In fact, they had precisely the opposite effect.

Early in 1945, Eisenhower was much disturbed at Churchill's suggestion – virtually a decision – that Alexander should replace Tedder as Deputy Commander, SHAEF. With Alexander at his side, the Supreme Commander would have found it considerably more difficult to refuse Montgomery's demands, which were almost invariably backed by the British Chiefs of Staff. We know from Eisenhower's papers that Marshall had told him to withdraw US Ninth Army from Twenty-First Army Group for the final victory; this, Eisenhower knew, would be bound to infuriate Montgomery – who would have the full support of Churchill – so he did not want to have Alexander breathing down his neck, thus making his task in dealing with Montgomery so much the harder.

Eisenhower visited Montgomery twice in February 1945, at Namur and Zondhoven, and on each occasion the latter instructed Dawnay to put detailed accounts of the conversations in the Log. From these it is clear that Eisenhower gave the impression that US Ninth Army would stay under Montgomery's command until the end of the war; furthermore,

---

* The German Generals Westphal, Blaskowitz and von Zangen (respectively Chief of Staff to von Rundstedt; GOC, Army Group H; and GOC, Fifteenth Army) had by then made surrender approaches to the Allies.

he sought the Field-Marshal's help in persuading Churchill not to bring Alexander to France, arguing that the existing command arrangements were satisfactory. Accordingly Montgomery, in contradiction of his earlier views, firmly told the Prime Minister that he did not think it would be a good idea for Alexander to come to SHAEF in place of Tedder. Churchill, although extremely annoyed, was compelled to accept this, much to Eisenhower's relief. Plainly Montgomery was utterly unaware that the Americans intended to remove US Ninth Army from his command, and that Eisenhower was, even then, already contemplating not attacking Berlin.

If Alexander had been appointed Deputy Commander, SHAEF, then Eisenhower would have been forced to give Twenty-First Army Group a much more important (and thus more glamorous) role in the final advance. The only possible conclusion is that the Supreme Commander used his considerable charm to fool Montgomery into thinking that their past differences were forgotten, and that the allotted American troops would stay under Twenty-First Army Group command for the final drive on Berlin.

Eisenhower's true intentions were revealed at the end of March 1945. Irritated by the somewhat overblown publicity for the British crossing of the Rhine, the Supreme Commander shocked Montgomery by peremptorily withdrawing US Ninth Army from Twenty-First Army Group, and by forbidding the British force to push on to Berlin, relegating it instead to the role of occupying Holland and sealing off Denmark from the Russians. Brigadier Williams's view is that:

Ike felt he had given Monty full rein, and the time had come to give firm orders to him. Ike's colleagues at SHAEF wanted him to clobber Monty and told him: 'Give him orders instead of arguing; never get into an argument with Monty because you are likely to lose it.' Ike was also fed up with Winston who was continually telling him what to do. He decided he was tired of Winston and now the war was almost won he would get on with it in his own way.

Despite the confusion and wrath of his allies, the Supreme Commander was set in his course, and would not alter his decisions. Marshall and the other US commanders, as well as

American public opinion, were all on his side, and American men and material were fuelling the defeat of Nazism to a far greater degree than the other western allies. Churchill was as angry as Montgomery, and protested vigorously, if fruitlessly, to both Eisenhower and Roosevelt about the abrupt change in the Allied plan. The Prime Minister did not take up the cudgels for long, however, for he had learned of Eisenhower's increasing impatience with him, and the war was too nearly over for more quarrels. Brooke, the staunchest of Montgomery's supporters, refused for once to involve himself since, with the European campaign all but won, his eyes were turned on the continuing problems in the Far East. He wrote laconically in his diary: 'It is all a pity straightforward strategy is affected by nationalistic outlook,' a comment which serves admirably as an epitaph on the later actions of both Montgomery and Eisenhower.

To his credit Montgomery, although he told Simpson that Eisenhower 'had double-crossed him', quickly learned to ignore the whole galling incident. As usual his mind was fully occupied with his fighting troops and with the plans for the hectic advance, and while the war continued he bore no resentment. He was, however, right in claiming that Berlin had importance, and that Twenty-First Army Group was well poised to capture it, for although the occupation zones had been agreed at Yalta, Churchill was prepared to re-open negotiations with the Russians over the allotment of these areas. There can be little doubt that if Twenty-First Army Group had taken Berlin, in accordance with the original Allied plan, then the map of Europe would be different today.

Field-Marshal Sir Bernard Law Montgomery, later first Viscount Montgomery of Alamein, helped shape that map, and no view of him can be entirely one-sided. Bedell Smith provided a clear assessment in a previously unpublished letter to Eisenhower, written in April 1948:

> When I last talked with Bradley and we drifted to the subject of Montgomery, he said with far more violence than I have ever known from him before: 'Montgomery is a third-rate general and he never did anything or won any battle that any other general could not have won as well or better.'
>
> As you well know, I am no Montgomery lover, but I give

him his full due and believe that for certain types of operation he is without an equal. On the other hand, he would not have been worth a damn for the wide sweeping manoeuvre where Patton shone so brilliantly in the public eye. Nevertheless his intransigent attitude and behind the scenes conniving to get his way with regard to military operations, to enhance his own prestige and to obtain a major measure of command, are certainly deserving of the most severe censure by any unprejudiced observer. Of course, I cannot claim to be an unprejudiced observer.[16]

It is sad that Bradley became so bitter and unfair about Montgomery, since during the Normandy campaign the two commanders had enjoyed a degree of trust and friendship; indeed, Bradley had commented of that period: 'I could not have wanted a more tolerant or judicious commander.' Probably the iron entered the American general's soul after the humiliating reverses in the Ardennes, and Montgomery's infamous press conference.

There can be few who would quarrel with Bedell Smith's verdict that Montgomery was 'without an equal' in well prepared assaults such as the cross-Channel invasion, and in sustaining his troops during prolonged and difficult operations. Any weakness he had as a commander lay in his occasional failure to seize the unexpected opportunity, and here his isolation was a contributory factor.

Again, Bedell Smith is probably correct in saying that Montgomery deserved 'severe censure' for his 'behind the scenes conniving to get his way' and a bigger share of the command and prestige. Certainly his dislike of playing second fiddle led to a shameful tale of bickering with Eisenhower throughout the campaign in North-West Europe. Nevertheless, the evidence uncovered can only lead one to believe that Brooke and Grigg, in their continual encouragement of Montgomery to seek sole command when, politically, such a course was impossible, were as much or more to blame.

Appendix

Important Eisenhower and Montgomery Documents

While Eisenhower was in Washington in January 1944, Montgomery was exerting pressure for 'Anvil' (the invasion of the South of France) to be abandoned. These signals to Bedell Smith and Montgomery in London show that the Supreme Commander accepted that 'Overlord' (the cross-Channel invasion) should be strengthened at the expense of 'Anvil', but that he obstinately refused to give up that invasion altogether. In the event, 'Anvil' did not draw a single German division away from the Normandy front, but Eisenhower always claimed that the port of Marseilles, liberated on 28 August, was an important help in supplying his eastern armies.

January 5, 1944

From Commander in Chief to General Smith for his eyes only.

Just as I am departing for a short journey, your W-9389 has reached me. I have agreed to the turnover of Allied Mediterranean Command as of January 8, and my opinions as to further operations there are advisory only. I agree that OVERLORD must be more broadly based, but I do not agree that a threat of ANVIL will be as effective as the operation itself. The right answer consists, I believe, in starting now to gather up and recondition all landing craft so as to produce the maximum number in May. This would mean abandonment of SHINGLE [the Anzio landings, 22 January 1944], but entirely aside from OVER-LORD—ANVIL considerations, that operation is open to grave objections under present conditions. Moreover we must resort to use of all types of unarmored craft for use of everything except assaulting waves, both in OVERLORD and ANVIL. We must insist on finding them now and planning carefully for their maximum use. I agree that some redistribution of armored landing craft in favor of OVERLORD as against ANVIL may be necessary, but in both operations we must develop the maximum in expedient and substitute to increase lift. Only in event that OVERLORD cannot possibly be broadened without abandonment of ANVIL would I consider making such a recommendation to the Combined Chiefs. I am passing your radio to OPD for examination during my absence from city with the special request that everyone turn on the heat in finding craft to support armored landing craft in both operations. Please let me know promptly of developments at your conference on January 8. Your recommendations of Morgan as Deputy Chief of Staff and Whiteley as G-2 are acceptable to me.[1]

January 13, 1944

To Theater Commander for his eyes only for Montgomery from Eisenhower.

I will go into the matters brought up by your W-9418, January 10 on my arrival which will be very soon. I have been discussing them intensively with the Staff here. The following considerations appear pertinent. The desirability of strengthening OVERLORD is universally accepted. However we must not lose sight of the advantages to OVERLORD which ANVIL brings. The fact that ANVIL presents the only opportunity for use of the large land forces in the Mediterranean to aid OVERLORD directly is important. This consideration is particularly applicable in the period from 10 to 15 days after launching the attack. Furthermore there are certain strong considerations not purely military which have been brought to my attention here and which must be weighed. My own conviction is that OVERLORD should be strengthened to the maximum possible but the abandonment of ANVIL should be accepted only as a last resort.[2]

At the beginning of July Eisenhower, prodded by Tedder and Cunningham, became increasingly worried that Montgomery's attacks around Caen were not being pressed hard enough; indeed Tedder told the Supreme Commander that they were 'company exercises'.[3] Eisenhower's letter of 7 July, and Montgomery's reply, demonstrate how far apart the two commanders had drawn in this most critical period.

PERSONAL

7 July 1944

Dear Monty,

Since returning here I have been studying our existing situation and future prospects, particularly in consultation with G-2 and the Air Commanders.

When we began this operation we demanded from the air that they obtain air superiority and that they delay the arrival of enemy reinforcements in the NEPTUNE area. Both of these things have been done. In the meantime, in spite of storms and hard luck, our ground build-up has proceeded rapidly and on the British side we are approaching the limit of our available resources. Very soon, also, we will be approaching the limit in the capacity of the ports now in our possession to receive and maintain American troops. Thereafter it is possible for the enemy to increase his *relative* strength; actually he seems to be doing so already.

These things make it necessary to examine every single possibility with a view to expanding our beachhead and getting more room for manoeuvring so as to use our forces *before* the enemy can obtain substantial equality in such things as infantry, tanks and artillery. On the left we need depth and elbow room and at least enough territory to protect the SWORD beach from enemy fire. We should, by all means, secure suitable air fields. On the right we need to obtain additional small ports that are available on the north side of the Brittany coast and to break out into the open where our present superiority can be used.

I am familiar with your plan for generally holding firmly with your left, attracting thereto all of the enemy armor, while your right pushes down the Peninsula and threatens the rear and flank of the forces facing the Second British Army. However, the advance on the right has been slow and laborious, due not only to the nature of the country and the impossibility of employing air and artillery with maximum effectiveness, but to the arrival on that front of [German] reinforcements, I believe the 353rd Div. In the meantime, I understand from G-2 that some infantry has arrived on the front opposite the British Army allowing the enemy to withdraw certain Panzer elements for re-grouping and establishing a reserve.

It appears to me that we must use all possible energy in a determined effort to prevent a stalemate or of facing the necessity of fighting a major defensive battle with the slight depth we now have in the bridgehead.

We have not yet attempted a major full-dress attack on the left flank supported by everything we could bring to bear. To do so would require some good weather, so that our air could give maximum assistance. Through Coningham and Broadhurst there is available all the air that could be used, even if it were determined to be necessary to resort to area bombing in order to soften up the defense. On the right, about the only way I could visualize helping out would be launching an airborne operation against St. Malo.

At one time this was reported to me as impracticable because of the strength of the defensive garrison at that point. I am having the matter re-examined in the light of information that the enemy has thinned out very considerably in that region. The First British Airborne Division is now available and if it could seize the port and a U.S. Infantry Division could follow in quickly by sea, they could, from that position, assist materially in getting your right flank rapidly down the Contentin Peninsula.

Because of the transfers that we have to make to the Mediterranean to help out in ANVIL, I think we cannot put on a full-scale three or four division airborne attack before early September. We are planning for this eventuality but in the meantime we will have the lift for more than a full division and the moon will again be right for such operations along about August 3rd or 4th.

I know that you are thinking every minute about these

weighty questions. What I want you to know is that I will back you up to the limit in any effort you may decide upon to prevent a deadlock and will do my best to phase forward any unit you might find necessary. For example, if you could use in an attack on your left flank an American armored division, I would be glad to make it available and get it in to you as soon as possible.

Beedle [Bedell Smith] tells me that he was prevented by weather from dropping in to see you the other day, but will be coming over soon. Possibly he will bring this letter. In the meantime, please be assured that I will produce everything that is humanly possible to assist you in any plan that promises to get us the elbow room we need. The air and everything else will be available.

If you get a chance to talk to Beedle, please give him any views you have on these matters, so whatever duties or planning may devolve on my headquarters can be expeditiously carried out.

With best of luck.

Sincerely
Ike

My dear Ike,   8th July 1944

1. Thank you for your letter of 7 July.

2. I am, myself, quite happy about the situation. I have been working throughout on a very definite plan, and I now begin to see daylight.

3. Initially, my main pre-occupations were:

    (a) to ensure that we kept the initiative,

         and,

    (b) to have no setbacks or reverses.

It was not always too easy to comply with these two fundamental principles especially during the period when we were not too strong ourselves and were trying to build up our strength. But that period is now over, and we can now set about the enemy – and are doing so.

4. I think we must be quite clear as to what is vital, and what is not; if we get our sense of values wrong we may go astray. There are three things which stand out very clearly in my mind:

(a) *First*

We must get the Brittany peninsula. From an administrative point of view this is essential; if we do NOT get it we will be greatly handicapped in developing our full potential.

(b) *Second*

We do not want to get hemmed in to a relatively small area; we must have space – for manoeuvre, for administration, and for airfields.

(c) *Third*

We want to engage the enemy in battle, to write-off his troops, and generally to kill Germans. Exactly where we do this does not matter, so long as (a) and (b) are complied with.

5. The first thing we had to do was to capture CHERBOURG.

I wanted CAEN too, but we could not manage both at the same time and it was clear to me that the enemy would resist fiercely in the CAEN sector.

So I laid plans to develop operations towards the R. ODON on the Second Army front, designed to draw the enemy reserves on to the British sector so that the First US Army could get to do its business in the west all the easier. We were greatly hampered by very bad weather and the offensive towards the ODON did not begin till 26 June, on which date the enemy commander at CHERBOURG was captured and the port was practically in First Army hands.

But this offensive *did* draw a great deal on to it; and I then gave instructions to the First Army to get on quickly with its offensive southwards on the western flank. There were problems of reorganisation, and re-grouping, and bad weather on the beaches; and First Army offensive could not begin before 3 July.

6. The First Army advance on the right has been slower that I thought would be the case; the country is terribly close, the weather has been atrocious, and certain enemy reserves have been brought in against it.

So I then decided to set my eastern flank alight, and to put the wind up the enemy by seizing CAEN and getting bridgeheads over the ORNE; this action would, indirectly, help the business going on over on the western flank.

These operations by Second Army on the eastern flank began today; they are going very well; they aim at securing CAEN and at getting our eastern flank on the ORNE river — with bridgeheads over it.

7. Having got our eastern flank on the ORNE, I shall then organise the operations on the eastern flank so that our affairs on the western flank can be got on with the quicker.

It may be that the best proposition is for the Second Army to continue its effort, and to drive southwards with its left flank on the ORNE; or it may be a good proposition for it to cross the ORNE and establish itself on the FALAISE road.

Alternatively, having got CAEN and established the eastern flank on the ORNE, it may be best for Second Army to take over all the CAUMONT area — and to the west of it — and thus release some of Bradley's divisions for the southward 'drive' on the western flank.

8. Day to day events in the next few days will show which is best.

The attack of Second Army towards CAEN, which is going on now, is a big show; so far only 1 Corps is engaged; 8 Corps takes up the running on Monday morning (10 July).

I shall put everything into it.

It is all part of the bigger tactical plan, and it is all in accordance with para 4 above.

9. I am not anxious to seize ST. MALO by an airborne operation if it can be avoided. I would much prefer to take it from the land and this is what I hope to do — vide my M505 dated 30 June. But it may happen that Bradley's southward move is very slow and requires help to get down the Cotentin peninsula, in this case an air and sea move against ST. MALO might become necessary, and it is being planned in case it is needed.

10. I am very anxious to secure the Quiberon Bay area so that we can get a move on with developing it for our administrative needs.

This would be done sometime about the first week in August — when I hope 8 U.S. Corps will have turned the corner and be heading for RENNES and ST. MALO.

This operation is being planned.

11. I do not need an American armoured division for use on my eastern flank; we really have all the armour we need. The

great thing now is to get First and Third U.S. Armies up to a good strength, and to get them cracking on the southward thrust on the western flank, and then to turn Patton westwards into the Brittany peninsula.

12. To sum up.

I think the battle is going very well. The enemy is being heavily attacked all along the line; and we are killing a lot of Germans.

Of one thing you can be quite sure — there will be no stalemate.

If the enemy decides to concentrate very great and overwhelming strength against us, that will take a considerable time; and during that time we will relentlessly get on with *our* business; we are very strong now and need not delay any longer for build-up purposes.

I shall always ensure that I am well balanced; at present I have no fears of any offensive move the enemy might make; I am concentrating on making the battle swing our way.

Yours ever
Monty[4]

On 14 July Eisenhower wrote again. His letter is evidence that he was hoping strongly that the main attack and break-out would be achieved by the forces on Montgomery's east flank, and not by the Americans in the west. The British general's strategy, however, was only to hold the enemy in the east, hoping for a break-out in the west. The letter was also an undisguised 'prod', an attempt to get Montgomery to attack as hard as possible.

14 July 1944

Dear Monty:

Through our recent exchange of telegrams I clearly understand the proposed timing of the impending operations.

With respect to the plan, I am confident it will reap a harvest from all the sowing you have been doing during the past weeks. With our whole front line acting aggressively against the enemy so that he is pinned to the ground, O'Connor's plunge into his vitals will be decisive. I am not discounting the difficulties, nor the initial losses, but in this case I am viewing the prospects with the most tremendous optimism and enthusiasm. I would not be at all surprised to see you gaining a victory that will make some of the 'old classics' look like a skirmish between patrols.

I saw your message today to Arthur [Tedder], sent in response to mine of yesterday. My only thought in suggesting that he or I come over was that there might be some particular point in which you wanted assurance from your rear. I know that the Air will be full out for you, day and night. I am sure, also, that when this thing is started you can count on Bradley to keep his troops fighting like the very devil, twenty-four hours a day, to provide the opportunity your armored corps will need, and to make the victory complete.

I have been going after the Cherbourg thing for the last two weeks. Prospects are some better, and Ramsay is over there today. You may be sure that we are using every facility and every talent on which we can lay our hands.

May good fortune attend you: I am looking forward to the happy chore of telling about your accomplishments as soon as we have put this one over. I hope you will forgive me if I grow a bit exuberant.

Warm regards.

As ever,
Ike[5]

On 20 July Eisenhower visited Montgomery, who was in a very confident mood having had a satisfactory interview with Churchill in the morning. The Supreme Commander was still unhappy about Montgomery's failure to risk heavy casualties in an all-out attack in the east, and he disliked the idea that it would be left to the Americans to make the main breakthrough in the difficult bocage country in the west. On the 21st he wrote of his misgivings, in a letter that also shows how firm both he and Montgomery were on the need to take the Brittany ports. When Tedder saw the letter he remarked: 'It is not strong enough. Monty can evade it. It contains no order.'[6]

21 July, 1944

Dear Monty:

Since returning from your Headquarters yesterday I have been going over the major considerations that, in my mind, must guide our future actions. This letter is to assure myself that we see eye to eye on the big problems.

I think that from the military side the case was well summed up in your letter of 8th July. There are also serious political questions involved, but in my mind they parallel, for the moment at least, the military factors. You said:

'1. We must get the Brittany Peninsula. From an administrative point of view this is essential.

2. We do not want to get hemmed into a relatively small area. We must have space for maneuver, for administration and for airfields.

3. We want to engage the enemy in battle to write off his troops and generally to kill Germans.'
(To this last one you might well have added 'We should like to kill them in big packets by means of breaking through his positions and cutting him off in sizeable elements.')

You stated this last thought in clear language in your M-510 of 10th July in Paragraph 5. You said:

'We are now so strong and are so well situated that *we can attack the Germans hard and continuously in the relentless pursuit of our objectives.* This will be done by both First and Second Armies.'

This is my view exactly. I think that so far as we can foresee we are at this moment *relatively* stronger than we can probably hope to be at any time of the near future. *Time is vital.* We must not only have the Brittany Peninsula – we must have it quickly. So we must hit with everything.

In late June, when First Army was cleaning up the Cherbourg Harbor area, Second Army was attempting to prevent any movement of German troops from the Eastern to the Western flank, in order that when First Army turned southward it would have the best possible conditions for a rapid advance to the base of the Peninsula. But because it had also to hold a firm defensive line, Second Army was not entirely successful in this – it could not have been done except by a definite, continuing, offensive. In any event, Bradley's advance to the southward has been disappointingly slow even though he has kept everlastingly on the attack with everything he can bring into action.

Then, a few days ago, when Armored Divisions of Second

Army, assisted by tremendous air attack, broke through the enemy's forward lines. I was extremely hopeful and optimistic. I thought that at last we had him and were going to roll him up. That did not come about.

Now we are pinning our immediate hopes on Bradley's attack, which should get off either tomorrow or on the first good day. But the country is bad, and the enemy strong at the point of main assault, and more than ever I think it is important that we are aggressive throughout the front.

The recent advances near Caen have partially eliminated the necessity for a defensive attitude, so I feel that you should insist that Dempsey keep up the strength of his attack. Right now we have the ground and air strength and the stores to support major assaults by both armies simultaneously. As Bradley's attack starts Dempsey's should be intensified, certainly until he gains the space and airfields we need on that flank. In First Army, the whole front comes quickly into action to pin down local reserves and to support the main attack. Dempsey should do the same. The enemy has no immediately available major reserves. We do not need to fear, at this moment, a great counter offensive.

I am sure that in this way we will secure the greatest results in the quickest possible time, which is our basic objective. Moreover, I am convinced that in this way we will have in the long run the least number of casualties. I realize the seriousness of the reinforcement problem for Dempsey. That is another reason, in my mind, for getting the business straightened out quickly. Eventually the American ground strength will necessarily be much greater than the British. But while we have equality in size we must go forward shoulder to shoulder, with honors and sacrifices equally shared.

I have taken up the air matters you suggested to me. We must preserve our organization, because the air, in the whole campaign, has performed splendidly, in support of the ground, in spite of adverse weather conditions.

Good luck!

As ever,
IKE[7]

The following letter from Montgomery to the CIGS, written ten days before the Allies closed the Falaise gap, paints a dramatic picture of the gains won and of the by then almost certain prospect of a tremendous victory. It also throws an interesting sidelight on Montgomery's character in his switching from describing the battle which was to change European history to pin-pricking criticisms of the Canadian Army commander and the British staff generals at SHAEF. The letter demonstrates, too, his supreme confidence that Brooke would take his side in any dispute arising from personality clashes.

9-8-44

My dear C.I.G.S.

Simbo takes this and will give you our news.

1. The enemy attack at MORTAIN was just what we wanted; it was held without difficulty; I put the 2nd T.A.F. on to it, as well as the 8th Air Force, and the pilots all had a great day. They claimed '120 flamers'; but I doubt that.

2. On the left, the Canadian attack is aimed at FALAISE. I have ordered them to hold that place securely, and from it to operate southwards towards ARGENTAN and westwards towards CONDE.

8 Corps, the right wing of Second Army, is moving on TINCHEBRAY today, but I do not expect this advance to progress far. Its main task is to hold the enemy to his ground.

3. The right wing of 12 Army Group, 15 U.S. Corps, is at LE MANS, where it will secure a bridgehead. I have ordered it then to operate northwards to ALENCON; this is a very important thrust.

4. I am aiming at closing in behind the Germans.

The Canadians should be able to fight their way to FALAISE; they will not have the easy time they fancied, but they should get there; at present their forward movement is not making rapid progress.

The Germans will fight hard for FALAISE I think. I don't think the Americans will have any difficulty in getting to ALENCON, as there is nothing there to oppose them.

If we can get FALAISE, and can also hold ALENCON strongly, we should then be able to close the gap in between — and that would be very excellent.

But the Germans will fight hard; it is good defensive country and we must not expect things to go too rapidly.

So far the Poles have not displayed that dash we expected,

and have been sticky.

5. The midday bombing yesterday by Eighth Air Force (Fortresses) on the Canadian front was most inaccurate. Bombs fell in 12 Corps area west of the ORNE, in CAEN itself, behind CAEN, east of CAEN, in the area of Canadian A.G.R.A., and on Tac. H.Q. 3 Canadian Div.

A few fell in the target area.

The Canadians had about 300 casualties in personnel, had about 12 guns knocked out, had a good many vehicles destroyed, and KELLER (Comd. 3 Cdn. Div.) was wounded (will be out of action for about 6 months).

The same thing happened on 25 July west of ST. LO; the Americans had 500 killed and wounded, and General McNAIR was killed.

It now seems clear that Eighth Air Force must never come down into the tactical battle.

6. Harry Crerar is fighting his first battle and it is the first appearance in history of a Canadian Army H.Q. He is desperately anxious it should succeed. He is so anxious that he worries himself all day!!

I go and see him a lot and calm him down.

He will be much better when he realises that battles seldom go completely as planned, that great patience is required, that you keep on at it until the other chap cracks, and that if you worry you will eventually go mad!!

He seemed to have gained the idea that all you want is a good initial fire plan, and then the Germans all run away!!

7. Rumours keep reaching me of bad influences at work at SHAEF.

My own feeling is that Bedel Smith [*sic*] is all right and not bad in that way. He is intensely 'national'; but I would say he is a good member of the Allied team.

His intense national pride may be at work to try and make it appear that the war in Normandy is being fought by two separate parties — a British party and an American party, with no connection between the two.

If this were so, we would NOT be where we are today.

It is of course one party, working on one plan, and controlled and directed by one HQ. IKE is quite clear on this aspect of the matter.

8. But I hear rumours that Gale is bad, in that he openly runs

down the War Office, and the QMG by name, at conferences at SHAEF. I shall check up on this, and if it is true I will tackle him on the matter.

I believe Morgan is suspect too, but have no evidence.

The senior British officers at SHAEF must realise that, in addition to being good allied chaps, they have definite loyalties to their own side of the house; and, in our side of the house, we must all pull together.

9. The P.M. visited me on Monday, and stayed one hour.

He asked me about this idea to switch DRAGOON [the invasion of the South of France, formerly 'Anvil'].

I told him as follows:

(a) I was not in touch with the strategical and political issues involved.

(b) The date for DRAGOON was 15 Aug and that is only 7 days off.

(c) We have not yet captured the ports in Brittany in to which the ships could come. The ports may be all mined, as was Cherbourg.

(d) From the purely military aspect it seemed to me to be too late to attempt a switch.

(e) From other aspects it would probably mean a quarrel with the Americans, and that would do us no good.

(f) Taken all round, I was in favour of deciding *well ahead* what we wanted to do – and then doing it. You cannot make big changes at the last moment.

10. The P.M. struck me as looking old and tired; he seemed to find it difficult to concentrate on a subject for more than a few moments; he seemed restless, and unable to make his mind up about anything.

11. I hear Dicky Mountbatten is in England. I would like to see him before he goes back, and hear his news about the war in S.E. Asia.

12. Ike came to see me last night. We discussed DRAGOON and I gave him my views as in para 9.

Yours ever
Monty

P.S. [hand-written] Latest reports are that 4 Cdn Armd DIV is well on. The Poles are still on their start line + thus exposing the eastern flank of the Cdn spearhead. I have told Harry [Crerar] to give the Poles a kick in the fork.

By 14 September 1944 Eisenhower had agreed to gamble three airborne divisions — almost the whole of the SHAEF strategic reserve — on the 'Market-Garden' drops, and to give priority in supplies to Montgomery's northern thrust, thus reducing the threat to Germany from the American armies. Yet the following letter to Marshall shows that the Supreme Commander had no faith in Montgomery's plan to concentrate on a northern thrust to enter the North German plain and reach Berlin. To a certain extent the letter detracts from Eisenhower's stature as a commander, since in effect he was telling Marshall that he favoured a different strategy to the one he was actually carrying out.

14 Sept. 1944

Dear General:

I think that by forwarding to the Combined Chiefs of Staff periodic appreciations as well as copies of principal directives you are kept fairly well acquainted with our situation. The fact is that we are stretched to the absolute limit in maintenance both as to intake and as to distribution after supplies are landed.

From the start we have always known that we would have to choose, after breaking out of the original bridgehead, some line which would mark a relative slackening in offensive operations while we improved maintenance facilities and prepared for an offensive operation that could be sustained for another indefinite period. At first it seemed to me that the German would try to use some one of the number of lines available to him in France on which to make a rather determined stand, but due to the decisiveness of our victory below the Seine I determined to go all out in effort and in risk to continue the drive beyond the German border, up to and including the Rhine before we began the process of regrouping and re-fitting.

While this was going on Montgomery suddenly became obsessed with the idea that his Army Group could rush right on into Berlin provided we gave him all the maintenance that was in the theater — that is, immobilize all other divisions and give their transport and supplies to his Army Group, with some to Hodges. Examination of this scheme exposes it as a fantastic idea. First of all, it would have to be done with the ports we now have, supplemented possibly by Calais and Ostend. The attack would be on such a narrow front that flanking threats would be particularly effective and no other troops in the whole region would be capable of going to its support. Actually I doubt that the idea was proposed in any conviction that it could be carried through to completion; it was based merely on wishful thinking, and in an effort to induce me to give to 21st Army Group and to Bradley's left every ounce of maintenance there is in the theater.

As opposed to this the only profitable plan is to hustle all our forces up against the Rhine, including Devers' forces, build up our maintenance facilities and our reserves as rapidly as possible and then put on one sustained and unremitting advance against the heart of the enemy country. Supporting this great attack will probably be subsidiary operations against the German ports on the left and against his southern industrial areas on the right. I have sacrificed a lot to give Montgomery the strength he needs to reach the Rhine in the north and to threaten the Ruhr. That is, after all, our main effort for the moment. The great Airborne attack which will go in support of this operation will be Sunday the 17th, unless weather prevents. It should be successful in carrying Montgomery up to and across the Rhine; thereafter it is absolutely imperative that he quickly capture the approaches to Antwerp so that we may use that port. The port facilities themselves are practically undamaged and we have there ample storage for bulk oil, something that we critically need.

Le Havre will be developed for utilization by U.S. forces.

During the early and middle summer, I was always ready to defer capture of ports in favor of bolder and more rapid movement to the front. But now approaches the season of the year when we can no longer afford this, especially in view of the resistance the German is ready to offer in Fortress defense, as demonstrated both at St. Malo and at Brest. Every day I thank my stars that I held out for ANVIL in the face of almost overwhelming pressure. Marseilles may yet be a Godsend to us.

My own belief is that, assuming continuation of the Russian pressure at its present scale, we will have to fight one more major battle in the West. This will be to break through the German defenses on the border and to get started on the invasion. Thereafter the advance into Germany will not be as rapid as it was in France, because we won't have the F.F.I. [*Forces françaises de l'intérieur* – the Resistance] in the German rear, but I doubt that there will be another full-dress battle involved. The big crash to start that move may prove to be a rather tough affair.

Recently Spaatz received a message from Arnold* suggesting the desirability of moving a lot of our heavy bombers to France immediately. This is simply beyond the realm of feasibility at the moment. Big bombers can still operate effectively from England and we need every ton of space and every bit of port capacity to get in the things that the ground troops and their shorter range air support units require. This will continue to be true for an indefinite period.

Sincerely,

Ike[8]

On 28 November 1944 Montgomery and Eisenhower had a discussion at Twenty-First Army Group Tac HQ at Zondhoven, after which Eisenhower stayed the night. The Supreme Commander listened patiently to Montgomery's demand for one land commander for the main thrust, and the latter took Eisenhower's silence for agreement, although Dawnay warned him later that in fact he was far from agreeing. Two days later Montgomery put his suggestions in writing, saying, among other things: 'We have failed ... Bradley and I make a good team ... to be certain of success you want to bring us together and one of us should have full operational control north of the Ardennes, and if you decide I should do the work that is OK by me.' He also asked for another conference with Eisenhower, suggesting that their respective Chiefs of Staff should be present but forbidden to speak. Eisenhower was furious, and wrote the following letter:

1 December 1944

Dear Monty

From my personal knowledge of appointments early next week, it appears to me that our conference will have to be

---

* General Carl Spaatz commanded the US Strategic Bombing Force operating against Germany; General Henry Arnold was Commanding General of the US Army Air Force.

held on Thursday morning, possibly about 10:30. I will confirm details later.

At first I thought no more detailed answer was necessary to your letter, merely leaving the various subjects to be discussed at our conference. However, you have stated your conception of the points that were 'agreed upon' during our conversation, whereas there are certain things in your letter in which I do not concur. Your letter does state your conception and opinions as presented to me the other evening.

I am not quite sure I know exactly what you mean by strategic reverse; certainly to date we have failed to achieve all that we had hoped to by this time, which hopes and plans were based upon conditions as we knew them or estimated them when the plans were made. The Ruhr is an important place, but let us never forget for one second that our primary objective is to defeat the German forces that are barring our way into Germany. The Ruhr itself was always given as a geographical objective, not only for its importance to Germany, but because it was believed that in that region the *German forces* would be largely concentrated to meet our attacks.

Specifically, I agree to the following:

a. We must determine how much profit there is in the continuation of our current attacks in the 12th Army Group, and whether they give real promise of reaching the Rhine.

b. We must recast our future general plans in the light of conditions as they now exist.

c. We must chose [*sic*] the best line of attack to assure success, including the maintenance of deception lines.

I also stated that from my personal viewpoint, it would be simpler for me to have the battle zone divided into two general sectors, in each of which one individual, could achieve close battle coordination. I expressed some doubt whether this zone should be divided on the basis of our rear areas or on the basis of natural lines of advance into Germany. There was some question in my mind whether the Ardennes or the Ruhr should mark the dividing line, if such a plan should be adopted.

I do not agree that things have gone badly since Normandy, merely because we have not gained all we had hoped to gain. In fact, the situation is somewhat analogous to that which existed in Normandy for so long. Our line as late as D plus 60 was not greatly different than what we hoped to hold in the first week, but I never looked upon the situation then existing as a strategic reverse, even though out of the circumstances of our long confinement in the narrow beach head have developed some of our greatest later difficulties. If we had advanced from the beginning *as we had hoped*, our maintenance services would have been in a position to supply us during the critical September days, when we actually reached the limit of our resources.

Moreover, I do not agree that more strength could have been thrown to the north than was actually maintained there during early September. Lines of communication in the north were so stretched that even delivery of five hundred tons to you at Brussels cost Bradley three divisions, the possession of which might have easily placed him on the Rhine in the Worms area.

We gained a great victory in Normandy. Bradley's brilliant break through made possible the great exploitation by all forces, which blasted France and Belgium and almost carried us across the Rhine. Had we not advanced on a relatively broad front, we would now have the spectacle of a long narrow line of communication, constantly threatened on the right flank and weakened by detachments of large fighting formations. In addition, we would have had a similar picture in the south, stretching all the way from Marseilles to Dijon. As it is, we now have a rear that is cleared of the enemy. We can look to the front.

I have no intention of stopping Devers and Patton's operations as long as they are cleaning up our right flank and giving us *capability of concentration*. On the other hand, I do not intend to push those attacks senselessly.

It is going to be important to us later on to have two strings to our bow. Don't forget that you were very wise in making a provision for this at Mareth, and it paid off.

With respect to the Chiefs of Staff attending the conference, it makes no difference to me whether your Chief of Staff attends or whether Bradley's does. Mine will be there unless some unforseen [*sic*] circumstance prevents. Bedell is my Chief of Staff because I trust him and respect his judgment. I will not by any means insult him by telling him that he should remain mute at any conference he and I both attend.

I most definitely appreciate the frankness of your statements, and usual friendly way in which they are stated, but I beg of you not to continue to look upon the past performances of this great fighting force as a failure merely because we have not achieved all that we could have hoped. I am quite sure that you, Bradley, and I can remain masters of the situation and the victory we want will certainly be achieved. But we must look at this whole great affair stretching from Marseilles to the lower Rhine as one great theater. We must plan so when our next attack starts we will be able to obtain maximum results from all our forces, under the conditions now existing.

Ike[9]

Montgomery read the warning signals and replied, humbly enough, that he had not intended to give the impression that the performance of the Allied army had been an overall failure, and that he had been referring only to the November offensive. This produced a typically tactful reply from Eisenhower:

2 December, 1944

Dear Monty:

You have my prompt and abject apologies for misreading your letter of 30th November. In my haste to answer I obviously read your paragraph 8 as a far more pessimistic statement than was justified. In any event, I am sorry if my letter gave offence; certainly I do not want to put words or meaning into your mouth, or ever do anything that upsets our close relationship.

Along with this message to you I am sending extracts from Strong's report, made only yesterday. You will find it most interesting indeed and thoroughly indicative of the great value we are deriving from present operations.

You will be happy to know that the prospects for U.S. ammunition are brightening. Apparently we are to get greatly increased allocations and a step-up in shipments.

Incidentally, I suppose you know that the R.A.F. is going to take shot at the Schmidt dam. I hope the try is successful, because otherwise both Hodges and Simpson believe they must halt on the Roer to clear up the risk of artificial flooding before they can go further. On the other hand, they are quite happy about the prospects of getting over the River if this added risk is promptly eliminated, and then of taking on the Panzer Divisions there in order to chew them up.

Again I say that I am sorry that in my hurried reading of your letter I made an interpretation that you did not intend. I now see clearly exactly what you mean.

Sincerely

Ike[10]

On 7 December 1944 Montgomery met Eisenhower, Tedder, Bradley and Bedell Smith at Maastricht. The Supreme Commander was now hostile to the ideas Montgomery put forward, and after the conference the latter wrote this frank and outspoken letter to Grigg:

7.12.44

My dear P.J.

Thank you for your letter of 6 Dec.

I have returned from my conference with Ike at Maastricht. The result was complete failure, and he went back on all the points he had agreed to when alone with me. Bradley and Tedder were there too; I played a lone hand against the whole three. That Tedder should take their side is too dreadful.

I have written the whole thing in a long letter to the C.I.G.S., and he will doubtless show it to you.

The American plan for winning the war is quite dreadful; it will not succeed, and the war will go on. If you want to end the war in any reasonable time you will have to remove Ike's hand from the control of the land battle; and Bradley's hand also. How you will do this I do not know; but unless you do so, the whole war will go on. I hope the American public will realise that, owing to the handling of the campaign in western Europe from 1 Sept. onwards, the German war will now go on during 1945. And they should realise very clearly that the handling of the campaign is entirely in American hands. We did quite reasonably well when it was in British hands.

One must keep on plugging away at it; possibly some miracle will happen. But the experience of war is that you pay dearly for mistakes; no one knows that better than we British.

We must keep on fighting all through the winter, and one would not mind if success came at the end of it. But success will not come. Come and see me some time. I will send my aeroplane for you at any time.

Yrs ever,
Monty[11]

With this letter, Montgomery enclosed a thirteen-paragraph résumé of his controversey with Eisenhower over the thrust line and the command problems, and he also sent a copy to Brooke. This clearly demonstrates his complete confidence that both Brooke and Grigg supported him to the hilt, and it was in this confidence that he returned to the attack over command in January 1945, with nearly disastrous consequences for himself. The résumé cited chapter and verse for the arguments:

The Thrust Line Problem

1. My note to Eisenhower on 22 August 44.

   '1. The quickest way to win this war is for the great mass of the Allied Armies to advance northwards, clear the coast as far as ANTWERP, establish a powerful air force in BELGIUM, and advance into the RUHR.

   2. The force must operate as one whole, with great cohesion, and so strong that it can do the job quickly.

   3. Single control and direction of the land operations is vital for success. This is a *whole time* job for one man.

   4. The great victory in N.W. France has been won by personal command. Only in this way will future victories be won. If staff control of operations is allowed to creep in, then quick success becomes endangered.

   5. To change the system of command now, after having won a great victory, would be to prolong the war.'

2. My telegram, M.160, to Eisenhower on 4 Sep. 44.

   'M.160 (.) TOPSEC (.) Personal for Eisenhower and EYES ONLY from MONTGOMERY (.) I would like to put before you certain aspects of future operations and give you my views (.)

   Para. 1 (.) I consider we have now reached a stage where one really powerful and full blooded thrust towards

BERLIN is likely to get there and thus end the German war (.)

Para. 2 (.) We have not enough maintenance resources for two full blooded thrusts. (.)

Para. 3 (.) The selected thrust must have all the maintenance resources it needs without any qualification and any other operations must do the best it [*sic*] can with what is left over (.)

Para 4 (.) There are only two possible thrusts one via the RUHR and the other via METZ and the SAAR (.)

Para. 5 (.) In my opinion the thrust likely to give the best and quickest results is the northern one via the RUHR (.)

Para. 5 (.) Time is vital and the decision regarding the selected thrust must be made at once and para. 3 above will then apply (.)

Para. 7 (.) If we attempt a compromise solution and split our maintenance resources so that neither thrust is full blooded we will prolong the war (.)

Para. 8 (.) I consider the problem viewed as above is very simple and clear cut (.)

Para. 9 (.) The matter is of such vital importance that I feel sure you will agree that a decision on the above lines is required at once (.) If you are coming this way perhaps you would look in and discuss it (.) If so delighted to see you lunch tomorrow (.) Do not feel I can leave this battle just at present.'

3. Eisenhower's reply to my telegram of 4 Sep. Sent off by him on 5 Sep.

'While agreeing with your conception of a powerful and full blooded thrust towards the RUHR and BERLIN, I do not agree that it should be initiated at this moment to the exclusion of all other manoeuvres. The bulk of the German Army that was in the west has now been destroyed. We must immediately exploit our success by promptly breaching the Siegfried Line, crossing the RHINE on a wide front, and seizing the SAAR and the RUHR. This I intend to do with all possible speed.

While we are advancing we will be opening the ports of HAVRE and ANTWERP.

Accordingly my intention is initially to occupy the

SAAR and the RUHR; and by the time we have done this, HAVRE and ANTWERP should be available to maintain a deeper thrust into Germany.'

4. Extract from Eisenhower's letter to me on 15 Sep.
   'we shall soon, I hope, have achieved the objectives set forth in my last directive and shall then be in possession of the RUHR, the SAAR, and the FRANKFURT area.'

5. Extract from my letter to Eisenhower on 18 Sep. in reply to his letter of 15.
   'It is my opinion that a concerted operation in which all the available land forces move forward to the RHINE and into Germany on a wide front is not possible. I consider we should put all our resources into one full-blooded thrust, and be defensive elsewhere.'

6. Extract from Eisenhower's letter of 20 Sep. in reply to my letter of 18 Sep.
   'Generally speaking I find myself so completely in agreement with your letter of 18 Sep. that I cannot believe there is any great difference in our concepts.

   * * *

   What I do believe is that we must marshal our strength up along the western borders of Germany, to the RHINE; insure adequate maintenance by getting ANTWERP working at full blast, and then carry out the drive you suggest.'

7. My telegram to Eisenhower dated 21 Sep.

'Dear Ike,
   I cannot agree that our concepts are the same and I am sure you would wish me to be quite frank and open in the matter.
   I have always said stop the right and go on with the left, but the right has been allowed to go on so far that it has outstripped its maintenance and we have lost flexibility.
   In your plan you still want to go further with your right and to capture the SAAR.

I would say that the right flank of 12 Army Group should be given a very direct order to halt and if this order is not obeyed we shall get into greater difficulties.

The nett result of the matter is that if you want to get the RUHR you will have to put every single thing into the left hook and stop everything else. It is my opinion that if this is not done then you will NOT get the RUHR.

Your very great friend, MONTY.'

8. Orders issued in the directive from SHAEF dated 28 October.

21 Army Group.

To attack the enemy west of the MEUSE, to advance to the RHINE and IJSSEL rivers, to deploy in strength east of these rivers and be prepared to advance on the RUHR.

12 Army Group.

(a) To advance to the RHINE and gain bridgeheads in the COLOGNE area, to deploy in strength on the east bank, and advance on the RUHR.

(b) To attack and capture the SAAR, and to secure crossings over the RHINE in that area.

6 Army Group.

To attack the Siegfried Line, to advance to the RHINE and secure bridgeheads, and deploy in strength across the RHINE.

The Command Problem

9. My note to Bedel [*sic*] Smith on 21 Sep.

'I consider that the organization for command and control of the operations to capture the RUHR is not satisfactory.

It is a task for one man and he should have the operational control and direction of all the forces involved.

To achieve success the tactical battle will require very tight control and very careful handling.

I recommend that the Supreme Commander hands the job over to me and gives me operational control over First U.S. Army.'

10. My 'Notes on Command in Western Europe' are attached as Appendix 'A'.
I sent this to Bedel Smith on 10 October.

11. Eisenhower replied on 13 October.
He did not agree with my views.

12. My telegram to Eisenhower on 16 October.
'Dear Ike,
   I have received your letter of 13 October.
   You will hear no more on the subject of command from me. I have given you my views and you have given me your answer.
   That ends the matter and I and all of us here will weigh in one hundred per cent to do what you want.
   Your very devoted and loyal subordinate MONTY.'

13. Eisenhower's reply to above.
'Dear Monty,
   Thank you for you very fine message.'

B.L.M.[12]

On 3 May 1945, as soon as he had finished speaking to the German delegation, Montgomery telephoned Simpson at the War Office. The latter immediately dictated this succinct minute of a historic call, and circulated it to the Prime Minister, the CIGS, and the Secretary of State for War.

CIGS
   1. Field-Marshal Montgomery has just telephoned to me (4.30 p.m.) to let me know of his discussions this morning with certain German representatives. He has reported the whole affair officially to SHAEF from whom we will presumably hear in due course, but he thought you would like private information of what took place.
   2. A German delegation arrived at his Headquarters this morning and consisted of the following:
   General-Admiral von Friedenberg, who is on the staff of Field-Marshal Keitel.
   General Kinsel, Chief of Staff to Field-Marshal Busch.

Rear-Admiral Wagner, staff officer to General-Admiral von Friedenberg.

Major Friede, staff officer to General Kinsel.

They had been sent in by F.M. Keitel himself, who had given them written authority to represent him, and had been told by him to see Field-Marshal Montgomery himself and discuss certain matters.

3. The discussions were carried out through the medium of an interpreter. Apparently, however, von Friedenberg understood some English as he said to the interpreter once or twice that he understood clearly what F.M. Montgomery had meant in certain of his remarks.

4. When asked what they wanted, they said that they had come to surrender to F.M. Montgomery three German Armies now withdrawing in front of the Russians in MECKLENBURG. They were also very anxious about the civilians in that area and wanted F.M. Montgomery to take some sort of action to prevent them falling into the hands of the Russians.

5. F.M. Montgomery told them that he must refuse to take their surrender and that they must surrender to the Russians. Of course, if any German soldiers came into the British lines holding up their hands, they would be made prisoners by the British.

6. The Germans then asked what could be done about the civilians, for 'the Russians would kill them all'. F.M. Montgomery says that his only reply to this was, 'I hope so'.

7. F.M. Montgomery then told them, if that was all they had to say, he must refuse to discuss the situation any further. He asked them whether they were prepared to answer any questions of his. They said they were prepared to discuss anything he wanted.

He then asked them whether Keitel was prepared to surrender all his forces on the Northern and Western flanks of 21 Army Group. They said this could not be done and they had not come there for the purpose of offering such surrender. They were, however, very worried about the fate of civilians in the battle area and were prepared to withdraw slowly in front of a British advance so that the civilians could be spared. F.M. Montgomery refused to have anything to do with this idea. He said that if that was all they had to say on that subject, he must bid them good morning and get on with the battle.

9. As they did not appear anxious to go, he showed them a small-scale map of the battle situation on the various fronts in Europe. They were entirely horrified at this situation and looked 'completely collapsed'. F.M. Montgomery then said he would like to make three points clear to them, viz:

(i) If they wanted to save German lives, they must surrender unconditionally all German forces in West Holland, in Friedland, including the Frisian Islands and Heligoland, in Schleswig-Holstein, and in Denmark.

(ii) Once such surrender is agreed unconditionally and in writing, F.M. Montgomery would authorise discussions on the best way of occupying the areas in question and dealing with civilians.

(iii) If the Germans did not agree, F.M. Montgomery was going on fighting with all the consequences it would have for German soldiers and civilians.

10. The German representatives said that they personally were prepared to agree, but they had no power to commit Keitel. They would go back to him and tell him what F.M. Montgomery had said and would recommend to him that he should agree. They hoped to return to-morrow evening.

11. Eventually von Friedenberg and Major Friede left to return to their own lines, but Kinsel and Wagner asked if they could stay behind. The latter two are now under guard at F.M. Montgomery's Tac. H.Q.

12. Von Friedenberg had said that Keitel was in a H.Q. South of Kiel. He was thought to be with Doenitz. F.M. Montgomery thought that Doenitz was probably in on this too. Von Friedenberg gave it as his personal opinion, in reply to a question of F.M. Montgomery's, that Doenitz and Keitel would agree to unconditional surrender.

13. F.M. Montgomery told me that he had been authorised by General Eisenhower to discuss unconditional surrender of the places mentioned in paragraph 9(i) above. If, however, there was any question of other places, such as Norway or the Channel Islands, being discussed also, it would have to be referred to SHAEF. F.M. Montgomery told von Friedenberg that he should find out, before he returned, whether Keitel was willing to discuss surrender in Norway

etc. as well. In that case he would pass the German representatives on to SHAEF for the purpose.

3rd May 1945   Frank Simpson [stamp][13]

*Documentation for page 22.

The following letter written by Field Marshal Lord Alexander to the C.I.G.S. on 3 April 1943 reveals his poor opinion of the fighting qualities of the U.S.A. troops in North Africa.

Headquarters, 18th Army Group.
April 3rd 1943.

My dear C.I.G.S.,
. . . . they (the Americans) simply do not know their job as soldiers, and this is the same from the highest to the lowest – from the General to the private soldier. Perhaps the weakest link of all is the junior leadership who just does not lead with the result that their men don't really fight. A few shells and they all stop because of the 'heavy shelling' – a few bombs and they all go to ground and call for air support . . . they are soft green and quite untrained. I handed them a ready made victory on a plate (sic Gafsa Maknarry) but their hands were too weak to take it . . . . Unless we can do something about it the American Army in the European theatre of operations will be quite useless . . . . they have little hatred for the Germans and Italians and show no eagerness to get in and kill them . . . if this handful of divisions here are their best, the value of the remainder may be imagined. Eisenhower and Patton and most of all Bedell Smith, know pretty well what is wrong – but even they cannot realize the true extent of their Army's weakness because they are not professional soldiers, not as we understand that term.
                    Yours sincerely,
                    H.R. Alexander

Sources

Observations from the following are taken from interviews or correspondence with the author in 1981 and 1982: Field-Marshal the Lord Carver; Lt-Col C.P. (Kit) Dawnay; Maj-Gen John Frost; the late General Sir Richard Gale; John Henderson, Esq., General Sir Nigel Poett; General Sir Charles Richardson; Maj-Gen G.B.P. (Pip) Roberts; General Sir Frank Simpson; Brigadier Sir Edgar (Bill) Williams.

Initials and numbers refer to papers in the Public Record Office, Kew, with the exception of EP which refers to the Eisenhower Papers at the Dwight D. Eisenhower Library, Abilene, Kansas 67410, USA.

All extracts from Viscount Alanbrooke's diaries and his letters and signals to and from Field-Marshal the Viscount Montgomery come from the PRO, Simpson Archives, Dawnay Archives, Grigg Archives, Bryant's *Triumph in the West* and Fraser's *Alanbrooke*; background material on Alanbrooke may be found in the Alanbrooke Collection at King's College, London. Quotations from General Sir Miles Dempsey come from WO 285, as do the signals to and from him – this file contains nothing but Dempsey papers.

1   Sicily and After

1. Montgomery, *Memoirs*.
2. Ibid.
3. Ibid.
4. De Guingand, *Generals at War*.
5. Moorehead, *Montgomery*.

6. Grigg, *1943: The Victory that Never Was.*
7. Eighth Army War Diary, WO 169/8494.
8. Ibid.
9. Frost, *A Drop Too Many.*
10. WO 169/8494.
11. Essame, *Patton: The Commander.*
12. Belchem, *All in the Day's March.*
13. Montgomery, *El Alamein to the Sangro.*
14. Butcher, *My Three Years with Eisenhower.*
15. Colonel J.G. Jeans, interview with author.
16. Grigg Archives, Churchill College, Cambridge.
17. Westphal, *The German Army in the West.*
18. Irving, *Hitler's War.*
19. WO 169/8494.
20. 3 Commando War Diary, WO 218/51.
21. WO 169/8494.
22. Ibid.
23. 5th Division War Diary, WO 169/8711.
24. Ibid.
25. WO 169/8494.
26. Buckley, *The Road to Rome.*
27. Eighth Army Intelligence Summary to 2400, 3 September, WO 169/8520.
28. WO 169/8711.
29. Bateson, *First into Italy.*
30. WO 169/8711.
31. XIII Corps War Diary, WO 169/8615.
32. WO 169/8494.
33. Ibid.
34. Montgomery, *Memoirs.*
35. WO 169/8711.
36. Buckley, *The Road to Rome.*
37. WO 169/8494, and for following passages.
38. WO 169/8711.
39. Frost, *A Drop Too Many.*
40. WO 169/8494.
41. Clark, *Calculated Risk.*
42. WO 169/8494.
43. WO 169/8497.
44. Chalfont, *Montgomery of Alamein.*
45. WO 169/8497.
46. Ibid.
47. Author's recollection

2 Montgomery and the Invasion

1. For this and the following paragraphs see Prem 336/3.
2. Ibid. Montgomery also told Churchill that it would be ninety days before the invasion of the South of France ('Anvil') would have any effect on the cross-Channel invasion.
3. The minutes of the 7 January conference and the following SHAEF conferences are in WO 205/12 and WO 219/255. For Montgomery's amendment of his remarks about commanding American troops on 10 January, see Brereton, *Diaries*.
4. EP 1475.
5. EP 1473.
6. WO 219/255.
7. WO 205/5g.
8. Ibid.
9. Sikorski Institute Files, Princes Gate, London.
10. Interrogation of German generals, WO 205/1020–1022.
11. Montgomery, *Memoirs*, and other books on D-Day.

3 Normandy Assault

1. WO 205/1020.
2. Vigneral Diary, Imperial War Museum, Lambeth Road, London. At 0200 on 6 June Madame de Vigneral took her children and servants to a trench in the garden, and she returned to the house at 0930 to bring out coffee and put the lunch on the stove. At 1200, when she brought the food out on a tray, German soldiers were in one hedge of her garden and Canadians in another. At 1315 she went back to get more coffee, and saw German soldiers running away doubled up and, soon afterwards, Allied soldiers lying flat on the ground. Sniping by Germans left behind went on for many days, however. There were tears and laughter as the Canadians gave chocolates to the children, and as soon as an officer had searched the house for booby traps Madame de Vigneral opened the champagne she had kept hidden from the Germans. But the Canadians became annoyed because she could not understand their French, and unfortunately a certain amount of pillaging took place on the pretence of looking for enemy soldiers hiding out in empty houses; Madame de Vigneral saw furniture loaded on to lorries, and even her sewing-machine was taken. Montgomery issued strong orders against looting, and on 9 July Madame de Vigneral was taken to the Town Mayor's office in Bayeux, where she identified and recovered almost everything that had been stolen from her.
3. Weighey, *Eisenhower's Lieutenants*.
4. Belchem, *All in the Day's March*.
5. WO 205/5b.
6. Simpson Archives.
7. WO 205/5d.
8. Simpson Archives.

9. WO 205/5d.
10. Ibid.
11. Grigg Archives.
12. Ibid.
13. WO 205/5d.
14. Ibid.
15. Grigg Archives.
16. WO 205/5b.
17. Grigg Archives.
18. Report from Panzer Lehr 6 June–12 July, Second Army Intelligence Report, 20 July 1944, WO 171/221.
19. Ibid.
20. Ahrenfeldt, *Psychiatry in the British Army in the Second World War*; also for Montgomery on the death penalty.
20. Belfield and Essame, *The Battle for Normandy*.
21. Ibid.
23. WO 205/5 and Grigg Papers.
24. WO 205/5.
25. WO 205/5d.
26. Irving, *The War Between the Generals*.
27. This and the subsequent Directives in the M series are in files WO 205/56.
28. WO 205/5f.
29. WO 205/5d.
30. Ibid.
31. Irving, *The War Between the Generals*.
32. WO 205/448 (G SD 4).
33. Irving, *The War Between the Generals*.
34. WO 205/5g.
35. Simpson Archives.
36. Belchem letters; see also Simpson Archives; Montgomery, *Normandy to the Baltic*.
37. Ambrose, *The Supreme Commander*.
38. EP 1827, 14 July.
39. Simpson Archives.
40. *War Monthly*, issue no. 7.
41. Wilmot, *The Struggle for Europe*.
42. Montgomery, *Memoirs*.
43. Belfield and Essame, *The Battle for Normandy*.
44. Speidel, *We Defended Normandy*.
45. Ibid.

4 Near-Failure and the Break-Out

1. Tedder, *With Prejudice*.
2. Ibid.

3. Charles Cruickshank, article in *War Monthly*, issue no. 76

4. Butcher, *My Three Years with Eisenhower*.

5. Prem, 3/339/11.

6. Cab 66.

7. Simpson Archives.

8. Ralph Bennett, 'Ultra and Normandy', *War Monthly*, issue no. 80.

9. Butcher, *My Three Years with Eisenhower*.

10. Ambrose, *The Supreme Commander*.

11. Tedder, *With Prejudice*. Tedder makes it clear that he was seeking Montgomery's dismissal, and was backed by Portal. Winterbotham in *The Ultra Secret* quotes a secret signal from Tedder to Churchill saying that Eisenhower was on the brink of asking that Montgomery should go.

12. Irving, *The War Between the Generals*.

13. EP 1844.,

14. WO 205/5d.

15. Butcher, *My Three Years with Eisenhower*.

16. Irving, *The War Between the Generals*.

17. Weighey, *Eisenhower's Lieutenants*.

18. Grigg Archives.

19. Ellis, *Victory in the West*, Vol. I.

20. Bucknall Papers, Imperial War Museum.

21. Simpson Archives.

22. Ibid.

23. Belchem, *All in the Day's March*.

24. Stacey, *The Victory Campaign*.

25. Belchem, *All in the Day's March*.

26. WO 163/498.

27. Rohmer, *Patton's Gap*.

28. WO 171/114.

29. Blumenson, *The Patton Papers*, Vol. 2.

30. Bradley, *A Soldier's Story*.

31. Stacey, *The Victory Campaign*.

32. Bradley, *A Soldier's Story*.

33. Irving, *Hitler's War*. Irving goes on to state that Lt-Col George Pfann, secretary to General Patton, says that Patton vanished for a day in mid-August. When he returned he stated that he had been trying to make contact with a German emissary who did not turn up. On 27 July 1945, however, Field-Marshal von Kluge's son-in-law, Udo Esch, German Medical Corps, interrogated later, said that von Kluge had discussed with him surrendering the whole of the Western Front. Esch's words were: 'He went to the front lines but was unable to get in touch with the Allied commander.' Blumentritt, under interrogation, stated that Keitel had told him of an intercepted Allied signal to von Kluge. Other Nazis, after the surrender, claimed that they had heard the same story – but it may well have been spread by leading Nazis who knew that von Kluge was in touch with the conspirators.

34. WO 205/1022.

35. Rohmer, *Patton's Gap*.

36. Second Army War Diary WO 171/200; see also Stacey, *The Victory Campaign*.
37. Bradley, *A Soldier's Story*.
38. Ambrose, *The Supreme Commander*.

5   Eisenhower Takes Command

1. Brereton, *Diaries*.
2. WO 219/1.
3. Ellis, *Victory in the West*, Vol. I. There is no evidence that de Guingand actually showed this provocative memorandum to Eisenhower. He may have kept it for his own background information in the discussion.
4. Ambrose, *The Supreme Commander*.
5. Ibid.; see also Wilmot, *The Struggle for Europe*.
6. Ellis, *Victory in the West*, Vol. I; Pogue, *The Supreme Command*.
7. Ibid.

6   Over the Seine

1. WO 171/441
2. Ellis, *Victory in the West*, Vol. II.
3. Horrocks, *A Full Life*.
4. Allied First Airborne Army Record, WO 219/4998.
5. WO 171/341.
6. Weighey, *Eisenhower's Lieutenants*.
7. Ibid. *et seq.*

7   The Fatal Wrong Decision

1. Bennett, *Ultra in the West*; see also Lewin, *Ultra Goes to War*.
2. WO 171/134.
3. WO 205/12.
4. Twenty-First Army Group War Diary, PRO.
5. Belchem, correspondence with Williams and Simpson.
6. Wilmot, *The Struggle for Europe*.
7. Tedder, *With Prejudice*
8. WO 205/247.
9. WO 219/448.
10. Weighey, *Eisenhower's Lieutenants*.
11. Ryan, *A Bridge Too Far*.
12. Brian Urquhart, letter to author dated 22 January 1982.
13. Wing-Commander Asher Lee, conversation with author.
14. Ryan, *A Bridge Too Far*.

8 Arnhem

1. Ellis, *Victory in the West*, Vol. II.
2. For accounts of the advance to Nijmegen and beyond see the regimental histories of the Irish Guards and Grenadier Guards. See also: Ryan, *A Bridge Too Far*; Ellis, *Victory in the West*, Vol. II; Twenty-First Army Group Report on 'Market-Garden', WO 171/118. For the plans, see XXX Corps' operational instructions, WO 171/341. For the airborne operation, see: Urquhart, *Arnhem*; Sosabowski, *Freely I Served*; Ryan, *A Bridge Too Far*; Gavin, *On To Berlin*.
3. Frost, *A Drop Too Many*.
4. Weighey, *Eisenhower's Lieutenants*.
5. Ibid.
6. Frost, *A Drop Too Many*.
7. WO 171/118.
8. Weighey, *Eisenhower's Lieutenants*; see also Brereton, *Diaries*.
9. Weighey, *Eisenhower's Lieutenants*.
10. Wilmot, *The Struggle for Europe*.
11. Ibid.
12. Belchem, correspondence with Williams and Simpson.
13. Lewin, *Montgomery as Military Commander*.
14. Belchem, correspondence with Williams.
15. Montgomery, *Memoirs*.

9 The Canadians on the Coast

1. For the events involving the Canadian Army and the personal exchange between Crerar and Montgomery, see Stacey, *The Victory Campaign*.
2. Bennett, *Ultra in the West*.
3. Montgomery, *Memoirs*.

10 After Arnhem

1. Belchem, *All in the Day's March*.
2. Ambrose, *The Supreme Commander*.
3. EP 1953.
4. EP 1957.
5. Ellis, *Victory in the West*, Vol. II.
6. Ibid.
7. Montgomery, *Memoirs*.
8. WO 205/147.
9. Ibid.
10. Simpson Archives.
11. See Appendix.
12. Minutes of Versailles Conference, WO 205/12. Letter to author from Wilbert Mahoney, National Archives and Record Service, Washington.

13. Grigg Archives.
14. WO 204/5g.
15. Grigg Archives.
16. EP 2032.
17. Pogue, *The Supreme Command.*
18. EP 2032.
19. Interview with Sir Frederick Morgan in Ambrose, *The Supreme Commander.*
20. Letter to Bedell Smith, 10 October, see Appendix.
21. Ibid.
22. Ellis, *Victory in the West*, Vol. II.

11   The Dreary Autumn

1. Ellis, *Victory in the West*, Vol. II.
2. WO 171/134.
3. Ambrose, *The Supreme Commander.*
4. EP 2145.
5. EP 2146.
6. Grigg Archives.
7. EP 2163.

12   Ardennes

1. WO 171/134
2. Irving, *Hitler's War.*
3. Simpson Archives.
4. Belchem, *All in the Day's March.*.
5. Ambrose, *The Supreme Commander*; see also Pogue, *The Supreme Command.*
6. Gavin, *On To Berlin.*
7. Wilmot, *The Struggle for Europe.*
8. Blumenson, *The Patton Papers.*.
9. Grigg Archives.
10. WO 171/134.
11. Ibid.
12. Ibid.
13. Blumenson, *The Patton Papers.*
14. Simpson Archives.
15. Grigg Archives.
16. Montgomery, *Memoirs.*
17. EP 2210.
18. Montgomery, *Memoirs.*
19. Ellis, *Victory in the West*, Vol. II.
20. Ibid.
21. Irving, *The War Between the Generals.*
22. Prem 3/334/6.

13 Rows Over Strategy

1. Montgomery, *Memoirs*. He wrote of US Ninth Army being left under his command: 'I clearly could not have asked for more.'
2. Alanbrooke Archives, King's College, London.
3. Ellis, *Victory in the West*, Vol. II.
4. Simpson Archives.
5. Ibid.
6. Ellis, *Victory in the West*, Vol. II.
7. Ibid.
8. Ambrose, *The Supreme Commander*.
9. Prem 3/336/6.
10. Ibid.
11. Ibid.
12. Ibid.
13. Letter from Montgomery to Nye, 14 February 1945, Dawnay Archives. In his *Memoirs*, Montgomery states that he put some of these remarks 'in a diary entry'.
14. Ibid.
15. Ibid.

14 Eisenhower's Revenge

1. Grigg Archives.
2. Eisenhower to Marshall, 21 March 1945, EP 2352.
3. Simpson Archives.
4. Prem 3/336/B.
5. Grigg Archives.
6. Bradley, *A Soldier's Story*.
7. Simpson Archives.
8. Weighey, *Eisenhower's Lieutenants*.
9. Pogue, *The Supreme Command*.
10. Alanbrooke Achieves.
11. Weighey, *Eisenhower's Lieutenants*.
12. Allied First Airborne Army Record, WO 219/2891.
13. Ibid.
14. Second Army Intelligence Summaries, WO 171/3958.
15. Simpson Archives.
16. Ryan, *The Last Battle*.
17. Ambrose, *The Supreme Commander*.
18. EP 2352.
19. Simpson Archives.
20. Dawnay Archives.
21. WO 205/5d.
22. Ambrose, *The Supreme Commander*.
23. Ibid.
24. Ibid.
25. Prem 3/198/2.

26. Weighey, *Eisenhower's Lieutenants*.
27. EP 2364.
28. EP 2363.
29. EP 2365. On reading Eisenhower's signal to Marshall, Churchill minuted: 'This seems to differ from last night's Montgomery which spoke of Elbe. Please explain.'
30. Ellis, *Victory in the West*, Vol. II.
31. Ambrose, *The Supreme Commander*.
32. Ryan, *The Last Battle*.
33. Simpson Archives.
34. Ambrose, *The Supreme Commander*.
35. Dawnay Archives.
36. Ibid.
37. Simpson Archives.
38. Alanbrooke Archives.
39. Churchill, *The Second World War*, Vol. VI.
40. Weighey, *Eisenhower's Lieutenants*.
41. Ibid.
42. Bradley, *A Soldier's Story*.
43. EP 2399.
44. Montgomery, *Memoirs*.
45. Second Army Intelligence Report, WO 171/3958.
46. Horrocks, *A Full Life*.
47. WO 205/273.
48. WO 106/4445. The main letters on the Anglo-American controversy are on Cab 32/64.
49. Montgomery, *Memoirs*.
50. Simpson Archives.
51. Dawnay Archives.
52. Ibid.
53. Pogue, *The Supreme Command*.
54. Simpson Archives.
55. Grigg Archives.
56. Dawnay Archives.

Conclusion

1. Liddell Hart, *History of the Second World War*.
2. WO 208/3575.
3. WO 169/8494.
4. Strong, *Intelligence at the Top*.
5. Liddell Hart, *The Other Side of the Hill*.
6. Churchill, *The Second World War*.
7. Liddell Hart, *History of the Second World War*.
8. Grigg Archives.
9. EP 1844.
10. Ibid.

11. Liddell Hart, *History of the Second World War.*
12. Ibid.
13. EP 2163.
14. Dawnay Archives.
15. Ibid.
16. EP 1016-52 (pre-presidential), Box 101.

Appendix

1. EP 1473.
2. EP 221.
3. Irving, *The War Between the Generals.*
4. WO 205/5d.
5. EP 1827.
6. Irving, *The War Between the Generals.*
7. EP 1844.
8. EP 1953.
9. EP 2145.
10. EP 2146.
11. Grigg Archives.
12. Ibid.
13. Ibid.

Select Bibliography

It would not be possible to list all of the huge number of books I have read and referred to in my research: only the main ones are cited below.

Ahrenfeldt, R.H., *Psychiatry in the British Army in the Second World War*, London, 1958.

Ambrose, Stephen E., *Eisenhower and Berlin*, New York, 1967.

——, *The Supreme Commander*, London 1969.

Bateson, Henry, *First into Italy*, London, 1944.

Belchem, Maj-Gen D., *All in the Day's March*, London, 1978.

——, *Victory in Normandy,* London, 1981.

Belfield, E. and Essame, H., *The Battle for Normandy*, London, 1965.

Bennett, Ralph, *Ultra in the West*, London, 1979.

Blumenson, Martin, *Breakout and Pursuit*, Washington, 1961.

——, *The Patton Papers 1885-1945*, 2 vols, Boston, 1972, 1974.

Bradley, General Omar N., *A Soldier's Story*, London, 1952.

Brereton, Lt-Gen Lewis H., *The Brereton Diaries*, New York, 1946.

Bryant, Sir Arthur (ed.), *Triumph in the West 1943-46*, London, 1959.

Buckley, Christopher, *The Road to Rome*, London, 1945.

Butcher, Captain H.C., *My Three Years with Eisenhower*, London, 1946.

Butler, Sir James (ed.), *The Mediterranean and Middle East*, Vol. V, London, 1973.

Chalfont, Alun, *Montgomery of Alamein*, London, 1976.

Chandler, A.D. (ed.), *The Papers of Dwight David Eisenhower*, Vols. III and IV: *War Years*, Baltimore, 1970.

Churchill, Winston S., *The Second World War*, Vol. VI, London, 1954.

Clark, Mark, *Calculated Risk,* London, 1951.

Cole, Hugh M., *The Lorraine Campaign*, Washington, 1966.

Cruickshank, Charles, *Deception in World War II*, Oxford, 1979.

De Guingand, Maj-Gen F., *Generals at War*, London, 1964.

——, *Operation Victory*, London, 1947.

Ehrman, John (ed.) *Grand Strategy*, Vols V and VI, London, 1956.

Eisenhower, Dwight D., *Crusade in Europe*, London, 1948.

Ellis, Major L.F., *Victory in the West*, Vols. I and II, London, 1962, 1968.

Essame, Hubert, *Patton: The Commander*, London, 1974. *See also* Belfield, E.

Fraser, David, *Alanbrooke*, London, 1982.

Frost, Maj-Gen John, *A Drop Too Many*, London, 1980, new, expanded edition, 1982.

Gale, General Sir Richard, *With the Sixth Airborne Division in Normandy*, London, 1948.

Gavin, James, *On To Berlin*, London, 1978.

Grigg, John, *1943: The Victory That Never Was*, London, 1980.

Grigg, P.J., *Prejudice and Judgment*, London, 1948.

Hamilton, Nigel, *Monty: The Making of a General, 1887-1942*, London, 1981.

Harris, C.R., *Allied Military Administration of Italy 1943-45*, London, 1957.

Horrocks, Lt-Gen Sir Brian, *A Full Life*, London, 1960.

Irving, David, *Hitler's War*, London, 1977.

——, *The Trail of the Fox: The Life of Field-Marshal Erwin Rommel*, London, 1977.

——, *The War Between the Generals*, London, 1981.

Keegan, John, *Six Armies in Normandy*, London, 1982.

Lewin, Ronald, *Montgomery as Military Commander*, London, 1971.

——, *Ultra Goes to War*, London, 1978.

Liddell Hart, B.H., *History of the Second World War*, London, 1970.

——, *The Other Side of the Hill*, London, 1951.

MacDonald, Charles B., *The Siegfried Line Campaign*, Washington, 1963.

Montgomery of Alamein, Field-Marshal the Viscount, *El Alamein to the River Sangro/Normandy to the Baltic* (one-volume edition), London, 1973.

——, *Memoirs*, London, 1958.

Montgomery, Brian, *A Field-Marshal in the Family*, London, 1973.

Moorehead, Alan, *Eclipse*, London, 1945.

——, *Montgomery*, London, 1947.

North, John, *North-West Europe 1944-5*, London, 1953.

Owen, Roderic, *Tedder*, London, 1952.

Parrish, Thomas (ed.), *The Encyclopaedia of World War II*, London, 1978.

Pogue, Forrest C., *The Supreme Command*, Washington, 1953.

Rohmer, Maj-Gen Richard, *Patton's Gap*, London, 1974.

Ryan, Cornelius, *A Bridge Too Far*, London, 1974.

——, *The Last Battle*, London, 1966.

——, *The Longest Day*, London, 1960.

Seaton, Albert, *The Fall of Fortress Europe*, London, 1981.

Shepperd, Colonel G.A., *The Italian Campaign 1943-45*, London, 1968.

Shulman, Milton, *Defeat in the West*, London, 1947.

Sosabowski, Stanislaw, *Freely I Served*, London, 1960.

Speidel, Lt-Gen Hans, *We Defended Normandy*, London, 1951.

Stacey, Colonel C.F., *The Canadian Army 1939-1945*, Ottawa, 1948.

——, *The Victory Campaign: The Official History of the Canadian Army in the Second World War*, Ottawa, 1960.

Strong, Maj-Gen Sir K., *Intelligence at the Top*, London, 1968.

Tedder, Lord, *With Prejudice*, London, 1966.

Thompson, R.W., *Montgomery: The Field-Marshal*, London, 1969.

Urquhart, Maj-Gen R.E., *Arnhem*, London, 1958.

Weighey, Russell F., *Eisenhower's Lieutenants*, London, 1981.

Westphal, General Siegfried, *The German Army in the West*, London, 1951.

Wilmot, Chester, *The Struggle for Europe*, London, 1952.

Winterbotham, F.W., *The Ultra Secret,* London, 1974.

Index